Hocking, William
Meaning of God in
human experience

THE MEANING OF GOD
IN HUMAN EXPERIENCE

THE MEANING OF GOD IN HUMAN EXPERIENCE

A PHILOSOPHIC STUDY OF RELIGION

BY

WILLIAM ERNEST HOCKING

NEW HAVEN AND LONDON
YALE UNIVERSITY PRESS

Fourteenth printing, June 1963.
Printed in the United States of America by
The Colonial Press Inc., Clinton, Mass.

Library of Congress catalog number: 12-14946

TO

A. B. O'R. H.

AN UNFAILING SOURCE OF INSIGHT

FOREWORD

by John E. Smith

The Meaning of God in Human Experience stands as one of the serious philosophical treatments of religion in the twentieth century. It is also Hocking's most representative work. The book exhibits not only that original synthesis of idealism and pragmatism which marks Hocking's thought, but it gives evidence as well of an important but lesser-known strain in his philosophy—a reliance on experience of a radical sort. *The Meaning of God* is a subtle book; the persistent tendency of its author to understate the case puts the reader on his mettle. The sense one has of participating directly in the problems it treats is due to the experiential standpoint from which it was written. Religious questions are posed in the form in which they actually confront us. The fact, moreover, that Hocking, like James, appears to be wrestling with the issues as he writes about them engages the reader and forces him to take a silent part in the discussion.

It was, of course, William James who set the pattern in American thought of treating religion from the standpoint of direct experience. There have been others, the so-called "empirical theologians" among them, who laid claim to the heritage of James. But their conception of experience was often too narrow—in an effort to emulate science, they thought only in terms of sensible data and facts thus losing experience in that larger sense which religion requires. Hocking is the true heir of James; he inherited the legacy and developed it further. Not only did he continue the line of radical empiricism, but he was in possession of a metaphysical outlook which James lacked. Hocking saw the metaphysical importance of experience; he knew how to go beyond description to the discovery of what experience can tell us about the general nature of things.

If Hocking has been the true heir of James, he has also been the genuine successor of Royce. Throughout *The Meaning of God* we are constantly reminded of Royce's speculative drive as we follow Hocking's persistent attempt to understand religion, to clarify the ideas central to it and to argue for its necessity in the cosmic scheme. It would be an error, however, to think of Hocking as primarily a rearranger of ideas or doctrines passed on by others. The marks of his predecessors are there, but his work has its own originality. Not only did he treat novel issues such as the problem of a world religion in a fresh way, but he was able to place religion within the framework of a more rigorous ontology than James, and his analyses show a greater sensitivity to experience than those of Royce.

Though written exactly half a century ago, *The Meaning of God* has a peculiar relevance for the current situation. Themes in the center of contemporary discussion are precisely those at the heart of Hocking's argument; merely to mention them is to move at once into the immediate present. As a counterpart to recent questions about the meaningfulness of the concept of God, Hocking sought for its "original sources" in experience. He refused to abandon experiential foundations and, like Peirce, his conception of experience is broad enough to enable us to say that having an idea is also having an experience. The Ontological Argument for God's existence, so often killed and resurrected, once again shows signs of coming to life; Hocking presents a novel recasting of that argument and at the same time shows the proper meaning of proof or demonstration in religion. In dealing with the perennial difficulty of showing the relation between religion as a generic feature of human experience and "positive" religion as represented by a specific Church or Communion, Hocking develops the "principle of alternation," the insight that, while religion has essentially to do with the *Whole,* the man of faith is always a concrete individual who lives in the world and who, when he comes to worship, finds it necessary to view religion as one more *part* or aspect of life beside others.

There is a growing sense at present that we must find ways of understanding the presence of God in Nature—the exclusively anthropological approach shows certain deficiencies. Hocking saw the point years ago and he argues that Nature is the universal mediator of the Divine. Our experience of Nature as shot through with mystery furnishes a starting point; as we come to judge the quality of the Whole we gradually discern in the workings of Nature a Power which takes on personal character. In seeking knowledge of Nature we discover our own limitation; in the sense that we are not alone in knowing Nature, we come to understand that what remains unknown to us is yet *knowable.* The original experience of God through Nature is best described as the sense that "I know not, but He knows." Science then becomes the quest for what God knows.

The strength of Hocking's thought is in its richness, its suggestiveness, and its profundity. His logic is a massive one; it is necessary to work through the whole in order to apprehend it. Having grasped the main thrust of his argument, one can go back to the details and carry the critical discussion from there. It is to be hoped that the return of *The Meaning of God* to the current scene will have its own powerful effect in leading on to a renewal of discussion about religion which combines metaphysical depth with experiential bearings.

New Haven, Connecticut
September 1962

PREFACE TO THE 1963 EDITION

AT the time of this book's appearance, just a half-century ago, its title carried a challenge to prevailing ideas about human experience. "Religious experience" was a common phrase; but God—as a being beyond the world whom "no man hath seen at any time" —was not presumed to be a direct factor in experience. There were "proofs of the existence of God"; and we do not attempt nor require proofs of an existence we can directly verify.

Our Western world was at that time under the spell of a notion of experience stemming as much from Locke as from Descartes, in which the stuff of sense-data together with the awareness of our own mental life were the basic ingredients. This pattern on all empirical knowledge was wholly successful in developing the methods of an expanding science of Nature, from which the notion of purpose was in principle excluded. The Modern Period, as we commonly term it, could almost be defined as the period of human self-reliance, aided by the techniques proposed by the sciences—a period of getting on without God, for all practical purposes.

The great technical failure of this notion of experience was its inability to account for one's knowledge of other selves. Ourselves we can experience, and nature; but minds other than our own were considered conjectures aided by language, whose meanings we can never directly compare or verify. On this basis, the social sciences, growing by leaps and bounds, have *no direct data*; and even psychology, hesitating to depend on introspection, must present itself as a science of "behavior." The term "behavioral sciences" is a flag of defeat.

Modernity completely failed to resolve the dilemma of "solipsism"; and with its inability to find an experience of other selves would follow its deeper inability to find an experience of God. I had for some time been of the belief that these barriers could be surmounted and that they would fall together. In my own experience they did; this book is to that extent autobiographical.

But it marks also a notable general turning away from the sense-data–mental-data pattern of admitted experience. The very vitality of the twentieth century is due to its rejection of that pattern, its appeal to experience neither physical nor ego-centered. Beside the vast fields of social enquiry, the experience of values aesthetic and ethical, there is a new recognition of the immense importance of our central and inarticulate awareness of existence which I have ventured to call "nuclear experience," rich in structure and meaning.

In this nuclear experience there are always three factors, an I, a Thou, and a common subject matter, let us say an It. Taken in its totality, this It is simply the world in which the I must work out its life. But the Thou, here discerned as always present, lends to the world, the It, a character which completely effaces the privacy-limit of Descartes' "I think, therefore I am": the It is no longer merely My world, the It is Our world. What I find true of it is true for everyone; my experience has a touch of universality: science is possible! The triumphant march of modernity is now understood.

And understanding it, we pass beyond it: we enter a postmodern era.

Nuclear experience calls for a wealth of interpretation. Under the names phenomenology and existentialism this task has occupied much of the present century. The nuclear Thou-art (whose encounter is the theme of the mystics of all ages, and whose dialogue with the self has been described with such discerning power by Martin Buber) is never experienced merely as a co-subject, but rather as a creative will sustaining my own being (hence caring for my existence), an activity inviting a response, a launch as of "animal faith," a summons to find in experience directives that indicate "this way lies your fulfillment, your task, your destiny."

The factual world confronting this "We are" presents no open path. As particular, it is necessarily "irrational," never deducible from a Platonic order of ideas nor from a Whiteheadian system of "eternal objects." There is in the situation an inescapable factor of adventure and risk in which life and death stand adjacent, with possibilities of tragedy and despair. Yet *Angst* is inadequate to the situation.

For with the certitudes of truth there are also certitudes of action, possibilities of rising beyond futility to control of the opening issues. In the inquiry into the conditions of the "prophetic consciousness" we have an answer to *Angst* and to despair, perhaps the most pertinent contribution of the book to the disturbed morale of an age of conflict and bent-to-death.

WILLIAM ERNEST HOCKING.

Madison, New Hampshire
February 1963

PREFACE TO THE 1912 EDITION

THE services of thought to religion have been subject to a justified distrust. Of uncertain worth, especially of uncertain recoil, are the labors of reason in behalf of any of our weightier human interests. By right instinct has religion from the beginning looked elsewhere for the brunt of support and defense — say to revelation, to faith, to feeling. A bad defense is a betrayal; and what human philosophy of religion can be better than a bad defense?

Present-day philosophy seems notably inclined to take this view of itself. Is it not Bradley, elder metaphysician to our time, who jots down that metaphysics is the finding of bad reasons for what we believe on instinct? Reason is not incapable of recognizing and confessing its own limits: it may even take pride in expounding them, an attitude which since Hume and Kant has become more or less fashionable. Our current science of religion may now assume without too much discussion that the grounds of religion are super-rational, or sub-rational: and we find philosophy undertaking to define what these other-than-rational grounds are — grounds moral perhaps, or psychological, or social, or historical; grounds pragmatic, or even mystic. Various and variously combined as are these several philosophic trends, they agree in accepting the judgment that religion lies close to the primitive moving-forces of life: deeper, then, than reason or any work of reason.

But a vague territory still is this Beyond-reason or Deeper-than-reason. Once singly-named Faith, now it has many names — instinct, the subconscious, the co-conscious, feeling, will, value-judgment, social sense, intuition, mystic reason, perhaps *l'élan vital* — as its border is touched in various scientific excursions. Some unclearness has come with the abundance of our learning, some confusion of categories, no doubt; we can hardly yet say that we know better than our forefathers what religion is, though perhaps we know better what it is not. The one impression which does distinctly emerge from the multitude of contemporary suggestions is a negative one: a general disaffection from the religion of reason, and from its philosophical framework, absolute idealism.

Some doubt the fundamental proposition of this idealism, namely, that all reality is of the same stuff that ideas are made of, that "whatever is is rational." Some doubt its doctrine that everything is known to one absolute Knower, whose being is thought, or Idea. And some there are who do not doubt these propositions; who will not deny logical force, even finality, to idealistic arguments — if one must argue: but who add the comment that whatever is vital in religion is missed in all logic-work, is necessarily and forever missed, thought and religion being once for all incommensurate. They do not find the Absolute of idealism identical with the God of religion: they cannot worship the Absolute. And they do not find that religion consists in our human knowledge of this absolute Knower: *Denken*, they think, *ist nicht Gottesdienst.*

In this general dissatisfaction with idealism, and in our

unclear efforts to win elsewhere a positive groundwork for religion, I find the sufficient warrant for such a study as this book undertakes. It enquires what, in terms of experience, its God means and has meant to mankind (for surely religion rises out of experience and pays back into it again): and it proposes, by aid of the labors of all co-workers, critics and criticised alike, to find the foundations of this religion, whether within reason or beyond.

This purpose is not over-bold; though no serious treatment of religion dare be over-modest. It is not over-bold, first, because it is a human necessity. We must reach some working clarity in these matters, every individual soul of us: the problem is there; we shall work it through well or ill, get our solution honorably or by default. Is there not in all positive living a similar necessity for what we may call presumption? The world too is there, with work to be done, votes to be cast, a new generation to be trained and harnessed, and other like requirements—all equally impossible. All such undertakings might well be postponed by any man under the true plea of unfitness: nevertheless all this is to be done, and all will get itself done in some fashion, creditable or discreditable. It is, in fact, an old ruse of nature's, this of clothing the necessary in the guise of the impossible, making a dignified way of escape for him who prefers to escape from complete living, calling for something like presumption on the part of him who will not escape. Let us rather say, calling for performance simply, categorical performance. Nature creates the requirement: let nature supply ways and means.

Our purpose is not over-bold, secondly, because, after all, the truth about religion cannot be in itself obscure or intricate. Subtle religion is false religion. Our difficulties are indeed made by our laboring philosophies themselves. The quaint words of Berkeley still hold good: "*We have firſt raiſed a duſt and then complain we cannot ſee.*" The truth about religion is to be had; but not by surpassing others in more mighty floundering and dust-raising: this truth is traditionally for "him that hath eyes to see and ears to hear" in a certain quietude of mind.

Only — be it at once said — the dust-raising in the present case is a much more important process than the words of Berkeley imply. In the new philosophies is new truth, and much of it — no mere new misunderstanding. Whatever murkiness there is marks, I believe, a genuine deepening of spiritual consciousness in our Western world: a new appreciation of faith, a new love of life and its variety, a new ability to be both bond and free — speculatively, spiritually, free, while not less scientifically bond, historically bond, even traditionally bond. It is a symptom of any such valid deepening of thought that men know less clearly what they want than what they do not want. The older philosophy has failed to satisfy; the newer philosophies have not yet succeeded in satisfying: the work of proposing and rejecting must continue until conscience at its profounder level can again rest.

It is just because of this veritable growth that cleverness and erudition poured out in abundance do nowadays visibly pall and fail of their usual effect: for cleverness and erudition operate within the already acquired conceptions of mankind — they stand ineffective before what is new-born. For this reason, in part, the weighty scholarship of Germany loses some little ground in these fields. If we know the kind of thing that a given type of scholarship has to offer, then even great virtuosity, though it be prolific of the Very True, must sweat to provoke an interest, still more to arouse our faith. The thing now required is a simple thing, a common word, a slight increment of ultimate sincerity somewhere that can reunite our roots with mother earth. We are as well off above ground as we can be until we are better off below ground. What boots it though a man can produce out of his inner consciousness a veritable banyan forest if there is, in all, no growth *downward?* There is, I say, a quiet and canny maturity of conscience abroad which knows surely what it does not want, a new-born thing in the world, the source of our new philosophies, — in particular of our pragmatisms, our realisms, our mysticisms, — the doom of the old, the doom also of the new that fail to arrive at reality: the lash at the back of the thinker, and the hope in his soul.

Meanwhile, the general deepening of consciousness, and of conscience, is a deepening of religion itself. The formulæ that were once potent here too begin to fail: ideas and phrases, gritty a generation ago, a decade ago, are already worn smooth and lend no more friction to any human work. A new calling has sprung up: that of creed-making, or of creed phrase-making; and many of our wise men take part in it. These too have their new Reality to face, merciless as a child. If the spirit of the age is but feebly responsive to new phrase or old, hasten not to judge that the spirit of the age is becoming irreligious: may not the opposite theory as well explain its indifference to *us* (though with less salve for our vanity)? Potentially, at least, men are becoming more religious. This development of religion is still a latent fact, mightier than any yet-visible shape or movement, discernible at times only as a cloud dim and vast, strained and full of repressed lightning. The release of these forces is no small human object.

In what respect, then, is idealism inadequate to these new demands? And what is the truth which the critics of idealism have to offer? It may be well to state at once (especially for the satisfaction of fellow-students in these fields) the substance of our belief on these points, outlining in rough summary the position in which the work of this book results.

The weakness in the armor of classical idealism has been made apparent, I believe, by pragmatism — or rather, by the pragmatic principle of judgment. *Idealism does not do the work of religious truth; ergo, it is not the truth of religion.* This judgment may be accepted without further commitment to the philosophy that pronounces it (for is it not also Hegel's principle that the true idea is known by its work in this concrete world?)

Idealism fails to work, I believe, chiefly because it is unfinished. Unfinishedness is not in itself a blemish; is professed even as a special excellence by that remarkable antisystemist, Henri Bergson.[1] But there are tolerable and intolerable kinds of unfinishedness. A thing is properly unfinished when *it* is finishable; when it has an identity that finishing will not change. Let an artist

[1] L'évolution créatrice, p. 209.

sketch a face with all conceivable haste and roughness: the unfinishedness of the thing is wholly justified if only it is a thing; if only it has a character and a significance which all later finishing does but develop without displacement or substitution. Our philosophies must meet the same test. Idealism can entertain much of what pragmatism, realism, and the rest have brought forward, and still remain idealism; whether it can entertain all, is doubtful. It is not incapable of admitting into its world-picture variety, change, growth, personality, freedom, also objectivity of a sort. The question is, of what sort?—whether the variety is a real variety, the risk a real risk, the objectivity a real objectivity, individuality and freedom real—or only shows of reality, infected by that illusoriness and approximateness which idealism tends to impose upon realistic experience generally. Can idealism entertain the Real, and still remain idealism? What pragmatism has specifically required of idealism in religion is more genuinely real opportunity, real freedom, real individual creativity. What realism desires is more valid objectivity, substantiality in the world beyond self. It is the latter want, I venture to say, which chiefly limits the effectiveness of idealism in religion: to satisfy the pragmatic test, idealism must become more realistic: for idealism in religion does not give sufficient credence to the authoritative Object, shows, so far, no adequate comprehension of the attitude of *worship*.

Idealism is unfinished, then, not having found its way to worship: it has not found its way to the particular and the historical in religion; to the authoritative and the wholly super-personal. The salvation it offers men seems still to be, in effect, a salvation from the particular in the general, the *ideal:* even though it names the *concrete* as its goal, it has not yet been able in this matter of religion to accomplish union with the concrete. It might seem that the idealist more than any other should appreciate the function of the positive and authoritative in religion; should know (as Hegel knew) that only the concrete can breed the concrete; should know (as Royce knows) that only the individual can breed the individual; should know, then, that only the historic can bear fruit in history, so that when the pragmatic test comes, a religion which is but a religion-in-general, a religion universal but not particular, a religion of idea, not organically rooted in passion, fact, and institutional life, must fail.

Idealism means, in name and in truth, the freedom in this universe of the thinker, the unlimited right of Idea in a world where nothing that is is ultimately irrational. But it is the exercise of freedom which alone discovers the rightful place of authority. Only he who has tried (or tried to imagine) a pure adventure knows that there is *no such thing as a pure adventure;* for when you have cancelled path, peak, sky, star, all distinguishable points in space, the adventure itself is abolished. The idealist who by right and intention is the pure adventurer in the regions of the spirit has not yet experimented his freedom if he remains unappreciative of authority, in religion as in knowledge. It is he who in the end must be called upon to expound the worth and use of church, dogma, creed, priest, mediator, the whole apparatus of God-worship which religious evolution has produced, and God-worship itself.

If idealism declines this responsibility, as being beyond its province, beyond *reason* in fact, belonging to the practical, or psychological, or anthropological, or historical aspect of the matter only, it does thereby acknowledge the foundations of religion to be beyond reason; implies that to comprehend the truth of religion, idealism must at last *abandon itself.*

The pragmatic test has meant much in our time as a principle of criticism, in awakening the philosophic conscience to the simple need of fruitfulness and moral effect as a voucher of truth. It is this critical pragmatism which first and widely appeals to the intellectual conscience at large. *Negative pragmatism*, I shall call it: whose principle is, "*That which does not work is not true.*" The corresponding positive principle, "Whatever works is true," I regard as neither valid nor useful. But invaluable as a guide do I find this negative test: if a theory has no consequences, or bad ones; if it makes no difference to men, or else undesirable differences; if it lowers the capacity of men to meet the stress of existence, or diminishes the worth to them of what existence they have; such a theory is somehow false, and we have no peace until it is remedied. I will even go farther, and say that a theory is false if it is not interesting: a proposition that falls on the mind so dully as to excite no enthusiasm has not attained the level of truth; though the words be accurate the import has leaked away from them, and the meaning is not conveyed. Any such criterion of truth is based upon a conviction or thesis otherwise founded, that the real world is infinitely charged with interest and value, whereby any commonplaceness on our part is evidence of a lack of grasp. Upon this basis (not apart from it), a negative pragmatism must be an effective instrument of knowledge.

This instrument is nowhere so significant as in the field of religious knowledge. What difference is made to you (and necessarily made to you) by your equipment of religious ideas and beliefs? If they are powerless, they are false. Whatever doctrine tends to draw the fangs of reality, and to leave men unstung, content, complacent, and at ease,—that doctrine is a treachery and a deceit. Note well that it is not pleasantness but force that sets the mark for truth: we have to require of our faith not what is agreeable to the indolent spirit but what is at once a spur and a promise. What do you think of hell? The doctrine of hell made religion at one time a matter of first-rate importance: getting your soul saved made a difference in your empirical destiny. If your idealism wipes out your fear of hell, and with it all sense of infinite risk in the conduct of life, your idealism has played you false. Truth must be transformed; but the transformation of truth must be marked by a *conservation of power*; herewith we have a more definite expression for the positive basis of our negative pragmatism. No religion, then, is a true religion which is not able to make men tingle, yes, even to their physical nerve tips, with the sense of an infinite hazard, a wrath to come, a heavenly city to be gained or lost in the process of time and by the use of our freedom. The flesh and blood of historical contingencies cannot be sapped up in the timeless issues of a certain type of idealism without loss of power, hence loss of truth.

What, again, do you think of God? The God of

orthodoxy is thought of as being so far like man as to have loves, interests, and powers which make themselves temporally felt: this God does things in the world which, if we like, we may call miracles or, if we like better, deeds of Providence. Upon this *differential* work of God, as contrasted with his total work, was based much of the urgency of former religious observance, prayer, and piety. Pragmatism rightly enquires what becomes of this differential work when God becomes the All-One of idealism; and what, if the historical will of God and the acts of Providence disappear from our creed, is to replace the immediacy and pervasiveness of the religious interest which those theories encouraged, and which in themselves (though not in all bearings) were good. In such wise, the pragmatic principle tends to confront idealism, as it has never before been confronted, with the substantial values of orthodoxy; compelling idealism to complete itself by the standard of these values (I do not say, of these propositions), even if at the cost of its philosophic identity.

This is the type of service which pragmatism can well render. As a positive builder it has little to recommend it. Founding truth ultimately on our human value is but another attempt, more radical than that of idealism, at the "pure adventure": it is an idealism become more subjective, freedom less bound by authority. It is the function of the pragmatic test (as of pain and discomfort generally) to point out something wrong; the work of discovering what is right must be done by other means. Knowledge may be obliged to wait long in a notch well known to be tentative and unsatisfactory because the satisfactory thing cannot be found *as truth requires*. I do not say that *action* must wait. Decision has its hour; and if knowledge is absent, the will-to-believe must come into play: but the will-to-believe is precisely a principle for action, not for knowledge. It has no place in the age-long work of speculation. The adoption of an hypothesis as a working-theory or postulate does not conceal from the adopter its true nature; does not obliterate for him the difference between postulate and knowledge.

But is there, then, no inaccessible truth? no permanent gap in knowledge (such as religious truth might hold), to be filled up *by choice?* There is no inaccessible truth. If any object has possible bearing on human interests, such as to make it matter of choice, it has a bearing on human fact also—there is some cognitive way to it. Truth is indeed variously accessible: there are regions of the world unsounded, long to be unsoundable, ample playground for imagination; but in truth-getting these very regions are to be approached (and are approached) with a more delicate chivalry just because of their comparative helplessness—with more care, not less, to restrain the impulses of subjectivity.

But, at last, is there no *unfinished truth?* No reality yet unmade, or in the making; no chance to co-operate with God in the work of creation, in determining what truth shall be? Have we not here the real meaning of positive pragmatism, and its true significance in religion? The world is infinitely unfinished; here lies the opportunity of freedom, the only excuse, indeed, for *time-existence* at all. But of the world, too, we can define a tolerable and an intolerable unfinishedness: the world must have an *identity* which the work of finishing does not destroy or from moment to moment displace. Unlimited co-operation with God in world-making we have; not, however, in ultimate *God-making*. The religious object offers that *identity* without which creative freedom itself would lack, for us, all meaning. Does it seem that super-nature is the plastic part of reality, nature relatively unplastic? — toward nature must we be relatively empirical, passive; toward super-nature relatively self-assertive, creative? I venture to point out that our creativity in any field follows faithfully the character of our passivity in that same field, varies with it not inversely but directly. Here, where our subservience to objective fact is most massive, here in the world of sense and nature, our practical creations are most massive also. And there, in the world of the religious objects, where myth-making, and world-picturing, even God-character-building, are most exuberant, — there the firm steadfastness of objective reality is at its summit also. An ultimate empiricism, a deference to what is given, not makable, just in these regions of the supersensible and the supernatural, is an attitude wholly necessary to human dignity, and to true religion. Far less than absolute idealism is positive pragmatism (radically taken) capable of worship.

If we are right in this, it may appear that pragmatism, taken in a constructive sense, is a self-refuting theory. The only kind of truth which in the end can comply with the pragmatic requirement that power shall be conserved is a non-pragmatic truth, a truth which has an absolute aspect; which proposition we shall try to make good in the course of this treatise. Pragmatism is a philosophy which cannot be finished without destroying its identity.

Whatever may be the deficiencies of idealism, pragmatism, if we are right, cannot supply them. How may it be with mysticism? Mysticism may have its absolute: but mysticism finds its metaphysics in experience; and mysticism is no stranger to worship. I believe, in fact, that the requirements both of reason and of beyond-reason may be met in what mysticism, rightly understood, may contribute to idealism. Not every mysticism will do. It is not the "speculative mysticism" of the text-books that we want; it is mysticism as a practice of union with God, together with the theory of that practice. Mysticism may introduce idealism to the religious *deed*, ultimately thereby to the particular and authoritative in religion.

There are mysticisms in which none of us believe. There is the mysticism of mantic and theurgy — mysticism of supernatural exploit, seeking short-cut to personal goods. There is another mysticism equally remote from our affections: world-avoiding, illusion-casting, zero-worshipping mysticism; living (in self-contradiction) upon the fruits of a rejected life. This mysticism has given the name its current color: making it necessary, perhaps, to ask that we be understood and agreed together in rejecting it. From the standpoint of just this sound disparagement of these types of mysticism, I have become persuaded that there is another, even a necessary mysticism. A mysticism as important as dangerous; whose historical aberrations are but tokens of its power. It is this mysticism which lends to life that value which is beyond reach of fact, and that creativity which is beyond the docility of reason; which neither denies nor is denied by the results of idealism or the practical works of life, but supplements both, and constitutes the essential standpoint of religion.

The mystic finds the absolute in immediate experience. Whatever is mediated is for him not yet the real which he seeks. This means to some that the mystic rejects all mediators: the implication is mistaken. To say that a mediator is not the finality is not to say that a mediator is nothing. The self-knowing mystic, so far from rejecting mediators, makes all things mediators in their own measure. To all particulars he denies the name God,—to endow them with the title of mediator between himself and God. Thus it is that the mystic, representing the truth of religious practice, may teach idealism the way to worship, and give it connection with particular and historic religion.

I have thus sketched, in highly crude and unmodified manner, the general philosophic attitude of this book. The philosophies of the present time, when they attain their own free conclusion, complete themselves in the same point. Pure thought, and pure voluntarism, share the fate of the "pure adventure": they must find rest in something other, limiting their freedom, yet required by it. It is the finished pragmatist who best knows the need of the absolute. It is the finished mystic who best knows the need of active life and its mediation. It is the finished idealist who best knows the need of the realistic elements of experience; the mystical and authoritative elements of faith. I know not what name to give to this point of convergence, nor does name much matter: it is realism, it is mysticism, it is idealism also, its identity, I believe, not broken. For in so far as idealism announces the liberty of thought, the spirituality of the world, idealism is but another name for philosophy — all philosophy is idealism. It is only the radical idealist who is able to give full credit to the realistic, the naturalistic, even the materialistic aspects of the world he lives in.

So much it has seemed right to say, by way of general philosophic orientation and confession. But in the work of the book itself no interest is taken in the criticism of thought-systems for their own sakes; our interest there is in the substance and worth of religion, to be found by whatever instruments of thought may be at hand.

As to the plan to be followed, I shall accept the pragmatic question, What does religion do? as a way of leading into the study of what religion is. In any case, religion must be understood and judged largely by what it accomplishes, by the difference it makes in human affairs. If we can at the beginning catch a glimpse of the sort of result which religion naturally achieves in history and in personal life, though only by way of a working hypothesis, we shall have a valuable guide for further enquiry into the nature of religion.

In taking up this enquiry, the second part of the book considers with some thoroughness the motives which have led to the retirement of reason in religion, and at the same time to a growing confidence in the worth of feeling. By deepening our conception of feeling we find

that our anti-intellectual tendencies can be funded for the most part in the "religion of feeling"; and in coming to terms with that view of religion we solve many of our problems at once. The issue of this enquiry turns largely upon reaching a new understanding (chapter XI) of the actual working-connection in consciousness between ideas and feelings. It will appear in what way the value of religion depends upon the religious idea and its truth.

Hereupon it would be in order to pass at once to the question of the truth of religious ideas, and especially of the idea of God as the central idea of religion. But here, too, it seems permissible first to build up our idea of God pragmatically, by considering in a series of free meditations (part three) what interest we may have, humanly speaking, in the unity of our world, in the presence there of anything changeless and absolute, and in the existence of a personal deity.

It is the work of the following part to deal directly with the question, how men know God; to show how God is found in human experience at large, and how this knowledge develops in the specifically religious experience of mankind. It is maintained (in chapters XIX to XXI) that our knowledge of fellow-men depends upon an original knowledge of God; not our knowledge of God upon a prior knowledge of our social world. But these two aspects of our spiritual experience do develop each one the other, according to a principle of alternation which is expounded in the ensuing part (part five), dealing with mysticism and worship.

It now becomes possible (part six) to set down in more adequate form what was taken as the beginning of our

study, namely, the work of God in the world, the way in which religion becomes fruitful in history, in morals, in the arts, and in the conquest of pain and evil. There is no creativity in human life without the Absolute as one party thereto.

If I have taken frequent occasion in this book to express dissent from the views both of Professor Royce and of William James, it is but a sign of the extent to which I owe to them, my honored masters in these matters, the groundwork of my thinking. I have differed freely from both, in the spirit of their own instruction, but not without the result of finding myself at one with both in greater measure than I would once have thought possible—or logically proper!

Most of the work of criticizing the original drafts of this book, and many an idea for their improvement, I owe to my wife: in so far as the path of the reader has been made plain, this is due chiefly to her. The manuscript was read by Professor George Herbert Palmer, whose criticism and generous interest have been alike invaluable; by my colleague, Mr. Charles A. Bennett, who has given substantial aid both in the thought and in the work of indexing; also, in large part, by Mr. Clarence Day, Junior, of New York, for whose careful, untechnical comments I am especially grateful.

WILLIAM ERNEST HOCKING.

NEW HAVEN, April 7, 1912.

Acknowledgment. — The editor of Mind has kindly allowed me to make use (in part five and in the last appendix) of parts of an article on "The meaning of mysticism" published in January, 1912. Two other appendices are due to courtesy of the editors of The Psychological Bulletin and of The Philosophical Review. These are acknowledged in place. I wish also here to express thanks to the publishers, who in many ways and without stint have aided my plans and contributed to the result.

CONTENTS

PART I. RELIGION AS SEEN IN ITS EFFECTS

PART II. RELIGIOUS FEELING AND RELIGIOUS THEORY

PART III. THE NEED OF GOD

PART IV. HOW MEN KNOW GOD

CHAPTER XVI

CHAPTER XVII

CHAPTER XVIII

CHAPTER XIX

PART V. WORSHIP AND THE MYSTICS

CHAPTER XXIV

CHAPTER XXV

CHAPTER XXVI

CHAPTER XXVII

CHAPTER XXVIII

CHAPTER XXIX

PART VI. THE FRUITS OF RELIGION

CHAPTER XXXIII

EXPLANATORY NOTES AND ESSAYS

PART I

RELIGION AS SEEN IN ITS EFFECTS

CHAPTER I

HOW THE NATURE OF RELIGION MAY BE KNOWN

WE are proposing to reach some definite conclusion about the nature and worth of religion — what it consists of in the way of experience, belief, and action; what comes of it in the way of support, outlook, and actual productiveness. As to the nature of religion, we are proposing especially to enquire how much it is concerned with theoretical propositions to be believed, metaphysical assertions, doctrines about unseen things and things past and to come — in short, how far the intellect is involved; how far, on the other hand, religion appeals to something in us deeper than intellect, — to faith, to feeling, to the subconscious, to the instinctive, to the essential will. Certainly, in our own time, the worth of intellect in religion is much discredited; various ways are suggested as to how we may take our creeds without taking them literally — as figurative or symbolic expressions of truths that cannot be exactly formulated, as postulates whose significance is primarily moral, as declarations of value, as determinations of the will. And yet one seems to require literality at some point in his creed; we wish to bring our religion at least into the same universe with our science (whose propositions are all 'literal') and to have them speak with the same voice when they verge, as at their limits they do verge, upon the same great questions of human destiny. Further, we do not believe that either science or religion is irrelevant to conduct, and when they bear upon the same fundamental issues of practice we wish to see a fair understanding between them. We are open to the opinion that religion does in some way take us beyond reason, and that religious truth must in some measure be clothed in symbols; but we are not open to believe that reason and our beyond-reason are separate and independent functions. As surely as any one person rides one consecutive route of experience through time, so surely must all the truth that belongs to one person come to the same court and enter into the same total system of his world. We are proposing, therefore, to interest ourselves especially in the parts that reason and beyond-reason play in the so-called truths of religion.

And we think that we shall be helped in determining what religion is by first fixing our attention upon what religion does, as if religion could best be seen not by direct inspection, but in its effects. Not only is it true that religion is itself an invisible and intangible object, best discovered as wind — and the spirit generally — are discovered, in what they move; but also, our interest in religion is due to an opinion of its value, or at any rate of its actual influence in the world, so that our identification of it and understanding of it are guided by these supposed consequences. This, we may say, is a pragmatic approach to our subject; and it will have the advantage of leaving open the question what importance theoretical propositions may have in religion; — it is possible, for instance, that the feelings may prove to be the working part of religion and the ideas a matter of derivative importance. But there are serious objections to this way of learning the nature of religion.

The first is that we shall be moving in a circle. The value of religion is half of our problem, perhaps the larger half; can we assume that we already know the value and works of religion as a guide to the knowledge of its nature, and then treat its nature as a source of the knowledge of its works? I only answer this objection by accepting it. In any living subject we have to assume that we already know something as a capital whereby to win a wider and more exact knowledge. And it is the usual procedure of science to use the phenomena as a means of winning a formula for the 'things', and the formula in turn as a means of discovering further phenomena. This circle, or as I prefer to put it, this alternation between inner and outer, is our own way of life, and the way of all knowledge.

The second objection is more specific. It is that the chief works of religion are as invisible and conjectural as religion itself, since they belong to another world than this. No historic religion has pretended to recommend itself to men solely on the ground of its value for the present life and social order. Most developed religions, on the contrary, insist on the comparative worthlessness of these goods, make it a point to draw away our attention and affections from them, and assert that the treasures to which they would introduce us are elsewhere. If such religions render distinct service to human society, it is an incidental service. The most widely influential of religions, Buddhism, must by its own logic regard itself a failure in so far as it tends in any way to make this present existence, whether personal, social, or political, more attractive. And Buddhism is not alone in this deprecation of things present.[1] Any attempt, therefore, to judge religion pragmatically, that is, by its effects in human experience, would seem to promise little to the point: at best, its estimate is threatened by defective proportion.

Nevertheless, it is true that religion has, for the most part, regarded itself as ministering to the welfare of two worlds, and not of one only. It seems to have gained a foothold on this planet originally by combining its invisible interests (so immensely real to the imaginative animal) with other interests of a practical and immediate nature. The gods were Powers, perceptible in field, water-course, and fruit; in cloud, in battle, and in bodily health or disease—though their great historical exploits may have belonged to regions behind the sun. Penalties visited upon the profane were physical as well as metaphysical; to be "cut off from fire and water" meant pain, probably death, to the body as well as to the social nature and the soul. And with the growing belief that the other world, whatever it be, is not a jealous rival of this present, but at least in relations of

[1] Neither Schopenhauer's nor Rousseau's interpretation of Christianity will be acceptable to everybody. But these words from The Social Contract are not all false; and may remind us how recently it has become absurd to take their view as full truth. "Christianity is an entirely spiritual religion, concerned solely with heavenly things; the Christian's country is not of this world. He does his duty, it is true; but he does it with a profound indifference as to the good or ill success of his endeavors. Provided that he has nothing to reproach himself with, it matters little to him whether all goes well or ill here below. If the State flourishes, he scarcely dares to enjoy the public felicity. If the State declines, he blesses the hand of God which lies heavy on his people."—Book iv, ch. viii.

friendliness and perhaps of organic union with it, the impression deepens in our common consciousness that the fruits by which true religion is to be known are such as ripen in part before our eyes. By virtue of some harmony of nature in the two worlds, nothing which is profitable in the one can, we believe, be wholly noxious in the other. And by virtue of some actual intercourse between heaven and earth, the effects of salvation may echo back and be noted in moral advancement, economic welfare, and the success of armies. Our increasing confidence that what we bind on earth is likewise bound in heaven, and that what we regard as good here is esteemed there in the same sense, makes it necessary for religion to submit to a type of measurement that must once have seemed unspeakably worldly and irrelevant. In proportion as any form of religion hinders, or fails to promote, what we regard as 'welfare' — that form is judged false: in no religion is authority now so far prior to social judgment that it could again impose upon Europe the human sacrifice or the sacred prostitution. When we now say that God loves men, we mean in part that God loves what we love; and when we refer to the will of God, we think we know that will chiefly through our knowledge of the conditions of social soundness and progress. We have all but lost our power to believe in the great reversal with which religious enthusiasm would once unhesitatingly confront any confessed ambition.

To be more definite, a certain large part of that primitive Other-world has been reclaimed as an integral part of this sphere of things. I do not mean simply that human ambitions have become capable of more idealism; so that the old contrast between the present and the beyond is largely reproduced in the contrast between the narrower and the wider interest, the self-seeking desires and the love of mankind. I mean that we have learned something of the sources of the older ideas about the Other-world; and that we can identify at least some of that Other-world with the human mind itself. For the human mind stands in direct contrast with nature; is somehow superior to nature, including it as in some god-realm remote yet intimate, a world of another sort. To the ancient beginner in self-knowledge, unfurnished with psychological ideas and unacquainted with the mysteries of introspection, his own mind appears to him — can only appear to him — as a part of supernature. He has no way to express what goes on within him save in objective terms, imaginatively chosen and projected. The gods who in ordeal choked the liar, showed themselves to the youth at initiation, who inspired the dance, swung-up the rage of fighting to omnipotence point, answered many a prayer, were in some part functions of his own soul — or of his sub-soul. Commands of the deity revealed to shaman and priest, — we may fairly call them instinctive forebodings of social good and evil, and say that supernature here is but remoter nature, impressing itself upon the sense of the keener-strung members of the race. It is simply the higher mental process that is read as a voice from another world.

So also with every new idea, with every product of "inspiration": those to whom at first, and rarely, such inbursts of reflexive insight came with definiteness and power could not have done otherwise than refer them to a supernatural source. Moments of deeper thought and intenser fancy distinguished above the commonplace of existence, moments of imagination and invention, — these moments have in all ages struck upon the mind as from a world beyond that of the visible career. No one upon whom reflection, the awareness of his own solitary self, has broken as an epoch in experience with the effect at once of revelation and command, can fail to understand how those early spokesmen of the spirit believed themselves both passive and at the same time more than human in the hours of their elevation; and how in declaring themselves media for the utterance of sacred oracles they were but recognizing that imperative impulse which an intense conviction always imposes upon the soul. The primitive prophet must have regarded the mystery of his insight with as much wonder and reverence as its expression would excite in those around him. Yet here also we are now able to recognize in large measure the natural operations of our own minds, conscious and subconscious.

In such ways as this much of the language of classic religion can be interpreted, and so much of the supernatural thereby *naturalized*, that we may question whether any significant part of the Other-world is left to be considered in a theory of religion.

For my part, I do not accept the notion that the Other-world can be wholly transferred to the present by these interpretations. There remains to me something literal in the supernature of the most material and credulous savage. I stand with him in the belief that religion would vanish if the whole tale of its value were shifted to the sphere of human affairs, however psychically or spiritually understood. But I accept the interpretations, as far as they can go. They prove enough to justify our method. They show an intermixture, anastomosis, and analogy between the Otherworld and this, so thorough that if we begin our study of religion by a rough survey of its working in our social structure and history we shall not go wide of the mark. Whatever other knowledge we might gain of religion, there could be no complete understanding unless it were also known in its bearing upon those interests we call humanistic.

CHAPTER II

THE WORK OF RELIGION IN HISTORY

IF we undertake to judge what religion is by what religion has done in history, some data are conspicuous, others obscure, — little is of sure purport. Students of *Kulturgeschichte* are more ready than they were to credit religion with certain definite achievements and services, especially at the beginning, in the rude business of nation-making, law-making, mind-making.[1] But as religion ceases to be the one salient social force its results mingle with the effects of other factors; clear tracing of the causal nerve is difficult. From the record, vast and igneous as it is, there appears also a certain contradictoriness in the effects of religion. It is credited with works of government, charged with works of war, — it sheds blood as generously as it promotes brotherhood. Religion has fostered everything valuable to man and has obstructed everything: it has welded states and disintegrated them; it has rescued races and it has oppressed them, destroyed them, condemned them to perpetual wandering and outlawry. It has raised the value of human life, and it has depressed the esteem of that life almost to the point of vanishing; it has honored womanhood, it has slandered marriage. Here is an energy of huge potency but of ambiguous character. From such a survey but one uncontradicted impression

[1] See Lippert, Bagehot, Fustel de Coulanges, Kidd, Hobhouse, etc.

emerges: the thing has been radical; it has had some grip upon the original instincts of human nature; it has known how to rule and to swirl into its own vortex all the currents of love, of hunger, and of self-defense; and it has been able to put these severally and together under its feet. It is this dynamic aspect of religion, an infinite resource, which has appealed to capable political intelligence since the days of Roman, perhaps of Persian, imperial policy; and it is this same aspect which appeals now to the scientist of society, whose eye is quick for usable elements of public power.

But religion, though a social force of unknown magnitude, has never been tamed to harness by statesman, diplomat, or sociologue: the word 'useful' hardly applies to it. Unlike the forces of nature, it is not now better known and more manageable for having been long dealt with. Statecraft has learned to fear it rather than to tamper with it; and having once hotly sought alliance now everywhere seeks separation. A thing so root-mighty cannot fail to excite the lust for power; but the exploiter has been at every point of contact stunned back by a touch of the uncontrollable. It is as if man's reason were trying to make bargains with man's insanity. As a social force, the *laws* of religious causality have not been discovered.

And in fact, from the side of its deeds in history religion remains a mystery. Its career is the swath of an agency immense, invisible, paradoxical. If its works are patent, they no more reveal its character than they becloud it. But the surface of historic fact which yields so little to an external inspection and use may respond more quickly to a simple hypothesis. What I have to propose is indeed something less than a theory at first, a rather unpromising tool, a figure of speech both commonplace and faulty. It is this. The effect of religion in history appears most comprehensible to me when I regard it not primarily as an actor but as a *parent*, a parent whose deeds are far less important than her progeny, and whose most notable activity is put forth only in course of her dealings with them. The distinction between utility and fertility runs throughout nature. It is a distinction which amounts to an incompatibility at some points in vital economy: it seems necessary that at these points life must choose between the useful and the fertile, so that the secret of the survival of many an apparently idle organ or social member is caught only in the rare moments of its creative action. It is vaguely, the distinction between worker and queen, leaf and blossom, male and female, science and fine art. Utility belongs to the middle things in creation, fertility to the extremes — the ugly, the rejected, the consummate, the perfect — to those things whereunto creation runs as to hopeless failure or to final achievement; and both the apparent failure and the apparent finality are denied in the moment when they become fertile. If the function of religion in the world should prove to be of the fertile rather than of the useful sort, the curiously paradoxical character of its overt deeds is in some measure accounted for.

Allow me to assert without detailed evidence that all the arts of common life owe their present status and vitality to some sojourn within the historic body of religion; that there is little in what we call culture which has not at some time been a purely religious function, such as dancing, legislation, ceremony, science, music, philosophy, moral control. I shall not enquire whether some of these human interests — which for the sake of simplicity I shall hereafter refer to in sum as "the Arts" — have not had independent beginnings, as for example ethical and legislative ideas may have had; for whenever this has been the case, the art in question has later found its way to amalgamation with religion, and has from this absorption emerged with a new character and animus. Religion, I shall say, according to this vague figure, is the *mother of the Arts:* this is its pragmatic place in the history of mankind and of culture.

If this figure is substantially right, the inference from the fruits of religion to the nature of religion itself will be more substantial and intimate than the inference from various effects to their cause, or from scattered deeds to the agent of them. For something of religion itself would have been communicated to its offspring, and might in all likelihood be recognized there. In attaining their majority, the children have not forgone the quality of the parent: they are still of her stock and substance.

It is true that in their successive struggles for emancipation, as in all adolescence, they were less conscious of their likeness to their parent than of their difference, and of the smothering necessity for independent fare and fortune. They have filled the air of Greek and modern times with cries to which we have become accustomed: "Art for art's sake," "Science for science's sake," "Right for right's sake," "Humanity for humanity's sake," and the rest — all of them heartily polemic against the notion that they exist for any god's sake. But note the stages of their growth to maturity. Originally, an Art, no matter which one — architecture, mensuration, law-giving, music — is regarded as a direct manifestation of the divine, subject to divine purposes only; then it is shown to be amenable to human control, and makes good its claim, as we have said, to serve as an independent human interest; later on, the question of its divinity or humanity loses venom, and it is acknowledged a free art, having a province in either sacred or secular subjects; finally, when all the causes for warfare have been won, the old spirit of kinship resumes sway, and someone sets up the cry that the art in question is really *the essence of religion!* No recent century has lacked men of weight who are prepared to discard the old progenetrix, and to assert with vigor that their religion, and quite possibly all religion, is now and hereafter identified with the cult of beauty, or of truth, or of righteousness, or of human good, or of all together.

Perhaps it is not too much to say that these several ingredients of our spiritual life constitute now for the world the bulk of what religion it lives by. At the beginning of history, religion is the whole of culture; at its end, it may seem, culture is the whole of religion. This relationship must be looked at somewhat closely.

Progressive historical subtraction, such as religion has been subject to in the maturing of the arts, looks like progressive analysis; and as this analysis continues the presumption grows that it approaches completion. Knowing as we do that all life moves toward the explicit from the hidden, it is more than a plausible hypothesis that religion has been simply the crude integral and germ of all these clearer essences; that her life has been prophetic and preparatory, her fertility is exhausted, her separate rôle is now outplayed. This impression is enforced by the observation that each of these arts fulfills in a substantial way the traditional functions of the older cult. Each one — poetry, or thought, or social service — has its type of *inspiration* upon which its devotee depends; each has its way of *saving* men from sensuality and selfishness; in each of them, this salvation is by way of *self-sacrifice* and devotion; and each of them is an imperishable cause, greater than individual aims, invisible and calling for a launch of *faith*, — yet for the same reasons more permanent than personal and visible things, a genuine *supernatural* order, capable of conferring a valid *immortality* upon the good and faithful servant. If there is anything in an identity of predicates, the identification of subjects seems irresistible. Religion is one with the Arts; it is *her* immortality to continue her life in them.

If we ask which of these causes contains the most of religion, the trend of the times furnishes an answer, as it were by instinct. It has frequently been observed that these several ideals or 'causes' have a remarkable power (due no doubt to their family likeness) to include and involve each other: the worship of beauty, for instance, carries with it normally a regard for the requirements of truth and sympathy, and conversely. We can see how any one of these, thoroughly worked out, might be sufficient for all: while still any one of them taken alone, as men are, would be likely to give life a skewed proportion in some places, since the supposed working-out is never finished — the artist may never arrive at a complete amalgamation of the moral with the beautiful, the moralist never fully unite grace and harmony with his ideal of right. It is the cult of social service that seems to be the most naturally comprehensive, and to engage most fully the whole religious nature of man. It tends at the present moment somewhat to displace the rest, and to suck up the enthusiasm of the new youth. It gives a better proportion: it can unite with beauty, but at a rate which does not part men from the actual dirt and disarray of social facts; it can unite with truth, but if it is a matter of the social good, or the religious education of children, or the like, — well, truth also can stand in its due order and degree, it may seem. But no matter which one of the offspring of religion is most appealing at any time; religion is exhausted into no one, — into nothing less than the totality of her children. The point is, that this totality, however found, seems an equivalent for passing religion.

A corroboration of this view may be found in the distribution of religion in the world, as compared with the distribution of the Arts. Where the Arts thrive as separate interests, religion is feeble. The zealous religion of to-day is at home in the life of the peasantry, of the bourgeoisie, — wherever life is still simple and unified.

For here it is still the whole of men's art, the whole of their literature, their philosophy, their poetry and their music: it is still the crude integral of their higher life, and should they lose it they would lose all that distinguishes their existence.[1] In so far and fast as they grow into possession of more individual forms of these same values they incline to let the separate practice of religion lapse.[1] Is it not fair to say that there are few of the developed individuals of our time who with either a powerful enthusiasm for a single branch of art, or a well-balanced appreciation of what we call our culture, retain in addition a vigorous religious life as a special direction of attention?

If we accept this theory of the function of religion in history and of its destiny to merge itself with the Arts, we can read with greater understanding the curious tale of religion's antagonism to progress, its inertia, obstruction, conservatism. We can readily put ourselves into the psychological position of the religious partisan, in whose consciousness the spirits of the several Arts dwell undistinguished, and all of whose inspiration has been indeed inseparable from his piety. We shall see it as inevitable that when the natural processes of growth and division have threatened to take away one by one architecture and sculpture, science and political control, from the sacred auspices under which they took their shape, it has seemed from the standpoint of the priest

[1] Höffding remarks, though with a different theory for the case, "The more men are absorbed in the business of self-maintenance, or the more they are given up to intellectual, æsthetic, and ethical interests, the more the strictly religious interest falls into the background — if indeed it does not entirely disappear." Philosophy of Religion, p. 111.

that these Arts were being cut loose from the source not only of their inspiration but of their life; and as though violence were being done not more to the priesthood or to the god than to the wayward Art itself and to the world beyond which fostered it. However much of 'priestcraft,' class-interest, and the like has mingled with these motives in the history of religious obstruction, there is a residuum of the genuine tragedy of all growth, so that the story of culture must henceforth be told not as a story of "warfare between science and religion," but as an infinitely human tale of growing asunder, with all the rending of veritable bonds and loyalties on both sides that such events have always involved.

While, then, we understand the historic attitude of religion to these changes, as dispassionate observers we must regard the process of taking human possession of any art as an advance; and hence as the necessary destiny of whatever religion contains, until *all* is free. The change is precisely analogous to the well-known psychological process of getting a clear concept or expression for what has been lurking in the mind as a feeling, unsatisfactory, haunting, mysterious, tantalizing. Once the adequate expression is hit upon, the cloudy fringes of the experience are lifted; the hovering sense of the infinite and ineffable disappear together with the humiliating consciousness of impotence: an 'idea' is born, and the human self is in *possession*. Such must be the career of all influxes to the spirit. And once the various possible directions of mental groping have been differentiated and established in our common life, the separate mission of religion is at an end.

Religion clothes itself to-day, indeed, in all the Arts, and in philosophy; but beneath these garments, what is there left to worship — unless, perchance, history itself? Instituted religion appears among us as a survival, decked out in relics of Arts that have won their freedom. Or, let us rather say, it is the spirit of the sacred past which organizes and sanctifies these relics, providing a place where the Zeitgeist may worship at the shrine of its own emancipation. Religion, as a separate object of attention, is an exhausted parent, cherished in her decay through some sentiment of recognizance by the Arts she has nourished, — the receiver, but no longer the giver of life.

The view of religion above sketched is a view more often felt than professed. It represents an argument more often found in men's lives than on their lips: suggested more by the tendencies of social movement than by any theories that are acknowledged among us. It is well to become expressly conscious of these facts of the progressive substitution of Art for religion, and of the view of religion which they imply. We have now to say what we think of this view.

So much must be admitted: that at every point of progress religion is a sort of remainder, — the *residual inspiration of human life.* And at each stage of subtraction, it becomes harder to see that there is any further residuum. What remains, if anything remains, is relatively formless, as compared with what has emerged. It is at a disadvantage for recognition. Especially when we have eliminated morality and philosophy from the special province of religion, does that province appear empty, mystical, barren ; and the position of those who ignore it may be made correspondingly solid, spiritually solid. To-day one need be no materialist, no mammonist, no foe of morality and order, no selfish or unspiritual mind, to dispense with the separate practice of religion ; it is precisely the humane and the ideal of temper, men of character and good-will, who by common consent and their own are likely to excuse themselves from the form, assuming that they have the substance — this is the most ominous fact that religion, as a distinctive thing in the world, has now to face. And rather than face it, many of her supporters hasten to save a weakening cause by accepting the identification — or near-identification — of religion with some Art — especially with morality or with human service. It is necessary at the outset of our work, in the interest of simple clearness, to recognize this tendency for what it is — a confusion and a breach of faith. Let religion vanish, if it is to vanish : but know that it is impossible — in any sense sanctioned by history, or faith, or clear reason — that religion should be merged with any Art, or with all Arts. The position of religion in the world is, and has been, unique ; and with the preservation of this distinction its very nature is bound up. The very work done by religion in the course of history has depended — despite her union with the Arts — on the clear eminence, above all her contact with affairs, of a summit which is No-art and touched by no Art.

What the inner nature of the unique element in religion may be, our present view of religion does not and need not show. Since it is No-art (and Art as we mean it includes everything that at any time is wholly naturalized and humanly possessed) it will be for any time somehow unpossessed and problematical, and may for the present be so to us. What our view of the effectiveness of religion in history does at once make evident as to its nature is — first, its necessary distinction; second, its necessary *supremacy*. These characters though external have been so essential to its fruitfulness, as to justify the statement that without them religion is not religion. A merged religion and a negligible or subordinate religion are no religion. If the importance of religion diminishes as Art progresses, religion must disappear. If there is any other way of life, if any other cause can act as a passable substitute, the case of special religion is lost. It is lost from the side of Art, because every Art is better off free, on its own ground, unencumbered by the peculiar apparatus and terminology of religion. It is lost from the side of life, because religion as a separate thing is the most difficult and expensive of all means to an end. But chiefly, it is lost from the ground of its own character, and the qualities which alone have given it its hold upon the human mind. Religion is already gone when it is weighed with or subordinated to some other and surer value. It can only be held to on the supposition that it is necessary. Shorn of its pride, its intolerance of rivals, its scorn of comparison, it is shorn of its honor also, and therewith of all that defines its value. Only that religion can hold attention which is always younger than the youngest of her children, more fruitful for what she has spent, more needful for the continued life of the Arts than for their inception.

It is here chiefly that our figure is defective. For the work of religion is a *perpetual* parentage; the status of the Arts is a perpetual dependence. All independence is conceptual, approximate, and relative. The inspiration, or breathing, of all the Arts, is, in the final tracing of their "compartments," a breathing of the outer and unlimited air: communication of this sort with the Whole, is religion. Or let us say, religion is the function of in-letting, or osmosis, between the human spirit and the living tissue of the universe wherein it is eternally carried. If many imagine that their Art is their religion, it is doubtless so far true, that their religion is continuous with their Art, and would be truncated and deformed without it. But their Art, in so far as it is still capable of creation, is continuous with their religion — a vital union which depends strangely enough on the consciously-held distinction between them.

Is our present age an age of originality, or is it rather an age in which Art gnaws its nails for sustenance? this age — in which every Interest has its own head and its own way as never before! Freedom to us means reasonableness; and reasonableness means that everything is referred to sources of its own kind. Thus, we refer public effects to public forces, — not to royal fiat, — and this is political freedom. We refer material effects to material causes, not to divine or human will, — and this is scientific freedom. We respect the family privacy of the different parts or groups of the cosmos, — thereby each such group is given its freedom. None but fine-art-considerations shall have an entrée to fine-art-work-shops. The rights of individuals to their own spheres and provinces, the right to be tried by one's own kind, even to be punished by nothing but the logic of one's own crime, — we care for these rights, but they are not by any means the only rights we care for: we treasure the private rights of Ideas, of Abstractions. Every Principle has its own belongings, every Conception has its own circle of Relations which must not be intruded upon by the unfit and extraneous. It is the technique of living to learn and feel all these personal and abstract Owns, — all the proprieties and freedoms, not to mingle Business with Personalities, not to lug in Politics when one is in Society, not to test Humor by canons of Science, still less bring Humor into the contemplation of Religion. One word is equivalent to our culture — 'Discrimination.' Yes, there was never so much freedom in the world as now, i.e., there were never so many Owns to be learned and respected. But this world of Owns is a noble mesh of surfaces that would be closed, but cannot be. It is in some sense a failure, a necessary and mysterious failure, likely to die of its tight-held freedoms and independences, its clear-cut-nesses and non-intrusions. Religion it is that knows the point of this failure. Religion holds self-sufficiency in derision; religion is the comprehensive irony of the world toward all Owns. In opening every Art toward itself, it opens each toward every other: through No-art all Arts become one, and one life courses through all of them.

Our arts are parcelled out much as we sometimes parcel out and enumerate human instincts. Every instinct naturally has an art — i.e., a way of finding satisfaction; on the other hand, every primary art, broadly speaking, corresponds to, and helps to define 'an instinct.' But no one can make a satisfactory *list* of the instincts, or of the primitive impulses, of man: for in the human being they have so far mixed and braided and fused, as their objects have developed, that listing becomes arbitrary. The truth is, they belong together; and in our modes of living find their way together: love and hunger meet in the family, hunger and defense in the civic community, love and defense in the war-gang. (This absurd list of instincts will serve as well as another to show the point.) Now in religion *all* instincts meet. Destined as they are to come to terms with each other in human society, religion engages them all, keeps them in yoke together until they make friends. Just as we found in all Arts the outlines of religious action, so every instinct, in what it deeply drives toward, shows the traits of religious aspiration. The life of an instinct and the continuous inspiration of the corresponding art are the same thing: *creativity* in some sort is what satisfies and alone satisfies every instinct, and creativity is precisely what religion calls out in them, in the process of holding them to their own unity.

Bergson has told us that all originality is derived from sensation: this is but part of the truth. Originality is derived from the primitive. Religion, "the crude integral of the Arts," is primitive as sensation is primitive, fundamental to knowledge as sensation is fundamental to knowledge — at the opposite pole: and creativity comes not from sensation alone (though not without sensation), but from sensation warmed and wet by the sky of religion. And back to mother-earth, to the cruder mind which knows its own integrity, shall we go, unless in holding to the severalty and freedom of our Arts and Owns, we are able to hold with equal strength to that which is other than all of them, the source of their creativity and the channel of their union.

Herewith, then, I have expressed quite dogmatically a conviction regarding the function of religion in history and society, a function which throws some light upon its nature. Only the completion of our whole task can bring adequate substance into these wide outlines. What the process of religion in the mind of man may be through which these creative results take place, we have not begun to enquire. We shall come nearer to religion itself in our next study — the effects of religion in individual life.

CHAPTER III

THE TRAITS OF RELIGION IN PERSONS

WE know religion when we meet it in persons. We are in no need of definition to guide our eyes, or to help in identifying it. We are perpetually seeing its fruits, or missing them, in our neighbors. We are sensitive even to its shades and degrees; aware of its more or less, its depth, its texture, its resistance. Indeed, we are instinctive connoisseurs on this subject, every son of Adam, — because religion is a human property, not a property of culture. An errand-boy can detect as well as any psychologist the falsetto in an assumed devoutness; is as keen to mark the fatal note of economy in an accent pious from habit; is cut as quickly by the leap of the true flame, no matter from what covering.

And this holds good in spite of the fact that a man's religion is the hiddenest thing in him. Hidden in large part from himself. Let him try with might and main to give a true estimate of his own, — his word for it is no better than mine: the thing is too close to himself to be well seen by him. But for that very reason our perception of it in him is conveyed immediately with our sense of the fiber of the person. It is as if a man's religion and his personal quality were in large measure interchangeable terms. We take our impression of it involuntarily, and this impression becomes one of the most stubborn of human opinions: if the alternative is pressed upon us of doubting a man in whom we have met this absolute worth, or of doubting an institution or tradition which damns him on its technicalities, we may find ourselves loosing our feet from the institution. In such and such an atheist or doubter of the Trinity or happy-go-lucky liver we may have caught some deep flash of the trait we call religious, and we sit strangely secure in the prospect of his future destiny. The power of religious dogmas is limited, and their edge slowly turned, by the unwaivable weight of this court which sits in permanent judgment upon their judgments.

Our perception of religion, like any other instinctive perception, can doubtless be sophisticated and work false. It holds its truth with difficulty in the presence of prejudice, theological interest, and passion. Even so, it is possible to describe in the large the kind of thing which in persons we pronounce the traits of religion. The world has not been poor in characters in whom the quality is present in such abundance as to carry our affirmative beyond a doubt; with these in mind we shall be able to characterize at least its outward appearance.

That which chiefly marks the religious soul is a fearless and original valuation of things. Its judgments emerge somehow from solitude, as if it had resources and data of its own sufficient to determine its attitudes without appeal to the bystander, as if by fresh contact with truth itself, it were sure of its own justice. It may treat objects which we pass as ordinary as if they were not ordinary; distinguished matters may seem reduced in its eyes to the commonplace. It lives as if seeing reality where neither physical eye nor practical judgment see anything; and it makes material sacrifices for this faith. Its original valuation is seen also in what it fails to do, equally with what it does. It seems not to display the common need to escape from some of the unpleasant facts of experience — to edge away from certain passages, to hurry through with certain inevitable others. It behaves as if no present experience could utterly oppress it, as if indeed all circumstance brought by history to its share might be received with respect, almost with deference, as significant and right, not accidental. It is not as one immune from suffering that the religious spirit moves in the severer passes of its career, but as one willing to accept and able to entertain suffering in the solemn adequacy of its own peculiar insight.

But this originality and this freedom are strangely united with an opposite quality, *necessity*. The certitude of the religious spirit is so poised by an inward bond that it conveys no impression of personal self-assertion. Its wisdom does not emanate from itself alone, is in some paradoxical fashion both original and derivative: it has the air of being less a product of individual force than a result of profound partnership with some invisible source of wisdom. The anxiety and burden of a self-maintained position are by this fact removed; the spirit is freed from itself by mooring in some objective reality constantly present to its consciousness.

And so also there is no sign of the strain which we associate with moral or courageous effort. The motive of religion is unlike that of an idea or principle which evokes a dominant sense of exertion and sacrifice: it is rather like that of a deep passion which possesses and supports the soul, and cancels with a margin of its own strength any opposing motion. In brief, this person has meat to eat which we who look on know not of; and here lies the mystery and the fascination of religion as it moves about in the world. It is the fascination not only of assurance, but of the sufficiency, the simplicity, the natural necessity, with which it utters its novelties, moves its mountains, and ushers in its revolutions.

If its relations to its invisible Object, held inviolate with anxious care, are such as to unbind it in some wise from men, they are also such as to bind powerfully to itself whoever enters the sphere of its action. It may seem that this Object is such only as men must serve if they will best serve each other. It endows the judgments of the religious soul, original as they are, not with a lower but with a higher human currency, — as if that Object were but reality itself. The burden of eccentricity is thrown upon our common behavior, not on that of religion. The words and actions of the religious man become *authoritative* for the world of men. In becoming free, he has also become obedient to some necessity; and in becoming obedient he has become universal.

Surely the religious spirit is living as if immortality were its share. What its source of judgment and power may be we have yet to discover, but in its valid originality, and in its emancipation from the stress and haste of the temporal current, we may see a present possession of that to which the secular spirit presses forward. That worth-of-life which is commonly held as imaginary, prospective, hypothetical, has become to it a matter as it were of sensation, immediate and inescapable. That which to men otherwise is but the word has to its knowledge become flesh. Such present possession of the distant sources of worth and certainty has been called "faith"; it is the characteristic of religion in all ages.

Here lies the essential distinction between religion and the Arts on the ground of personal experience. Art is long; religion is immediate. The attainment in every Art is future, infinitely distant; the attainment of religion is present. Religion indeed involves a present possession in some sort of the very objects which the Arts infinitely seek. Knowledge, for example, is an infinite quest in the order of nature, — and in it there is no absolute certainty but only a growing probability and approximation: but the religious soul knows *now* — and that without losing interest in the slow movement of science. Human brotherhood also is an infinite problem — men have to be *made* brothers, and the whole of history is requisite to tell the tale of achieving that end: but in religion men are already brothers and experience their brotherhood in the moment of common worship. So with morality: in time my moral task will never be finished, for my imperfection is infinite and my progress by small degrees; but religion calls upon me to be perfect at once even as God is perfect, and in religion somehow I am perfect. By this contrast we are helped to describe, still problematically, but with much greater nearness than before, the nature of religion.

Religion, we may now say, is the present attainment in a single experience of those objects which in the course of nature are reached only at the end of infinite progression. Religion is anticipated attainment.

This precursory definition of religion serves the purpose of such definitions — not to solve problems, but rather to open them. In religion, we say, men live *as if* in presence of attainment, of knowledge, of immortality: but in what respect is the attainment present when in the order of nature it must still remain at an infinite distance? What sort of present satisfaction is that which can still leave the individual involved in the unending struggle? We have indeed ceased to respect as religious any state of mind which withdraws the subject from sympathy or alliance with the age-long human labor. Whatever may be the nature of that anticipation of all attainment, genuine religion is not inclined — as far as hard work goes — to take advantage of its advantage. If being in the world it is not of the world, it is none the less with the world and for it — in brief, *in for it*, and with no loss of power. That is an extraordinary attainment which one must still labor forever to possess: but just this paradox is inherent in the religious consciousness, and opens the way to a fundamental question as to its nature.

For something of this same paradoxical character we find in certain kinds of *knowledge:* there are insights which come in a moment, and yet have to be kept by endless vigilance — as men keep their liberty. The peculiar possession of religion is often spoken of in terms of knowledge, as wisdom, vision, revelation, truth. But there are reasons for doubting whether religion is, literally speaking, a kind of knowledge. Whatever it is, it cannot readily be translated into valid ideas and language. Its secret is one which the religious spirit tries not to keep but to give away — and cannot. But what is a knowledge that cannot be expressed, communicated, or thought? And further, thought is but one of those same Arts which (as science or philosophy) is a product of religion, together with politics, poetry, and all other forms of human expression. How then can religion itself be a matter of knowledge?

When we speak of religion in terms of thought, is it not according to that loose and general usage which applies the word thought to all that is inward and free in men? 'As a man thinketh in his heart, so is he'— that is to say, as a man orients himself, as he 'makes up his mind,' as he feels his way in the practical antitheses of existence. Is it not more probable, in terms of psychological fact, that religion consists in a practical attitude of mind, or a mode of feeling — say in practical confidence, optimism, good-will, enthusiasm for what is real, the power to penetrate shams that goes with these things? A disposition of this sort, an inward certitude or faith, is indeed an anticipated attainment, 'the substance of things hoped for' — but in more primitive form than knowledge, in the form, briefly speaking, of *feeling*.

We have now to deal with this view that religion is a matter of feeling. We may agree to use the word feeling for the present in a very wide sense — as a name for whatever in consciousness, deeper than explicit thought, is able to give a bent to conduct. Feeling is not, as we sometimes think it, a wholly vague and uncertain principle: it is capable of bearing much responsibility in the direction of practical living. In the form of moral disposition, it may be the highest, as well as the most individual, determinant of conduct and bearing. The question whether religion belongs to this realm of practical and responsible feeling rather than to the realm of thought is an issue of greater practical interest than may appear in this formal statement; it will engage us for some time.

PART II

RELIGIOUS FEELING AND RELIGIOUS THEORY

CHAPTER IV

THE RETIREMENT OF THE INTELLECT

THE intellect has evidently been assuming too much importance, not only in religion but in life at large. Hardly otherwise would so much satisfaction be taken in showing this quite human organ to its subordinate place, so much eagerness in putting our valuables into some other custody. Wherever our likes and dislikes are concerned, as in appreciations of beauty, moral rightness, and other values, logic is *persona non grata* — at least in its own name. Since the impressive effort of Kant to mark out a strictly limited province for the valid use of the theoretical reason — a province which all our major human interests lie safely outside of — thinkers of the first rank (with exceptions, but with singular accord) have added some stroke to the picture of reason's retirement, representing it as servant of the will, or as tool and creature of some darker and more primal reality — blind impulse, immediate feeling, the unconscious. In religion more than elsewhere the intellectual disaffection is sweeping. One who now ventures to discuss religion from the side of cosmology as a "theory of original causation" seems to be strangely remote from the point; the inoffensive words, creed, dogma, theology, are almost words of reproach. The whole apparatus of reason in religion has retreated in importance, in favor of a more substantial basis — which we have agreed to call feeling.[1]

This retirement of the intellect is not altogether a result of free research. So far as religion is concerned, it strongly resembles a forced conclusion. It comes from holding tenaciously to the immense importance of religion, while despairing of finding for it any intellectual content having equal importance, or equal stability or accessibility. The *ideas* of religion, whether in the form of metaphysics or of revealed truth, have not been able to command that respect and loyalty which is readily given to religion itself. We are driven to confess that we actually care more for religion than we do for reli-

[1] The following may be taken as typical expressions of the tendency to give feeling the primacy in religion:

Es ist seit Schleiermacher ein anerkannter Grundsatz, dass der innerste und eigentliche Kern der Religion im Gefühl zu suchen sei. E. von Hartmann. Religion des Geistes, p. 28.

Not only can religious knowledge never cast off its subjective character; it is in reality nothing but that very subjectivity of piety considered in its action and in its legitimate development. A. Sabatier. Outlines of a Philosophy of Religion, p. 310.

I believe that the logical reason of man operates in this field of divinity exactly as it has always operated in love, or in patriotism, or in any other of the wider affairs of life in which our passions or our mystical intuitions fix our beliefs beforehand. It finds arguments for our convictions, for indeed it *has* to find them. It amplifies and defines our faith, and dignifies it, and lends it words and plausibility. It hardly ever engenders it; it cannot now secure it. William James. Varieties of Religious Experience, p. 436.

Religious experience is essentially religious feeling. H. Höffding. The Philosophy of Religion (tr. Meyer), p. 106.

What the future of religion is to be no one can tell. Of this, however, I think we may be sure: religious belief will stand or fall with what I have called the Religion of Feeling. J. B. Pratt. Psychology of Religious Belief, p. 302.

gious theories and ideas : and in merely making that distinction between religion and its doctrine-elements, have we not already relegated the latter to an external and subordinate position? Have we not asserted that "religion itself" has some other essence or constitution than mere idea or thought? We are in need of some other foundation for our faith.

The proposal, then, that religion may be sufficiently founded on feeling comes with too great promise of relief to be lightly dismissed. Grant it, and all dogmatic authority loses its pressure at once. We are set free to be religious beings without the infinite argument and haggling over unreachable and untestable propositions. Creeds we wave aside ; — or else, we carry them lightly, knowing that they are at one stroke dehorned, put out of conflict with truth as otherwise established. We need not any longer take their clauses to task seriatim and verbatim; we are free to utter the *whole*, if we will, as a single expression of the feeling we call faith, as the historic voice of a total confidence in destiny. Who can deny that we do thereby come nearer to the intimate sense of our creeds? Further, if the essence of religion is feeling, it is to be judged by feeling and not by argument, — it is to be judged as beauty and right are judged : we are not only at liberty to bring our instincts to bear, we are compelled to bring them to bear, — a responsibility from which we too easily escape when religion is gained by accepting a creed. Who will say that this requirement is not more adapted than the old one to keep alive the spirit of genuine religion? That forced conclusion which has driven religion from intellect toward feeling may thus prove a literal god-send to religion. But there are other grounds for this change; it is, in fact, the outcome of converging tendencies so various that they can only be called the labor of an age. Some of these we shall pass in review.

The *comparison of religions*, whenever historical movements (whether crusades, or conquests, or missions) have made comparison inevitable, has always led to some doubting of the face-value of creeds: for the alien religion has always made some appeal to that instinctive knowledge of religion which we have said is a possession of human nature. Especially is this true of that deliberate scientific comparison of religions which in our own time has yielded so great wealth of historical knowledge. For this wealth has required of us a penetrating effort to conceive the essence of religion in its world-wide identity: in which effort we have been steadily drawn back of religious ideas to something more fundamental. Men's religions, we cannot help seeing, are much more alike than the explanations and expressions they give for them. Diverse as are myths, prophecies, eschatologies, angelologies, and the rest, religious feeling is much the same the world over. When identical values thus attach themselves to quite different ideas, it cannot remain in doubt where the substance of the matter lies. Theories which have varied so much might vary further *ad libitum*, and religion still do its common human work. The thing is indispensable; the ideas that have been connected with it are, with all their mystery and ambiguity, perennial causes of discord, misunderstanding, division without compensating benefit. It is a pious wish to be rid of them all, if it were possible, and let mankind flow to its proper unity in the substance of religion, in the feelings which all men share.

A similar impression is made by the *life-histories of religious movements*, as we are now able to understand them. Religion renews its life in great bursts of impulse which emanate not from new thoughts, but from rarely impressive personalities, capable of inspiring exalted and passionate devotion in their friends and followers. Their utterances are poetic, oracular, couched in figure and parable, not in theses. While their power and meaning seems to be propagating itself by the mediumship of words and thoughts, it is in reality propagating itself immediately, by infection, by contact, by the laying on of hands, by the leaping-across of an overmastering fire. In the presence of such men, leaders and carriers, others are lifted, not to high knowledge, but indeed to a high degree of moral potency which is capable of executing great deeds, sometimes upon the most visionary basis. With the rise of the critical business of thinking and philosophizing the decline of religious vitality keeps even step. As passion cools, theology spreads; and as theology spreads, passion cools still more. Remoteness from religious leadership can infallibly be read in the conditions of religious life in a given place or age. The stream which at its source is impetuous, fierce, channel-plowing, here at its mouth lies lazy, divided, straggling off to the dead-level of religious homogeneity, through the arms of shallow, reasoning sects, where (by the very multitude of distinctions between the believers) there is hardly any more distinction between river and bank, saint and sinner.

The making of creeds, it is true, has never been a

purely theoretical interest; creeds have had important social functions: but these functions, we think, do not lead us to love them more. For creed-making belongs to the eras of political-religious propagandism stage through which especially the religions of Buddha, Jesus, and Mohammed have passed lingering. Creeds have served as weapons of warfare and persecution and inner partisan rivalries. Disfavor towards the polemic method of religious promotion thus adds itself to the distrust of intellect, in the rise of the religion of feeling.

But these comparative and historical judgments upon religion are themselves results, and hard-won results, of longer circuits of human labor; circuits which flow wide of any special religious interest, impinging upon religion only after coursing through the whole range of scientific experience. It is not our religious instinct alone, but something much like an *acquired scientific instinct* which sends us looking to-day among the feeling-roots of religion for its ultimate essence.[1] Into the building of that scientific instinct have entered many strands, of which it will be sufficient for us to consider four — the psychological, the biological, the pragmatic, the critical.

[1] Is there not much eloquence, for example, in the high value which is accorded to simple and emotional religious experience in the psychological workshop? What is it but an instinctive expression of the deference which intellect pays to religion *as to a foreign power*, that the investigator looks so eagerly into the humblest corners to bring to light its pearls — or seeks to lure it into his presence by means of the wily questionnaire? Surely, if the material of religious life must be thus sought, it is something other, in essence, than the thought which seeks it. This humble, empirical attitude of the scholar toward religion is indeed the most convincing acknowledgment that thought finds here something other than itself.

I must speak broadly in all these matters; dealing with general tendencies, not with the work of individual men: dealing also for the most part with older tendencies, such as have had time to pass into our mental habits, not with views now rising.

First, then, of the *psychological current* of thought: our world is thoroughly leavened by the conviction that *nothing is real unless it belongs to conscious experience.* Philosophers wonderfully agree in accepting the term "experience" as a comprehensive name for whatever is either real or significant. Facts and events may have their independent external existence; but they gain living certainty and importance only as they impinge upon consciousness. Unless a fact is caught in the circuit of a self; unless somewhere it reports to the sensitive, irritable, responsive thing we call a mind, it is nothing. It is the inner event that is solid: the status of matter, of energy, of all external objects, is doubtful; the 'outer world' is best understood by relation to the inner world, as a stimulus, or as even less than a stimulus.

The result of this conviction is that we incline to unravel every science from its inner end, from its psychological insertion. Where have we to look for the sources of public events, the making of states, the development of crafts, the making and managing of political movements, the shaping of ideals? To human instincts, to "human nature." There is no theory of politics, of economics, of law, of morals, nor of religion either, that can now dispense with its psychological groundwork. Skill in self-knowledge, in tracing the psychical factors of all institutions and of all history: this is the predominant habit and technique of our scientific age. No such surefooted exploring of the inner man has ever before been known.

But all this psychological habit (lineal descendent of a subjective sort of idealism) brings with it the depreciation of idea in favor of feeling. For ideas and thoughts are the tools of our intercourse with external objects. They are attempts at externality: they are at the same time the medium of outgo from the mind to the outer world, and the medium through which that outer world maintains the posture of externality to the mind. If it is only the subject that is important, an end-in-itself, and also a beginning in itself, then the objects of thought and theory — together with thought and theory themselves — are there only as *means*, factitious, troublesome, and circuitous, through which the subject must win its satisfaction. The real substance of that subject is something else than intellect — a natural self with spontaneous affections and repulsions, needs and desires, beliefs and illusions, consistencies and contradictions. That which in human nature is fundamental, intimate, genuine, private, and wholly owned, is feeling: in feeling we substantially exist.

Then there is the *biological current*, which easily abets and coalesces with the psychological trend of thought. There is something in the logic of biology (though certainly it is no part of biology itself) which has helped along the conviction that *nothing is real unless it is aboriginal and germinal.* Biology must find the explanation of the characters of living things in some interaction between these things and their environments: but what is the "thing" which takes part in this interaction? Naturally, it must be something which is identical throughout all the transformations of the organism, the same in the germ and in the mature individual: but that which is identical in the greater and in the less must be the less, one might fairly suppose, or even less than the less. Hence in identifying the living thing, we naturally look toward nucleus and germ, behind the differentiated and explicit.

Now if it is true, as it seems to be true, that conscious life is a shape which has been taken on by some more primitive reality; and that intellect is a more or less advanced instrument assumed by conscious life in its later stages: it would follow that this conscious life itself is something else than intellect, — something presumably of the nature of feeling.

It is true that inferences of this sort are hazardous: the same logic would lead us to seek the explanation of consciousness in something less than consciousness. Psychology is always attracted by biology, in the search for its own unit, into a twilight region where physical and psychical incline to blend, and can no longer for lack of light be distinguished. Mistaking its own ground, it is in danger of lingering and groping about in a sort of half-world, where the mind never knows how far to admit itself a group of tropisms, nor the brain how far to allow its chemistry to dally with the influences of the mind. But as to the position of the intellect and its ideas there is no confusion. They are, as it were, feelers, sparks, signals, thrown out by the deeper reality, and subject forever to its own ultimate ends. Ideas crop out like leaves; if they are cropped off, the root lives on — and produces more leaves. A psychological sociology accepts this instruction from biology, and forms its theories upon these principles. What is the substance of the family, for instance, if not in certain heavy-loaded human instincts which survive many a dynasty of customs and custom-supporting theories. The independent variable, in its slow march through the ages, lies far deeper than the idea. The real is the permanent and the ancient, as well as the germinal and creative. But only in the form of feeling can consciousness accompany the organism, as it is traced back to its simplest forms or to its beginnings.

The pragmatic current, the third of these scientific tendencies, is much older than present-day pragmatism, which is but "a new name for some old ways of thinking." Its conviction is that *nothing is real which does not do work.* And in proportion as it appears that the working element of human nature is value-consciousness, not fact-consciousness, pragmatic tendencies assign feeling a higher degree of reality than idea. This is but to make into a universal principle the repeated observation that 'essences,' when we get close to them, are *energies* — and nothing else. If we look for mental substance, what do we find except the energy-charge of action, which is feeling. Ideas can apparently float idle in the mind; facts and truths can deserve the epithet 'mere'; and if they do not deserve it, if they have any *grit*, it is no inherent quality of their own, but added by some gift from our own will. Especially are our ideas about metaphysical things liable to become thus 'mere' and dead. All available information about heaven and hell, and more, one may receive unmoved. In a certain military establishment, the pious are called "hell dodgers," implying that a soldier should be ready to take hell like a man. If any stirring of concern or plan of action comes out of the idea, that is an additional fact, not bound to it by any definition; and religion lies in the stirring, not in the view. Enlightened religion has perceived this from afar, and has called on men not to acknowledge certain truths, but to love certain realities.

In this judgment biology strengthens the pragmatic tendency, just as it abets the psychological tendency. For an idea is (biologically) a product of friction and hesitation in conduct: a token of failure in spontaneous reaction. Creatures become conceptually conscious, it appears, in proportion as they have need to extract an identical value from an ambiguous or non-committal environment. Hence, an idea stands for a pause between perception and action. It is an eddy into which the mind enters, a product of doubt and a means of parley. But religious impulse has no need thus to learn its line of outflow. It has no mission to special plans of action, but rather a set and spirit to infuse into the whole active being. Religion is one with its application; it *exists applied.* Hence, it does not pause to hang up in the exhibit room of our ideas the program or scheme of its meaning, as if it were something to be deliberated — definite, defensible, and so debatable. It is more like the breath of life, its existence its own defense. Such immediacy and centrality belong only to feeling.

All of these currents so far described are founded upon a common insight, namely: that *ideas have at all points to be tested by a higher authority.* This insight is itself the burden of yet another current of thought, much older and broader than the others, which it sustains and makes possible: it is *the critical current*, coextensive almost with modern times. To John Locke we owe our prompt confidence that it is possible to set up limits and standards for thought; it was he who first deliberately made bold to examine our ideas *from the outside* — in the attitude of a physician; it is "Dr." Locke who first accomplishes *an idea of an idea* — a more or less physical idea of an idea — and sets the fashion of assigning reasonable limits to the use of reason, in view of the humble origin and restricted function of our ideas. That we may and must look thus physicianly upon our ideas from the outside is no longer an open question; it is only to be questioned what that greater thing is which surrounds and subordinates the ideas to itself. That higher authority, the three currents above considered have agreed to find in the region of feeling. And so far at least we must follow them: in every human interest the rationale, the exposition, is weaker than the vital meaning of the thing as retained in feeling or instinct. And all observations of this sort are more conspicuously true of religion than of anything else, because in religion the status of ideas is less certain than elsewhere, and the tap root of human instinct more deeply involved.

It seems to me a weighty consensus, — this group of tendencies which we have thus hastily reviewed. It is, of course, no new discovery that religion is an affair of the heart rather than of the head. Among the axioms of that instinctive human knowledge about religion is this one: that religion must be accessible to all sorts and conditions of men, to the unlearned as well as to the learned. If scripture and all appearances do not deceive, babes have even a certain advantage in this matter over the wise and prudent; which could hardly be the case if religion depends upon the results of thinking. Religion does not as a rule show itself strongest in the most thoughtful; nor can the reasoner develop it in himself by his reasoning. All these are observations of long standing in the history of the spirit. What distinguishes our present age is that this old truth now appears as a philosophical conclusion, as a result hard-won and independently won. Our sketch of some of the factors in this conclusion, imperfect as it is, may make more definite to us the meaning of the claim that feeling is the essence of religion. A general conception or picture of religion emerges, something as follows:

Religion is to be understood as a product and manifesto of human desire; and that of no secondary and acquired desire, such as curiosity, but of deep-going desire, deep as the will-to-live itself. Its non-rational character may be seen in the fact that in satisfying the religious craving, an individual serves the race more than he serves himself: as in the desires of sex and hunger, nature uses a well-centered impulse to produce a far-reaching effect. The religious motives of men have contained the secret of political loyalty as of other costly, death-involving loyalties. If we should venture to name this deep-set desire which we call religious it might be represented as an ultimate demand for conscious self-preservation:[1] it is man's leap, as individual and as spe-

[1] Lippert unites many strands of theory in deriving religion from the fundamental need of "Lebensfürsorge." Kulturgeschichte, chapter I.

cies, for eternal life in some form, in presence of an awakened fear of fate. Religion is a reaction to "our finite situation," a natural reflex of small and highly aspiring beings in a huge — perhaps infinite — arena. This reaction seems to be, at its heart, as instinctive as a start or a shudder. It is (in its first shock) an immediate and penetrating, even appalling, recognition of what and where I am in the universe; it may issue in some sense of footing, and of the direction in which safety lies: in any case it is, in itself, a great emotional response to the felt perils and glories of the weird situation. The unlighted vagueness of outline in this vast setting, the necessity of moving by the most elemental of instincts rather than by vision, the almost animal panics and animal assurances of the adventure (as we see them in religious history), make the language of reason inept — even false. If we resist the impulse to refer the whole experience to a special faculty, different alike from thought, from feeling, and from will, in short to a "supernatural sense," we must certainly choose the realm of feeling as fittest to contain so unique and intimate a transaction. The history of religious agony and despair, of hope, attainment, exultation, the whole gamut of the intense inner drama, shows beyond doubt the locus and the eternal spring of the vitality of religion.

Such feeling is peculiarly able to retain the position which religion must hold in our living, — the position which reason is always exposed to losing. There is something unspoiled and original about human feeling: it lies beyond the reach of dispute, refutation, and change. Religious feeling is the adequate counterpart of those metaphysical first principles upon which so much used to be hung, in everything that made those principles attractive. It has the same primordial and original character, the same cosmic scope and dignity; and it has in addition what these principles had not, — the energetic property which fits it not alone to guide but also to instigate and to sustain what it has produced. Men have always been more or less clear that the essence of religion cannot be far from the brewing-place of action, and that the most sensitive test of genuine religion is in its ethical consequences. Prophets have always been obliged to recall idle mankind — keen to evade a hard requirement — from the extraneous to the central elements in their religion. Of such extraneous elements, rite and ceremony were prominent in the earlier ages of prophetic rebuke; but in these latter days it is the seduction of the religious *idea*, with the same illusory promise of security formerly offered by the rite, that is the chief antithesis to genuine religion. Practical and responsible feeling bids fair to give a clear and sufficient answer to the various demands which are made upon religion. But perhaps one point should be further dwelt upon.

For surely he is bold who asserts that religion, which we may grant to arise out of feeling, has its satisfaction in feeling also? In a former chapter we defined religion, not by its origin, but by its successful completion, — as a form of *attainment:* and can it be said that feeling satisfies feeling? It has been assumed from ancient times that these cosmic hopes and fears contain within themselves as necessary ingredients certain theoretical questions, which questions can only be satisfied with theoretical answers. It was supposed that men wanted to know whether there be, in very fact, a god; and whether, in historic literalness, men's souls endure after the death of the body. These and other questions are categorical enough, it might seem; and the plain-speaking man will not be put off with other than categorical answers.

But we are pointedly reminded by advocates of the religion of feeling that if we have indeed such wishes as these for express knowledge, these wishes have never been fulfilled: and the various good reasons for supposing such questions unanswerable are so many good reasons for doubting whether we have any such theoretical needs and wishes. These alleged wishes for knowledge have in all times been quieted by answers that can be easily shown empty; which would imply that the wish itself is something other than it takes itself to be, is only one more case of a common thing in human nature—a misunderstanding of our own wants.

For example: we have at times set great store on the doctrine that God exists—letting pass as relatively unimportant the further question about the *nature* of God: but clearly unless we have some tangible inkling as to what God is like, it profits us little to know that he *is*. May it not be that the real meaning of that desire to be assured of a God is absorbed in settling our own good-will toward our own destiny, satisfying ourselves that in acting morally we are not playing the fool? Similar things have to be said of the interest in a future life, often so zealously insisted on apart from any enquiry into the possible nature and endurableness of a permanent existence. Perhaps into these questions themselves we have imported more of *the earth*, with its own personalities and its own time-order than we could support.

There is such a thing as greed of the spirit — so we are told by those who find religion in feeling — which not only claims more than it can use, but heaps up for itself trouble by overreaching its powers. We learn in time to be content with the "revelation" we have; and to read that revelation more modestly than we used, accepting the fact that in all questions of supernatural physics and psychology the same obscurity is the lot of man in all ages. For revelation, as we come to see, is reticent, and slow to clarify in these matters. If there are any coherent messages to be read, we must gaze long into the glass to make them out. We are more diffident about lump-communications from behind the veil than our forefathers were. To say that our satisfaction comes in the form of feeling rather than in that of categorical propositions seems more simply conformable to the facts. It is in harmony also with what many men of exalted piety have reported of their own attainments: namely, that the contents of religious insight are indescribable; that as we specify them, we falsify them; that feeling alone is right. According to these persons, as religion becomes more true and self-knowing, it becomes more silent; as it becomes perfect, it becomes dumb. It is our practical and responsible feeling which alone can give body and substance to that which in terms of idea is nothing.

Let us not disguise the fact that only a much altered conception of revelation can comport with this religion of feeling, a conception somewhat as follows: If it may be said that God in religious attainment touches and satisfies the spirit, his dealings are not overt and visional, nor verbally expressible without transformation and risk of error. In admitting the soul to new certainties, revelation leads by the path of premonition, not by that of inserted information. The transaction of God with the soul (if there be any such transaction) is not in the form of conversation, in which could be imparted (though only by whisper) statements, and inside advice, direction to the way of life, and true descriptions of destiny to come. No: any such dealings must occur in the unlighted chambers of consciousness, whose only report to the vocal self is in the raw-material of feeling. And when the attempt is made to interpret the impression thus received, it must first be projected from us, and read as at the remote end of an unsteady beam. We cannot but find in this projection a flickering, uncertain record, corrupt with imagery taken from the mind's external store, or tricked out in dress accepted from an older custom and tradition. If such is, and has been, the nature of revelation, we may understand the sources of the inveterate variety and dissonance of religious ideas. We see that it is well when men are beaten back from the idea, as from a vain quest, to return to the genuine import of revelation in terms of feeling with its definite bearing upon action.

With this understanding of revelation, it may reasonably be held that religion, which has its origin in feeling (of one kind), has in feeling (of another kind) its satisfaction also.

Thus, I have stated — in a very summary fashion, but I hope with rough justice — the more general grounds for the retirement of the intellect in religion. I am not wholly in accord with the conclusion to which these tendencies have led; I have been the more desirous of presenting them in their cumulative force.

CHAPTER V

RELIGION'S DILEMMA IN RESPECT TO THEORY

CONSIDERATIONS of the sort we have reviewed flock to the support of him who asserts that religion is a way of feeling. The intangible nature of religious objects; the obscurity of revelation; the lack of proportion between religious power and religious theory; the direct and personal conditions of religious growth; the identity of religions beneath diversity of ideas; and finally, the large consensus of scientific judgment in subordinating thought to some more ultimate reality as its authority. If anything could add to the weight of all this, it might be an immediate consciousness of what we mean by religion in ourselves; hardly a compendium of theology, but rather a governing disposition of some sort, which may do its work as a state of feeling whether or not we are fluent with the theory that could justify it.

But I doubt if we find substance enough in a religion of feeling. It has advantages of a positive sort; it makes religion a matter of experience, present and concrete. But it also has advantages of a negative sort which are highly questionable; it solves too many problems by avoiding them; it escapes too completely the labor and hazard of thinking. There seems to be some natural necessity whereby religion must try to put itself into terms of thought and to put its thought foremost. Religion seems to begin in feeling; and it seems everywhere to surrender by an inner requirement the advantage of this simple and strong position, to risk itself in the field of ideas with all its instability and wreckage. If only as students of history we must come to terms with this conspicuous fact: *that religion has never as yet been able to take itself as a matter of feeling.*

Especially in its prophets and originators has the religious consciousness been stubbornly objective: it has concerned itself with metaphysical objects, with God and the other world and the laws thereof, with our remotest and most external objects: and it has intended to propagate itself by fixing the eye of the mind on these things, not on its own inner states. Doubtless the prophet is mistaken if he thinks that he moves men only by the truth he offers them: it may be that the actual forces of religious propagation are much nearer his own personality than he imagines, much nearer, certainly, than these remote objects. Yes; but would not the prophet lose at once in power if he should deliberately abandon his objects and begin to exploit his own personality? Is it not true that the prophet has personal power, in part at least, because personal power is *not* his direct concern? The strength of religion in the world (so we thought in an earlier chapter) depends upon the fact that the religious man is free from himself. And are we to believe that the work of religion in the world depends on a self-deception, a permanent discrepancy between what such men suppose themselves to be doing, and what in fact they are doing?

I cannot believe that this is the case. The thread of history is, to some extent, a thread continuous within the intentions of the actors in history. However rich we may become in knowledge of the deeper causes of historical results, we forgo all understanding of history if we forget this inner continuity, — i.e., the conscious intentions of the participants in history-making and their consciously known successes. And more than any other element of history, religion demands to be understood from the inside. Granted that the more exalted the prophet, the more his work will be mixed with passion and the more his success will be due to his intensity of feeling: yet just because of this passion, we shall be less at liberty rather than more at liberty to translate his fervid assertions about God, man, and destiny into terms of feeling. We shall be impelled, in spite of ourselves, to attach importance to his metaphysics, if only because he himself attaches primary importance thereto.

I will go so far as to say this: That he who sees in the output of theory and doctrine in religion only a natural blunder, the prophet's misunderstanding of his own psychology, does quite as completely renounce all insight into history as if he held to that older explanation of religion by intentional priestly deception and priestly craft. Unless the idea in religion has some necessary and central function, we are wholly without explanation for this lavish and persistent yield of "revealed truth." And still more perverse and inexplicable must seem the universal insistence on these intellectual by-products; the persecution and slaughter uttered in maintaining them. Slaughter and intolerance are aberrations, sometimes; but they are aberrations founded at least on convictions. They may belong to the Dark Ages, but they do not belong to the Dead Ages, of religion. Some right sense there must be beneath all this over-violent emphasis on doctrine. There is no possible psychology of history which can escape the judgment that these intellectual ingredients of religion are in some way vital.

And when we say that it is a declining religion which prizes the subtleties of theology, we must make a distinction between one kind of thinking and another. There is such a thing as a congestion of cleverness consistent with a great dearth of profound thought. Clever and intricate theology does usually mean trivial religion; but mighty religion and mighty strokes of speculation have always gone together. Something like a religious impulse is needed to sustain the flight of powerful and far-reaching thought: and presumably the converse is also true, that a religious impulse must exhibit its force in some fundamental cognitive achievement, some Sultan's turret caught in a noose of light, — even though this achievement may have little in common with the noisier conquests made by the logical weapons of the forum. Deficit of mind must always, I venture to think, be a weakness in religion, and must rob that religion at last of all mordant power. A great religion will produce, and demand of its adherents that they reproduce, some great idea or system of ideas. Such, I say, is the evident purport of history.

The intellectual elements of religion must be vital; yet the embarrassments which religion suffers on account of them have hardly been overstated. Is it not probable that in this matter of theory religion is in a genuine predicament, unable to maintain its ideas in face of scientific criticism, yet unable to dispense with them? Religion seems to labor under a double necessity: the necessity of making much use of thought, and the necessity of discounting all thought. Kant's theory regarding our knowledge of God, immortality, and other religious objects, does fairly describe our apparent situation. Our human mind, thought Kant, is forever obliged to attempt the impossible in these matters: it must attempt to express its religion in theoretical terms, and it must deny the resulting ideas all scientific validity. Humanity must give conceptual form to its religious ideals and governing principles, because these must hold their own with all other experience and theory: but since our only resources for framing ideas are such as pertain to this world of natural experience, they can never truly represent to us any object which is beyond such experience. Religious speculation is inevitable; yet it always falsifies the religious object, turns it into something humanistic and material, something which interferes with the clear sweep of scientific thought and at the same time brings the religious object into the world with which it should stand in contrast. We are thus caught in what Kant calls the "dialectical illusion"; and religion is unable to evade either of the two opposing requirements.

If there is any such dilemma as this in the nature of the case, religious history will show it: for every such difficulty within the mind is bound to appear in history as a division between parties. Now just such a division seems to break out in mediaeval Europe when scholastics and mystics fall apart. On one side, the scholastics hold to the theoretical validity of religious doctrines. On the other side, the mystics are more impressed by the hopeless defects of the idea in religion and call for its renunciation. And each of these two parties has a characteristic way of recognizing the grain of truth in the position of the other. The scholastics are unable to ignore the profound difficulties in religious truth; they incline (with their genius for slippery distinctions) to invent a third status between truth and falsehood wherein certain parts of religious dogma must consent to dwell. Religious truth has standards of its own, somewhat different from those of other truth: a statement which is scientifically false (as a story of creation or of virgin birth) may yet be religiously true and binding. The mystics, for their part, are equally unable to ignore the necessity for using ideas, even while the ideas are defective: but as an upright and downright lot, they are unable to reckon with shades in the status of truth. They therefore take refuge in *paradox*, which is but another way of confessing the same dilemma. God is real, they assert, yet he is nothing, infinite emptiness; he is at once all-being and no-being. The other world is real and objective; yet at the same time it is within myself — I myself am heaven and hell.[1] The predicament in question is thus fairly attested in religious history: the scholastic and the mystic are facing a genuine

[1] As in the lines of Silesius:

Gott ist ein lauter Nichts, ihn rührt kein Nun noch Hier.
Je mehr du nach ihn greifst — je mehr entwind er dir.
(God is a perfect Naught; no Now nor Here attain him.
The more thou striv'st to seize, the more thou fail'st to gain him.)
Cherubinischer Wandersmann, I. 25.

Ich selbst bin Ewigkeit, wann ich die Zeit verlasse,
Und mich in Gott und Gott in mich zusammenfasse.
(I am Eternity when I have Time forsaken,
And self comprised in God, and God in self have taken.)
Same, I. 13.

dilemma. And a problem set thus deep in religious consciousness cannot be met, as in the religion of feeling, by a simple retreat from the cause of the trouble, the necessity of the idea.

We must find a solution which will give the idea in religion positive and unambiguous standing. The suggestions of the mystic and of the scholastic are all valuable, but so far as we have noticed them they still leave us groping. Is there perhaps some hope in a point of view which is both older and newer than this mediaeval discussion and which pervades it all: namely, in holding to the simple validity of religious knowledge while making a distinction among our *faculties* of knowledge? The ancient distinction was made between reason and faith. In Kantian and post-Kantian times, this same distinction often takes the form of a contrast between intellect and insight, thought and intuition, *Verstand* and *Vernunft*. May it be, perhaps, that religious truth is to be known by faith or *Vernunft*, a higher sort of intelligence than common understanding?

To my mind, all such distinctions as these leave us precisely as we are left by the scholastics with their twofold truth and the mystics with their paradoxes. A distinction in the faculties of knowledge only substitutes one problem for another. We cannot permanently relieve a split in our world of idea by making a split in the soul to account for it. All of these devices are but various ways of stating and perpetuating the problem; and though this is itself no small service, it is but a tentative one.

The best hope lies in a different direction: namely,

in attacking the division already set up between feeling and idea. The advocates of the religion of feeling are not mistaken in referring our various religious ideas to a higher authority, which they call feeling : the mistake is, as I think, in not observing that *the higher authority is itself still idea.* Idea can only be judged and corrected by idea; but these most authoritative ideas are so much more intimately related to experience and to feeling than other ideas as to justify nearly all that the religion of feeling asserts. It seems probable that in religion idea and feeling are inseparable; and that whatever valid ideas religion may have are to be found in that region of human nature where the cleavage between idea and feeling, never more than a tendency to diverge, no longer exists.

The religion of feeling depends on an artificial conception of this cleavage. It depends in fact on three assumptions (to summarize its various motives somewhat violently): first, that feeling may be happily independent of theory; second, that theory may be drearily independent of feeling; and third, that valid theory in religion is not obtainable. A study of the inner nature of those states of mind which we call feeling and idea should rectify these assumptions, and indicate the direction in which we may look for valid religious knowledge. It should leave us not so much with a refutation as with a better interpretation of those motives which have led to the retirement of the intellect. This study we shall now undertake, beginning with the first of the three assumptions mentioned, and then (in chapters vii to xi) dealing with the third and the second assumptions in the order named.

CHAPTER VI

THE DESTINY OF FEELING

IF these ensuing enquiries into human nature are often occupied with feeling and idea as if for their own sakes, while the special interests of religion fall momentarily into the background, it is because we are obliged here to some extent to work out our own way in independence of the usual paths of psychological theory. I must bespeak the patience of the reader to that end.

Of this present chapter, the thesis is a simple one, namely this: that there is no such thing as feeling apart from idea; that idea is an integral part of all feeling; and that it is the whole meaning and destiny of feeling to terminate in knowledge of an object. If these things are true, they will help us to understand why a religion of feeling always and rightly tends to transform itself into a religion of idea.

We have already noticed how closely feeling is connected with action. This is one of the great advantages of interpreting religion in terms of feeling. Some of our feelings are indeed less obviously active than others. The feelings of absolute dependence, of awe, and of reverence, which Schleiermacher regarded as the essence of all religion, are of a relatively quiescent and contemplative sort. Yet these feelings also (though they are not the whole of religious feeling) do powerfully regulate action, even if they do not seem at once to excite action. In all feeling, if we look closely, we shall find activity and the guidance of action.

But to say that feeling is the immediate cause of activity is still to put it too far away from action. In feeling, action is already begun: feeling is itself activity. Feeling is always in transformation — as if it had need to escape from itself. Its very existence seems to consist in a kind of instability in consciousness, a nascency and unfinishedness of mind which requires continuous change. Emotion is a name usually reserved for certain of our more complex feelings; but speaking literally, all feeling is e-motion, a flight from what is to something beyond. And thus all feelings, I venture to say, are forms of desire — not forgetting those feelings which seem to terminate desire, as joy, triumph, and relief — and all have at their center a sting of restlessness.

It follows that that which can satisfy feeling is something which will destroy it as feeling. As much feeling as is present at any time — just so much unrest and pushing onward elsewhere for satisfaction. In the movement of life feeling is always present, for the destruction of one feeling is as a rule the inception of another: one feeling debouches in another, or the appeasement of one hunger sets in motion the springs of another. Thus emotion maintains a perpetual circle while life lasts. But it remains true that to satisfy any given feeling is to bring that feeling to an end. And if the attainment which religion offers is indeed a satisfaction of all desire, and not of some fragment of our nature, it must intend a living escape from this perpetual circle: we should expect to find in religion the destruction of all feeling as such.

What is that other-than-feeling in which feeling may end? I answer, consciousness of an object. Feeling is instability of an entire conscious self: and that which will restore the stability of this self lies not within its own border but beyond it. Feeling is outward-pushing, as idea is outward-reporting: and no feeling is so blind as to have no idea of its own object. As a feeling possesses the mind, there also possesses the mind as an integral part of that feeling, some idea of the kind of thing which will bring it to rest. A feeling without a direction is as impossible as an activity without a direction: and a direction implies some objective. There are vague states of consciousness in which we seem to be wholly without direction; but in such cases it is remarkable that feeling is likewise in abeyance. For example, I may be dazed by a blow, neither realizing what has happened nor suffering any pain, and yet quite conscious that something has occurred: the experience waits an instant in the vestibule of consciousness, not as feeling but purely as fact, until idea has touched it and defined a course of response. At that same moment it is felt as painful. If we are right, feeling is quite as much an objective consciousness as is idea: it refers always to something beyond the present self and has no existence save in directing the self toward that object in whose presence its own career must end.

These statements are most obviously true of the feelings to which we usually apply the name of desire: for desire is clearly desire of some object or condition not now present, and in obtaining the presence of that object desire ceases. But how can these statements be applied, as we said, to the feelings of satisfaction themselves? Are joy and triumph also unsatisfied states? Is pleasure, dwelling hard on its present object, such a seeking-process as we have here pictured?

As to pleasure, it wants *more of the same*—more than it now has: that is what defines it as a state of feeling. It is an old and well-worn analysis of pleasure which identifies it with a tendency to approach more nearly the object which gives the pleasure. When pleasure ceases to require further approach, it becomes simply a vehement cognizance of its object: its character as feeling is dissolved into a state of knowledge. As to the feeling of triumph—triumph, "unable to contain itself," has certainly much to do. It may wear itself out in shout and song. More probably it becomes aware of a destination which is common to most of our positive feelings—namely, a *social aim* of some sort. The restlessness of triumph will usher the subject along toward his friends or his populace, until in physical contact with their responses (a flood height within balanced by an answering flood height without), the internal tumult is appeased and feeling disappears—into what? Into clear, animated *cognizance:* cognizance genially distributed over the new situation created by the event of triumph, and the common knowledge of it. All the "feelings of satisfaction" so far as there is feeling left in them, in the same way move on to cognizance. Heightened feeling hastens to fund itself in heightened consciousness, that is, in a keener sensitiveness, a more unshrinking objectivity.

All positive feeling, I dare now say, reaches its terminus in *knowledge.* All feeling means to instate some experience which is essentially cognitive: it is idea-apart-from-its-object tending to become idea-in-presence-of its-object, which is "cognizance," or experiential knowledge.

And thus knowledge, which of old has had the dreary character of feeling-quencher, must also be accepted as feeling-goal, the natural absorbent and destiny of feeling. All positive feeling is at heart some marriage quest which ends in knowing. And such knowledge, so far from being less a 'value-consciousness' than the feeling which has led up to it, is but the more excellent condition of that very value-consciousness embodied in the feeling. Such feeling so far from being less a "fact-consciousness" is, in its guiding idea, throughout a prophecy of the fact; as if the object itself were pressing to be known in presence. In the satisfaction of feeling, the guiding idea coalesces immediately with the object then known as present: to the including mind there is perfect continuity between prophecy and fulfilment — the feeling is unaware of death. In truth, it is not dead, but risen (aufgehoben): cognizance and feeling are but different stages of *the same thing.*

These observations (superficial as they still are — and over-general) [1] must modify somewhat our impressions

[1] I have made no distinctions between the several meanings of the word 'feeling,' though few terms in the language are so highly ambiguous. Nor do I think that I have fallen into obscurity on that account. The mind (we as psychologists should admit) is as intricate as we choose to take it — and as simple. The truth about our inner states does not wait until we have found the "psychical atom." Some truth about feeling may be conveyed, even without definition.

of the pragmatic contrast between feeling and idea. It is true that ideas apart from feelings do no work: but it is also true that a *feeling does no work apart from its guiding idea.* Though feeling is close to action, is incipient action, it is not without incipient idea: and as this idea becomes adequate, the working effectiveness of the feeling is not diminished, but enhanced. If the idea is vague the feeling may waste itself in spluttering activity with little satisfaction; there is economy of conduct in proportion as feeling (so to speak) learns its own mind. Thus, whether fear leads to wild flight or to simply climbing a tree may depend on the "presence of *mind*" in the feeling. We cannot properly draw a contrast in regard to working-power between idea in general and feeling in general; because the working-forces of consciousness are neither ideas nor feelings, but always idea-feeling couples.

Instead of contrast, there is a very obvious equivalence

It may be asked whether any such account as this does not omit whatever makes feeling distinctive. What becomes of the color and quality of our psychical states — the nuances of joy, grief, gaiety, ease, kindly expansiveness, and infinite others, which temper the mind's atmosphere from moment to moment? Whatever ideas and transitions toward knowledge may be involved in these, is it not the quality and flavor which we lose, just as the qualities of nature are lost in the language of matter and motion? It is true that such quality, in itself, is precisely what no description or explanation can capture — or need to. For these colors of the mind are to be predicated always of the *whole mental state*, never of any elements of it. Feeling-tones of this sort do not float about in the mind-current like fish in a stream, nor take part as strands in a total movement: they are best placed, I believe, as the interest which the mind at any time is taking in its own existence. They are the total impression which living, from moment to moment, is making upon the ultimate liver. Our own discussion is concerned with what goes on within the actual mental movement: feelings as we are concerned with them are distinguishable working-elements in that movement.

between feeling and idea in this respect, such that idea may gradually substitute itself for feeling while doing the same work. The guiding idea of any repeated feeling becomes by degrees more adequate: as this occurs, the feeling itself seems to diminish, as if it had been, in part, absorbed or transformed into the idea. Thus, the emotional side of love inclines to transform itself into an "understanding," in which the meaning of the feeling is carried out in the system of ideas and actions which constitute permanent friendship. This system of active understanding is precisely what the original emotion *meant* and prophesied; the feeling which seems lost has its living equivalent in what we may call the *creed* of that relationship. And it will reassert itself as feeling if those habits of friendly action are interrupted.

Or again, a feeling of distrust toward some person, at first without tangible grounds, succeeds — we will suppose — in defining its basis. Thereafter, conduct toward the distrusted person need be no wholesale rejection or avoidance: I may make definite negations on definite grounds; and on the other hand, I may accept with confidence other relations in which the defined trait plays no part. Such definition is a relief; a degree of mental friction disappears; feeling is less intense: the new working-couple (lowered feeling, heightened idea) does the same kind of work as the older working-couple, but with more efficiency. Knowledge of human nature tends to *place* men instead of hating them or blaming them: and the traditional impassivity of this kind of wisdom is no absence of feeling, but only a relatively complete translation of emotion into a working creed.

In practice, we reckon a feeling of aversion toward

any project as equivalent to some reason against it: and a feeling of attraction counts as some reason in its favor. In any public arena, feelings and thoughts thus mingle upon the same footing; they are added and subtracted as coin of the same mint in all the actual transactions of persuasion. But in any such arena, to become explicit is a gain. One often yields his feeling to the pressure of tangible considerations with the impression that the feeling must have been victor if it could have met the tangible on its own ground. The prejudice which can get itself formulated in language has an immense advantage in the struggle for existence. Or, it is known for what it is, and done away with. However great one's faith in the un-idead regions of existence, that faith is newly-born when through some stroke of conception, outlines of a felt foundation loom for the first time out of obscurity into relief. The feeling has been an anticipatory thought, a fact throughout of the same nature.

A large part of what we call *thinking* is nothing other than the effort to gain this kind of possession of our more helpless meanings. Poetry (playground of ideas) is the form in which the feeling or spirit of an age wins its first breath; and philosophy (idea hard-labor-ground) attempts the complete transformation of the feeling into literality, which means connection with earth. In all this, we have continuity and equivalence between idea and feeling, quite as significant as in any physical 'equivalence and transformation of forces.' To make an aspiration or a motive visible in idea is not to render it more abstract, is not to alter its identity or its character or its pragmatic bearing; it is simply to give it status among other expressed tendencies. This pragmatic equivalence is a confirmation of the substantial sameness of idea and feeling; of the destiny of feeling to fund itself in idea.

These general characteristics of feeling hold good of religious feeling. Feeling is known as religious, rather than as some other sort, by the peculiarity of its objects and ideas. Fear is a fundamental element in religious feeling; but what distinguishes a given type of fear as religious? Why is it that such fear appears only in the human being, not in the animal? Because it is roused by a situation which it requires human imagination to grasp. Some conception of the Whole of things, some super-stition is necessary before *that* fear can take hold of the mind, even though it be excited by purely natural happenings. The same of religious hope and worship. The same of religious attainment, and the feeling of assurance which comes of it. In a human being, to "feel sure" and to know one's ground are one and the same thing — perhaps in different stages of distinctness. If religious enthusiasm comes to rest in a state of 'peace,' this state is a state of feeling only in that same metamorphosis by which all feeling in its satisfaction vanishes in cognizance, the sting of restlessness having been drawn. The Stoic's summit was *apathy* — non-feeling: religion also wins a non-feeling — but a positive sort — let us say, *metapathy*, a state beyond feeling, not beneath it. What feeling was has not ceased to be; but it exists as a heightened value diffused over all experience. The measure of life is increased; and that measure is perhaps well enough described at present as a measure of cognitive penetration. Religious success becomes, I think, precisely this: an unshrinking objectivity.

The strains of religious feeling belong especially to that period of life in which one is working out his Weltanschauung. Conversion is in part at least the grasping of an idea; such an idea as can thereafter infuse itself with peaceful dominance through the system of conduct and belief. Starbuck calls attention to the value of intellectual points of fixation in tiding over the storms and stresses of adolescence: without some ideas through which feeling can win an interpretation, "one is torn by he knows not what." And the storm and stress itself may be regarded as a process of deep thinking, carried on by the whole organism.

Religious feeling, then, like other feeling, is all idea-material, idea-activity. Dissolve out the idea-tissue of religion, and no feeling, and so no religion, is left. Holding our pragmatic test to religion, requiring of it that it do its work, we will have no religion without a theory; we will have no religion without a creed.

Religion as feeling must aspire to complete self-understanding and ultimately to a complete transformation of all its emotion into a present knowledge of its desired object, whatever that may be. This truth prevents us from resting satisfied with feeling: but it is fair to observe that it does not provide us, as yet, with any substitute. We have not yet enquired what the essential meaning of religious feeling is; nor have we at all shown that such sure self-understanding and ultimate satisfaction can be obtained. It remains possible, so far as we have yet shown, that our religious impulses must continue, so long as we are human, to grope for their own meaning: and it may still be held that the ideas which religious feeling makes use of must always be partly mistaken, tentative, and mythical.

The supposition that religion must put up with imperfect equipment of theory does no violence to human nature as we otherwise know it. It is a notorious fact that feelings may frequently find their satisfactions through misfit ideas. My ill-temper, in search for its own theory, is more than likely to adopt a false one and expend itself on some innocent head. If a nation is lusting for war, no one can foresee on what pretext theories of offended national honor or of manifest destiny may make fatal alliance with the belligerent impulse. Such mistaken self-interpretation is not always the fault of feeling, but often its fate: for it can only press into service such ideas as are at hand. The deeper and obscurer cravings and discomforts of body and soul must frequently be diagnosed by the sufferer almost in the dark, with a slender gamut of hypotheses; it is not surprising if many a self-made invalid results from a faulty theory of one's own feeling, fit to be cured by a course of bread-pills or other placebos. And who will say that the various religious doctrines of mankind, ministering as they do to the obscure spiritual cravings of the race, have not acted rather as *placebos* than as literal interpretations and satisfactions of these feelings? Harmless remedies for the most part, because very likely there is no such explicit truth here to be had — none, therefore, to be conflicted with: they serve their function in setting the mind at peace, and harmonizing the active impulses of the empirical self.

Let us be at one with our saints, as in reality we are one with them, in the drama of their moral will. And let us be free of the allegory in which they depict to themselves that drama, free to take other allegories as well, or to put forth our own. I read Augustine with wonder: but with the greater nearness when I see (as who can fail to see) that his spiritual crises hang upon, and swing about, intellectual snags irrelevant to the real issue — whether God is extended in space, whether evil is a substance, whether Paul contradicts Moses and himself: why dost thou halt upon these matters, friend Augustine, if not to delay the course of that dreaded moral requirement so great in thee? The settlement of thy problem, which looks so much like a theoretical result, — is it not in truth an inevitable moral decision, governed from afar by thy deep religious feeling, playing itself out in terms of speculative issues which only symbolize the inner meaning of the process?

This well-known point of view is quite compatible with what we have said about the destiny of feeling: and it can only be dealt with by a direct enquiry into religious knowledge. But one or two remarks may be made before beginning that enquiry.

It is obvious, I think, that no one would adopt such a position as this if he believed that a more satisfactory status of idea were possible. And further, no one can in reality make use of religious ideas which he believes to be thus mythical. It is quite possible to adopt a mistaken theory, believing it to be true; but it is not possible to adopt a mistaken theory believing it to be mistaken, or even allegorical. Our real theory is the *meaning* of that allegory as we understand it, and not the allegory itself.

Feeling is a thing which cannot, in its own nature, remain in the dark. Whatever our Most Enlightened View about the nature of religious truth may be, that Most Enlightened View becomes, willy nilly, the rule for our feeling. The more vehement the feeling, the more it resents darkness (and certainly all deliberate parasol-protection) and pushes for clarity. In their demand for idea, our major feelings rather possess us than we them. More especially the race-old feelings we call religious will hold to their service all of our new and best insights, all our detections-of-general-religious-mistake, all our suspicions of subjective-intention-in-objective-myth: they will identify themselves with these insights, partial and unsatisfactory as they are, until we provide an idea-system which is fit, necessary, and adequate to our present stage of self-conscious attainment.

NOTE. In the four following chapters (chapters vii–x), dealing chiefly with the competence of the idea, it will be necessary to consider certain adverse positions, as of Bergson and Höffding. These chapters though as little technical as possible may have for the general reader a difficulty which I cannot wholly avoid. If any such reader finds that these problems are not his own problems, I may advise him to omit these chapters, passing at once to chapter xi, which resumes the argument as we now leave it, stating a proposition regarding the organic relation of idea and feeling which is fundamental to our whole view of religion. Then in chapter xii, the theory that religious truth depends on the will is discussed in detail, both in the form in which James states it — the well-known will-to-believe — and in the form in which Royce holds it — namely, that reality is the fulfilment of an absolute purpose. This chapter, again somewhat refractory, concludes the laborious controversial part of our work.

CHAPTER VII

HOW IDEAS OF IDEAS MISREPRESENT THEM

WE have said that feeling has need of idea; that it can get no pragmatic hold on us without idea; that it has no existence except as it were a suicidal one — to disappear in knowledge. We might further have said that except through idea feeling cannot consciously *communicate itself*. Our feelings we do, for the most part, instinctively seek to share: few feelings are not improved by social reflection. But if we have a pleasure or a grief to express to another, we do so (if we can) by *telling the tale*, or by pointing out the object, on which the feeling depends; not by simply showing the feeling, or explaining *it*. If we must give the clue to the fun, or to the sorrow, or to the admiration, by our own prior grimace or gesture (not to say *word*), we know there is loss in passage: if we are so far overcome that we have nothing but emotion to give, we are pitiable — or ridiculous.

It is seldom, indeed, with our limited control of idea, that an emotion passes from mind to mind by idea alone, or can so pass: but the communicator is bound in good faith to bring forward what idea he can, with all promptness, and to rest his case on that. There is an ethics in the communication of whatever feeling, binding the communicator to the limit of his powers to be *objective*, to make no conscious exploit of his own affectedness. This *rule of first intentions* must hold, I fancy, with extreme rigor in the case of religious feeling. It would be no crime in an actor if he should try to make me weep by himself weeping (though he would do better to show a great effort at repressing his tears): but what outrage when the like occurs in religion! The spirit of the prophet who has communicated his religion, and his feeling therewith, by the circuitous way of idea and doctrine is right — is alone right. Passion in history retains its soundness and force just so long as it forgets itself and holds to its objects. All else puffs out, or putrefies. The taint of emotional exploitation on the part of the more sophisticated trustees of religion must long since have killed the church had it not been for the sound objectivity of the people. Their exploitableness is their moral superiority.

Attempts on the part of 'the enlightened' to take with the same objective good-faith the words of the prophets must meet with many defeats; to find the tenable ideas of religion is indeed no easy matter: but it is the temper of defeat to cry too early, All is lost! The mutual cancellations of our divergent religious thoughts and theories leave no idea in the whole field unquestioned: but it has yet to be shown that all idea is thereby eliminated and impossible. Idea has many lives, is of tougher substance than we think; and has perhaps greater resources for grasping the remote and supersensible parts of reality.

We need to enquire into the capacity of our instruments of knowledge. Most of our prevalent doubts regarding our ability to reach knowledge in religion are based on false conceptions of what an idea is. These false conceptions are natural enough; it is hard to make an idea of an idea that will not misrepresent it. For it is natural to think of ideas as we think of *things* —men, bricks, magnitudes, events. We cannot think of any idea that is not an idea *of* something: and in thinking of the idea, that something shines through the transparent substance of the idea itself, and our thought of the idea becomes mixed with our thought of the idea's object. We need constantly to remind ourselves that our ideas are what we think *with*, not what we think *of*, in the order of nature. When we try to think *of* an idea, we are proceeding in some way against nature, taking nature backward: it is not surprising if in our attempts to do this the resulting conception of the idea is denatured to some extent, and so misjudged.

The first objects which are taken up in great numbers into our knowledge are objects of the physical world, fixed in outline, mechanical for the most part, and finite: it seems to us, then, that our ideas of these objects participate in these qualities, and the consequences of this impression are far-reaching. For if ideas have about them some inherent rigidity and finitude, if intellect is indeed a mechanical affair, they can do no justice to *reality* in its infinitude and its incessant flux and change. The kind of knowledge of ultimate things which religion has supposed itself to need — nay, the very conceptions of those objects, the familiar terms of religious doctrines — are scientifically impossible. I wish, then, to examine our ideas of ideas; and to consider in the first place the supposed rigidity of ideas.

An idea, it seems, is a piece of one's mind: a piece so delimited, outlined (découpée), that it can be individually used, handled, referred to. One cannot handle the ocean: but water-buckets-full, casks-full, tanks-full, taken out of the ocean can be handled well enough. Such water-bucket, or other vessel, has *known contents:* it is a bit of the ocean, bound, measured, put under control, lifted into relief from out of the general wash of waters, and set to work. Such is "an idea" in the general flux of consciousness: a vessel of known contents, manipulable, destined to some work. And to what work? In part, at least, to such work as is performed by *coins*, vessels of value: namely, to possess me of my valuables in convenient, storable form; to measure and assess the worth of new facts, recognizing them in their bearing upon my actions; also to serve as unit of exchange, whereby such pieces of my mind may be passed on to others. What better simplest image or symbol of idea could be devised than *the circle* — an enclosed bit of space of known contents — precisely such symbol as is in common use among logicians?

This, I think, fairly describes our usual conception of an idea. And such images as these of the water-bucket, the coin, the circle, contain all that is true in our usual conception, together with all that is false. They contain enough truth to be exceedingly useful, enough also to be exceedingly seductive. So far does the correspondence between ideas and the logician's circle-diagrams hold good, that logic itself may appear to be nothing more than a sort of space-play or topology, our thinking processes a sort of "geometrizing."[1] Our conception of the

[1] Bergson's epithet. It is indeed sufficiently remarkable that our thought-relations can be represented at all in terms of space-relations — not to say so completely represented. It has often excited speculation that

idea begins to partake of the rigidity, the lifelessness, the finitude of these inevitable images. And we can hardly better win a true idea of idea than by enquiring how far these spatial symbols, circles and the rest, are appropriate and valid; and where they begin to work false.

In the first place, our spatial symbols represent truly the *definite inclusions and exclusions* of our ideas. One is said to have an idea of an object when he can recognize it, and tell it from every other thing in the world. Ideas do not always accomplish this infallible identification of their object. Most ideas of actual things have doubtful boundaries — as of animal from plant, or of river from brook — their lines are less sharp than the circle; but the *ideal idea* knows its own, and excludes even more sharply than any actual circle-outline; more sharply, in fact, than any except the boundary of the *idea-circle.* The power of perfect definition is *conferred on the circle by the idea,* not on the idea by the circle. In this matter of definite inclusion and exclusion, then, the circle does not misrepresent the idea.

In the second place, each idea has its own *changeless*

some deep-going vital unity must obtain between the structure of space and the structure of intellect. It has been a great point with idealism; supporting the notion that space is but the mind itself, externalized, and readable by the mind as a foreign object. F. A. Lange, in particular, was much impressed by this correspondence. And most recently M. Bergson has thrown a biological light on the matter by reminding us that intellect and physical world have grown up together in the course of evolution; that they have been modeled for each other, to some extent also, *by each other;* that the intellect inevitably "geometrizes" because it is its primary nature, not to know self or reality, but to guide our physical conduct to its physically practical ends. The correspondence, then, has attained a certain philosophical celebrity.

identity, a character fitly represented by the circle, or by any other fixable object. To suppose an idea to change is to suppose it to become another idea. We could never recognize an object as being the same object unless we infallibly *meant the same:* nay, we could never know a thing as *not the same* unless we were sure of a sameness of meaning. Permanence of meaning, taken in total, is but our own mental integrity, our personal identity itself. The permanence and sameness, then, of any poor chalk-circle, or world-orbit for that matter, is infinitely *unfit* to symbolize the unwavering sameness of idea, save for a short span, and by leave of the idea itself. It is the *idea again that confers identity on the circle,* not the circle that confers identity upon the idea. In this matter of changelessness, then, the circle cannot misrepresent the idea, for it has no other changelessness than that of the idea itself.

If, then, we admit these characters of the idea found in the symbol — its changeless identity, and its aim to be perfectly defined and exclusive — do we not also admit that the idea is *rigid,* even as the symbol is; and therefore equally unable to deal with this living world as it is?

M. Bergson is at this hour most impressively insisting upon the fatal discrepancy between a reality which is fluent, passing, ever-growing, and an idea-world which is static, rigid, conservative, mechanizing what it touches. There is something about change, especially about life-change, which never gets caught in our ideas: this fact the history of thought has repeatedly been compelled to notice. The idea seems not only to fail, but somehow to falsify, when it intends to grasp a living thing: as if in fixing it, it had also transfixed it, and could carry about but a dead image.

Now, I must confess that in all such criticisms of the idea I seem to see pointed out rather defects in our human industry and loyalty than any inherent defect of the idea itself: for if an unchanging idea is sufficiently true to its object, it must entertain every change and development in that object. *It must change just because it is constant;* it must change in content because it is changeless in meaning. I can see that there is much human idleness to be overcome in keeping our ideas fresh while their objects are developing; I can also see that a satisfactory life-theory, mind-theory, world-theory, will require of us infinite racial labor. But I know not how to describe this labor except as the labor of idea-making. The "inherent discrepancy" eludes me; seems, to speak plainly, a demonstrable confusion. For that with which the "rigid idea" is contrasted is the "fluent reality" held up to contemplation — of which "fluent reality" then we have some idea: and can it be that this idea of the "fluent reality" is itself also rigid? Is this fixedness, or unbending idea-quality, idea-starch, such that no valid meaning is contained or containable in those conceptions we name 'change,' 'growth,' or even 'wilting,' 'deliquescing,' 'melting,' 'dissolving,' and the like? On the contrary, no ideas are more useful and more used than these ideas of change by M. Bergson and the other authors in question. To know these things, it is said, we must revert to immediate experience. But whatever can interest in experience is already caught in idea: *there is nothing in experience which cannot become content of idea,* for what else is the (empirical) idea but selected experience, in shape for memory and communication? Idea is a universal tool, making *no demands upon its subject-matter.* It takes the contour with perfect faithfulness, perfect transparency, perfect non-interference, of whatever can hold (through whatever movement or metamorphosis) the same interest. Give me an interest in a cloud, or in a revolution: at no point do I find my pursuit of that shifting object barred by some stiff-joint of my *idea.* Give me an interest in the thing you call reality, and if it is to be met with in experience at all, nothing can prevent idea from holding *it,* in all its flux or creativity. Whatever character you give this reality, in mentioning that character you have already confessed an idea of it. Indeed, it is futile to define any region of the world as the exclusive or favorite region of idea: for the only force which can confine idea to such domain is the force of idea itself.

I do not suppose that these considerations are unfelt by such a thinker as M. Bergson. Not only is he aware of them; he anticipates them. It is not impossible to think change, he says, but only *almost* impossible. It is counter to our mental habit (habitude statique de notre intelligence); it is like climbing backward the slope of our confirmed intellectual direction (remonter la pente, etc.). While ideas of qualities (adjectives) and ideas of forms (nouns) clearly choose to mean only *states,* still-states, of our world, ideas of action and change (verbs) have a tinge of the non-static in them; yet they too are interested not in the process per se, but in the terminals thereof; they present chiefly a picture of the ends of the movement, and a still-chart of its course. "L'ideé du changement est là, je le veux bien, mais elle se cache dans la pénombre. En pleine lumière il y a le dessin immobile de l'acte supposé accompli . . . Adjectifs et substantifs symbolisent donc des états. Mais le verbe lui-même, si l'on s'en tient à la partie éclairée de la représentation qu'il évoque, n'exprime guère autre chose." [1] Significant "guère." Significant "pénombre." Bringing into some question that striking definition of the idea (though only of the Greek εἶδος) as a flash-view, or instant (la vue stable prise sur l'instabilité des choses). Bringing into some question also that famous figure of the intellect as a moving-picture apparatus, dealing essentially only in such instantaneous views, mechanically fused together (mécanisme cinématographique de la pensée). For what is it that rejoins these separate flashes of the actual moving-pictures into a continuum of movement? Not, for us, the mechanical apparatus; for that emits nothing but discontinuous flashes (with due interval, to be sure, and regularity.) What rejoins them if not our own way of interpreting, perhaps of sensing, the succession? But hardly of sensing, nor yet of perceiving, if M. Bergson is right: for perception, according to him, rather turns motions into states, than states into motions (notre perception ne doit guère retenir du monde matériel, à tout instant, qu'un *état* où provisoirement elle se pose.)[2] One knows not where to look, if this is so, except to our own *ideas*. At all events, the continuous-change character is something not here found in the data of immediate experience, is something added *by us* to those data out of our own meanings. Some idealistic path seems to open out here — "idea-creator-

[1] L'évolution créatrice, p. 328, 3me ed. [2] Ibid. p. 325.

of-its-own-world," or the like: into this path we shall not enter. But must we not perforce admit change and rest, static and non-static, to full coördinacy, so far as our idea-power is concerned?

Idea does no doubt enable us to store change in memory, as hardly it is storable in fact. Thus stored, we are able to dwell upon it, retrace it, in such retracing to alter its rate as we will,—pass from beginning to end with indefinite speed (change intense), or from end to beginning, or pause to take the time of its passage through this point and through that—but in all these liberties taken, we are under no deceit. Unless time could be remembered *as it is*, there could be no mind; if keeping the past in present view denatured time, and turned it into a sort of space—time itself would drop out of meaning, and out of reality, for us. A present idea, and an idea of a present, are not necessarily the same; a changeless idea and an idea of only-the-changeless are not equivalent phrases. Has not M. Bergson fallen into the error from which he himself would warn us, that of applying to the idea the characters of its (physical) objects?

And if we wish to know the real source of such difficulties as the mind falls into in gaining an explication of reality, shall we not find it rather in the exigencies of finishing our idea-systems than in the incompetence of the individual idea? The paradoxes of Zeno are due, not to the difficulty of grasping motion in idea, but to the difficulty of putting *the idea of motion* into terms of *the idea of rest.* The incommensurables are *both in the region of ideas;* the dilemmas arise from the necessity of clarifying our ideas by relating them to other ideas; eventually, of explaining a thing in terms of what it is not. Thus may it not be with reality also? If it appears in experience, then also in idea: but whether the idea can make connections with other ideas is not thereby decided. These other ideas try to gain relations to the idea of reality, that is, to set up *predicates* for our idea: but the predicates may not fit.

It is chiefly our idea-connections and systems that threaten to stiffen and falsify the living thing. To be forewarned that any such idea-connection is liable to need revision is to escape the consequences of rationalistic rigidity, without abandoning the needful work of system-making. We cannot cease to observe that S is P; but we can enter the caveat — "with reservations and conditions, not yet wholly known." System-making cannot cease, because in part it is the life of the mind itself — expressible as an automatic process in part. Every idea, we might say (again with justified psychical mechanics), attracts every other idea — tempts it into some union or other, for which it may or may not be fit. The number of mechanical ideas we possess is hereby a perpetual menace to the integrity and virtue of the non-mechanical. Ideas of life and of living things are thus constantly exposed to *mésalliance,* need continually to be guarded from mechanization. This, as it seems to me, is the real meaning of the complaint that our ideas are rigid and cannot do justice to reality. We have a greater population of mechanical ideas than of others — they are "the masses" in our mental State — whence a certain instability of the others in their rightful place. The remedy is first, in simply knowing the danger; second, in holding the non-mechanical ideas to their own character; third, in producing more of the non-mechanical sort. This is in every way the result of such work as Bergson's, except for his too physical idea of idea.

The general name for this process of making connections among ideas is *reasoning*. We would therefore agree with Bergson and others that it is not by reasoning, in this sense, that reality is first known. Reasoning, or thinking, is a process which insists first on connectedness of ideas; is willing to reach new territory only from old, and by approved truss-work, in cantilever fashion: "intuition," or immediate knowledge, is capable (relatively speaking) of ignoring connections, of seizing a bridge span in mid air and holding to it while truss and abutments *grow*. But in the one case as in the other it is *idea-work* that we witness, — nothing different. So of "instinct" which is often appealed to as a more adequate organ than idea for knowing reality. What is there about reality which instinct can divine while idea must remain confined to its clear-cut and barren circles? If any real What, significant of anything, then ipso facto idea, though the work of wooing that idea into our systems and reasonings may well be the work of ages and of races of men.

It is only in very recent years that religion has directly suffered from this particular aspect of the distrust of ideas: for religion has, in the main, been content to conceive its God, its world, its various objects of dogma, as unchanging — in view of which, idea may be as rigid as we please, without detriment. It is only as the necessity has arisen in the speculative mind to recognize flux and growth in everything, even in God himself, that loyalty of idea to its meaning becomes felt, in religious discussion also, as the idea's rigidity and incompetence. Modernism feels it; such writers as William James, and in popular vein as Mr. H. G. Wells, complain of it in religious context. But a deeper and older ground of distrust — perhaps at the bottom of this very prejudice regarding rigidity — is the sense that the idea is *finite*, fitted to cope only with the simpler, poorer, exhaustible phases of reality. To this more fundamental difficulty we must now turn.

CHAPTER VIII

THE ALLEGED FINITUDE OF IDEAS

ALL pictures of the idea which we are likely to frame to ourselves — circles, coins, counters, ocean water-buckets — would agree in at least this one point: the finitude of the idea. The essence of the idea is *known contents*, marked off from the infinite unknown. An idea is a mental achievement, a success of some sort, *un fait accompli*, a usable possession: whence that which is unconquerable and unpossessible, the infinite, must be left outside the idea. Efforts, indeed, the mind is continually making to encompass gulfs, seas, the ocean itself; or let us say, to decoy limitless genii into stoppered bottles: and in these enterprises certain partial successes seem always on the eve of happening — some robe corner or perchance a toe of the genius approaching the bottle, actually in the bottle; just enough encouragement to prevent sanguine mortals from forgoing the quest of the infinite altogether, and yet no authentic triumph. These are, to speak most hopefully, prospective ideas; and do but serve to show what finitude is implied in the achieved idea. It is clear enough what bearing this finitude of idea may have upon religious thought, which must needs try to think the Infinite: this bearing has been sufficiently exhibited by all those philosophers whose point of pride is their humility and candor, since Herbert Spencer, and also before him.

How the religion of feeling is concerned in this issue none has shown so well as Professor Höffding.[1] Religion cannot reach its goal in the form of thought, he reasons, because religion must aspire to be conclusive; whereas thought, in these matters, is necessarily inconclusive. The religious object, in order to fulfil the requirements of the religious life, must possess finality (no complaint here of the 'rigidity' of ideas), must furnish "an absolute and objective conclusion for our knowledge": but no ideas in the field of religion can claim these qualities. However comprehensive they may be, reality in its infinitude breaks away from them. What satisfaction in idea can there be for religion unless, for example, we can frame valid ideas of "God," and of "the world"? But this we cannot do. What is to be meant by "the world" but a symbol for a completed work of fact-finding and law-finding brought to perfect unity? — which work shows no sign of being finished till Doomsday, and can by no right be treated as done before that time. Indeed, the finding of a principle which could unify the physical world-laws alone seems to be inherently impossible, involving endless retreat of the object, endless regress, endless rainbow pursuit. As for the idea of God, there is no need to question completion when so much question besets our poor *beginnings*. And were we able to think both God and the world, this would not satisfy the requirement of religion, which (if it depends on ideas) must have some idea of the relation between its God and its world: whereas, any supposition we make, or perhaps that can be made, only plunges us into further infinities. Not

[1] Philosophy of Religion, chapter II.

accidental unfinishedness, but inherent unfinishableness of this God-and-world-problem, is what we face. By whatever concept we try to compass finality, reality opens through its wall an alley of "infinite regress," and escapes — mocking. "All limiting concepts contain a certain element of raillery." Thus instructed by the self-invited discomfiture of the idea, does religion pass (through analogy and symbol) to its secure seat in feeling, with its postulate of faith, — "the conservation of value."

We cannot but endorse this conception of religion's demand for finality in its objects. Have we not already described religion as "anticipated attainment"; reaching ends (of which the world-knowing end is one) for which men must otherwise infinitely wait. But because we accept that demand, we cannot despair of it; nor resort to feeling for a finality denied to the idea. I shall not by any means attempt here to do justice to Höffding's thought in its deeper bearings; I can deal only with the one difficulty, — the finitude of the idea, the infinitude of the task of knowledge.

Consider first, that *all ideas contain an infinity*, — though an uncounted infinity. Within the contour of the blank circle-face alone is there not an infinitude of points? — which infinitude does not render less serene our finished possession of the circle's meaning. In a tree, there are leaves which could be counted, also cells, atoms, infinite infinitesimals; but my idea of that tree does not await the result of the counting and studying. Every idea, at that instant in which it is distinguished from other meanings of the mind, is *finished at once*, from its inner end, its intention: at that instant the universe is dichotomized, even to its borders (as a bill may become law throughout a nation at the stroke of the clock) — though the work of its application be never finished, or so much as entered upon. No consideration of the immensity of the object, nor of the long labor or impossible labor of finished acquaintance, can balk the ease and timeless facility of the idea. No one shall tell me that my ideas of Russia, or of physics, or of walrus, or of my friend, are but feelings because my ignorance of them is measured only by eternal time: if at the name I know to what object that name refers, I have a valid idea of that infinite object. In international affairs, a State may be recognized and dealt with if it has but a determinate place and foreign office: all else may be problematic — population, extent, resource, even government. An idea likewise has existence and standing when it has a determinate *place in the mind*, determinate *external relations* (distinctions from other ideas): internal exploration, development, spinning out of treaty web-work, may pursue its own slow course.

One sort of completion, and one only, an idea must have — the complete distinction and identification of its interest (or of its problem): it must be an individual interest in a mind-full of interests. One sort of finitude it must have and one only: the finitude of not being the only idea in the mind, of having a genuine exterior, a wholly mental exterior, of other interests. So far as the idea's *object* is concerned, it seems to me *doubtful whether there are any finite ideas at all.* Choose your idea of the minutest possible object, an object defined as being without internal detail, atom-atom: this poorest idea in the mind must, like other ideas, be *on duty forever*, ready for infinite recurrences of its object — which possible infinitude is already part of the sense of the idea. So with our ocean water-bucket, which, though it would, cannot close to itself the prospect of endless other buckets-full; a vista involved in its own limited cubic contents. So with all other ideas; they must contemplate an infinitude of application having a rough inverse proportion to their own internal poverty. Indeed, I am prepared to say that the chief function of an idea is to serve as a vessel, or as a center of attachment, for infinite growth of knowledge: that any idea *not* infinitely capacious, infinitely ambitious, is already a dead idea. To the question, Can we think the Infinite? let me propose the answer, We think nothing else.

Religious ideas, then, have nothing to fear from the general charge of infinite ambition. But perhaps the real occasion for the diffidence of the candid-humble philosopher is not so much infinite contents *per se* as it is the special case of infinity involved in *totality:* for the religious idea (of God, or of world, or of eternity) must be in its own way all-comprehensive. Ideas may have an internal infinitude, and beside this an infinite swath of application; but all this is as nothing to the infinitude beyond their interest: the dark stretching expanses of reality left out by all ideas — *not-x* to all of them.

In meeting this objection, it is fair to notice that in describing this unlighted region, *not-x* to every idea, one has made it or confessed it a definable interest, already an object of idea. Some marginal interest always goes to the *not-x* of whatever idea, — which marginal interest, heaping up from all ideas on any region which is *not-x* to all of them, must acquire much positive weight in time. But this observation hardly satisfies the objector, and ought not to satisfy him, — nor the defendant either: for the religious interest in the Whole is no marginal interest; and the supposed religious attainment of whole-knowledge no dim reflected luminosity. The religious idea will be as positive and primordial as any; will insist that it is possible for idea to *begin with the Whole*, as readily as with any fragment. The real source of doubt lies in some unclearness about the way in which knowledge grows. We must give some attention to that.

It is not a true account of knowledge to say that it proceeds (always) from the part to the whole. The progress of knowledge has rather more in common with the development of a germ-cell than with the building of a brick wall; something of the whole present and active in that cell from the beginning. But we must always reject helpful metaphors, inimical metaphors unless we bundle them off in time, and refer to the idea itself: we may draw a line about a germ-cell — none about a germ-thought; an idea of the universe can never have been wrapped up in small compass for gradual unfolding; we do not learn *to see space little by little*. The child's space is as great as the man's, — namely, whole-space. He who comes into the world at all comes at once into the presence of the whole world. I am introduced to a person, not by piecemeal, but all at once, with a positive impression and judgment contained in my idea: not denying that there is much to learn and correct through long-growing acquaintance. So of my introduction to reality: in its full infinity and wholeness it is now before me and has been so from my conscious beginning, the same from birth to death — the same space, the same time, the same natural order and particularity, the same history and social context, the same God, too, if there be a god, the same world-laws or law, the same conditions of life and death, success and failure.

What grows in knowledge is the under-standing of all this, the internal complexity and detail, middle-world experience and thereby middle-world ideas, and especially the power to put ideas together. That fundamental difference already noticed between having an idea and having it in terms of other ideas, between knowing your object and reasoning about it, is here again in evidence: for the great volume and business of what we call the growth of knowledge is growth of connection, growth of treaty-making between ideas. (Each such new treaty-connection is doubtless itself a new idea — as we count ideas — and brings with it internal development of the ideas thus newly related, but without altering their place in the mind, which *place* is their identity). The connecting of ideas goes on apace: for our loquacious, marketable knowledge is in proportion, not immediately to our ideas, but to the couplings we can make among them, unions as of subject and predicate. Every new bit of experience, taken in idea, makes chance and demand for new couplings, — couplings, in fact, with all previously present ideas: such a process has no end — of all possible couplings only a relative few can be effected. Meanwhile, knowledge keeps getting smaller and finer, more tangled, more systematic all the time:

there are more threads and pins in the loom, more shuttles in the air. Such is the general aspect of the growth of knowledge—a mid-world growth as we have said. But with what does all the growth and weaving begin? In the beginning was at least *the Loom;* and always remains, the simple-total frame of things. Huge, inevitable, abiding Loom, loom-motion and loom-law: these, we may say, are *given*; stuff also to weave with, and withal the command to weave. Such total world-fact, always present in idea, *contains* the growth of knowledge—is not in its wholeness any mere final achievement thereof.

The whole, then, is knowable: is the one thing permanently known. Any first idea of any dawning consciousness, whatever its stimulus-object, must be at the same time idea-of-the-whole, never to forsake that consciousness while it remains such. But there is no lack of growth and change in this idea. Once given a whole-idea as a positive possession, every addition to knowledge must add to it also; every change in the intricate structure of mid-world knowledge must have some answering effect upon it. Suggestions about the character of the world as a whole are continually steaming up from the general intellectual workshop; since every idea that man gains casts some reflection or other upon that world. Every other idea, let me say, is a possible *predicate* for that permanent *subject;* that is to say, a possible *commentary* upon its nature and character.

And men have always been eager to bring their new knowledges in all fields into connection with their whole-idea, framing new judgments about it. Thus the reputation of the whole is always in the making: there is no absolute stability in the qualities or *predicates* which have been attached to it — as whether it is just or unjust; caring about men or not-caring; unconscious perhaps or super-conscious; unitary, or struggling for unity, or a mere scene of struggle. In so far as our knowledge of the whole comes through such judgments from the progress of our day's-work, bringing explicit predicates to that whole-idea, that knowledge of the whole might well be *subject to greater contingency than any other*. And this consideration, I think, may help us to understand the historical instability of religious thought. As the growth of other knowledge falls into tangle, it suggests discordant predicates for the whole; and judgments once secure fall into doubt, to be set up again later with greater assurance and added meaning, or to make room for some truer judgment. Intellectual business is, as we have seen, an eminently dust-raising pursuit: it seems at times as if our whole-idea, which like all permanences is non-intrusive, were passively obliterated in the general murk; as though we might lose not only the predicates, but the subject as well.

Herein, no doubt, lies the advantage of the child in religion: not greater power, but a freer atmosphere. To some extent, intellectual advance must always involve loss to religion: readjustments within the whole-idea are required; the simplicity and firmness of our former predicates are disturbed; the solid proportions of the whole-idea of childhood can with difficulty, or never, be recovered. One sees in part why religion and 'intellect' are prone to fall into contrast. For the religious idea suffers whatever genuine losses are involved in all progress; and furthermore cannot be clearly discerned amid the bustle of scientific labor: it needs in a measure to be looked-away-to; it is best found in the pauses of the weaving process, a matter for the most part of holiday survey.

The whole-idea, then, while ever present, has its vicissitudes, its fortune to make and ever re-make, its frequent seeming life and death struggles. It is no idle spectator of mental progress, but partaker of all mind-growth, mind-revolution. And all this is consistent with, nay implies, the truth that this same infinite whole-idea is that with which every rational existence begins.

CHAPTER IX

THE RETREAT INTO SUBJECTIVITY

IT needs still to be explained what positive character this whole-idea can have, if no predicate can permanently adhere to it. The instability of any given predicate must often appear as evidence that the idea in question is impossible: on this account our whole-idea has often been put down as a no-idea: everything, so far as idea can grasp it, being equivalent to nothing. The mystic has often been charged with this conclusion, even while he maintains as the true mystic must that his whole-idea is the most positive of all.

In spite of the difficulty of fixing predicates for the whole, circumstantial evidence does strongly discountenance the notion that the idea is a negation, or a pure problem: for hardly would such persistent ferment and vicissitude center about *it*, if there were no positive individual interest and content at stake. The most striking circumstance in the history of this idea is not, I think, that all predicates have been beaten back; but that in spite of all difficulties the assault continues, unremitting, through all mental eras. And if it were true (as it is not) that in this persistent attempt to capture the whole in predicate-idea no single predicate had gained permanent hold — all of them struck down by Something — we should still judge this fact the poorest possible evidence of Nothing There! When we reject a predicate, it is because we know, better than this predicate can say, what the character of our world is.

The principle here chiefly concerned is this: that the *denial of any predicate does not leave behind no-predicate;* a simple enough principle, but much hindered by mechanical ideas of ideas — for the erasure of a circle does certainly leave behind precisely no-circle in its place. If however I deny an idea, I leave behind endless possibilities, or even responsibilities, some of which are very near to the negated idea itself. For instance, I deny that potatoes are red or that the Earth is a sphere: yet these denials leave possible much redness in potatoes and much roundness in the Earth's shape. So when discordant opinions cancel each other, what is left is no mere feeling, but some very real idea, if we can but name it. Neither the whole-idea nor any other is at first *quality-less*, getting its character by the attachment of predicate after predicate from without: a new predicate does no more than express what was and has been true of the subject, not hitherto say-able, but needing and requiring to be said. The retreat into subjectivity (for that is what the feeling-resort is) means an abandonment of the effort and responsibility of naming the idea that *is* tenable, letting subject as well as predicate sink beneath the threshold waters of conscious existence.

A rough parallel may show this: religious opinions differ from age to age and from people to people hardly more than do the foods of these same ages and peoples. Have we then any positive, objective, food-idea — since scarcely anything used in one place would not be rejected in some other? — shall we not say that the real meaning of food is a *feeling* of some sort, say of hunger and the relief thereof? Doubtless this feeling-sequence is a constant amid all the variations of menu, and enters into the meaning of the term; but there is another constant, amid all the varieties of foods,—and that is *food*—physical, eatable, digestible object-matter, as well as subject-matter. Behind every such diversity of idea, there is an identity of feeling (which it is well to note); but also—an identity of Idea. Men may lose their gods, and have God left. Behind Indra and his drivers is Prajapati; and behind Prajapati, there is Brahm.

It is fair to observe, also, that the displacement of old predicates by new (admittedly an infinite process, in the case of our whole-idea, or of our God-idea) *does not imply the essential falsity of the old.* There are among predicates no precise fittings of any subject, nor yet precise mis-fittings (if a predicate wholly coincides with its subject, it ceases to be a *garment* therefor): what is fit depends upon what is required. My predicates hurled at Deity and the World are like broad missiles that hit the mark—*and more*: as my marksmanship becomes finer I may adopt finer weapons, substitute arrows for clubs and stones, but still hit only the same mark. I cannot accuse my stone-and-club-throwing successes of substantial error, but only of rudeness, of anachronism if persisted in. Arrows too must be displaced—in time perhaps by light-rays: yet each, in its own way, may strike true. Nothing in all this difficulty of predicates then (even if it were, which it is not, a pure chaos), need justify the abandonment of the whole-idea as a no-idea, at most a feeling.

It is not our present purpose to say what we know about the World or about God; we are enquiring only whether such knowledge is possible, and how it is possible. So far as explicit predicates of the whole are concerned, our answer may now be put in this way: If there are any permanent achievements of knowledge in any direction, in the progress of science and the Arts, every such achievement may be the basis of an equally stable judgment about the whole. At one time, we were questioning whether the emergence of the Arts were not the silencing of religion: we may now see that it is the emergence of the Arts that chiefly aids, and even compels, religion to become vocal. When the Arts had no language, religion herself was necessarily helpless, un-literal, speaking the speech of myth and figure, lacking fixed objective moorings. The question of *truth* in religion did not arise, and could not consciously arise, until there had come into the world an independent science, philosophy, art, and artisanry. Now that these have made good their independent faculties, they lend to religion their new-made powers: religion becomes articulate in the same measure in which she gives articulateness to the world.

We have, then, a growing body of positive knowledge about the whole, as well as a permanent whole-idea as subject of these judgments. But it remains true that all knowledge of the whole is of the simplest order. In the presence of the ultimate we shall always remain primitive: we can never become civilized in respect to God. All our accounts of the larger realities fall back in language to the elements of speech, the rudiments of numbers, the conceptions of infantile mechanics.[1] Childhood lies always within our reach, as we pass outward from the world in which we move with skill (because we have set up in it the stage and reaction-board suited to meet our powers) into the field of the larger interests of the cosmos. It is because of this necessary simplicity, and not because the type of hold we have on these larger interests is not a grip of *idea*, that we bow our minds in well-considered humility as we approach the infinite, that religion belies itself when it expands in verbiage. For speech, at its best, is only partial wisdom; whereas the wisdom of religion is entire.

But as for this other humility — that of the candid, humble philosopher, who will have no idea of the infinite, especially of the Total-infinite — that is, in truth, the poorest virtue in the catalogue. A labor-saving virtue, I fear: also at times, sadly enough, a guilty virtue, parting too readily with its birthright. Such a thing there is as impatience in knowledge, also presumption; not to be cured however by renouncing courage, effort, and withal the capital-possession of humanity — the idea which with simplicity embraces and knows the infinite. Every living infinite-total, and not the world only, has for knowledge this same unitary-simplicity; the Person, Nature, Society, History, the State: the knowledge of these, open to the "poor in spirit," is the justification of democracy, of modern life at large. We are not human until we claim and use these ideas-infinite, the essential organs of a genuine personal life.

[1] We may notice a similar thing in all the maxima of life — say in world-politics, whose "depths and intricacies" are chiefly the mysteries of closed doors, whose "complex principles" chiefly the abstruse policies of boys and savages.

It remains true also — and what we have been saying will help to explain the fact — that religious knowledge, of the kind with which revelation and prophecy are concerned, is not commonly found in the course of theoretical reflection. That which so profoundly stirs feeling has been in its psychological origin a product of something very like feeling, and very different from common thought. Abeyance of ingenuity, a fostered passivity, reliance upon the primitive in the mind, the coöperation of what psychology prefers to call the subconscious and instinctive: all such *non-thinking* has been requisite for winning truth about super-nature. To retire into the wilderness for forty days, to make yourself pure and empty, to throw off your skill and your shrewdness, to forget the proportions of men and of men's outlooks: these have been found fit preparations for the reception of prophecy. But let us be clear that this negation of common thought-activity, the intense passion and subjectivity of religion thus shown, is but a measure of the immense scope of its intention. The most inner is called on only to reach the most outer. The bow-string is pulled in to its limit only that the shaft may also reach its limit.

Religious wisdom impresses us as an affair for the subconscious subject because it stirs subconscious depths: an impression which the psychological attitude can hardly shake off; yet the inference is exactly topsy-turvy.

Nothing can stir the "depths" of mind, but total out-of-doors. We call "depth," last dregs, etc., that in man which only ultimate facts and happenings can interest; that which the near and usual can neither rouse nor ruffle. Somewhere in each man, we imagine, there lies an *ultimatum*, to be backed by all his energies from all reservoirs, ordinary and extraordinary, — what can elicit from any man such ultimatum and ultimatum-backing? — nothing that has not somewhere in it the word *All!* There are such things, we think, as ruling passions, "deepest desires," in any man some nameable or unnameable last ambition — what can set such a depth on fire? — nothing but some *total opportunity* (real or believed real), discovered in the wide world beyond the self.

Drama, dreaming likewise, can detach itself at once from reality and power of excitement: but objectivity is the very food of passion. Passion necessarily *realizes;* apart from some experience of passion one hardly knows what *fact* is.

Religious passion, at length, is the best illustration of all this: for this is the mark of religious passion, that a specific *view of the whole* makes conscious connection with one's practical ultimata. The "deepest of all inborn impulses," says Professor Pratt,[1] "is the 'instinct for self-preservation'": and what is to set *that* impulse trembling? — "a belief in the impossibility of real annihilation." Belief founded on what? — founded back on the instinct itself? — doomed then to death and silence. Founded on vision perhaps? If ever upon the stupid day-length time-span of any self, or saint either, some *vision* breaks to roll his life and ours into new channels, it can only be because that vision admits into his soul some trooping invasion of the concrete fulness of eternity. Such vision doubtless means sub-

[1] Psychology of Religious Belief, p. 292.

conscious readiness, and subconscious resonance too,—but the expansion of *unused air-cells* does not argue that we have ceased now to breathe the *outer air*:—the very opposite!

No. The so-called wisdom of feeling is of the same stuff and substance with other wisdom, positive, objective, belonging to our world of ideas. The religious vista is large and open : in integral continuity with the field-lines of our overt existence (not narrowly caught by peering up back-chimney-flues of consciousness). Whatever is thus continuous with the real known in idea is itself known in idea,—not otherwise. There are vague ideas, and unfinished ideas, uncertain predicates, qualities only dimly divined—known most certainly by their difference from others, their negative bearing — but none of this haze and floating outline affects the intent and category of the scene-contents. Whatever is, or can be, predicate of idea is itself idea-stuff, whether or not yet successfully defined and connected.

We have dwelt long on the question of the idea's defects, the most persuasive of the supports of the religion of feeling. For some touch of finitude must cleave to all things human: and none of our ideas, religious or other, can be more than the idea of some poor mortal. Yet, we do here claim that the ideas of mortals may entertain the infinite and the total as their valid objects, and do always entertain them, though unawares. Whoever says that the foundations of religion lie deeper than idea speaks true: deeper, indeed, they lie than the current idea-level; deeper than most of our predicates, taken as these are chiefly from the sphere of the day's work.

The result we have reached is simply that *deeper than idea is Idea.* There is nothing of reality, whether the infinitude of its livingness and change, or the infinitude of its extent, to which we must be related through feeling because of the incapacity of idea. Retreat to the inner man (retreat for which idealism has itself set the example) is not imposed upon us by any yet-mentioned defects of our organs of knowledge or, let me say, is *not permitted* to us: driven back from any stated idea, we must still remain in the idea-world.

CHAPTER X

THE IDEA-WORLD IN ITS AIM TOWARD FREEDOM FROM FEELING

ASSUME, then, that we have overcome the most serious and actual of the obstacles to our confidence in the possibility of knowledge in religion. Let us agree that religious feeling, in its necessary effort to win a theory of its own meaning, is not inevitably balked by the incompetence of our organs of knowledge, the ideas. If we can accept this as a definite result, though wholly general and preliminary, we have dealt with one half of the problem which the religion of feeling puts before us. Another half remains: for while we must try to work out a religious theory and have good hope of success, it may still be true *that the vitality of religion lies in the feeling and not in the idea.* As long as our ideas retain their living connection with the feelings which they are naturally meant to guide, they are sound: but idea has a way of severing that connection and setting up as a thing separate and sufficient in itself. We have ourselves asserted that feeling tends to vanish as idea becomes more adequate: and yet it is certain that religion without feeling is nothing. All feeling needs idea; but it does not follow that all idea needs feeling or can win it: in fixing attention upon the idea, we are in danger of detaching ourselves from the sources of life.

It is idle to deny that he impoverishes himself who

tries to live by idea alone. What we have to do is to study this evident tendency of idea to separate from feeling and become external. We cannot doubt the tendency, though we may doubt whether it is the last word in regard to their relations. The union between idea and feeling seems to me to be organic, not accidental or external, so that idea in the last resort can no more free itself from feeling than feeling can free itself from idea. But whatever may be the nature of this union, it is not to be found by minimizing the fact that the world of ideas does aspire to be independent of the current flux of feelings. We must rather give full scope and credit to this aim, and think it through to its conclusions. What, then, we first ask, seems to be the nature of that ideal of independence?

In the first place an idea must be permanent, whereas feeling is essentially transient. An idea may guide a feeling to its goal and its cessation; but as the experience passes, the idea does not cease to exist, — as for example the idea of food when I am *not* hungry. On the contrary, it seems now to begin its most characteristic existence as idea.

For the more common uses of the idea, in memory, in reflection, in communication, are best fulfilled when the idea can be referred to without unnecessary stirring of subjective interests and emotions. We want our ideas to be so held in the mind that any vital connection with feeling must come as an additional fact. We want them so far insulated from ourselves that whatever their momentary importance may be or become, we must first make an application to our own case by a separate act of inference. Picture me a destroyed San Francisco: this is a fact distantly regrettable, but still a mere fact: but remind me now that I have friends there, or investments, and immediately the bond with feeling is accomplished. Apart from such separate act of application the idea exists in its normal freedom, fit to be dealt with in what we call the purely theoretical manner, the characteristic life of the idea.

In this theoretical condition any idea of mine finds itself in a permanent and fairly complete *world of ideas*. This idea-world at any moment must contain the idea-concerns for all possible feelings, past and future — not merely for those accidentally present; and even to some extent for all mankind, not for myself alone, in so far as I undertake to understand the feelings of all mankind through my own magazine of ideas. Only a few of these ideas can be in use at any time; for feeling is nothing unless present feeling; hence for the most part one's idea-world stands undisturbed by feeling, a liberal and adequate field for free conscious existence. Were it not possible to lift the eyes from the movement of affairs in course to other idea-regions without at once experiencing the full feeling-effect of these ideas, human life could scarcely move in any such roomy spiritual place as it now possesses. The permanent and instant command of our whole-view is perhaps the distinguishing mark of our species. Whatever independence of feeling is implied in this undisturbed access to every idea-meaning is the clear tendency and purpose of the idea-world, and to a great extent an already accomplished fact.

And further, whatever we can call a spiritual possession has its place here. For surely we should give religion, or any other human interest, both ampler and firmer terrain by establishing it in this permanent idea-world than if we could find for it, so to speak, only a sea-faring life on the incessantly shifting surface of feeling. Whatever is to be established in this world must be established in idea, for only the idea admits of establishment.

And now, in the second place, this free theoretical status of the idea in memory and reflection becomes an ideal even for the use of the idea in concrete cognitive experience, in so far as this too has a theoretical aim. We are sufficiently familiar with the way in which feeling interferes with this work, mars the equanimity of its operation, and warps its results. This work must be done in a certain equilibrium of mind, an equilibrium whose difficulty is itself a testimony to the strong natural bond between idea and feeling. But this equilibrium is possible, at least as an ideal, and it is this ideal that now concerns us. Through the need to be anti-emotional, the attitude which we call the empirical attitude takes on a definite moral aspect. What we will to know is reality, and reality is a word having the force of feeling-rebuke — "stern reality" is its name.

Thus, in sum, our ideas have many other uses than those of the immediate guidance of present feelings; and for all these other uses a freedom from feeling-entanglements is as desirable as in its own place a ready union with feeling is desirable. There is a liberality about idea which does not comport with its being always in harness to feeling; and the idea cannot be identified with a relation which now appears to be but a special and occasional relation. The idea is normally independent of the flux of feelings. But has not this independence some further and more general relation to feeling?

There is no doubt that it has a further account to give. This power to hold our ideas in theoretical equilibrium is no mechanical matter; it is a hard-won accomplishment, and it becomes marked only in the higher stages of evolution and of culture. It is an acquisition of much importance, having a decided biological value as well as the general spiritual interest which we have suggested. This status of the idea is thus itself a matter in which our feelings must be in some way deeply involved. Very likely the apparently independent idea is but a pseudo-independent idea; a highly explicable, and even copiously explained, product of evolution.

There is certainly little agreement at present as to the exact sequence and description of the stages of mental evolution; but there is some approach to agreement in the opinion that the theoretical use of idea is a comparatively late invention of nature's and a thoroughly practical and instrumental affair. Primitive idea-making is seemingly most un-theoretical; and developed idea-making is at bottom the same, though under high disguise. There is a well-known theory to the effect that *all ideas*, in the last resort, *mean some action or plan of action;* so that in their very meanings they are bound up with the feelings which normally announce and accompany those actions. Through whatever remote and devious paths the idea in question finds its way into practice, its whole significance can be reduced to the *difference in conduct* which belief in its object tends to provoke. Idea means action or purpose. This we may call the *action-theory* of idea. In this theory I do not find any complete satisfaction; yet it moves so far in the right direction, in bringing the theoretical idea into relation with feeling, that it will be well to follow its path and define our own belief with reference to it. Let me then bring to mind a typical sketch of the evolution of the apparently feeling-free idea, as interpreted by this action-theory.

When the world may be simply classified for any organism into the eatable and the non-eatable, the terrible and the non-terrible, idea directly means action, and idea-difference means action-difference. Development, which means at each stage dealing with a bigger world, must bring into view objects whose bearing on action is more and more indirect and distant, as follows:

First, we must acquire ideas of *ways and means*, not of ends only. Before we can eat we must chase, and long series of signs and way-marks must be added to our idea-stock — all practical enough, but without original interest in themselves.

Then it appears that some things are *means to more than one end*. The same path leads home, and also leads to water; the same water may be source of food supply and drink supply. In such ideas the various suggestions of action tend to cancel or inhibit each other. Many-purposes may seem to the mind much the same as no-purpose: here begins the apparently action-free idea. Of this sort are most of our present stock of substantive ideas, because nothing concrete has its value all in one direction. And further, in all real objects, as in all real men, there is a mixture of benefit and injury. The action-value of any concrete object taken by itself is nearly neutral, a grey in which all colors mix.

My world extends in time and not in space only: and as memory and prudence accompany the widening of my world in its time-extent, I interest myself in *possible values*, and not alone in actual values. Every concrete thing, under such a broadened area of purpose, has a speculative importance. Thus arises the idea of a *thing*, the most finished achievement of our assumed attitude of indifference. The *thing* has no defined suggestions of action; its reputation is all to be made; our value-judgment is perfectly reserved; we have become, to all appearances, purely theoretical.

Two new emotions, caution and curiosity, mark the upper reaches of this development; indeed, they are probably provided by nature fairly early, but come to flower late in that feeling which is sometimes called the *love of knowledge*, which interests itself in things ostensibly for no other reason than that they exist. But this love of knowledge, like all preceding stages of recession from the immediately useful, is still practical; it is best regarded, perhaps, as a form of the love of power, which in acquiring new data feels a diffused delight hailing remotely from the sense of possible action.

"Dispassionate investigation" is an office created by this practical curiosity. It is the best value-policy to treat our world as if we were interested in it for its own sake. But dramatic self-sacrifice like this does not conceal the fundamental relation of all meanings to feelings. Is it not a commonplace of experimental psychology that action-shadows and fringes attend all ideas at all times; are there not incipient, tell-tale muscular movements always to be discovered accompanying all thinking-movements, inhibited, but none the less verifiable? Supporting the proposal that some motor-outraying is the essential meaning of every idea.

Theoretic use of idea, then, is a use in which we say to the idea, in effect, "Action-meaning—yes, but *not now.*" And in this power of restraint or inhibition we are mightily aided by a growing social experience, which lends much practical significance to the attitude, "Action-meaning—yes, but *not mine.*" Society imposes upon me the habit of regarding actions through the eyes and muscles of others: I learn to regard objects irresponsibly, as one reads the newspaper. There is much that excites action-impulse, — but it is not my affair, and I check myself. The unmoving idea, the idea regarded theoretically, is simply in a socialized condition: it is set over into the world of an actor who is, in thought, some one else, any one else than myself.

Thus we understand how, on purely practical considerations, it comes about that we have a pseudo-independent world of ideas. Feeling does not markedly accompany a thought except in so far as that thought touches the springs of my own musculature: feeling is the idea doing work in me. By whatever policy I can prevent this motor-connection from being made, I add to my power over the theoretic idea. But in all such theoretic status, we have to recognize at bottom the fundamental action-meaning held in abeyance, and for a limited duration. All theory is sustained throughout by a powerful current of feeling, the interest in possible action: and any one active impulse is prevented from displaying itself only by other impulses which for the time rule my assent·

This is a crude and over-simple account of the action-theory of idea-meaning, such as I will attribute to no one thinker. For our purposes it sufficiently represents the view in question.

Suggestive of much truth is this evolutionary picture; showing the existence of some close bond between all idea and all action: yet not on the whole a just picture. It seems to reduce the idea everywhere to the service of action: but in all justice it only shows the idea in its struggle for independence hampered at the edges by the persistent fringes of action. The rightful inference, I venture to say, from such evolution-tracing must show idea connected with feeling universally indeed — but still *externally*, as to something intrinsically different. Idea, we find, is always accompanied by feeling: will have various feeling-promptings, hints of valuable action, associated with it — by way of annex; but still always as additional and extraneous fact. Every idea-object must indeed have some appeal to the imagination, its vividness depending largely on these communicating rills of value-fancy, more or less overt. But the idea-meaning remains *that-upon-which* these value-fancies turn, *that-from-which* these action-vistas open out: is itself something else than these fringe-leadings; cannot by any evidence so far brought forward be identified with them, as value-meaning or action-meaning.

From the beginning, our ideas give cues to action, but they give, it seems, always somewhat more than the cue: and in this somewhat-more they seek to lodge their meaning — not in the accompanying cue to action. Thus the idea of wine carries with it very definite suggestion of action — wine is something to be drunk : yet wine cannot be so defined and identified. Wine must be defined, officially and otherwise, by its relation to the grape, ultimately by its root in *nature:* apart from this particular source in nature wine is not wine, though perfectly imitating all possible wine-feelings and wine-reactions. To lodge meanings somewhere in Nature seems to guarantee their genuineness ; as if all meanings must be made to touch base in a *region of indifference* before they may spin lawful alliances with feeling and action.

Nature is the typical region for the feeling-free anchorage of the meanings of ideas. But this region of indifference can be more generally described. If we have to make a distinction between ideas (as of wine from vinegar, friend from foe) we can do this only by making, or having, an idea of the common ground which these objects occupy: which common basis (common man-shape of friend and foe, common white granule mass of salt and sugar), precisely *not* to be acted upon, becomes the refuge of hesitation. Refuge of hesitation, however, just because common ground, will constitute the stem from which the divergent idea-meanings must spring. Whatever the impulsive foreground of idea, there will thus necessarily be a *non-impulsive background,* and in this our idea-meanings will rest.[1]

This non-impulsive background gives its character to the foreground also : our action-cues are but features *belonging to it,* only fortunately and accidentally avail-

[1] In symbol : we distinguish between x-conduct and y-conduct, not by means simply of x-idea and y-idea ; but by means first of a non-motor idea, A, capable of the varieties Ax and Ay. The A-idea is, in practice, only relatively non-motor ; but since the formula is entirely general, it indicates an ultimate purely non-motor basis of meanings.

able for our discriminations. Through serving all idea-differences, this background looms large; background and all foregrounds merge into one vast non-impulsive *World-object,* infinite complex magazine of object-fields and field-contents:—space-field, cosmic force-field, spectrum-series, tone-scale, effort-scale; human-desire-gamut, too, taken as objective fact; social scale, moral-value field, and many others, together with all their contents and the motions thereof; all motions and changes of contents against one ultimate background-field of infinite time; all contents rooted in one ultimate background-stuff, which we may call — problematically — Substance. Infinite complex magazine, capable of serving all action-differences actual and possible, yet with infinite unused resource, superior to and apart from all such use, — essentially *unused* by it. Such World-object, in its complexity, is partially summarized in our idea of Nature; more completely, as objective Reality, whose problematic *Substance* sets the last goal for all idea-meanings.

In such external World-fact do our idea-meanings seek lodgment; as if, I repeat, it were necessary to *touch* the passionless ground of things, before affiliating with any particular actions and feelings. The structure of the whole system of ideas and actions becomes indirect, *triangular:* there may be no direct passage from perception to action, but perception must first be related to substance, and from substance pass on to action — with freedom of will.

Now this idea of a non-impulsive background, which at last gets the mysterious name of Substance, the external goal of all idea-meanings, is *in no wise a result of development.* It is rather the aboriginal fact of consciousness. Environment, and environment complexity, have extended immeasurably; but externality has become no whit more external. From the beginning, our idea-making must have held itself in independence of impulse. For without such prior independence, action development could not so much as begin. We are able to find cues for divergent lines of action, *because we have already been interested in something else than the actively important features of our world.* [1]

Nature has early separated the organs of perception from the organs of action; and in the freedom of perception, with its liberality of interest, care-free play and exploration, idea-making has freedom also. Idea-outlining follows *shapes*, perceptive unities and uses, not the unities and uses of our own action. Perception shows us, we think, the immediate clothing of Substance; and shares in that externality which idea-meaning requires. Perception is no doubt to be regarded biologically as a means of adaptation : but as such alone it must be judged immeasurably wasteful, supplying us with entire fields, infinite manifolds of objects, in order that a few discriminations may be made (supplying also that whole super-useful region of perceptive beauty, whose extraor-

[1] Especially is the idea of the thing-with-various-uses visibly dependent on such liberality of interest. For if idea meant to us just so much action-plan and nothing more, action routes might cross ad libitum without ever exciting any knowledge of the fact of their crossing. The notion of an intersection presupposes an interest in the lines for their own sake, in some independence of the ends reached by those lines. Thus we know *water* as the same thing in this use and in that only because in any use of it characters other than those used have freely engaged our attention ; qualities appealing to eye, touch, and the like.

dinary art-development escapes so far from biological explanation).

In spite of all important evidence showing to what extent perception-interest is governed by active-interest, it remains true that in idea-outlining perception has a prior and independent head. So much so, that when we make to ourselves *ideas of activities* themselves, we incline to make them in terms of "external" perceptions, rather than in their own proper coin (for instance, our idea of *walking*, which represents to us commonly walking-as-seen, attribute of outer Substance, rather than walking-as-inwardly-known in terms of feeling and impulsiveness, attribute of Self). Feeling and action find in the perception-substance-world some requisite mise-en-scène; varieties of feeling and action find here a unity, coherence, relatedness, intelligibility, which on their own ground they lack; especially, they find here unlimited *room to grow in*, the dome of perception never narrowed down to the scope, or even the prospective scope, of conduct.

It is not surprising, therefore, that the ideas we make as ideas of *single objects* should show no close correspondence to action-need; should share in the superabundance of the perceptive fields themselves. From a given desire can never be inferred the idea of the object which does, in concrete fact, satisfy that desire (from thirst alone, what actual beverage can be deduced). Ideas, we say, do by aboriginal instinct fix their meaning in the ultimate non-impulsive Substance of the world; and idea-outlining tends to follow the hints which perception gives of the unities belonging to that reality-not-ourselves.

But here we encounter a type of demurrer, leading direct to the heart of the matter. Idea-outlining according to perception-unities is not, we are told, so independent of action-reference as we suppose. Ideas are made not indeed in the interest of specific actions, but still in the interest of *types of action* of very general sort. Spatially closed figures are regarded as single things, because solid outlines form, in general, the limiting lines of our own physical movements (consideration finely employed by Bergson). Detachable and movable objects, especially moving objects, have evident biological importance; are indefinitely liable to concern one's own vital status: must naturally become practical idea-units.

Significant here is not so much the interest alleged (which is real enough, but still demonstrably after the fact, still external) as the immense *generality of the interest.* Why may I not say, on the same basis, that *objects* interest me, because forsooth objectivity-in-general is practically portentous? What is to give into the hands of biological induction terms of just such high generality ("spatially detachable objects," "moving objects," "physical bodies," "forces," etc.) as expressive of *that in which* momentous issues reside; what if not some prior idea? May we not say just this: that perception *generalizes the conditions of conduct;* provides generalization in advance; and is able to do this because of its relation to our original idea of Substance? What fundamentally interests men is, in truth, just reality —nothing more special, nothing less. Around this original meaning gather all practical concerns; in this all importances are funded. Interest in reality is the idea-making, idea-outlining function of the human mind.

Interest in What Exists, not more because it is mine than because it is not-mine. Doubtless all practical motives lend their weight to this peculiar limiting interest; but it is not constituted by them. Some passion for objectivity, for reality, for Substance, quite prior to other passions, there is at the bottom of all idea; a passion not wholly of an unreligious nature, not wholly un-akin to the love of God.

The nature of that passion, if we could know it, would afford the answer to our question regarding the organic union between idea and feeling. It is an inability to believe in the possibility of such a passion, a passion for what is merely because it is, that closes the way to that solution. It is by accepting the apparent paradox that we shall now come to our understanding of that union.

CHAPTER XI

IDEA IN ORGANIC UNION WITH FEELING

FEW ideas we have that do not freely mix and entangle themselves with feeling, and lend themselves variously to the service of action. But all ideas, so we have now concluded, have a natural and original independence of those stirrings of emotion which accompany our current activities. The child, the savage, and no doubt also the crayfish, the sponge, the polyp, if they are idea-builders at all, have an interest in their world which we must call 'purely theoretical.' No creature can construct ideas except through a genuine non-practical interest in what is around him simply 'because it is there.' Every idea, however rich in practical association, is attached in its ultimate 'external meaning' to the idea of reality, the center of all this free, dispassionate interest.[1]

[1] Whatever release any mind can win from its own present interests and passions, for memory or reflection or scientific effort, is accomplished through holding instinctively or consciously to its own idea of reality, or of substance, in whatever form this idea presents itself to him. It is in its religious form that the idea of reality has been the chief culprit in all abstraction of the mind from the current of feeling and action. From the beginning, religious ideas have exhibited a certain aloofness. The seers have had their practical and moral recommendations to make ; but in their cosmologies and theologies, in their myth-spinning generally, they have been curiously free from relation to human values. All such ideas have appealed to no other visible interest than this ancient interest in reality, interest of a purely theoretical nature. I cannot defend the religious idea against this charge, nor the metaphysical idea either. I

And now, it is here if at all, in this center of the idea's independence, that we shall find the essential union between idea and feeling. For that same idea of reality which has so little to do with the beginnings of our actions, and the stirrings of feeling that accompany those beginnings, has as I believe everything to do with the building of their *ends*. The values which our actions aim at seem to me to be the direct and continuous creation of that idea. How this is the case is a simple matter if we can win the right view of it; but the winning of that view has its own difficulty.

Our actions drive on incessantly to their ends, and these ends we call values. We take these values, our various human interests and concerns, for the most part as self-justifying and self-explanatory: that this thing is a source of pleasure, and that a source of pain, we accept as ultimate facts, our practical first premises. We understand, in general, that in the pursuit of these various satisfactions, nature is luring us on to live, and to increase life. But we seldom enquire why our living itself is of interest to nature; as apart from these same values we think it would hardly be of interest to ourselves. Our values, then, remain essentially unexplained. They remain too without clear relation to each other. We like beauty, and we like company; we enjoy music, and care for children, and appreciate a courtesy. These are facts of instinct and human nature, and we adopt them as our several ends. It was for the sake of winning

see and acknowledge the futility of much, perhaps most, of this curiosity-work. But I see also in that power of detachment the worst in close conjunction with the best.

these scattered values that we were supposed, by the action-theory, to be concerned in making ideas.

But if we can so readily accept these ends as final facts, there is no need of explaining the interest in reality. We may simply say that this also is a value, and is its own justification ; and this is often said, as if it were enough to say. If in our theories of human nature we no longer think it necessary to reduce altruism to a transformed egoism ; if we have long since learned that care for another is quite as native and original as care for oneself, that love is one of the instincts ; it can do no violence to our scientific principles to accept the love of reality as *another instinct*, an ultimate fact of value like the rest. But it ought to do violence to our scientific principles to fall so readily into finalities. Our values need to be explained ; our interest in reality not more than our interest in food or in society or in imitation. And it is probable that if any value could be explained, they would all fall into some sort of system. The key to that system may well be furnished by this same interest in reality. For in separating that interest from all others, we have by a sort of distillation separated out as it were an instance of pure value. We cannot explain this interest by any other ; but we may be able to explain all other interests by this one.

For there can be no doubt that the interest we have in reality is somehow substantially bound up with the interest we have in all other ends : there is a discernible relation between the *quantity* of these two types of interest. The passion poured into the construction of an independent idea-world is in some close connection with the sum of passion poured into the practical pursuit of all other things. The more interest there is in life generally, the more devotion is spent upon knowing reality for itself and vice versa. Let the Renaissance serve as an illustration. If, then, the interest in reality is not derived from the interest in other things, there is a strong suggestion that the interest in other things may be derived from the interest in reality. I have no doubt that in actual working order dependence is mutual; that passion spent in either pursuit becomes a cause of the zeal-level of the other: but interest in reality has the priority. Whatever energy is spent in understanding experience, in attaching its meanings to the reality-idea, is so much recoverable energy for all other valuing. If this is the case, then work done by us on the idea is no work on action-cues perhaps; but it is work done on the worth of living itself, it is the creation of the very fabric of value. Now let us consider how this may be.

It will be generally admitted that the value of any object depends as well upon the thinker as upon the thing. Values vary with the man; and within the man's life, they vary with his powers of attention, and what he can bring to the subject. They vary with what psychology has called his 'apperceptive mass'; if you enjoy Widor's music and I do not, it has something to do with your greater knowledge and experience in the world of music. A state of keen enjoyment is a state of high mental activity: the resources of memory and invention are loosened, the mind becomes a free field for quick and accurate connections powerfully focussed.[1]

[1] The same may be said of anger and of certain other negative emotions. In so far as these are states of enthusiasm they are also percep-

Pleasure is evidently a *mode of being aware of the world;* a way of taking and attending to things, transferable from one object to another, tending to propagate itself and continue itself. Delight develops attention; and attention develops more delight. That same object which under a cold gaze reveals no interest may under an eye already kindled with pleasure develop unlimited value. Hence wit and fun once started can sustain themselves with little fuel from outside; any trifle becomes a matter of extraordinary feeling. Any object or task strenuously attended to begins to glow with some heat of value after a while; there is something like spontaneous generation of values under the focus of attention. And everything we enjoy for a moment prepares us to like something different in the next; because it brings under way in us that mode of regarding things wherein the secret of value lies.

In some way, then, value is conferred upon the object by that with which we can meet it. But what is it that a man brings with him which can determine the feeling-worth of his world? His 'apperceptive mass,' indeed; and this consists of what? Of instincts in part, organic capacities for enjoyment? Experiences also, and all sorts of associated fancies and memories and ideas? But all of this is nothing other than idea; idea being but experience itself in all its life and infinitude prepared for this very work of meeting new experience with justice. What any conscious organism can bring to a new experience is but its prior experience *referred*

tions of value and need not here be separately analyzed. The problem of pain, and negative feeling in general, is considered in chapter xxxii.

to reality, held, that is, in idea; whether ancestral experience, embodied in structure (instinct-idea) to be made the individual's own by re-thinking; or his own experience taken up into his own thought: in one case as in the other — idea. It is this thought-over experience, experience already organized into idea, which measures the power of any mind to appreciate new experience, to find in the world objects of value. Value varies with idea-resource.[1]

These considerations all but compel the simple hypothesis which I have here to offer. It is that all valuing (and so all feeling) is a way of knowing objects with one's whole-idea. In some way, in valuing, appreciating, enjoying, we are using this idea-mass; yet not in the effortful way of deliberate thinking: an object of value is an object in which my whole-idea finds some peculiar ease and sufficiency of application. The worth which any object or end can have for me depends on mutual fitness between my idea-mass and that object — the fitness of my idea to comprehend the object; the fitness of the object to engage the idea.[2] Let me state this theory more fully, and then illustrate it at length.

Let us summon up such true conception of idea as we

[1] To put the matter roughly: to be more alive is both to see more and to feel more — and these are not two separate things, but at bottom one.

[2] In a former chapter (chapter vi) we suggested that feeling might be explained as a transition from one state of knowledge to another. Now we have to complete this view by explaining the original instability in our knowledge-field at any time. This instability, I think, is due in part to the varying capacity of objects for the total idea-mass, and partly to the varying potential of this idea-mass itself, due to work done upon it. See for more detail than this chapter can give the explanatory essay on Idea and Value in Biological Context.

can now muster; idea, as the living and infinite thing *with which* we meet and know our experience. Note what can be easily noted: that any successful working of the idea in knowing its object is a pleasure — especially the finding of an idea, and the use of a new-found idea (as a child repeats the new-learned word with recurrent satisfaction). Note that of all ideas, the idea of reality is most of all thought with; as all ideas seek their meaning-terminus in reality, so all idea-use is at the same time use of the idea of reality. With our reality-idea we think, not only reality itself, but also, so far as we are able, every particular object of experience. Spontaneously, not deliberately, we endeavor to see in each object of attention a *case*, more or less complete, of what reality means to us. Now suppose that the *value of any object of attention is nothing other than the entering of that reality-idea into the thought of the object.* Suppose that the degree and sign (positive or negative) of that value is a measure of the success or unsuccess of this idea-use; the fulness with which that object-vessel can contain that wealth of background meaning, always pressing to *know* — not to be known. Would it not at once become clear that our reality-idea, our whole-idea, must determine the level[1] at which all our values will stand, must be, in a definite sense, the reservoir of all value for us?

All idea at work upon its object is a source of feeling. As for the idea not at work upon its object — let us here once for all note that *there is no such thing.* The unused idea, lying latent and un-feeling in the

[1] Strictly speaking, must constitute one determinant of that level. What the objective determinants may be, we need not here consider.

mind, is the most obstructive, yet emptiest of all psychological superstitions. The life of the idea is in its use, not as being thought of (one must repeat) but as thinking; and not alone in thinking its own-named object; but also in thinking every other object upon which it may even remotely bear — in the end, every other object; in the process of thinking any object before consciousness no idea can be wholly inactive. With what idea, pray, do I think *hat?* With the hat-idea, to be sure. Yes, but is the clothing-idea unconcerned? — or the city-street-idea? or the civilized-society-extraordinary-requirements-ideas? or the man-and-woman-ideas? or the whole mass of æsthetic notions, and political, historical, even religious opinions? With all these, and with all other ideas summing themselves up currently in my whole-idea, *hat* is thought. If hat has a practical meaning as something to-be-put-on, or to-be-taken-off, or to be otherwise dealt with, it is because hat through these other ideas has already acquired a more intimate significance and value than these extraneous action-hints can suggest. A value measured by the degree, proportion, and facility with which my whole idea-equipment can find itself in hat. Probably this direct feeling-value of hat is not large; probably a primrose, a bit of music, a single human being, would involve my idea-world more adequately and immediately: if so, the feeling-value of these objects is higher. But in one case as in the other, whatever may occupy attention, occupies the man; it is *he* as a total self, mind-total, who for the moment gives himself to that object, discovering in it what value it may have for him.

The meaning of these proposals may best be seen

where value varies visibly with idea. As where ghost-terror is created by idea-anticipation; or where with the growth of knowledge an interest seems to develop out of no-interest, value created from nothing by the rise of idea and idea-application.[1] To become a connoisseur, an *amateur*, in any field is a self-furthering process after the first few conceptions have been won, the first elements of a collection made, and the idea, now fairly alive, becomes hungry for its own food. Acquiring some bit of skill, and delighting in the use of it, is a value creation of the same type, though the units here are idea-action couples, not ideas alone; the delight is in the meeting of situations, the union of confidence with challenge and novelty, the instantaneous judgment that my idea is meeting the various phases of the new case as they arise, even while my hand is carrying out the part assigned by the idea. What one does well, one likes; what one does not like, dancing, speaking French, public ceremony, is in all likelihood something one does less than well, feeling therein an inadequacy, shall we not say of "habit," modestly suggesting "lack of practice"?—shall we not rather say (tracing our feeling to its lair) primarily an *infacility of idea*, a felt inferiority not of the animal but of the spirit. In all such matters

[1] The whole history of value we cannot here follow. In the more momentary spot-values of pleasure and pain, or of direct satisfaction of instinct, the work of idea is not quickly seen. Such values seem fixed by Nature in the physical frame ; a certain value-capital, one might think, sufficiently free from idea. Yet not meaning-less; rather, spots of instantaneous meaning, whose idea-elements are separated with difficulty, becoming slowly interpretable as the idea-world thickens about them, as poetry in time, then philosophy begin to voice the meaning of sex-love. In greater detail this theory of value is presented in the final essay on "Idea and Value."

rapid subsumption is the inner kernel of delight. The pleasure found in a generalization, even in mildly lifting the conception of ordinary things into a wider sphere of relation (flowers as modified leaves, or neuron-idea embracing all nerve-forms); the discovery of genial resemblances wherein so much of the pleasure of literature consists; that noting of more hidden likenesses which has been said to mark genius — all this value-making is but the idea-making process in its own natural freedom.

Note also how values change as life matures. The ends which men pursue are less tangible than those spot-splashes of pleasure-color hypnotic to the eye of childhood, though not excluding them. Family, and status, and power, and the doing of human work, and whatever else, are ends whose appeal can be seen to vary visibly from man to man, not so much with instinct as with experience, and not so much with experience alone as with digested experience, *Weltanschauung*, whole-idea. The significance of any given event will be estimated variously, a given circumstance will give pleasure or pain, chiefly according to the 'way of thinking,' the 'point of view' of the subject. The critical question put to me by any happening is, "Can my conception of reality accept and place that happening, or can it not?" That alone will please me in the end which is according to Nature as I conceive Nature; that alone can hold me prisoner wherein Nature itself, or reality, or Deity, becomes visible or vocal. Experience is a course of perpetual conflict between my Idea and my circumstance, each modifying the other until my idea of reality can cope with circumstance and all its issues. No man can be content to accept evil as finality: each must have his *theory of evil*, as a means of bringing that evil under the conception of the whole, and so — of disposing of it. To win such idea, and to use it effectively, constitutes certainly not the whole, but a large part of the achievable satisfaction of any mature human life.

Consciousness is essentially cumulative; experience becomes memory, becomes idea, whereby as Bergson justly insists, no new event can have the same meaning with any previous event — for none can be received into the same soul. All such cumulation, however, builds itself into the fabric of the permanent whole-idea, thereby contributing, in any person, to a quality of character, a general value-tone, or flavor, which becomes relatively stable. That which we first sense in any person is the operation of this whole-idea; that which we value is some excellence in its operation. Burke elevates whatever subject he touches; his place is secure among the minds of earth because the vigor of that whole-presence casts a nobility over all valuation, makes human existence another and better thing than at our common ease it inclines to be. To see the significance of things trivial is the prerogative of greatness, to see everything as bearing upon the whole is both genius and happiness, to see all things *sub specie æternitatis* is the joy of religion itself. To conceive a thing largely, to throw over it a generous dome — this is the very physiology of human worth. It is not necessarily the express logical reflection upon things that endows a life richly with this human quality. It is not even the clear-held memory of special circumstances. It is rather the spontaneous after-working of experience once well-met — which is Idea, holding idea and event together until they answer "Done": this experience-well-met it is, which entering into the bone and blood of the Idea (for the most part unreachable in speech) builds human quality and human worth.

Love itself, then, if we are right, is not a thing apart from knowledge. That which we love is not indeed learning, or logic-skill, but some reality-thought at work upon an actual experience, creating there the very material of beauty and value. No one will be loved blindly; no one will be loved as other than an intelligence, human and universal, sharing in that same reality which all men share. Love and sympathy we often think of as feeling, in direct contrast to idea. It is clear however that they both are cognizances of *another*, do in some way make the leap between my own soul and the soul of some one not-myself, intend to put me in veritable rapport with what thought is passing there, the very *tour de force of objectivity*. We note further that that sympathy which is not exact knowledge of the other, is of feeble and ineffective quality; that we incline to measure the worth of sympathy by the extent of its gratuitous and extraordinary perception of the other's situation. Sympathy notes what the casual eye ignores: for sympathy is objectivity of mind, and objectivity of mind is *knowing*. Interest in objectivity, which we have found at the root of all idea-making, is love itself directed to reality; and conversely, the interest in reality is the measure of all possible love and appreciation, toward humanity, or in the Arts.

Love and sympathy are the activity of the idea. And

in their exercise, the idea is enlarged. The lover widen his experience as the non-lover cannot. He adds to th mass of his idea-world, and acquires thereby enhanced power to appreciate all things. Is not this the sufficient solution of that long-standing difficulty between 'egoism and altruism?' The altruist alone can accumulate that treasure of idea through which all things must be enjoyed that are enjoyed. No one has, or can have, any 'egoistic' satisfaction except as a consequence of so much effective love of reality as there is in him by birth or acquisition.

If what is here said does truly represent the organic bond between idea and feeling, we may now confirm — but with better understanding — the extraordinary intimacy between the ideas of religion and human feeling at large. It is not alone the specifically religious feeling with which the religious idea is bound up: it is — as an interpretation of our whole-idea — a factor in all human feeling and value. And that, *immediately* — not by way of any external arrangements in which the work of God may meet and supplement the work of men: not excluding these — not waiting for them. The use of the God-idea (which if one have cannot but be the most-used of all ideas — not as thought-of but as thinking), the use of this idea will be the *chief determinant of the value-level in any consciousness.* Whether or not the terminal-object of one's faith be called God, whatever object comes before the mind of any man must inevitably be judged at last by that man's sense of the nature of the reality with which he has, in the end, to do; and thereby must the current-worth of his experience be continuously determined. And very probably the religious feelings themselves, religious fear, religious hope, religious worship, are in part instinctive recognitions of the immediate vital bearing of such idea-possession upon every conceivable human value: not only as conserving those values (from internal decay) but also as presiding over their perpetual increase. The meaning of the religious idea is so far inseparable from this fateful value-bearing as almost to justify the statement that religion is the region where fact and value coincide: where there is no idea apart from feeling, as there is no feeling apart from idea.

We have then no cause to fear that labor and interest spent on religious truth will be lost from the side of feeling. It is only by a recovery of "theoretical" conviction that religion can either maintain its own vitality or contribute anything specific to human happiness. In the attainment of knowledge, feeling — in so far as it is connected with agitation and active-impulse — is silent: but the end of feeling is at the same time the beginning of a new world of value, wherein all feelings are reborn through renewal of their source. Through losing its life, and only thus, can feeling save its life.[1]

[1] This is true whether religious knowledge is won in the course of metaphysical reflection, or as the mystics have often won their insight through a process which looks very different, through worship. In worship also, feeling as a spur to particular action comes momentarily to rest. Schleiermacher's interpretation of religious experience in terms of dependence, awe, reverence — relatively quiescent and contemplative feelings we called them — is not far from the truth; but above these feelings and including them stands the impulse of worship, in which all these other feelings unite and finally vanish into a present sense of reality and worth. Worship conducts religious feeling to its terminus in cognizance: and thus worship stands at the node of a rhythm or alternation through which the

We may now perceive, in bare outline, the more literal sense of our former figure which represented religion as a parent rather than an agent in history. For the religious idea bears upon the Arts, not so much through particular instigations of thought and action as through a more internal fruitfulness, watering and sustaining all those perceptions of value, in which the work of the Arts must terminate. It is through devotion to the Idea, to the reality of the world — a devotion which, whatever else it may be, is also a theoretical devotion — that religious feeling and all human feeling must be kept alive.

values of our lives pass — disappearing and reappearing. The principle of this alternation is further developed in Part V.

CHAPTER XII

THE WILL AS A MAKER OF TRUTH

WHATEVER value religion has for man will be funded, we now judge, in the religious ideas, especially in the religious world-idea or reality-idea or substance-idea—the idea of God. Judging religion solely by its effectiveness in human affairs we will have no religion without metaphysics, which is but a knowledge of reality. Religion does its work by way of its truth. Creed and theology become again important to us; become the essential treasures of religion: for in them the race preserves from age to age the determining factors of all human worth.

Such is, in fact, my own belief. But there is one formidable question to be met before we can either rest in this conclusion, or wholly understand its meaning. We have been assuming that reality is a finished total which it is our place to recognize and adjust ourselves to, without presuming to alter its general aspect. We have been assuming that if there is a God at all, God is a fixity in the universe; a being whom we must accept and not undertake to change. We have been assuming that the objects of our religious interest are all made up in advance, and that our own wills have no part to play in determining what *is*; in short that as knowers of reality we must be passive, receptive toward the truth as it is, taking it as we find it, in experience and in idea. But this general assumption of ours, that reality such as religion deals with *is what it is* in independence of our own wills, not to be created or destroyed by anything we may resolve or do about it, — this general assumption is open to doubt.

There are certainly some regions of reality which are *unfinished.* We are endowed with wills only because there are such regions, to which it is our whole occupation to give shape and character. In such regions the will-to-believe is justified, because it is no will-to-make-believe, but a veritable will to create the truth in which we believe. What I believe of my fellow men goes far to determine what my fellow men actually are. Believe men liars — they show themselves such; determine yourself upon their essential goodness, and they do not disappoint your resolve: your belief is not one which can ever be refuted, for the characters of men are not finished parts of reality; they are still being built, and your will is a factor in the building. Where truth is thus waiting to be finished or determined, the will may hold the deciding play.

Every social need, such as the need for friendship, must be a party to its own satisfaction: I cannot passively find my friend as a ready-made friend; a ready-made human being he may be, but his friendship for me I must help to create by my own active resolve. So of the great political reality, the State. This also is nothing which man has found ready-made. The State is a reality which is what it is by dint of the combined resolves of many human wills, through time: we individuals find the State as something apparently finished, standing there as something to be empirically accepted; but at no time does the existence of this object become so independent that it can continue to hold its reality apart from the good-will which from moment to moment recreates it. May it be that the objects in which religion is concerned are in some ways like these, belonging to the unfinished regions of reality?

We find our religion much as we find our State, an inherited possession fixed in its main outlines by no will of our own; yet an expression, perhaps, of the racial good-will of men, depending like the State on the continued good-will of all individuals for its validity, even for its truth. Religion throws over human life a unity like that of the State, but vaster: it provides a canopy under which all men may recognize their brotherhood: in the good-will of religion a totality of spirit is *brought about* which apart from that good-will has no independent existence. In holding to this qualification of my whole-idea — by the idea of a spiritual totality which I must coöperate with other men to make real — I find an immeasurable and substantial enlargement of my field of vision and so of my whole level of values. Is not this spiritual unity, though a function of the will of man, a large part of what I mean by the name God? Through religion, too, a still greater totality is accomplished: a world beyond is brought into conjunction with our present interest, and our mortal lives are endowed with prospects of immortality. Yet I strongly doubt whether immortality is any such predetermined reality that it exists for any person apart from that person's will to make it real. The future life may well be such an object as my decision can make real or unreal, so far as my own experience is concerned. And in general, when we consider closely the kind of object which religion presents for our faith we find it such as might well be plastic to the determinations of the will, more plastic even than friendship or the State. For these objects are not to be found on earth like the friend ; nor are they to be set up in visible form like the State : they exist wholly in that region of the spirit, whose coming and going is immediately sensitive to every variation of loyalty and disloyalty on the part of the souls in which alone it has its life.

Further, the difference between a religious view of the world and a non-religious view lies chiefly in the quality or *character* which is attributed to the world as a whole. It does not lie in the circumstance that the religious mind has a whole-idea, while the non-religious mind has none: every man must have his whole-idea, and such as it is, it will determine what value existence may have for him. But the critical difference appears in the judgments *about* the whole ; whether this reality of ours is divine, or infernal, or an indifferent universal grave-pit. These differences, we may say, are differences in *predicates*, rather than in the subject; and it is precisely in the matter of the predicates which can be applied to the world as a whole that we found the primary difficulty of religious knowledge to lie.[1] Every one begins with his whole-idea ; but it is the function of religion to *interpret* this whole as divine; in brief, to make the transition from the whole-idea to the idea of God. These other words of ours, non-committal in regard to quality — "the whole," "substance," "reality" — do they fairly name that with which religion has to do? Is not

[1] Pp. 100 ff. above.

the problem of religious knowledge a problem of the *attributes* of reality;[1] and are not these attributes indeterminate, apart from the will?

For it is not simply the case that these attributes which religion ascribes to reality (divinity, beneficence, soul-preserving or value-conserving properties) are invisible, spiritual, inaccessible to observation: it is the case that these ideas, so far as reasons go, are in apparent *equilibrium* — neither provable nor disprovable. The world would be consistent without God; it would also be consistent with God: whichever hypothesis a man adopts will fit experience equally well; neither one, so far as accounting for visible facts is concerned, works better than the other. I have often wondered whether in these supermundane matters the universe may not be so nicely adjusted (and withal so justly) that each man finds true the things he believes in and wills for; why should not every man find his religion true, in so far as he has indeed set his heart upon it and made sacrifices for it? However this may be, the religious objects (the predicates given by religion to reality) stand at a pass of intellectual equipoise: it may well seem that some other faculty must enter in to give determination to reason at the point where reason halts, without deciding voice of its own. The birth of the idea of God in the mind — the judgment "Reality is living, divine, a God exists" — is so subtle, like the faintest breath of the spirit upon the face of the waters, that no look

[1] The earliest ideas and names for the Deity seem to have been rather adjectives than nouns. Among the Aryans, the divine was expressed as "the shining," "the illustrious"; among Malays and Indians and very generally elsewhere, "the wonderful," "the powerful," "the immense."

within can tell whether God is here revealing himself to man, or man creating God.

It is because of this position of subtle equilibrium that the religious consciousness is *evanescent;* faith is unstable as empirical knowledge is not. Though at any time I find my world sacred, it only needs a touch of passivity on my part and it will again become secular: I cannot recover nor understand its former worth. My faith in God is subject to fluctuation as my faith in other objects is not, even though these other objects are equally inaccessible (as my faith in China or in the conservation of energy). And noteworthy about this fluctuation is that it passes from extreme to extreme, not pausing in the intermediate stages of probability: the existence of God is to me either wholly certain or wholly absurd. Likewise of immortality: it seems to me at times that a man is a fool to believe it, at other times that a man is a fool not to believe it. I have no power of weighing shades of probability in these matters. It must be so, it can't be so: these are the only degrees of which my own religious faith is capable. But alternatives like these belong rather to the will or disposition of the spirit than to the estimating mind. And further, the one thing which is most sure to dispel faith and substitute the secular world-picture is precisely intellectual scrutiny. Faith is not only difficult for reason; it is distinctly diffident toward reason. Its origin, then, and its firmness must be due to some other power, presumably to will.

It would help our thought on this point if we could trace the mental processes in which the idea of God first arises in human consciousness. It is more than doubtful whether any such tracing is possible; and largely because of the circumstances which we have pointed out: the thought of God comes and goes; is often lost and often recovered, both in racial and in individual experience; it appears also in various ways to various minds. No historical nor typical origin of the belief in God can be shown. Nevertheless, taking as a beginning a mood of secularity which often recurs in human experience, there may be some measure of typical psychological truth in such a picture as this which follows:

There is a grim and menacing aspect of reality which remains commonly unemphatic as our lives go but which events may at any time uncover. We are obliged to witness this vast Whole, of which we speak so easily, threatening existence or destroying the things that make our existence valuable. Against such threats our usual methods of protection avail exactly nothing. The merciless processes of nature, of disease and death, of fate generally, are not impressed by entreaty or by effort, are not to be beaten off with clubs nor frightened away by shrieks and gestures of defiance. All these weapons will be tried; and trial best convinces of futility. Fear and hope normally inspire action; fear and hope show themselves alike empty in this situation. That with which one has to do is reality itself; and toward this only some less external attitude can be significant. But in the human creature at bay there are other depths; the recognition of futility is the beginning of human adequacy. For despair ends by calling out a certain touch of *resentment*, — resentment having a tinge of self-assertion in it, even of moral requirement directed against reality.

Such a being as I, by virtue of this very power of realizing my situation, by virtue of my whole-idea and my self-consciousness, has some claim to urge upon the reality that surrounds me, threatening; the reality which, after all, has brought me forth. Though by the slightest movement of this deep-lying sense of right, one does, in effect, demand justice of his creator: and thereby, without premeditation, finds himself with the idea of Deity already constituted and possessed. For toward what can moral resentment and demand be addressed but to a living and moral Being? In that deep impulse of self-assertion there was involved, though I knew it not, *the will that my reality should be a living and responsible reality*. And in time I shall find that in imputing this quality to my world, I have already lifted the burden of those anxieties, so helpless upon their own plane. The God-idea thus appears as a postulate of our moral consciousness: an original object of resolve which tends to make itself good in experience.

For the proof of this new-found or new-made relation to reality, expressed in my God-idea, is this: that in meeting my world divinely it shows itself divine. It supports my postulate. And without such act of will, no discovery of divinity could take place. Men cannot *be* worthy of reverence, until I meet them with reverence: for my reverence is the dome under which alone their possible greatness can stand and live. Of the world likewise, — it can have no divinity but only materiality or menacing insensibility, unless I throw over it the category under whose dome its holiness can rise visible and actual. God cannot live, as divine and beneficent, except in the opportunity created by our good-will: but given the good-will, reality is such as will become indeed divine.

In accord with this conjecture as to the position of religious truth, namely that it is determined by the movement of will-to-believe, is an old observation of religious experience. It is written that he who seeks finds: the connection between seeking and finding is infallible. Such infallible connection may be many-wise understood, but it may be thus understood, that the *seeking brings the finding with it.* "Thou wouldst not seek me hadst thou not already found me," said Pascal: and to Sabatier this thought came "like a flash of light . . . the solution of a problem that had long appeared insoluble."[1] The religiousness of man's nature is the whole substance of his revelation. Whatever we *impute* to the world comes back to us as a quality pre-resident there — is not this the whole illusion of reality? Impute then to the world a living beneficence: the world will not reject this imputation, will *be* even as you have willed it.[2] Your belief becomes (as Fichte held) an evidence of your character — not of your learning. He who waits his assent till God is proved to him, will never find Him. But he who seeks finds — has already found.

In all these respects there is the strongest resemblance between the religious idea and human value. The world

1 Outlines of a Philosophy of Religion, p. 32.

2 The Chinese have long had a saying "If you believe in the gods, the gods exist: if you do not believe in them they do not exist." Whence pragmatism as a theory of metaphysics may be said to be of Chinese origin. See A. H. Smith, Chinese Characteristics, p. 301.

is consistent without Deity (so it is said); the world is *consistent* also without beauty, or other charm. Before reason, religious assurance is evanescent: so also with any pleasure or other worth when by introspection, or analysis, we determine to seize its secret. The world-body to the eye of Fact is grey, even dead with all its working; if it is to be reanimated with worth, it must be by that miracle which continually repeats itself in our experience — the Spirit breathes upon it from its own resources the breath of life. Thus the birth of value and the birth of God-faith are alike; as indeed we have every reason to believe, if the conclusions of the last chapter are valid: is it not possible that they are the *same thing,* — in both cases the work of an ultimate *good-will* toward our world? If the union which we have proposed between idea and feeling is indeed so intimate and equal that "without feeling the ideas are false; even as without the idea the feelings are meaningless," it is at least possible that some deeper faculty fundamental to both idea and feeling is here *giving laws to reality itself:* deciding what the truth, and therewith the value, of my world shall be.

A new conception of faith appears here: faith is more than passive feeling, more also than the sight which seizes upon the reality of the world as it is — faith is the loyal determination and resolve which sees the world *as it is capable of becoming,* and commits its fortunes to the effort to make real what it thus sees. The religious creed or world-view becomes a postulate rather than either an empirical discovery or a revelation to be obediently received.

I know not whether this presentation of a voluntaristic foundation for religious truth has been able to provoke any acceptance on the part of the reader: it is a paradoxical doctrine, yet it has in it great power, and especially great relief for the difficult situation of the religious idea. To my mind, I must admit, nothing more illuminating has ever been put forward than just such interpretation of many a religious doctrine; nothing truer to the way in which religious picturing and myth-building does actually take place in the human consciousness.

Taking religious ideas literally and fixedly is, in fact, a modern and Western peculiarity. The Oriental mind realizes that the spiritual atmosphere in which either men or gods may breathe, must be *created*; it knows nothing of empirical truth in matters of religion, truth passively taken; and postulate joins hands with poetry in constituting the medium in which all spirituality may live. (The freedom of the religious poem or myth or parable may be regarded as the will-to-believe at play.) The Oriental mind speaks understandingly of miracles and virgin births, because it sees in them poetic means of lifting what it will pronounce divine above the commonplace of profane event and indolent human character. We also, of the West, have our own style of poetry and imagination; of which we see well enough that it must be understood with imagination and humor also after its kind. But we approach, in religious matters, the poetry of the Orient often with a literal-minded savagery, which must accuse us of some deeper defect than simple lack of humor — a lack, namely, of spirituality itself, which knows that the language of the spirit must be read by the spirit also, and is not to be rudely transferred into empirical text-books of physics and of medicine. I do not doubt that in religion as in human experience generally, each will sets the level of its own life, determines in large measure its own destiny, and helps to create spiritual reality for all other human life. A faith without a large ingredient of will, is no faith at all.

Nevertheless, I must believe that the great heave of the West to get a literal and objective grip upon its major religious objects is an advance, and not a retrogression. We only drive men to make their religion all prose, when we threaten to make it all poetry and postulate. For poetry and postulate are pioneer stages of truth, and live by the ounce of literality and truth-independent that is at their heart. The large scope for our own will and creation is not denied: the world is such as to make this creativity possible. But then our religion attaches itself to the literal truth *that the world is such,* already such, *as to allow these developments* and to respond thus sensitively to our acts of will. This prior element becomes our religious creed; the region of our wills to create becomes the province of art and of morals.

The destiny of religious truth to become universal and imperative must detach it at last from all salient subjectivity; must state and define the *scope* of our creative possibilities *within the frame of that which independently Is.* Literality is an accomplishment of deepening self-consciousness; it marks an achievement of personal equilibrium and stability, which is able to recognize corresponding stability and identity in the world with which it deals, — not as limiting its own freedom, but as upholding it. It has required a Western integrity and self-respect to submit in obedience to the observation of Nature; it is this same integrity which requires in its religious objects that to which it must be obedient, as the basis of whatever creativity and command it will claim.

Early religious objects are like play-objects of children, whose character is partly real, and partly conferred by the player. This, says the child, shall be a soldier, — this a good soldier, and this a bad one — and behold they are such. To hold interest, playthings must become more autonomous as the child grows, more locomotive, more realistic and difficult to manage. In time they are all to be displaced by objects of the same name, — but *real*. As for these real objects, they are more dangerous, more refractory; they have independent inner purposes of their own; our success in dealing with them is uncertain, whereas with the play-objects, whose inner thoughts were such only as we imputed to them, our success was a forgone conclusion. Play is the necessary prologue to life, because, chiefly, it is necessary to meet life with the *habit of success*. Not wholly different may it have been with the maturation of the religious life in human history. Let the religious instinct have its full swing and success in its traffic with divinities and world-auspices which are in large part the work of its own will, if not of its own hand. Thereby may it be prepared to meet with the temper of success the ear of a Deity wholly *himself*, wholly identical in his own counsel. Christianity marks the first great inburst of the Orient into consciousness of the literal world, with its literal human problem and world sorrow, the first worship of the literal God of that world. The work of literalizing our creed is never to be finished; for imagination and postulate move more rapidly than the leaven of objectivity can spread; but they move under the protection of the major literalities. Upon these major literalities religion must henceforth and forever be built. For maturity is marked by the preference to be defeated rather than have a subjective success. We as mature persons can worship only that which we are compelled to worship. If we are offered a man-made God and a self-answering prayer, we will rather have no God and no prayer. There can be no valid worship except that in which man is involuntarily bent by the presence of the Most Real, beyond his will.

The problem of loyalty in religion is not different from the problem of loyalty elsewhere. It is true that we cannot be loyal to any tie that has been imposed upon us without our own consent—this is the first premise alike of love and of government. On the other hand, we cannot be loyal to any tie that has been fabricated by a needless stroke of our own will. Any object which can hold our allegiance must therefore be at the same time an object of free choice, and an object of necessary choice. In the expressions of romantic love it is hard to tell which is uppermost: that this bond between the lovers is wholly their own, their exclusive knowledge and will, the highest work of their own freedom; or that this bond is the work of Fate, such as the stars of heaven from all time have destined to effect. Unless God is that being for whom the soul is likewise inescapably destined by the eternal nature of things, the worship of God will get no sufficient hold on the human heart. Religion is indeed a manifestation of the generous and creative side of human nature; but its generosity is not that of creation out of whole cloth, — it is the generosity of the spirit ready to acknowledge the full otherness of its objects, and to live divinely in a world which *is* divine.

It is still possible that reality in its whole constitution is a matter of choice, though not of *our* choice. The results of your choice become data to me; your will is my fact: it may be similarly that everything which is fact to our human consciousness is the creative choice of a supreme Will. On such a supposition, voluntaristic views of reality would be true for God, but for no other. It is true that creativity is the essential quality of the will; and in the constitution of reality, man's will is to coöperate with whatever other creative will there may be in the universe. But man has religion because he is not wholly identical with God; and his religion will be founded upon that relation to reality in which he is less creative than dependent, — or more exactly, in which his creatorship is a result of his dependence.[1]

For in truth, our human life is only an apprenticeship in creativity. The small launches of postulation which we make depend on being quickly caught up and floated by a tide of corroboration hailing from beyond ourselves.

[1] There are two uses of the word independent which need to be distinguished. One kind of independence is mutual, a symmetrical relation: A is independent of B, B is independent of A. The other kind is not symmetrical: A is independent of B, B is dependent upon A. It is in this latter sense that we refer to 'the independent variable,' in mathematical and physical systems. Reality has an element of the latter kind of independence of finite purposes, not of the former.

We leap; but unless we are soon borne up from beyond we make but a sorry flight. And however far my creativity extends, my own creations never become truth for me, until seen through the eye of another than myself they are recognized by him as fact, and so made valid for me also. My best creativity must win the consent of the independent before it can take the status of truth, even in my own eyes. The word truth has in it some reference not to be suppressed to a wholly other than myself, to a will wholly other than mine, as a condition of the reality of anything created. Thus, all finite creativity contemplates this other, which by implication is not a product of its will; it is this radically independent reality which religion seeks to know, and which alone it can worship.

How, then, is religious truth to be known? Are the realities of which religion speaks to be discovered in experience? Or are they matters of hypothesis, or of inference, that is to say, of reason? Our answer has been implied in what has gone before: religious truth is founded *upon experience.* In that imaginary picture of ours of the psychological birth of the idea of God — in which it seemed to us as if our resentment, a stroke of moral will, had spontaneously made or recognized our world a living and responsible being — we may discern beside the stroke of will an experience of discovery.[1] If there is any knowledge of God, it must be in some

[1] Of some such subtle but veritable experience I believe that all "revelation" is built. Revelation is knowledge real and empirical (i.e., received in relative passivity), which is more certain in itself than in its assignable connections with the main body of experience. The logic of the matter is worked out in Parts IV and VI.

such way a matter of experience. This implies that our experience of reality is not confined to sensation. Sensation itself also brings us into contact with a reality which is independent of our will; sensation is a metaphysical experience. And religious faith must be built upon an experience not wholly different from sensation; but a super-sensible experience, like our experience of our human fellows; an experience which recognizes the reality given in sensation for what, in its true nature, it is.

And whatever is matter of experience must also become, in time, matter of reason; for reason is but the process of finding, by some secure path of connection, a given experience from the standpoint of other experience assumed as better known. The proof of God's existence is (as Hegel put it) but the lifting of the mind to God from out of the affairs of secular business. Such proof, or mental direction, is called for, not because the religious objects are inaccessible to experience, but rather because they *are accessible*; and being found in experience, it is necessary to establish their systematic relations with the rest. It is through reason that the original and evanescent experience of God becomes established as veritable truth.

This, then, is the result to which our labors so far have led. We cannot find a footing for religion in feeling: we must look for valid religious ideas. And these ideas are not to be taken at liberty, nor deduced from the conception of any necessary purpose: we are to seek the truth of religion obediently in experience as something which is established in independence of our finite wills. So far we have done no more than orient our search. The task itself we shall take up in a later part of this book.

In the meantime, while voluntarism cannot define truth for us, religious truth least of all, it remains the most important and valuable of all tests of truth and ballasts of judgment about truth. The question, "What kind of world would best satisfy the requirements of our wills?" can never finally determine what kind of world we, in reality, have. But such questions may go far toward clearing our mind about those requirements themselves; they may give some not-unimportant hints of what we have to expect of reality. To this pragmatic type of inference we shall devote the next few studies.

NOTE ON PRAGMATIC IDEALISM

IN the foregoing chapter we have appealed from that which we can voluntarily determine to that which independently Is, as the necessary basis of religious truth. And this appeal is on the whole valid and intelligible. But voluntarism may recur to its most searching and general question — a question which we have already dealt with by implication [1] but which may now with advantage be considered by itself. It may require of us an account of that independence which we expect to discover, doubting whether anything in this universe can be essentially independent of any other, doubting whether any real object of ours is independent of ourselves, doubting whether in the last resort those most real objects of our best maturity are not also there, in all their inner freedom and autonomy, by dint of *some deeper will* of ours, some necessary or absolute will. Have we not even now said that we must *desire* that our religious objects have such independence, that we need it as a support for our loyalty? and in confessing these needs have we not admitted that this independence may still be regarded as the free deed of our own deepest will, and so no absolute independence?

It is in *experience* that we meet with the supposedly independent realities of nature and society with that total volume of Fact which is there whether we will or not. But experience has long been known to be no such passive affair as it seems. Idealism has made clear to us how much the mind must contribute to make its experience what it is: how little is actually *given*, how much is *made* on the basis of this little — or nothing — from outside. We think we find our fellow men, for example, as independent metaphysical entities; we treat them

[1] Both in the above chapter and in chapter x, in discussing the meaning of ideas.

as if they were such. But even as we observed how far the qualities and characters of men are determined by our own resolve, so we may now see, striking deeper, that their very metaphysical selfhood, their individuality, is real by consent rather than by given fact. Neither they nor we *find given* any substantial soul or individual in this world, whether theirs or our own; but our *purpose* is to live in a world of real persons, and so far as possible to be real persons ourselves. According to this necessary aspiration we act, and cannot help acting. But in its nature our whole environment of "metaphysical reality" is no independent fact, passively received, but a determination of our own absolute will.

Such, in brief, are the considerations pressed upon us by volitional idealism, especially in the form in which that idealism is presented by Fichte, and in our own time by Royce, by Münsterberg, by Rickert, and others.[1] There is nothing true for any subject in which it is not possible to trace the sign of the subject and of the deepest will of the subject. Reality itself can have no other independence of the thinker than that which he wills it to have.

But valuable and morally important as all this is, to know how much of what we passingly regard as independent Fact is in the making of our own wills, the case of the (pragmatic) idealist is not — I must think — complete; nor can it be completed. There may be no assignable feature of my world in which I cannot trace the work of my own will: it still remains possible that there may be no assignable feature of my world in which I cannot trace *also* the work of something not-my-will. Let me illustrate this situation:

Independence may be symbolized by *discontinuity* in geometry, — let us say, by a point that stands off by itself. There

[1] For our present argument the differences between these thinkers, important as they are, need not be discussed. A summary statement of the position in question may be found in Royce, The World and the Individual, vol. I, pp. 320-342. The position itself may be labelled voluntaristic idealism, or pragmatic idealism, or, as Royce calls it in his last book, absolute pragmatism. (William James and Other Essays, p. 254.)

are no independent points in a circle: every one is perfectly bound and held by the central rule. In ellipses, there is a struggle apart of centers, so to speak, — a certain mutual independence in the two focal points, which loosens the attachment of the curve to either. The central government of other curves as defined by their 'equations,' is variously strong: in some of them, single points become detached; in others, whole regions break out in double boundaries. Wherever a hump or projection or departure from the perfect round is visible, there is the sign of rebellion, of incipient independence. In the *angle*, we have a complete rupture of central control; two independent equations describe the two independent lines. With this picture of dependence and independence in mind, we might undertake with idealistic eyes to examine the shapes of natural objects. In nature, our supposed idealist might report, we find no straight lines and no angles: everywhere, if you examine closely enough you find the round, the mark of subjection to some center. In any given organism you find repeated everywhere the same curve — in eye, in nostril, in spinal and muscular wave — the same reference of every element to the type-cell and its central forces. This is the report of the idealistic eye, which is always on the lookout for signs of centrality; and which may truly say that there is nothing real and concrete which does not betray these signs in every nameable feature. But now, look at the same shapes with other eyes, with those of an imagined realist, believer in the independent reality. Perhaps there are no straight lines in nature, he might report, but on the other hand there are no circles; and the higher the effort of nature, the less is the circle apparent. Nature, in fact, progresses out of roundness toward angularity. Primitive animals, and simple orbits, may be nearly round; but no developed animal is round. In elliptical and elongated shapes we see signs of rebellion, a new center struggling apart from the original one. Humps, horns, heads, tails, autonomous internal organs, are so many evidences of promising home-rule. In animals which we regard as highly developed we find actual corners and discontinuities of line: — see the square-blocked blooded bull; compare the man with the infant; note the loose play of limb in quadrupeds as compared with the tighter bound organs of bird and fish. So in the works of art that follow nature; contrast the moon-faced people drawn by a school-boy with the cross-hatched sketches of any master hand. Or observe the line of progress from the round huts of the ancient Saxon, the igloos of the Eskimo, the charcoal-burner's huts of Scotland, the Indian wigwam, and the like, — from these to the square walls of the romanized English dwelling and our modern house. Roundness is, in fact, the hopeless thing in nature. So far as the organism is round and continuous within itself, in so far it must live upon its own resources and inertia, and has the promise of death. But wherever it crosses reality, even the most primitive of organisms, wherever it touches the sources of its continued life — in eating, in knowing, in giving birth — there is a breach in its body-wall; there it confesses discontinuity and dependence upon the independent. So the report of the realistic eye, on the lookout for marks of independence, might answer and supplement the report of idealism. To every sign of dependence which the idealist can show, the realist can show a corresponding sign of independence. We can decide, on such showing, neither for one nor for the other.

To come now from our illustration to the matter itself: It is not enough for the idealist to show that the mark of the ego and its purposes is on every object of knowledge, and on every phase of the object; he must also consider whether the mark of the non-ego is not equally pervasive. In so far as he fails to do this, he leaves us dissatisfied. His argument savors much of the logic by which Thomas Hobbes proved that by virtue of the social contract, all acts of the Leviathan are in reality my own acts, expressions of my own will — no matter what the Leviathan may do, short of threatening my own safety or existence. There is a Leviathan of our living universe also, to whom we are bound perhaps by some cosmic 'contract,' i.e., by some necessary consent of our absolute wills — presumably further a wholly benevolent Leviathan: still his enactments strike upon my consciousness with the novelty of independence — fruits of a purpose which may include mine, but is not included in mine.

It is in vain also that pragmatic idealism shows that the universe is everywhere what I would will it to be if my will were wholly self-knowing; or that when the scientific mind submits itself empirically to the independent fact, it expresses not alone its own purpose but its harmony with a great spiritual fabric of conspiring purposes: these things may be true, but they do not answer our question. There is nothing in reality but that my will helps to make it what in my experience it becomes: but is there anything in reality that I could wholly have created? is there anything that my purposes can wholly define? The universe fulfills my will; but it is not definable as the fulfilment of my will: it is *That Which* fulfills my will — and much more besides; first fulfilling its own independent will. The universe has its own soul, and its own counsel which is not mine. This is its independence.[1]

We admit the positive side of the idealistic argument; whatever is real for us is real with our consent and coöperation. As for its negative part, that nothing in reality is independent of our will, we would turn tables on the idealistic argument. In denying the reality of this independence, does the idealist not implicitly acknowledge that very independence? For he means to make a statement to which we must assent, consulting not first our wills and purposes, but solely the truth as it is. By reality, idealist and realist alike mean that which first is, and afterward is in accord with our purposes.

He who says that individuality is a postulate, not a fact;

[1] This point is further discussed and illustrated in the explanatory essay "The knowledge of independent reality." The geometrical illustration above used was originally a part of the article from which this essay was taken.

he who declares that metaphysical being is an aspiration or purpose, not a matter of experience ; is bound to account to us for the source of these ideals and purposes. Ideals do not come out of the void : postulates and moral principles are not whispered to us in the form of "innate ideas" : it is on the spur of experience that our wills adopt their aims and their deepest meanings. Whatever is present in ideal, is first present in independent reality. In the order of existence we are first passive and then active : though no analysis can separate our passivity from our activity.

PART III

THE NEED OF GOD

A SERIES OF FREE MEDITATIONS

PART III

PRELIMINARY

WE do not know, in detail, what kind of world we would desire to live in. Wisdom to devise such a world we slowly acquire, and in infinite time may possess; meantime we tend to assume that our perfectly enlightened wish would correspond not too remotely with the general description of the world as we find it — at least that it would more nearly approach these curious and mysterious arrangements than we now fathom. Further, there are certain major features of our world whose value, or part of whose value, can be made out. In adorning the figure of God the wishes of men have certainly had large play: it is not unimportant to enquire how much of this wish and will is permanently valid, how much is the passing work of a fancy too little self-conscious. We have been told in these latter days that a pluralistic world would be better than a world of One Being; that a world without an Absolute would be wholly as good as with one; and we have often been assured that God is no certain addition to human happiness, most lately by Mr. McTaggart. Emboldened by these representations we may make a few tentative excursions into this pleasant field of world-willing before girding ourselves to the more strenuous labor of truth-finding — not forgetting, however, that the question what we need is also a question having a true answer.

CHAPTER XIII

THE NEED OF UNITY: MONISM AS BEARING ON OPTIMISM.

MONISM may be optimistic or pessimistic, as we conceive the One Being to be good, bad, or indifferent. Schopenhauer's One was blind, and its products fit only to be swallowed up again. But monism at least permits optimism, since a world that is One has a chance of being safe. It may even be *too safe*. To the minds of pluralistic writers monism offers too little scope for freedom and adventure; there is not enough leeway for risk and radical disaster; not opportunity enough for ultimate enterprise and knightly peril; not enough summons to courage, to world-winning or world-losing wagers and commitments. Because of all the surplus protection of monism, men are made flabby; their skins are safe, but their morals are in danger; hence, the world of monism proves no such safe world after all, when you consider the whole man. A true optimism must take the side of pluralism. This seems to me a fair and fruit-promising issue; for surely we will have no world in which it is not possible to be optimistic, and without danger to our moral fiber. Let us then attack our subject in this way: considering different brands of monism (for there are different brands), and enquiring what brand of optimism (for there are different brands of this also) is compatible with each brand of monism.

I

A few elementary observations may be made at the outset, and got out of the way.

First, no optimism is possible without some kind of monism. For in order to think well of your world, and expect good from it, your world must at least have *a character*. It must afford a basis for expectations or probabilities. If the world were simply random, there would be no such thing as probability in it, nothing to build a reasonable hope or prospect on. There is no pluralist who does not limit, and very profoundly limit, the sort of chance and accident which he admits into his world-picture. Change occurs, new things are born, forces of many kinds drive at large, free individuals assert themselves freely: but all this variety and novelty takes place in *digestible quantities*. New creations are to be noted; but they begin small, in a more or less considerate manner, appearing in homes and other places where they can be taken care of. The pluralistic universe does not blurt and burst out in erratic and unmeasurable Facts, of unheard-of Kinds. The most revolutionary things that happen there are *revolutions:* each quietly contained for a time, in the form of a new idea, within the compass of some man's head. *The Mind* is in fact the hearth and brooding-place of such wild Force and Novelty and Freedom as the pluralist most wishes to make way for. And the fortunate circumstance that these things have any brooding-place at all shows how important it is, even in pluralistic eyes, that the new should come with some reference to the old; the Many be not too fatally disruptive of the One. The world that any of us want to live in has, then, some character of its own, innate or acquired, and hence some unity upon which any man must build his hopes.

Second, no optimism is possible without some kind of doubt whether things are what they seem; without looking behind appearances. If the character of the world is Good, or has good possibilities, this does not appear upon the surface of experience. No justification for either optimism or monism can be found there. The surface of experience is pluralistic enough, tossing, various, distracted, challenging sanity if one lets himself go. And this surface, if it has any general character, is not more good than bad. The idea of evil did not arise in the mind without illustration in experience: it is from this surface that good and bad get their flavor and burden of contrast. No man can be an optimist, then, without going behind the superficial returns. The character of the world upon which he bases his judgment must be a *real* character, as opposed to apparent character: your optimist must be something of a metaphysician, something of a seer. He is an optimist only because he has caught or achieved some glimpse of the Whole, and some Idea therewith, which permits him a confident judgment about the ultimate forces and grounds of sensible experience: the facts he has about world-character must be *bottom facts*, or they are worthless as a basis for expectations.

Every optimism, then, involves a judgment about a Reality, which has a character, and is therefore One. It may appear to the judger that the unity of the world is only achievable, not an accomplished fact: but if the world is even achievably One, then it is already One in a real, though more attenuated sense; it has a character which makes it capable of being pulled together.

II

Optimism, we have said, must come from getting our world into so much of a real unity that we can pass judgment upon it as a whole. We may now observe that this unity must be of a fairly substantial sort. There are types of monism too attenuated to justify any genuine optimism. Let us describe one or two such.

Our world has, for example, a certain *formal unity*. This unity is to be seen in the fact that all objects of experience, however various, are all alike *objects of experience:* must have so much in common as is implied in their being thinkable by the same subject, all containable within his comprehensive background of objectivity and time. No one can mention any possible degree of frantic chaos, but that in mentioning it as an *idea* of his, he has made a unity of it; has even presented it to us *in a frame*. Beat the bush of self-contradiction with sufficient skill and persistency; always some such unity can be corralled in the liveliest pluralism statable. But any pluralism may grant you *these* bonds, without substantial menace to liberty: all fish of the sea are also already caught in the fisherman's *idea*, and if not further caught need not resent their captivity. But our world must be further caught, if we are to be optimistic pluralists; this degree of unity if it goes no farther can support no concrete expectations. For anything, however disastrous, that could be fancied, would by the same reasoning fit into the same frame of unity. Our optimism must affect the *contents* of our picture; the unity must obtain in the designs of the object, as well as in its external relations to the subject.[1]

But there are also objective and concrete unities which are still too attenuated. Idealism knows of such unities, discoverable by applying this same method of self-contradiction but more thoroughly. It may be shown that this world of ours has a one-ness of Life, or even of Purpose. If the real world has a conscious selfhood, there is very substantial basis here for expectations. But hardly enough for expectations of any definite human color. For would we not have to enquire what reference such world-purpose might have to our own special situation; further, what fixes the course of such purpose, spreading its career out in time as if by some resistance; whether, then, *in any finite time* the purpose reaches fulfilment; and whether any segment of history, such as may concern humanity, is to move toward or away from the goal of our Good, in the immeasurable rhythms of cosmic history? The fact of the simple *existence* of a sympathetic purpose at the bottom of Reality may have some positive value, quite apart from any practical expectations; a question which we may later on enquire into.[2] But considered from our present standpoint of *expectation*, any such unity might consistently admit into its outline a retrogression, damnation, or even extinction of human experience, if there is nothing more known of it. Has not the good God existed for long ages in the same world with hell

[1] And such like external relations between its own parts as are involved in that common relation to the subject, external to all of them.

[2] Chapter XV.

and all devils, hell getting steadily fuller?—and may not your One-purpose do as much, or even more? There would seem to be still plenty of risk in such a world for the most reckless pluralist. The Great Hunter crashes through the World-forest in pursuit of *His* quarry — not spoiling nor heeding our small chase, adding if anything one more and chief excitement thereto, that He do not tread on *us!*

In fact, must it not be said of any purely meta-physical monism that it leaves our human situation and problems much the same as before? It is astonishing, when we stop to consider, how much monism we can define without affording any substantial footing for optimism —hence without cancelling any of the *undesirable* risks of existence, to say nothing of encroaching on those *desirable* risks which pluralism wishes to preserve. We see how it is that pragmatic objections to monism have been of two opposite tenors: one, that the world of monism is a "block-universe" closing up all avenues of chance; the other, that Unity is a wholly ineffective and meaningless bond, making no difference whatever in our outlook upon experience. It is worth while, as against the first objection, to bring forward the second: a *single* organism certainly does not *ohne weiteres* imply a *petrified* organism. It is open to doubt whether the fact of unity, by itself, implies anything significant about the *working-character* of the thing unified. Let us put the matter thus: if our monism is such as to pinch the universe together *only at that point from which it emanates* — whether in one cosmical and temporal point of beginning, or in one permanent basis and *pre*-supposition — such monism gets no control over the wild horses of *Becoming*, whether in our favor or against us. Enough of this kind of monism.

III

If monism is to be of service to our expectations, it must affect the apparent as well as the Real; we must indeed go beneath the surface of experience, where good and bad meet on equal terms, but only for the sake of prophetic control over that same surface in its further developments. Monism begins to offer significant basis for our prospects when it seizes upon the actual processes of the world, and declares that they are all cases of One Process. In the nature of that One Process can be read something of the presumable outcome.

All the processes that we know are operations carried out against resistance; the unification of the processes may well begin by a unification of the resistances, bringing all practical problems together into one practical world-problem. Unifications which thus begin with unifying the resistances seem to set up dualisms instead of monisms—as of light against darkness, Persian God against Persian Devil, spirit against matter, and the like. But such dualisms are not far from monism. For clearly there can be no well-founded hope for good unless there is some estimate of the resistance thereto; and there can be no estimate of the resistance unless such resistance has its own unity.

Any theory of the world which represents all the forces of the world as cases of one Force; all laws as cases of one Law; is thus unifying our problem, and helping man to see his task as the task of spirit everywhere in a world of Nature. Such is the monism of natural science: and indeed might not science be fairly described as the effort to reduce the practical problems of man to one problem? Our apparently hundred-headed problem is One, and this one problem is the only problem there is in the cosmos. Whatever the 'trend of evolution,' whatever impulse there is in the life of the world, all becomes merged in, and subordinated to, the human undertaking: the world-problem is our problem. Whence it appears that human preferences and aversions as they become self-knowing are absolutely valid — there being no Great Hunter with object other than our own.

Such monism as this of effort and resistance is the necessary beginning of any concretely significant monism. So long as resistances are plural, we are slaves to each one severally; the mastery of one gives no aid in the mastery of another. There can be valid hope only in a world in which the conquest of one difficulty is already a partial conquest of another. Monism of this sort does actually wipe out certain conceivable chances for heroism, if heroism consists in infinite willingness to begin again at Zero. But it does not eliminate the freedom and variety of life — it alone makes such freedom and variety possible. For the Many, in such case, are more tyrannous than the One; in winning subjection to one master we gain foot-looseness from indefinite tyranny of the mob. In cosmic as in political affairs, man has many powers over him; and unless he find some one power in which the powers of capital, of custom, of church, of the mandarinate, of social pretence have their match and solvent he is slave indeed, though he live under a "free" constitution. Freedom from the powers is found in subjection to Power; as freedom from the ten commandments is found in subjection to the one and great commandment. Hence monism is at once fixity and freedom from fixity; the only possible condition under which freedom in the world of concrete enterprise can be won.

It is necessary, then, to any optimism, that there should be unity in the conscious processes of the world; and especially a unity of the resistances or evils, which such processes have to meet. But this is not a sufficient foundation for optimism. Optimism requires a further judgment, namely, *that the Real is the good, and not the evil:* i.e., that evil is an essentially conquerable thing, not a reality co-ordinate with the purpose that is against it. And herewith, as monism begins to be significant, it begins also to justify the pluralistic criticism: by reading the outcome into the prior constitution or nature of the case, the world is made too safe, — and the nerve of our responsibility, as well as the zest of our personal importance is relaxed.

It is obvious that this judgment, that the Real is the good and not the evil, stands at a critical pass in this problem of monism. It is a judgment of many shades, and some conclusion as to its worth may be gained by considering how it is actually used in human affairs.

IV

The implicit assumption of the scientific view of things is that every evil is to be remedied in time by our own efforts. Conversely, there is a type of reaction to every definable ill of our human condition which we might well describe as *the scientific reaction;* that is, the effort to refer the ill in question to *causes*, to conceive it as a form assumed under definite conditions by the one world-energy, and by mastering the conditions to master the ill. The evil, in short, must be thoroughly examined and known; to overcome it, we must first become fully conscious of it.

But our world seems to be so constituted that many a bad condition is not best cured that way. It happens at times that an invalid may make a better bid for health by ignoring his disease than by enquiring into it. As for our moral faults, it is quite impossible to reach a cure by the scientific reaction alone. If we tend to ignore our own sins and win our moral salvation in large part through determined self-respect—there is in this instinctive attitude much moral lethargy, no doubt, but some modicum of natural health of spirit. Willingness to confront every evil, in ourselves and outside ourselves, with the blunt, factual conscience of science; willingness to pay the full causal price for the removal of the blemish; this kind of integrity can never be dispensed with in any optimistic program. And yet we cannot radically cure evil that way: the method of *justice* works perfectly only in the world of scientific objects themselves, world of unconscious things. Wherever consciousness enters we have to combine the scientific reaction with another, one which involves turning away from the defect and asserting in effect that the evil is less-than-real, that the real is the good. There is a self-righting tendency in conscious beings which has only analogies more or less distant in nature. The system of movements in such a group as the solar system has a certain self-righting tendency; a gyroscope will resume its own plane after disturbance not too great; any living organism has still more remarkable self-restoring properties: but when we are dealing with consciousness on its own ground, or with any product of consciousness, with systems personal or social or political, self-righting becomes the essential thing in all righting. This is the grain of truth in the former *laissez faire* theories. This is the important truth in the instinctive dislike of attacking the social evil and its affiliations with the hammer and tongs of scientific procedure and publicity. In these regions, our world upholds a policy of working out the good by over-attention to it and under-attention to its opposite. The world behaves as if the good were the real.

I venture to say that there can be no real optimism on the scientific basis with its type of monism. For not alone are evils too numerous to be disposed of in this way. It is also true that progress, with its income of new pains and troubles, would involve continually greater and not lesser suffering. If it were the destiny of human life to pursue all evil by proportionate attention, becoming first fully conscious of it and of its conditions, a just consideration of the way in which life deepens both in sensitivity and in demand must open the prospect of our knowing pain and evil not less intensely, but more intensely forever. Men differ much in their disposition to yield the scientific method to the more monistic method of ignoring evil. Some are unable to enjoy a good until they think they have earned it, which earning is another name for knowing the conditions and complying with them, conditions fixed in the unity of nature. Others demand without earning, and receive much of what they demand. But even the most earning natures earn less than they think. For on the level of experience-surface there is an overcrowding of possibilities, too many features of the world to be attended to; every man must choose which aspects of his world he will look upon, forgetting the overwhelming majority; and every man is led (even though he like to be a pessimist) to select those aspects which best suit his habit of thought and make a world-harmony for him. Every one must fall back at last on *vis medicatrix naturæ* when working out his destiny, making mute appeal to the proposition that the real is the good, and the good the real *par excellence.*

V

Optimism, I say, requires this degree of monism;—belief in an individual Reality not-ourselves which makes for rightness, and which actually accomplishes rightness when left to its own working. Does this, then, eliminate moral courage from the universe? making things, on the whole, too secure? It must be answered that there are right and wrong ways of taking this principle, which in itself permits moral laxity and also admits moral enterprise, as in a world of free men we should desire — for what moral worth can there be in a strenuosity which is a necessary condition of existence itself, as in a pluralistic universe it must be?

If ignoring evil becomes a conscious principle for saving personal effort, it is bad — and also defeats itself. Evil self-savingly ignored is *not* cured: the monism in question is not *mechanical* in its operation. When seeking forgiveness and getting it becomes routine, it ceases to minister to moral progress. The ship of state has large inherent tendencies to go right, even if the helmsman is tipsy and negligent — else what state could last: but when the helmsman begins to exploit this quality, adopting *laissez faire* policies for his own holiday, the way to shipwreck is not long. Selective emphasis becomes insolence when the goodness of Reality is made a personal perquisite.

The true use of the principle seems to lie in this direction: that the evil is not merely forgotten, but *genuinely disposed of* by that to which the attention is turned. If I assume of my neighbor that the reality of him is good, and that his faults are relatively non-real, this assumption is justified only as I actually grasp his faults as the seamy sides of his virtues, having their reality and their ultimate relief in the heightened life of those same positive qualities, — his wrath as part of his *spirit*, his hesitation as a phase of his self-consciousness — to be relieved by more self-consciousness, his shiftlessness an incident of his ideality — to be remedied by a more vigorous ideality, not by mere battle against shiftlessness. Of ourselves, we know that when life is at low tide our very strength stands against us and becomes our fault and our viciousness; whereas, when life is full, our sin becomes our character, and fights for the good we seek. Ignoring, then, is justified when the ill is *known;* known as an alterable aspect of a reality which is good. The whole necessary policy of efficient living, that of concentrating upon a few positive aims, to the neglect of much detail, is morally and practically justified (where it is justified) only by a conscious monism of the sort we have been describing. In fine, any and every radical *commitment* to a single aim, heroic adoption of a cause as one's own fate, ultimate risk and wager against destiny, can be justified whether before morals or even good sense, only if the meaning of the commitment in question is this: that this thing to which I give myself is a character of the One which is real and good, destined to endure, held in place when established by all the self-righting forces of the universe. The moral good which pluralism demands can only be had, I say, on the basis of the kind of monism here defined.

Justice and science pit wrong against wrong to make right; thereby making good commensurate and homogeneous with evil. Justice and science must smell full deep of every ill-odor in order to discard it. If we doubt the universal worth of this method, it is because we judge evil to be a shade less real than the good, something that can be displaced to some extent by simply finding its place in a positive view of things — reducing its evil-ness to an error of position. This gives us our responsible right to discontinuity. Such a view, we may note, also involves a judgment that Reality is akin to consciousness; for in terms of the causal network, there is no other than the scientific method possible.

VI

It remains to be noticed that the monism here described leaves a degree of pluralism in the universe. Any principle of selection, which admits certain elements of experience into the Real and excludes others, is incompletely monistic. The mind is a unity in process of being made up; in which process much that presents itself is bundled out, discarded, as not to be knitted in with the unity here being constituted: and whatever is true of the single mind, if the mind is an integral part of the universe, is true also of the universe. If any materials of consciousness appear to the mind as loosely attached, detachable, actually detached and excluded — then in Reality they *are* thus detached and excluded. Any experience dropped by us is dropped absolutely. Even though the One may attend to what we let go, our letting go is one of the absolute facts; a stitch dropped by ourselves is dropped by the World, irrevocably dropped. The scientific method of disposing of evil is more completely preservative of the outcast elements, hence in this respect more monistic: science regards well what it will exclude, whereby the thing to be excluded gains a kind of immortality in memory, at least in the records and working of the mind — scientific exclusion is thus no wholesale exclusion. But otherwise the mind deals more ruthlessly with its contents. *Forgetting* drops much experience-stuff out of sight that has not been refused in the movements of attention. Discontinuities abound in our inner history, snapping off of thought-threads, wanderings, unfinished business — never to be finished; moral discontinuities also, in forgiveness and self-forgivenesses. Sleepings and wakings, the fresh starts without which every finite will would speedily be brought to despair, — through all such our mental and moral world, so far as its contents are concerned, takes on the aspect of a series of geologic *faults* — departs from a scrupulous monism in which every item is an equally valid member of the Whole, by quite unmeasurable amount. There is no monism on the level of events. History falls by quantities into the abyss, and this is the unstinted opportunity for our sifting — even yet all too un-radical.

The only hope of finding the Real to be one and good is in such sifting-right, in the circumstance that the universe is not utterly organic, and that we are not compelled to absorb into our structure all the false scaffolding we have raised. Unless our monism were thus saturated with pluralism and absolute death, we should have no power to move under the burden of our past. As old men, dying, free the race from their formulæ, so our deeds and memories die, and leave us new from point to point; links drop out of sight in evolution and in history; whole vistas of character evaporate into the night, unpreserved, unpreservable by diary and memoir. Whatever the ultimate goal of Reality there is leisure for working it out; the creator has been generous with time, with the material of existence, the cloth of history, and most of it is wasted. It looks at times as if he had been equally prodigal of men. Only the Nature of things is One and Good; all the "empirical stuff" is as yet unmeasured and unjudged.

There is, if this view be valid, no fixed quantity of evil fortune mapped out in advance for every one; no fated "peck of dirt" for each one to eat: there is room for just such hastening or retarding the One process as there seems, in our consciousness of freedom, to be. The One stands there, as our opportunity, not as mechanical necessity. The monism of the world is such only as to give meaning to its pluralism; our belonging to God such only as gives us greater hold upon ourselves. True, the heights of monism and of necessity we have not scaled; nor shall we here attempt them. Suffice it to have shown that for the good of men, for their good-hope as also for their rightful darings and commitments, some concrete conscious monism is a necessary condition.

CHAPTER XIV

THE NEED OF AN ABSOLUTE: REFLECTIONS ON ITS PRACTICAL WORTH

HAS the Absolute, or the thought of an Absolute, any human value of practical sort? What interest has that which is changeless to a world of movement and change? what function in a world which deals everywhere with contingent realities could be performed by a reality (if there were such) which is subject to no contingencies, final, resting in itself — having no *outside*, nor beyond, and so nothing to fear or to expect from any external possibilities?

We know of no absolute stability in our physical universe, and yet we get on very well with our relative stabilities; build on the spinning surface of the earth, walk on ship's decks, having mastered the art of treating any relative foothold as if it were, for the time being, absolute, and yet without being deceived. Even the falling aviator feels that the earth is moving upward to him. It is not otherwise with our truths in every department of practice; we learn to use them *within* their range of validity, treating them as if they were absolute, but not misled by the practical worth of that assumption, always ready (or almost always) to subordinate them to another truth when their limit is reached. We can treat our atomic weights as permanent, without needing to deny conditions under which the dogma fails to hold good. May it not be the same with Reality also, — that a *floating* reality, a slowly changing and growing world, a developing God, even — with finite and revisable thoughts and purposes, — may it not be that such a universe would serve as well as one that is based on an Ultimatum, an Eternal and Necessary Fact? Nay rather, may not such conditional reality be the *only* sort we ever do or can make reference to?

No better summary of the failure of the alleged Absolute to make connections with human needs can be given than these words of William James: "The absolute is useless for deductive purposes. It gives us absolute safety if you will, but it is compatible with every relative danger. Whatever the details of experience may prove to be, after the fact of them the absolute will adopt them. It is an hypothesis which functions retrospectively only, not prospectively."[1]

Like those too formal unities which we were recently considering, the Absolute seems to be tolerant of any kind of world-contents and experience-contents whatever: and therefore the idea of the Absolute seems to throw no light on the kind of destiny one may expect, suggests not one course of action rather than another, in short "is useless for deductive purposes." "I have noticed," once said an artist to me, "that perfection is nearly always barren: a touch of ugliness is needed to give life, action, instability." When one speaks of the

[1] A Pluralistic Universe, page 111. This is not William James' only word on the worth of an Absolute. I quote these words as the best statement I can find of a typical opinion, not as a complete statement of his opinion. In Pragmatism and later books, James became, consistently or not, more or less tolerant of the Absolute, finding it useful as providing 'moral holidays,' etc.

Absolute, we are reminded of some such well-closed perfection, all too successfully placed beyond the exigencies of all living and striving; we doubt whether it corresponds with any significant reality; whether it is not a name for some sort of logical problem, a name handed back to us as an answer.

I cannot imagine any issue more vital to us than this. Under various names we have been dealing with Absolute Reality. Under the name of Substance, it appeared as the anchorage which all idea-meanings seek; it was credited with internal relations to value of utmost importance. Whether it had any bearing upon action (such as "deductive purposes" imply) we did not expressly enquire, though the name "non-impulsive background" so far corroborates the comments of William James. I am inclined to agree with the requirement that our First Principle must be useful *for practice also*, that it must mean something in particular to the exclusion of something-else-in-particular, that it must be a principle from which deductions can be made. I wish therefore to enquire whether the Absolute is an object or concept that we could do without. Let me put down certain scattered reflections on this subject.

.·.

Something like the Absolute appears from time to time in the history of religion; but it is noteworthy that it is not worshipped. There is no temple to Brahman. The Algonquins did not pray to Manitou. Unkulunkulu, as most primitive near-Absolutes, is too far off and has no interest in the affairs of men; whence petitions must be addressed to the nearer and more finite spirits. The same judgment occurs a hundred times in the various religions of the world. In all religions have mediators of some kind corrected the tendency of the great God-father to fall in with the Absolute, giving the Deity effective human sympathies and fighting interests. Ahura Mazda must have his group of nature-gods and his retinue of Amesha Spentas. Even Jahweh as he tends to be thought of as Absolute ceases to deal with men in person and works only through messengers or through the Logos. What we need to worship is the seminal, disturbing, creating, and destroying principle of Reality: for which purpose would not *Siva* be a better Deity than Brahm, the ineffable and indifferent?

Must not Reality be a Real Force, a Real Mover, and no Eternal Fact of changeless order? Whether for worship, or for theory, or for common practice, we need to reach an Ultimate which is no ultimate indifference: something, rather, like an ultimate *grit*, a principle that lends friction between wheel and belt, which gives bite to the tool, plunge to the earth-dive of the plow.

.˙.

Still, we cannot dispense with a Changeless Ultimate in our world. For practical life is not interested solely in making differences. Indeed, action is never interested in simply producing something different: it is always interested in making *improvement*, which is to say, change in a situation which itself is permanent. The permanence of the frame of change has a value of its own, if only this—that we find ourselves at home in it.

In the altered place we recognize ourselves because we recognize our environment: these two things, self-identity and world-identity, go inseparably together. And the degree of alteration which we can endure, even for the better or best, is not indefinitely great. Any permanent feature of the world will always have at least this value for action: it is a part of that which we are forever moving *toward* — there will be something at the last day which was also there at the first.

It may be well for us that the only changeless Being in the universe is the Absolute, if there be an Absolute. For no more definite shape could be so attractive but that in time we should lose zest in moving toward it. The Absolute binds us to no *particular* conservatism; impedes no possible rate of progress in terms of concrete experience. Here the unlimited hospitality and indifference of the Absolute to contents of experience is an advantage: "compatible with every relative danger" — compatible, then, with every relative improvement. Offering all the advantages of changelessness, with none of the disadvantages of conserving the undesirable.

It is the presence of a Changeless Absolute that alone could set us wholly free to grow. For otherwise we would fix upon some concrete thing as a Changeless, something which ought to be forever revisable, and then we must either stagnate, or *break*.

Not only my own identity, but the identity of the human mind as a species, is bound up with that changeless identity of the ultimate object. We pass judgment upon the intellects, and estimate the world-guesses, of Newton, and Paracelsus, and Thales, and Lao Tze, and Moses: we are able to do this only in so far as they, and we all, have been aiming at *the same mark*, thinking the same world (not even, at bottom, a slowly changing world), testing character upon the same nature. If a man's philosophy is to be a faithful expression of his "temperament," he must in that philosophy single-mindedly seek — the Absolute: for individual differences can be individually significant, or even measurable, only as they accept the same aim and standard.

Identity of mind in the species is a consideration of the same moment with sanity in general. We cannot dispense with a Changeless Ultimate.

∴

As a First Principle, the Changeless is of course insufficient. Our Ultimate Reality must have qualities of both changelessness and change. Or, may it be that the principle of change is furnished *by ourselves?* Let us consider this.

No Eternal Fact can of itself foster any practical conclusions or deductions; what one will do about it depends on how one is disposed to take it. There is no conclusion from one premise alone; and in these practical affairs conclusions are drawn by concentrating the changeless Facts in one major premise, while we carry with us the minor premises which determine how we shall respond to them. Let me illustrate:

Among the relatively stable features of our existence, there is this one, that "Life is short." Well, — what is to be done about it? That depends upon the imagination of the individual; but in every case something is done about it. One man pulls a long face; becomes a pious miser, begrudging every minute not spent in profitable meditation — and when *he* says to a neighbor that life is short, he expects to see the same practical consequences. But hear old Omar announce to us this same eternal truth, and notice his conclusion: parsimonious also, toward the finite number of moments, but for fear he may not live to drink his fill. His originality lies in his minor premise. But indeed the shortness of life need mean neither one conclusion nor the other; need mean no time-parsimony of any kind. Why, for example, might it not suggest leisureliness — since all fever-haste makes time run the faster: only the typical Oriental knows how to prize time — namely by *taking time* about everything. If we rebel against the announcement of eternal facts, it may be in part because those who have brandished them have not allowed enough for these differences of imagination, for the need of a minor premise: our proper retort being that the eternal fact, by itself, has no consequences at all. Not, indeed, unless there are some *necessary* minor premises.

The Absolute, whatever else it may be, is the quintessence of Eternal Fact. May it be that the minor premise which makes that object significant for action is — the Self? We must develop this consideration further.

∴

Every circumstance, however trivial, which becomes a spur to action, has something of the Absolute in it. Is my corn ripe? — then I move, because my Real World is unchangeably a world which presents to me on this date ripe corn, an absolute and relentless fact of history, never to be undone while reality is itself. But beside the Absolute, my Self is necessary to account for my motion — all namely, that imagination presents to me on the advent of ripe corn. The minor premise lies in my Self. The world has its *nature;* the Self has its *character:* when nature and character come together, action results.

But nature and character are not two separable facts. There is no such thing as character in men apart from nature in objects. For character forms itself on the reliabilities of the world; is nothing else than my way of response to the world's way of approach. My character is only seen and known in my actual dealings with the habitual straits evolved by the nature of my world. Since every deed is an exhibition both of nature and of character, all behavior is symbolic, if we know how to read the symbol. As one handles his bat, or his fork, so will he treat his friends, his pecuniary obligations, his holidays. Among other things, character is well shown, perhaps chiefly shown, in one's grasp of nature itself: given a congeries of facts, how much *nature* (that is, absolute objective character) can you extract from it — is not this a test of the man? Hence it may be said that there is for us no such thing as *nature* in things apart from character in men; and my descriptions of nature betray its reference to my approaches. Things are described as hard, heavy, stubborn, yielding, imposing, difficult, and the like: which of these qualities of things (not to mention the primary and secondary qualities of the classics) would have existed apart from the conscious character that has to do with them? Nature and character are fitted to each other, evoked by each other, relative to each other throughout; and this by virtue of the steadfast identity and absolute relation between them. Given the Self and the Changeless, is it somehow *conceivable* that all the rest should spin itself out between? Is it not at least possible that in this situation, character confronting nature, some principle of differentiation may be found which will take away the reproach of the Absolute?

We shall come to this point again.

∴

The Absolute ought not to be barren, for it is supposed to be reached in answer to significant questions; as a last reply to enquiry. To say that it is useless for deductive purposes is to say that it *does not answer the questions put.* It will be enlightening to compare a number of lines of enquiry which end in an Absolute, to observe, if we can, why the questions are not answered; or why they are thought not to be answered.

∴

Consider, first, the epistemologist's enquiry: What can I surely know?

The meaning of the question is practical: nothing is more costly than error, and who can understand his errors?—only he who knows what he may be sure of. But error seems to be incident to all judgments made about external things, things physical, things social, even things scientific and rational. The world waits for a Descartes, who pursues these uncertainties to the end and exhausts them: who finds his *absolute assurance* at last. In doubting all things, I cannot doubt that I doubt; and doubting, (that is, thinking), *I exist.* Surely here is an Absolute. But is it useful for deductive purposes? Descartes does not find it sufficient: it is a great truth, but he uses it — not at all.

What is the trouble with Descartes' Absolute? Is it not this: that this existence-of-self is certain, whether my knowledge of external objects succeeds or fails? But the task set before me, the task that stimulates my original question, is that of *knowing objects*. It does not answer my question to know that I can be sure of the *Subject*. Hence it is that Descartes has to appeal to the knowledge of God, through the "ontological proof" — a way of leaping from the subject to the object, from the idea to the objective fact.

What we want is absolute *objective* certainty; and this, Descartes' I-am fails to give us.

. . .

Descartes' mode of argument reappears in manifold interesting forms in modern thought. As in reply to the skeptic or agnostic, who asserts in despair that there is no absolute truth. The dialectician retorts: Then at least your own assertion must be absolutely true. There must be some absolute truth, for you cannot assert that there is none without self-contradiction. As in Descartes' case, the doubter is *reminded of himself*. There, in his own assertion, is a certainty from which he cannot escape.

This turn of thought which reminds the enquirer of *himself*, we shall call the *reflexive turn*. It reappears in all discoveries of the Absolute. It is clinching — but is likely to disappoint, even as Descartes' result disappoints. For the skeptic finds that he also was in search of *objective* truth: and that the absolute truth of his statement is *irrelevant* to his quest. Whence his skepticism toward objective truth remains unanswered.

∴

Consider the question of the moralist, who likewise has an Absolute to seek — an absolute rule of conduct.

Rules against killing, appropriating property, and the like, have their exceptions. Moral principles vary with social conditions and times. Everything is *relative:* is there not some underlying principle that will standardize all this relativity, and give a substance to moral certainty? The world waits for its Kant; who provides the reflexive turn in morals. No empirical rule is absolute; but one fixed rule there is, — observe Rule. It is, as Professor Palmer puts it, the "law that there shall be law." Let your conduct be law-abiding, law-recognizing, law-constituting; if you have exceptions to make from any rule, let them be made "on principle," principle in general. For the absolute rightness lies not out there among deeds, but in the self, in its fixed principle of duty.

Shall we not herald Kant as the savior of an absolute morality? Yes; — but what exception to rule is not made on some principle or other? Kantian morality is regarded as rigoristic, but does its rigor come from its first principles, — or from its *second principles,* alleged deductions from the first, but of doubtful parentage? Kant, like Descartes, must emerge into the world of objective situations, must appear with a principle that has somewhat to say about dealing with objects, with beings beyond oneself. Treat persons as ends in themselves, says Kant; and herewith, in setting up an objective principle, he confesses that his reflexive turn does not afford sufficient answer to our ethical enquiry.

. · .

Consider the metaphysician's question: what is the absolutely real? That, namely, which exists by itself, not depending on any other being for existence; but conferring being on every other.

Here again, trial of various would-be realities, like matter, or force, or energy, shows that they cannot be what we seek. Matter disappears, on analysis, into activity of energies; and energy seems to disappear into a definition, or formula, regarding what we may expect from experience. No nameable thing can answer the demand for an objective Substance. The world waits for its Berkeley: who hits upon the *reflexive turn*—everything is dependent on consciousness *except consciousness itself*. To be, says Berkeley triumphantly, means to be perceived, or to be a perceiver; reality is consciousness and its world.

Such discovery, following much despair about finding Substance, cannot fail to excite much joy. The reflexive turn is wonderful, unanswerable: yet strangely paradoxical, is it not?—as if for bread one were given a stone, one can hardly say how. At last it appears that what one sought was an absolute reality *beyond oneself;* for one's ontological interests come from questions about Fate, questions about what I may expect from the action upon me of that which extraneous to me is real. I start from the fact that *I do not determine the contents of my own experience;* and no matter how much you assure me that the Absolute is Self, it must still be beyond *this self* which knows its own ignorance and so its dependence. What you have offered me for reality is but another Cartesian I-think, which must indeed (as Kant puts it) accompany all experience (or be able to): but just because it is a coefficient of all experience, it is a determinant of none — "compatible with every relative danger." Useless for deductive purposes. No genuine answer to our question.

.˙.

There are not a few other such enquiries and absolute solutions that do not solve. There is the quest for an absolute good, or happiness, which brought out perhaps the first pure case of the reflexive turn in history — the Stoic answer, namely, that I myself am my own absolute good. Then there is the religious quest itself, the quest for "salvation," which is a search for an absolute security against death: and which at times, especially in these latter times, has received the answer "I myself am heaven and hell": or in more adequate Spinozistic reflexion, my knowledge of the Eternal is my own eternity. Compatible, all such answers, with *too much.*

The same principle is involved in all of them. It is the reflexive turn that makes the trouble and creates the disappointing illusion of finality. We have reached in each case a universally valid answer — but it is not an answer to our question: it is an irrelevant universal. It has the fault of *retreat into the subject;* a well-exposed fault in the case of Stoicism, and of Berkeleian idealism, and of Kantian morality (as criticised, somewhat unfairly, by Hegel), a fault still mightily influential, however, wherever dialectic and idealism flourish. It is this reflexive turn and its products which rouses the pragmatic ire. If I forsake matter for form, one may say, I surrender my right to regain any touch with matter. If I slip from the object into the subject, let me candidly forgo any power over the object. If I leave the world of physics to consort with pure spirit, let me not claim any other than a Platonic relation to empirical reality—relation without fruit or progeny. That too safe thing which in denying I affirm is, after all, something that I have not denied nor ever doubted. I sought an Absolute in the field of man's work.

∴

Of all these irrelevant universals, found by the reflexive turn, one surmises that they have a certain significance, if not that which is claimed for them. It cannot be worthless to have pointed out that while our world of objects is refractory, baffling, and offering no point of fixity or perfect assurance, there is a world within where abiding satisfaction obtains: we object only to the substitution of this latter world for the former, as a co-ordinate and difference-making affair. Reflexive turns are backward glances; and all these considerations have a worth looking backward which they do not possess looking forward. They "function retrospectively only, not prospectively." In the same way, the pious soul thanks God, looking backward, for everything that has happened: everything that has happened is *good*,—not so everything that *may* happen. When next I have to thank God, let it be for something different; and in the meantime the guide to my conduct will not be that God-idea which has proved "compatible with every relative danger." Some principle we must have which charges those forward-looking paths with contrast, which acts like the physiologist's stain, distinguishing tissue from tissue. That which is thus to function prospectively cannot be this Absolute.

∴

Yet there are situations in experience in which form becomes matter, and the reflexive turn does acquire practical significance.

In the work of science, for example, a formal arrangement of the materials of a problem is the beginning of an *explanation*. To classify data, to establish external connections among them, is the beginning of mastery; is a very substantial practical mastery. The assemblage and comparison of unknowns generates known-ness, as friction of cold and dark objects may produce heat and light. Science has begun to question whether any other conquest of Nature is either possible, or desirable, than just this of establishing order and law among phenomena — not trying to penetrate their objective interiors, doubting at last whether there be any such interiors, external to ourselves; doubting whether *we* are not the interior of Nature. Here the product of the reflexive turn is accepted by nearly everybody as the only practical thing in sight.

In moral affairs, also, we recognize the substantiality of the form in certain limiting cases. A person who wills to have a good will, already has a good will — in its rudiments. There is solid satisfaction in knowing that the mere desire to get out of an old habit is a material advance upon the condition of submergence in that habit. The longest step toward cleanliness is made when one gains — nothing but dissatisfaction with dirt. Surely the work is not finished — but the obstacles that remain are material only; the fateful question was whether one could get the *idea* of cleanliness, or of truthfulness, or of the good-will generally. In that idea is the *reality* of the condition; the practical questions are all resolvable into this one, — the maintenance and development of that idea.

There is, then, in these matters some absolute finding in the seeking: salvation is, to seek salvation, for in seeking it one has already abandoned his mortality and his sin. In religion or in morals the question can never be, How much is empirically finished? but rather, What beginning is made? for any beginning is the birth of an idea, and the *anticipation of attainment.* To cast off an old type of conception and forge a new one is the greatest of all practical moral achievements. Compatible with every relative vice, is this Absolute? Compatible with everything it *rises upon*, and there is presumably nothing so vicious that the absolute cannot rise upon it in the form of idea: yet not compatible with remaining therein. This merely formal conceiving of the facts of one's own wretchedness is at the same time a departure from them — placing them in the *object.* It is not idle, therefore, to observe reflexively that in that very Thought, one has separated himself from them, and is no longer that which empirically he still sees himself to be.

In many other connections do we find "mere" forms making practical differences. Nothing is more indifferent to all its contents than *time;* yet time is one of the greatest *agents* in the social world. Long-standing, whether of customs, of offices, of friends, of peoples, is no merit, one might say: yet it is everywhere operative as such to some degree (not preventing French revolutions but delaying them). Age of service, quite apart from brilliancy of service, claims gratitude and honorable discharge: old age, of itself, apart from its contents receives respect; and antiquity is all but equivalent to sanctity. The mere mechanical and empty infinity of space and time may introduce the spirit into the presence of Deity; and to survey the Whole, in any capacity, will work differences in the judgment of details.

In all such cases, that which is found in reflexion,—retrospectively,—functions prospectively also.

∴

In truth, the reflexive thing is the easiest in the world to ignore; because it does require this almost un-natural reversive glance of thought to discover: and ignoring it leaves out an essential in all ultimate solutions. I do not say that it is a sufficient solution of any problem; I point out that it is a necessary ingredient of the solution.

Offered as a sufficient answer, the reflexive turn is indeed the essence of *sentimentality:* hunger is not relieved by Stoical reflexion on the inward conditions of happiness (mentally inward). But to offer the hungry a meal without any of that spaciousness of idea which the sentimental soul too fulsomely invokes; to omit, I say, your reference to the Absolute, somehow spoils the value of your practical charity. I agree that it is well to be meager of sentiment: but I merely indicate a fact of human nature when I say that the thing done "in the name of Christ," or by one who wears the cowl, or in the simple presence of humanity to Idea, leaves a tinge of worth behind it which no amount of practical Aid, apart from the "irrelevant universal" could accomplish.

∴

It is no sufficient solution of grief to say that grief must have a solution; but the only hopeless grief is that which abandons the postulate that grief has any meaning. Point out that in holding to that postulate there is already a superiority to the condition that depresses one; and you reveal a situation which caught in idea does materially lighten the grief. To know that suffering is a common human lot may not empirically change the contents of pain; yet there is no reflexion which more substantially relieves the pressure of actual distress. Let me take my bereavement, said Epictetus, as I take the bereavement of my neighbor: yes, but not because you look coldly on his trouble — rather, because you are free to reflect in his case what must enter as idea into your own, that this is the lot of man, — through which irrelevant universal fact, see mankind actually held in closer unity. To see in the man before me my brother does not help me to deal with him; does not substitute for judgment, discretion, antagonism in its place; does the idea then do no work? Let him answer who is able to hold the fact of brotherhood before his mind, in the midst of his antagonism.

∴

So long as the mind is admitted a part of reality at all, it must be a material part. Differences which are made to mind must tend to become differences to matter. The presence of reason, though it does no more than throw its noose of idea over the contents of experience, makes different every experience. Reason has the function of leading to pleasure and avoiding pain; but the default of reason which exposes to pain adds still another pain — the pain of the defect of reason. Self-consciousness, like other psychoses, leaves tracks in the brain; our physical groundwork takes notes of our reflexive doings as of other doings, and transmits the habits of our ideal attitudes. The irrelevant universal to all our experiences is collectively named, the Self; the Subject, present to all experience, inclusive of all, compatible with all; yet if this self were indeed indifferent to all, useless for deductive purposes, Self could never have become its own *object*, self-consciousness would be impossible. In being thought *of*, the self is made a member of the world of experience, and acknowledged as active there. It is thought *of*, because in being thought *with*, it has had differences to make.

And here may we not observe how the internal relation of idea to value becomes also an external relation, determining differences of conduct? The maintenance of the idea of the Absolute in any subject-matter is a matter of effort and of will; the degree of value which any situation or prospect may have is dependent upon the actual operation of an irrelevant universal which a reflexive turn of thought might discover. But an alteration of value is an alteration of conduct. This is the substance of our answer to the question regarding the worth of the Absolute.[1]

∴

The absolutes which are found in the reflexive turn of thought are not useless, even prospectively. But their functioning has seldom or never been understood, even by those who have hit upon them: and this is, in part, because they have often failed to observe that the reflexive turn reveals never alone the Absolute within, but always the Absolute within *in conjunction with the Absolute without.*

The whole tale of Descartes' discovery is not told in the proposition, I exist, knowing. It is rather told in the proposition, *I exist, knowing the Absolute;* or, I exist, knowing God. The self, taken alone, or in presence of contents of experience as they come, is a fairly irrelevant universal. But set before that self in its dealings with experience an Absolute Object; and its own existence becomes fruitful of differences. For note:

The self might conceivably be a passive spectator of the contents of experience, accepting "the colours of good and evil" as unalterable fact. That which starts the search for the Absolute is an unwillingness to take things in this way. Beside the love for the satisfactory contents of life, there is a most remarkable *love of life itself*—in distinction from its contents, even if the contents are generally bad; some in whom this love of existence is strong have said that they would prefer to endure hell rather than to be extinguished—a most inexplicable attachment, this, to the bare fact of exist-

[1] See further, Part VI, The Fruits of Religion, chs. xxxi and xxxii.

ing, being conscious, without reference to the contents of consciousness. Surely, if ever there were a blind valuation of an empty husk of irrelevant universal, it is here. Yet, with our interpretation of value,[1] is not this same celebrated and mysterious "instinct of self-preservation," the most fundamentally rational of all practicalities? For *life* is but a certain consciousness of the Absolute, in process of application; and the application of this Idea is the substance of all positive worth, conferring upon "contents" what quality they have. Attachment to life is simply attachment to the source of value; and that which appears evil does so appear because the Real cannot be recognized in it, creates a problem of which the living thing already holds the key. Evil becomes a problem, only because the consciousness of the Absolute is there: apart from this fact, the "colour of evil" would be mere contents of experience.

∴

It is true, then, that What Is makes no difference; that which produces difference is Consciousness of What Is.

This pair of Absolutes, or Absolute-pair, which we above described as Character in presence of Nature, is well capable of producing practical difference; might well be described as the original source of all difference, perhaps. For if we begin with simply a consciousness, and its object-absolute (not Sein and Nicht-sein, but Sein and Bewusstsein) we have all that is necessary to develop change (Werden). It is notorious that what endures before consciousness does *not* endure the same;

[1] Chapter xi, above.

this fact has its psycho-physical explanation, its Weber's law, and the like: its essential explanation may be this, that any object of consciousness, simply as object, i.e., as case of Reality, is so far *good*, and therefore — to be approached, or increased in vividness. Whereas what simply stays as blind datum is in its mere persistence *bad*, to be withdrawn from, diminished in vividness to zero. Briefly, Sein and Bewusstsein together give Werden.

∴

The Absolute, after all, is not an escapable practical problem; and no showing that wrong solutions have been forthcoming will destroy the practical worth of the right solution. Knowledge of the Absolute remains as practically significant as the question which perennially gives rise to the search for it.

And this question always calls for just such an indifferent object as the absolutes, in each of our various cases, turned out to be. If we could accept the differences of experience as they stand, there would be no problem of unity; but if we cannot accept them, there is nothing to look for but an in-different. Either we are content with conditional certainties, or we seek a certainty that holds everywhere, — and is thus compatible with everything. If the absolute good were not compatible with every relative evil, it would not be the absolute good. If the Absolute were not compatible with every relative danger, it would not be the Absolute. That which holds good, no matter what occurs, — that is precisely the object of our search.

∴

Such an object is no modern discovery. From the beginning of religious thought, in the very conception of a creator, there has been present to the mind of man a Being who is present alike in good and evil. In quite ancient times, as times go, we may find a wholly explicit definition of such a Being as the desire of all mankind. The founder of a popular religion held up to the minds of a spell-bound multitude, as his own original revelation, a God who "maketh his sun to rise on the evil and the good, and sendeth rain on the just and the unjust." Upon this basis he defined the "perfection" of God, and summoned men to the same perfection, the same absolute bearing. Thereby he defined an attitude of mind which was indeed new in that world, an attitude of equal treatment toward friend and enemy, toward good and bad, — an attitude much garbled and misunderstood, but an attitude wholly intelligible in the light of that unmistakable description of the Absolute God. For how could the new attitude be better defined than as an attitude of *absolute justice*, a thing quite alien to the *proportionate justice* of the Greeks, wonderfully similar to absolute in-difference and in-justice? Is this attitude then actually in-different, and useless for deductive purposes? On the contrary, it is the only radically creative attitude yet known to humanity. Its operation was dimly announced some six hundred years earlier by a solitary Chinese sage, who said: "I meet good with good, that good may be maintained; I meet evil with good that good may be created." Do we not here discover the Absolute functioning prospectively?

The secret of this creativeness we shall in time pursue

in some detail,[1] at present it is sufficient to refer to our own doctrine of the substance of Value. There is we may presume, something in the mere fact of divine attention to objects which confers value upon them; or to put it in the language of Professor Royce, it may be that divine attention is the same thing as divine love, and that love of this sort is the one thing in the world that is creative.

∴

We could not live without the Absolute, nor without our idea of the Absolute. I do not say that the Absolute is equivalent to God; I say that God, whatever else he may be, must needs also be the Absolute. Thus, accepting fully the pragmatic guide to truth, we conclude that the only satisfying truth must be absolute, — that is, non-pragmatic. Wherewith, pragmatism ends in consuming itself; appears as a self-refuting theory.

[1] See especially chapter xxxi.

CHAPTER XV

THE NEED OF A GOD[1]

IN our usual conceptions of God, the One and Absolute is raised to the level of personality and moral quality. These latter characters are indeed more conspicuous, both in current meaning and in history, than either unity or absoluteness. They may well be regarded as the most humanly valuable attributes of the divine nature. Yet they are the oftenest subject to criticism and doubt. More in their case, perhaps, than in that of the others will it be important to enquire whether they are needful features of our Whole-idea.

In a recent book by Mr. McTaggart, called "Some Dogmas of Religion" this question is discussed[2] in so clear, frank, and radical fashion that we shall gain much by stating our view in relation to his.

I

If the thought of God is of any worth to us, says McTaggart, it must be either because of what God is, or because of what God does. It is conceivable that to believe in the simple existence of a being having such character and powers as we suppose God to have would make life better worth living for us. It is also con-

[1] In somewhat different form, this chapter was read as a critical paper before the Philosophical Union of the University of California in 1907.

[2] In the concluding chapter, entitled "Theism and Happiness."

ceivable that apart from his character and attributes, we should set store on the thought of what God does or can do for us and for the world at large. Let us estimate each of these two conceivable values of the God-idea, beginning with the supposed works of God.

God's presence in the universe means to most believers the presence of a very powerful champion of certain righteous causes of immense historic range. We think of God as a vindicator, working out that deeper justice which shall bring together at last the innermost merit and its external recognition. We think of him perhaps as causing happiness and brotherhood to prevail among men at some future time. Or we think of him simply as security to our souls that in some hidden way all is well, or will be well, with the world.

But every legitimate hope or confidence must have some foundation in experience or reason: the sort of thing we are pleased to believe must be at least not-inconsistent with what the world as it is shows us. If God exists, there are certain conditions existing in the same world with him which throw light on his character and powers. Unmerited, random, and general suffering are conditions, not theories. Iniquity and degradation are conditions. Nowhere do we have to search for evil amid the good: we have to search for the good amid the evil. Further, what good we have is unstable in its whole fabric, as if it were upheld *against* the nature of things: life is a constant fight against decay; civilization a perpetual struggle against dissolution; and virtue itself incessant strain against the clamor of flesh and the devil. Now God — if he exists — has either permitted this, or else it exists in spite of him: in either case what can we reasonably depend upon for the future?

It is the same dilemma on which McTaggart has often insisted. If there were an all-powerful God, the defects in his world would show defects in his character. Whereas, if God is wholly good, and therefore not all-powerful, it is at least possible that the mass of evil in the world may prove greater that he can cope with. In either case, the works of God are of no very tangible value.

In truth, these supposable works of God would be of no value at all for human happiness until we had some further knowledge about them. We should have to enquire, as best we can, how this world is constituted; and what are the actual forces at work; we should have to estimate from the basis of our own experience what the likelihood is of any conquest of evil whatever. We must carry our science to the point of metaphysics by our own unaided efforts before we are warranted in taking any satisfaction in the contemplation of what God may do for us. And in the progress of this metaphysical work, we are likely to discover — so McTaggart intimates — that good can gain the upper hand of evil without the assistance of a God. Idealism, which resolves matter into spirit, and shows that against spirit matter must be ultimately powerless; especially personal idealism, which puts the power of spirit into the joint possession of a co-operating society of persons such as this world of ours in some measure already is, and may in larger measure become, without limit, — especially personal idealism may give us all that God has been supposed to offer, and without the moral detriments involved in relying upon a supernatural ally for doing the work of men. Happiness depends (so far as events are concerned) on grasping that total law and tendency of things, wherein we can read the ultimate doom of all existing defects in our condition; and it is more than possible that this law may be found in our own personal and social nature, if we but penetrate to its foundations.

So much for the appearance of God in the sweep of human history. But how about that part of individual destiny that lies beyond human sight? It has been believed that men cannot be wholly happy without the expectation of immortality, and the supernatural compensations that have become associated with that belief. In reply, McTaggart points out two things. First, that immortality is no more an unquestionable benefit than are the visible works of God. Certain great religions of the East, as well as certain philosophies of the West, have led men to find their highest good in personal extinction. And secondly, hope of immortality does not depend on belief in God. It is possible that the soul is intrinsically superior to the crises of material bodies, even if it were a solitary being in the cosmos. The prospect of individual immortality must be gained if at all by the same painstaking scientific and metaphysical enquiries as justify our confidence in human welfare: we must learn of what stuff we are made, and what sort of contingency that stuff is intrinsically subject to. An immortality thus established would be much more satisfactory to our thought than one dependent upon the good will of a finite God: for it would be founded upon the nature of things. God and immortality are wholly separable articles of faith, and no interest which we may have in the one can lend any interest to the other.

The works of God, then, do not at once recommend him to our needs. But we may still have an interest in his existence, for the sake of the guidance, or the encouragement, or the love and worship which his presence in the universe would provide. Let us again look closely and consider what these things are worth.

As far as guidance is concerned, the moral ideal is one which we can never discover unless we already bear it in ourselves. Given a God, we should first needs pass judgment upon him, on the basis of our own knowledge of good and evil, before adopting him as our standard. It is true that we need the suggestion of a quality, oftentimes, in something beyond us, before that germ which is in us can awaken to life. But this type of suggestion is much more available in our fellow men than in the mere thought of a God whom we do not see, and whose acts we can only infer. Guidance must stand very close to us to be of any value. The circumstance that God is god and not man makes any application of his character to our own case difficult, even if we perfectly knew his character. Hence men have been fascinated by the conception of the God-incarnate, visible in the flesh, in all points tempted like as we are. But just in so far as even the divine man fights evil with the weapons of God, and not with those of men, his case fails to be applicable to mine; and the guidance fails. What is done by man we can call upon men to reach; what is done by the god-man stands just beyond the region of my responsibility. What goodness, in the end, can effectively guide and inspire us but the goodness which we observe and recognize in those whom we must judge to be in all essentials such as we ourselves are?

But there are still other interests than this one of moral guidance to which the existence of a God might minister. There is the encouragement which some minds find in considering that there is in the world one morally sublime person. There is the comfort which others find in the thought of a moral leader whose survey is great enough to include the whole field: if I am too weak to fathom the total meaning and drift of things, it is good to think that there is one who does. Loss of such value as this encouragement and comfort might bring would not be wholly made good by human substitutes: yet the gap that would appear in the world would, in all probability, not be irreparable. Remember that God, if he exists, is at best an imperfect Being. God cannot escape his share of the imperfection which, in this universal society of imperfect spirits, is a running stain. What men can lose in the loss of a God like this, is only such value as they may regain, in some degree if not in full, in their fellows. When men believed in the divine right of kings, they could not but apprehend that the spirit of loyalty must vanish in the spread of democracy. But loyalty lives, not less but possibly more, in the government of society *by itself* than in the alleged divine kingdoms. So with the loss of the conceived God, something of spiritual shelter and canopy is removed, without which the soul may well for a time feel naked and alone: "There will be no one to worship, and there will be one person less to love." But reverence and love are not left without objects: and who knows but that the necessity of confining the range of these highest of human sentiments to the members and causes of visible society will in time exalt *human* relations, and accelerate the attainment of perfection?

"Whether the friends whom all men may find could compensate for the friend whom some men thought they had found is a question for each man to answer. It is a question which can never be answered permanently in the negative while there is still a future before us." Thus McTaggart closes his argument.

II

This argument makes remarkably vivid to what degree the values commonly centered in God are reproduced in kind in other relationships, to nature, to friend, and to society. Mr. McTaggart has mentioned no value of God unique in kind except the value of worship, and even this seems to him fairly well recovered in human reverence. One might question whether all possible values of a personal God had been considered; whether the primary worth of such a being is not unique in kind, such as the worth of these other relationships would not substitute for. But without pressing this point, I wish first to call attention to certain logical peculiarities of the argument.

One is struck by the fact that the argument is highly tentative and hypothetical, calling for further metaphysical investigation, and depending for its proposed substitutes for the worth of God on what metaphysical investigation might probably show, if we once vigorously put ourselves to it.

I cannot but assent to this call for metaphysical enquiry. I believe with McTaggart that men have no right to the satisfactions which their religion affords them except as they earn that right by successful metaphysical thought. We cannot pass at once from our needs to the satisfaction thereof, without considering what that reality is from which we must obtain satisfaction. "What people want," says McTaggart, "is a religion they can believe to be true"; than which nothing could be better said. Yet right as McTaggart is in referring us to metaphysical thought to find the objects on which we shall hang our major values, just so wrong is he in basing conclusions on what such enquiry *may probably show*. For in advance of the actual enquiry, there can be no probabilities in the case: metaphysical thought will show one thing, or it will show another; but forecastings of what it *may* show signify simply nothing. In order that there may be any probability in a given field of enquiry, something in that field must be *certain*. Probabilities support themselves invariably on known laws. Hence any enquiry which attempts to find the basis of all certainty, the ultimate thing, is in advance of all possible use of probabilities; it is trying to pave the way for them—they cannot pave the way for it. Hence *no metaphysical hypothesis is antecedently more probable than any other*.

It follows that as long as we have only probabilities and hypotheses to refer to in these matters we have nothing at all. If the belief in God is simply an hypothesis, as for McTaggart it seems to be, we should be more radical than he; we should say outright that it is worth nothing at all. Ideas have certain sustaining powers, even though they are wholly our own fabrications; but no idea that is such a pure launch of our own imagination into the unknown—and nothing more—has any permanent sustaining power. We must take McTaggart strictly, therefore, at his own word, and demand that all attempts at circumstantial evidence on questions of dogma be excluded as irrelevant; that religion shall at all points be built on metaphysical knowledge and nothing else. God can be of any worth to man only in so far as he is a *known* God.

Happily, metaphysical knowledge is the most universal kind of knowledge; the infant's first thoughts are metaphysical, that is to say, thoughts of Reality—though not by name and title. The chance for finding God of general human value is built on the prospect that God may be found *in experience*, 'experience' being the region of our continuous contact with metaphysical reality.

Now God can appear in experience only through some working of his. If no effect of God were visible in the world, his existence must be always a matter of conjecture. Or if God works in the world, but in such manner that we can never identify any work as his, his existence must be a matter of conjecture. If God's whole office in our behalf is that of touching only the august and inaccessible points of destiny,—to decide our birth, to sit in remote judgment upon our deeds, to record the secret fact of our salvation, or otherwise to carry into effect our fortunes in the other world—his existence must be a matter of conjecture. It is because McTaggart thinks of the "works of God" in some such way as this that it seems to him necessary to reason around and away to them; that he can balance so speculatively the chances that such a Being exists. It does not occur to him that the metaphysical knowledge of God might be empirical, i.e., based on his manifestation in human concerns. Yet I venture to say that unless God does operate within experience in an identifiable manner, speculation will not find him, and may be abandoned. The need for metaphysical thought arises (I venture the paradox) just because God is matter of experience, because he works there and is known there in his works. I must enlarge upon this assertion to some extent.

If we consider the first out-croppings of the God-idea in history, we do not find that men begin by connecting God with unseen effects. He is the invisible cause of very evident effects. Were it not for these effects, it is difficult to think that the idea of an invisible cause would have arisen. Men do not first imagine a God *in abstracto*, then speculate about his possible powers, and then at last enquire whether such a Being exists. They begin at the other end. They find their God (as James puts it) *in rebus*. They are impressed by powers which actually operate in Nature and society; they attribute to these powers substantial, that is metaphysical, being. They learn in time that various powers can be manifestations of a single power. They come to see that in the struggle of powers among themselves, one power must be supreme, and only one can be supreme. If they have called the several powers gods, they call the supreme power God; and God is thereby defined in terms of the interest which the human mind cannot but have in whatever power is supreme in man's own world. In such a development of thought, there can be no place for an enquiry whether God exists, or whether belief in him has any importance: for the existence and importance are the fixed points in the problem, — the uncertain elements being the fancies as to the nature of God's inner being, his private life. Doubts must attach themselves not to the question whether God is and works; but to the question what his works in reality are; what we shall think of their tendency and quality; what we can know about the inner nature of that Being which we have identified simply as The Supreme Power.

Am I willing to accept the full consequences of the position here taken, — namely, that if the personal and moral aspect of supreme power has any worth, that aspect will be found in experience also? I am willing. But we shall have to search well in order to identify such an experience.

III

The essential value of the personal attributes of the Supreme Power is not to be found by those who simply look forward. It is important to know what we may expect; it is important, as we were saying, to be able to be hopeful. But for human nature much more than good prospects are necessary to happiness. One must be able to approve the world as it is; one must even be able to look *backward* without a shudder. We must provide for the safe-conduct of the excursions of the human *mind*, not alone for those of the actual human being — such is the universality, or shall I say generosity, of that side of our nature to which religion appeals. We must find some worth in God that we cannot find in the forward look of evolution.

Let me put the matter thus: we must be free to open ourselves, wholly, in imagination and in fact if need be, to the *whole* of human experience. If there is anything which destiny may thrust upon us, or has thrust upon others, and which we have to hide from or banish from thought, we are not happy. If beasts must suffer to supply my table, and I cannot open my mind to the fact of their suffering, I cannot be unqualifiedly happy at my table. If men have been tortured to establish the civilization I enjoy, and I cannot face the reality of their torture, I am not happy in my historical position. If I can reconcile myself to the certainty of death only by forgetting it, I am not happy. And if I can dispose of the fact of human misery about me only by shutting my thoughts as well as myself within my comfortable garden, I may assure myself that I am happy, but I am not. There is a skeleton in the closet of the universe; and I may at any moment be in face of it. Happiness is inseparable from confidence in action; and confidence of action is inseparable from what the schoolmen called *peace* — that is, poise of mind with reference to everything I may possibly encounter in the chances of fortune.

Now this perfect openness to experience is not possible if pain is the last word of pain. Unless there is something behind the fact of pain, some kind of mystery or problem in it whose solution shows the pain to be other than it pretends, there is no happiness for man in this world or the next; for no matter how fair the world might in time *become*, the fact that it had been as bad as it is would remain an unbanishable misery, unbanishable by God or any other power. If we are bound to be as fixedly final in our valuation of evil in general as Mr. McTaggart is, taking it at its face value, as pure *bad* and nothing more, then we must not only accept his conclusion that the supreme power in this world is of very mixed worth, such as only the continued perpetration of mixed products can be expected from: we must also accept such an imprisonment of *thought* in its contemplation of the world and of destiny as must ruin the peace of any out-living soul. The fact is, that men have never taken their troubles that way: they have always assumed that pain is to be explained. And if this attitude is in any degree justified, important consequences follow — namely, that no degree of evil whatever can constitute an absolute condemnation of life; for it would be always possible that further application of the same solvent would transmute that evil also. Whether a given evil can be understood "is a question (to borrow McTaggart's language) which can never be answered permanently in the negative while there is still a future before us." If this attitude is *in any degree* justified, the whole groundwork of McTaggart's argument is undone; built as it is upon the dogma that pain is incurably the last word of pain.

Now it can hardly be denied that the attitude in question is in some degree justified. For it does not occur to us that pain is not the last word of pain, apart from *experiences in which we actually discover pain changing its character*. Do we not find simple pastness or remembrance changing the quality of ill for the better? do we not find excitement doing it, love doing it, wrath doing it? Early man probably knew these strange transmuting experiences better than we do. He knew how wounds in battle are scarcely felt. He knew how rage could carry him gladly into certain injury. He knew how pride could stop the sting of very torture. And he knew how the frenzy of religious ecstasy made mutilation not only endurable, but even *necessary*, to give grist to the great exhilaration that stormed within him. James notes "the remarkable fact that sufferings and hardships do not as a rule abate the love of life; they seem on the contrary to give it a keener zest." Inhabitants of Greenland and Labrador do not leave their difficult countries, though they might; and seamen return to the hardships of the sea with an unbreakable attachment which is no mere habit. There exists then even widespread in human experience a justification for the assumption that pain has in some degree a further account to meet; and if in some degree, then possibly in all degrees. That complete openness to experience, necessary for happiness, cannot be shown impossible.

IV

Consider, now, by what means this occasional transmutation of evil could become a certain command of all possible evil — whereby an openness to all experience might be possible. "All possible evil" is a large, undefined, even growing and rapidly metamorphosing object. What we should much like to find is a power which is, not simply as a fact but in the nature of the case, necessarily efficacious in this work of pain-transmuting, which *anticipates* the nature of possible obstacles without knowing them in detail. Where can such a principle be looked for?

If a given power stays in the same field with other powers and competes with them, its chances of subordinating them are precarious; its supremacy at any time is a simple matter of fact, which may give place to another matter of fact. But one power can obtain certain supremacy in a field of power if it can in some way get outside that field and survey it from above. Thus man, as a physical force among forces animal and natural, has little chance with them; but as intelligence he has some possibility of coping with the best that nature can bring against him. There is competition also among intelligences, among ideas; is there any possible supreme power here? No intelligence can be sure of success so long as it remains in the existing field, striving simply for a more effective arrangement of old ideas; but if it is able to *reflect* upon the whole idea-situation, and from that reflection derive a *new idea*, all other intelligences must become its dependents. It is the same with competing passions. Anger pitted against anger can never be sure of conquest: but a "soft answer" enters the situation as a new idea. If it conquers, it is because, refusing to compete, it *includes* and itself stands outside the arena. Without further illustration, may I suggest the principle that the supreme power in every case is a *non-competing* power, one which may seem at first glance even irrelevant to the point at issue. Not otherwise will it be with any principle which can give us assured mastery of those obstacles collectively named "evil."

In the cases above mentioned, in which we can see a transmuting principle at work, let me call to mind the prominence of *association.* That pain which is taken in common, like effort which is carried on in common, is found through the association to lose its harshness.[1] One does not quite see *why* misery loves company, perhaps; but no doubt the fact of association does something to change the color of the experience. There is only one situation in savage life when pain seems wholly unendurable: namely, when vanquished, dishonored, and abandoned, the wretch must gasp out his life in utter solitude. Hardship gives zest, but under what conditions in particular? Chiefly, under conditions of significant association. The general condition for the transmuting of hardship seems to be this: that the sense of *union with something not-myself,* which I judge worthy of this very hardship, and which somehow demands it for adequate expression, shall be dense and compacted in the moments of suffering. This is naturally the case in the moments of war and excitement, and it must have gone far to make history less painful than the reading of its literal pages in cold blood makes manifest. The laws of the multiplication of human power by association have never been worked out; but no one has failed to measure in frequent experiences what incredible enhancement of the value of any experience may occur in a single touch of endorsement from without. Worth of all sorts begins to acquire another dimension as it enters a

[1] Even remembrance is a kind of social relation between my present and my former self.

career of actual universality, such as the merest nod of assent from an Other may convey. Association is a principle which stands outside of and includes whatever may become content of individual experience; there is some possibility that in association a sufficient mastery of evil may be found.

But unfortunately, association has its own evils. Human companionship can, in the way we have noted, do much to transmute every other kind of pain into something else; it cannot transmute its own kind of pain, that which comes from its own defects. As imperfect knowers of themselves and of each other, fellow-men are the source of the severest evils we men have to endure; and by virtue of our precarious hold on human existence the closest association may cause the bitterest pang, because its loss removes also *that by which* any loss is made less grievous. Far, indeed, must we be from perfect openness to experience if there is not some power over these evils also.

V

From what we have judged of supreme power, it would follow that only something outside the field of human association, not competing there, could afford sufficient armoring against these greatest evils. It must be another than any finite self, something which reflects upon and in its reflection includes all finite selves and their circumstances, something, nevertheless, with which any finite self may become associated in some infallible manner. This seems to me the point in which a God becomes necessary. In God we have the notion of an Other-than-all-men, and an Other whose relation to me is not subject to evil through its own defect; one from whom therefore I can anticipate no pain that must refer me to still another for its transmuting. It is not the power of God, as mighty in comparison with other forces in their own fields, that is of value to us; it is not God as miracle-worker, tumbling Nature-masses about through Herculean or Jovian command of energy; it is not even God as vindicator, doer of particular justice, meeting and overcoming the inequities of men's judgments by a more penetrating judgment; it is rather God as intimate, infallible associate, present in all experience as That by Which I too may firmly conceive that experience from the outside. It is God in this personal relation (not exclusive of the others) that alone is capable of establishing human peace of mind, and thereby human happiness. Something paradoxical about the Supreme Power there is; something in this non-competitive character which thinkers early seized upon:—as Lao Tze glorifies the Tao that never asserts itself, as Christianity presents for adoration its God in the guise of an infant, and infant of the humblest. The authentic voice of God, if it is to come to man with a wholly irresistible might of meaning, must be a still, small voice.

It is scarcely open to question that the deepest assertion of the religious consciousness is of its *experience* of precisely such relation to its supreme Other. Just such companionship we seemed to see the human will spontaneously creating for itself, in its early resentful outcry against destiny; to find later, perhaps, that here was rather a discovery than a creation, strangely relieving the pressure of its initial burden. Just such companionship we find the developed religious consciousness celebrating as the source of its "victory over the world." Further than this it is not my function here to demonstrate the validity of these alleged experiences. The problem of God's reality, in its metaphysical setting, will occupy us in the pages immediately following. We have shown that such God as theism presents to men is necessary to their happiness, and we have shown that such a God must be found in experience, if at all.

It will not be amiss to emphasize in conclusion the entire justice of McTaggart's contention that the finite God is of no worth. When we talk of experience of God and companionship with God, we run a danger hardly less seductive than the danger from atheism. Indeed, atheism may be said to live on the perils and failures of theism. The experience and companionship of God are not a substitute for relations with humanity. The guidance and encouragement of God, devotion and love toward him, are false when they appear as competitors in the field of human alliances. If we have been near the truth in our description of the immediate work of God, it can only be to render the individual more perfectly *open to experience*, human and other. If the experience of God does not, on the whole, enhance the attachments of human life, one must judge on these principles that the experience is not of God. What these terms of human association can mean when applied to God is the most difficult of practical as well as of theoretical problems; tending, presumably, to a mystical interpretation of worship. The personality of God must be, we think, personality whose bonds are broken in "passing through infinity"; denying this infinity, McTaggart finds rightly that he must reject the rest as comparatively useless; finds that his finite God becomes an intruder, and an obstacle to the loyalties of the spirit. The balance between the denial of God and the right perception of God is most delicate, and difficult to maintain. We shall not find it until we have realized what Kant meant by the "regulative idea." But the positive appreciation of what God means to men is the first step toward finding that balance; and further, "all things good are as difficult as they are rare."

PART IV

HOW MEN KNOW GOD

CHAPTER XVI

THE ORIGINAL SOURCES OF THE KNOWLEDGE OF GOD

GOD is to be known in experience if at all: to this result both of the preceding parts of our study have led. And now we have to interrogate experience, in the hope of a categorical answer whether the reality which here we encounter in experience is in any literal sense a living and divine reality, directly knowable as such.

The habit of receiving our ideas about God through tradition is likely to grow at the expense of any original sources of this knowledge which we may possess. We more readily believe that "God spake in times past unto the fathers by the prophets" than that we have any natural human organ for recognizing that presence. But it must be a postulate of our own study that in whatever way God has been known and heard by any of the prophets, or by seers of more ancient date, or by the first remote God-discerning mind in this planet's unrecorded history, in fundamentally that same manner is God known by all God-knowing men at all times. The habit of looking backward to older origins, for revelation authoritatively transmitted, is just and right: because the knowledge of God is capable of development, and no man could wish to begin again at zero. But *that by which he is able to recognize and accept his authorities* is his own knowledge of God, especially that more elementary sense of his that a God exists, and has left his word in the world. It is of this universal and primordial knowledge that we wish to take possession; far simpler and less wealthy than the contents of "revelation," but for that reason the more apt to be neglected, and thereby the means lost by which alone revelation and tradition can be either appreciated or criticised. We shall be satisfied at present if we can find and verify those original sources of the knowledge of God which we have in common with all men at all times, the universal revelation. And it is fair to surmise that these original sources, advanced in God-knowledge as we may be, remain sources of new knowledge also, inexhaustible, neglected at peril.

To judge from the history of religions, God has been known for the most part in connection with other objects; not so much separately, if ever separately, as in relation to things and events which have served as media or as *mediators* for the divine presence. We find the early knowers of God worshipping him under the guise of sun, moon, and stars; of earth and heaven; of spirits and ancestors; of totems, of heroes, of priest-kings; and of the prophets themselves. Speaking broadly, there are two distinct phases of experience wherein God is apt to appear: in the experience of Nature and in social experience. Not everywhere in Nature, but at special points, well-known and numerous enough, the awareness of God seems, as it were, to have broken through, or to have *supervened upon* our ordinary physical experience of those objects. When man has acquired so much imagination that he is capable of being stirred by Nature, he seems capable at the same time of something more than imaginative stirring—namely, of superstition, of religion. If that element of the man is present which we call the *sense of mystery*, then the apparitions of heaven begin to work upon it, and to co-operate with it; the infinitudes of space and time are teeming with presentiment and omen; and man's nature-world is on its way to be judged divine.

So of social experience: it is not everywhere, but at special junctures and crises, that the awareness of God has come to men; at the events of death and birth, of war and wedlock, of dream and disease and apparition. Given the imagination, the sense of mystery, and withal so much self-consciousness as is required to make the idea of soul, or double, or shadowy spiritual counterpart; and these crises of social experience become clothed with a significance not limited to this visible context: the unseen world becomes peopled with spirits, and in time, with gods. Spirit-worship and ancestor-worship develop side by side with the greater and lesser nature-worship, as if here also man had found access to a knowledge of God.

But although we have here two different regions of religious suggestion, destined to great historic careers in relative independence, it is evident that in looking for original sources we cannot keep them apart nor assign to either a priority over the other. For the religious experience of Nature means nothing if not finding Nature living, even personal, thereby socializing that experience. Whereas the religious meaning of social experience arises in the first place only as birth, death, and the like are regarded as the work of that same inexorable power displayed in Nature; and survival theories become religious only in so far as the surviving spirit becomes a power in Nature. What is the Fung Shui of Chinese family religion but the collective ancestral Force, bearing on family fortune through the nature-powers of wind and rain—in effect a family Yang and Yin, even Tien and Tao. What would the Hindu Sraddha be without its nature myth? In all early religions the dead are thought to pass into Nature, and in that passage to change their character, taking on the menacing aspect of nature-powers, requiring therefore to be propitiated no matter how nearly allied in life. Further the *unity* that belongs in kind to the religious objects, and must become theirs in form also, is chiefly conferred upon them by the god of Nature. Spirits are essentially pluralistic and swarming: at death, losing much in individuality, souls were thought to mix with nature and the winds in floating multitudes, or to huddle in dismal nether-world societies, without hierarchy of form or purpose. But heaven and earth and sun have a natural universality and unity; are fitted to give shape and character to the plastic spirit-mass; and at last to lift that mass into their own singleness of order and power.[1] Social experience, then, becomes religious experience only when it is at the same time an experience of Nature power. And nature experience like-

[1] Thus the conquest of Egypt under the banner of Horus, god of the rising sun, prepared the way for such monotheism as Egypt approached, and even for a moment attained. The focussing and defining influence of nature in the religions of Persia, Greece, India needs hardly be pointed out. In the Hebrew religion, indeed, the progress to monotheism was of another sort; but in this religion the imaginative elements are little in evidence, whether on the side of nature or of social experience.

wise is religious only when Nature becomes an object of social apprehension. *Spiritism* and *Animism* are at bottom the same.

Such experience of Nature as arouses a fear with supersensible reverberations, suggestions of unseen presences;[1] such social experience of human crises as arouses an awe, likewise reaching into the supersensible, an awe having close kinship with that Nature-fear: it is such experience as this (not wholly unknown to any age or to any man) that is called *religious,* and that brings us close to the original source of religious knowledge. But it is clear to us that this experience is *not the original source itself.* In these distinctive religious feelings of fear and awe we have already recognized the operation of idea-masses prepared beforehand in some more elemental experience; some vast and intangible idea-mass probably, which man tries to give shape to, but most miserably fails to express, in his language about the "spirits." As small sounds in the night convey mighty meanings, and feelings therewith, to minds well-stocked with images of the weird and sinister; so if the phenomena of experience, trifling as well as majestic, call forth startled reactions, it is because man has already begun to consider and judge the Whole. Neither men nor children are able to fear the dark until they have made much progress in intelligence and imagination. In that "sense of mystery," which we thought must first be present, we may see the idea of God already at

[1] For a most skilful differentiation of this peculiar fear from other types of fear, see F. B. Jevons, Introduction to the History of Religion, ch. viii.

work. The original source is here, if we can discern it. God has come upon man's world-scene in quiet; and man's terror results when in some use of his whole-idea he suddenly notes God standing there. Through no historical re-tracings shall we discover the silent entrance into Nature of that presence. But what external evidence may refuse, some analysis may yet afford us a glimpse of.

In all experience of the type considered, we have found man vividly conscious of his own limitations. And all man's limitations, whether of knowledge or of power or of worth, are brought home to him by his contact with Nature in some form or other. Nature concentrates within itself all that is menacing and hostile to man; and also all that reminds him of his pettiness and weakness. Primary religious experience is so burdened with this consciousness of limitation that we may almost say: What man fears, that he worships.

But we may notice that what he both fears and worships is always something more than the World which limits him. His religion has added to the natural terrors of existence new terrors of its own. Whatever his fundamental religious experience is, it has brought him little consolation. He goes about in a subjection to his world which he had not before known; a breach has opened between him and his reality, — as if now it belongs to a stranger, whereas before it was, if brute fact, still *his* fact. The redskin, says Brinton, is oppressed by the sense of something invisible at work everywhere about him; a sense which leaves him anxious, full of alarms. And further, every touch of supernature is at the same time in some degree a sudden stroke of accusing self-consciousness. Among the Bechuana people, when it thunders they exclaim, "I have not stolen, I have not stolen; who among us has devoured the goods of another?" In first judging his world, man seems to find his world *judging him;* and every experience of the divine is a day of judgment, a moment summoning to instant, summary review of self — which review seems from the first to have yielded little of reassuring nature.

Now the epitome of all man's limitations is his ignorance; and it is fair to presume that man's speculative troubles are the secret of all these more practical troubles. For the idea is (biologically) the scout of experience, and doubtless a knowledge of dependence has touched the soul in advance of any full appreciation of what that dependence implies. The *knowledge of ignorance* may well be the first warning note, sending its premonitory shudder through the frame of human values. The sense of a limitation of knowledge, even in Paradise, might tempt man to explore his boundaries; might make him desire "to be as the gods, knowing good and evil." He realizes that his knowledge is his great weapon and defence, standing between him and fate; he soon chafes at the persistence of any region of ignorance; early proceeds to fill any such void of knowledge with creatures of assumed-knowledge — even long before he sees definitely how his ignorance is to hurt him. Nothing could have been better timed than the appeal of the serpent in the Garden.

But the knowledge of ignorance is of itself no religious experience. Religion is bound up in the difference between the sense of ignorance and the sense of mystery: the former means, "I know not"; the latter means "I know not; but *it is known*." And I dare say that man first realizes his ignorance only in so far as he becomes conscious of mystery; the negative side of his experience is *made possible by some prior recognition of a positive being*, on the other side of his limitation.

It seems to me then, that the original source of the knowledge of God is an experience which might be described as an experience of *not being alone in knowing the world*, and especially the world of Nature. In such an experience, if there be such, would be contained all the possibilities for harm and for good which religion has exhibited.

So long as the unknown of the world is simple *mystery*, a mere "It is known," man is made more a servant than before by his religious experience. His worship will take on depressing and violent aspects; his consciousness will become a perpetual celebration of his own inferiority. He will become a devotee of the fearful and the immense, which have always for their own sake an inherent fascination for man; a fascination which we understand when we consider how the operation of any whole-idea is a creation of value. It is psychologically impossible for man to face the infinite in any shape without exultation. Any positive view of the universe beyond my ignorance has power to excite infinite devotion; not failing to tempt the spirit to an infinite disloyalty to itself. Hence in all ages of the world, the mere sense of mystery, as the discerning of something beyond the bounds of ignorance, has claimed its victims; there are always those who are capable of throwing themselves beneath the wheels of a cosmic Juggernaut, finding in pure abandonment to the infinite if not a cure for human trouble, at least an anæsthesia for all ills. And indeed, no man has found his religion until he has found that for which he must sell his goods and his life; the enthusiasm for martyrdom, for radical self-sacrifice, is the work of the idea in all of us: and a universe of mystery, though it can afford no more, can at least afford opportunity for *this*.

But if that original experience of the presence of God in the world can reach to some permanent hold on its object, so that it might be expressed, "*I know not; but He knows*," the entire aspect of religion is altered. The reconciliation of men with such a world is no longer degrading nor disloyal; for the breach which is opened up between man and his world by the entrance of the unseen Claimant, may be through that same presence completely closed.

From the knowledge that "He knows" will be inferred the thesis that the unknown of Nature is knowable: and the endless task of science will receive its necessary and sufficient warrant and encouragement. Religion offers science the power and the stimulus to proceed *ad infinitum* without fear of ultimate obstacle. That this proud liberty has been no meaningless gift, the beginnings of science may clearly show. For man's first science is *magic* — his first systematic assertion that nature is subordinate to the spirit; man's first inductions are the magical inductions of the Name, the Symbol, the Imitation. By his knowledge of God he knows that there is nothing in the world that will prove wholly refractory to the work of idea-making; his knowledge of the absolute Knower is an attainment, though a *vicarious attainment*, of the end of scientific effort.

And so with whatever other and more concrete consciousness of limitation may be incident to natural or social experience: if that by which one knows his limit is a positive knowledge of the Spirit, then it is a success of incalculable importance. "*I cannot, but He can*," lifts man over his first formidable obstacles, and sets him on his feet as *man*, endowed as a race with infinite faith and with infinite patience, because already tasting the cup of ultimate achievement. Such knowledge of ignorance, and the fear of the Lord therewith, is the beginning of wisdom; such knowledge of impotence, the beginning of concrete mastery; such knowledge of unholiness is already a touch of the untouchable and a beginning of holiness.

Religion is often described as the healing of an alienation which has opened between man and his world: this is true; but we may not forget that it is religion which has brought about that alienation. Religion is the healing of a breach which religion itself has made: and if we would reach the original sources, we must find them in man's awareness of an *Other than himself*, an Other who may be a companion, but also an enemy more deadly than death, more dreadful than Nature in herself has any image of. It is religion that reveals to man the disparity between himself and his world, sets him at odds with that from which he came, brings him to that pass to which the animal cannot come — an unwillingness to take his world as he finds it, a consciousness of the everlasting No, and a defiance of it or perhaps a subservience to it, — as if *this* were his god. And what man has to learn by difficult degrees is, that it is his original knowledge of God that has made this alienation possible. "Thou couldst not seek me (nor fear me, nor be resentful toward me) hadst thou not already found me": this is what religion always knows, yet has forever to re-learn.[1]

This primordial knowledge of God has never been wholly obscured; some sign of that known companionship has never been absent from religion. Man records this consciousness not only in tradition, but also in act and token; he sets up his holy places and their strange appurtenances as memorials that the Spirit has here been met on friendly footing, and may probably be met again. He carries with him, inseparable from his person, his *fetich*, material medium for his spiritual attendant and confidante, loss of which may be loss of all that makes life worth living.

At the source of all religion, so far as our analysis can discover, we find an experience of God as an Other Knower of our World, already in close relation to self,

[1] It is reserved for fully developed religion to read truly the paradoxical history of man's religious experience, both in the race and in the individual. Are not these lines of George Herbert true of these early racial gropings also?

> Lord, Thou didst make me, yet Thou woundest me;
> Lord, Thou dost wound me, yet Thou dost relieve me;
> Lord, Thou relievest, yet I die by Thee;
> Lord, Thou dost kill me, yet Thou dost reprieve me.
> I cannot skill of these Thy wayes.

and also in some natural bond with our social and physical experience. Such is the report of the elementary religious consciousness; it is this report that we have now to pass judgment upon.

CHAPTER XVII

THE KNOWLEDGE OF OTHER MINDS THAN OUR OWN

OUR enquiry into the knowledge of God has led to this as the central issue: whether in the midst of experiences of Nature and of human extremity, using these in some way as mediators, there can be a veritable experience of infinite Spirit other than myself. We do not mitigate the difficulty of this question by pointing out that the knowledge of any other minds than our own, even in plain human intercourse, has its difficulties also. But in so far as the difficulties are similar, it will be an advantage to bring them together,—the more so since, in spite of any difficulties of theory, we believe our experiences of our fellow's minds to be real,—neither illusory nor simply working-hypotheses.

All the (substantive) objects of human attention and experience may be put into three fundamental classes: the physical objects, which with their relations we sum up as Nature; the psychical objects, which with their relations we sum up as Self; and the social objects, or other minds, which with their relations we sum up as Society, or still more comprehensively, as our Spiritual World, ourselves being included. These classes of objects seem clearly distinguishable; not mixing nor blending at their borders—when I mean another mind

I distinctly do not mean either my own mind or a physical thing. Each has its own science — physics, etc., psychology, sociology. And each has its own organ of perception.

But no. We have an *outer sense*, says Locke, for things of nature; we have an *inner sense* for things of our own minds, our thoughts and feelings; but Locke mentions *no sense* by which we can discern another mind. And neither, be it said, does any later philosopher. Sociologists speak of "the social sense," social instincts, "consciousness of kind," and the like; but these practical designations are not intended to name an actual organ of knowledge differentiated for perception of other minds. *We have no such organ.* Sociology is an extended psychology, made possible by the fact that Society, as we noted, includes Self, — is built up really of psychical objects, and from the center outward, by help of ideas which work well in practice: other theory than this of social experience we shall not find in the Books. This third class of objects is, by some strange device, made knowable without a special perceptive organ: — or, perhaps we are mistaken in assuming it literally knowable.

This absence of a perceptive organ makes it probable that we are mistaken: it suggests that our social knowledge is built on hypothesis, and not at all on experience. It compels us to examine our so-called social experience directly, to see whether we can find any point of actually present and certain knowledge of another mind. Such an examination yields little that is satisfying. What I do directly experience is the physical presence of the other person; and his expressive signs and language, which are also physical. From these I infer his reality, and nothing in experience tends to shake that hypothesis; everything confirms it. What I have, then, is a perfect hypothesis. For all practical purposes, I am as certain of my social environment as I am of my physical environment: indeed, the reality of this social world of mine is the last thing I should doubt. The practical certainties here are unshakable. But if you ask for more than practical certainty; if you require a genuine social experience, in the literal sense of the word experience, I am at a loss to discover it. I am inclined to think there is no such thing.

And I must acknowledge that even this sense of practical certainty does sometimes desert me. My social consciousness is subject to extraordinary fluctuations; my sense of the presence of other souls comes and goes in an unaccountable way; it flits in its substantiality from one extreme to the other, much as does my belief in God. When I seek to grasp it, it eludes me.

There are times when my consciousness is burdensomely public, and not my own; when the social world is all too real and immediate; when I can find no seclusion in my thoughts, no privacy even behind barred doors. At such times, I can get no hold on myself, because of the incessant pressure of the other men in me, voices, postures, beliefs that pursue me and harry away all risings of individuality on the part of my self. I escape into the wilderness, and Nature becomes a chorus — there is no shape which may not take on animation — even the stones may sermonize. And yet at other times, if I deliberately *seek* contact with that world of other mind, an oppressive solitude cloaks me in. I bury myself in the rush of men; but am no better able to bridge chasms, or reach vitality of give-and-take with them. I make designs against my neighbor, I hunt him to his secret castle, I hold him at the point of my sword, I seize him bodily — he vanishes, and I have nothing. I cannot make him open himself to me; I cannot so much as open myself to him: I am a prisoner, and without ability to find where I am bound. I see that the doctrine of *monads* is no futile myth.

Such is my current social experience so-called, and it seems clear to me that if there were any absolute certainty in it, these variations would not occur. That which at times may so escape me can hardly be an empirically given presence.

Then I reflect that in the nature of the case it could hardly be otherwise: the other mind must be beyond my powers of direct experience. It can be no object of sensation, because it is not a physical thing. It must be such as I am, a thinker of its objects, not an object among objects; and as such thinker, or *subject*, it can only be *thought*, not sensed. That which makes him himself, and other-than-me, is (by definition) the fact that his thoughts are not my thoughts; so long as he remains other-than-me, his thoughts can never become identically mine, though I may conjecture them and approximately think them *after him*. Of myself, I find, and desire, an infinite thought-fund inaccessible to others, and inaccessible through all finite times to myself; it cannot be otherwise with him — he has in him an infinitude of character, only gradually developed and *made general* — infinitude at which I may only guess. Souls, by their own nature, cannot touch each other; cannot experience each other: their relations do not rise to the point of *knowledge*, — they remain excursions, adventures, hypotheses, wonderfully sustained by their results, but none the less, launches from solitude in the direction of an assumed reality; which reality, if it exists, is no less solitary.

I look down from a cliff upon a beach below; the black fleck wandering there excites in me the consciousness of fellow-being: I turn away with the impression that there has been in my life a social event, an experience of another mind. But I have *verified* nothing. And if I climb down and discover that object to be in fact a human shape, what have I now verified? A physical object, — nothing more. What made that glance from above more than physically significant was clearly a contribution from within. In Kantian phrase, I had imposed this *concept* upon the appearance; I had *begriffen* it that way, and my own Begriff gave me the only sociality I experienced, — all that in fact I ever can experience.

There are more intimate relations, and less intimate relations: more work, or less, for my Begriff-social to do — but what my Begriff is *given* to work upon, as actual stuff of experience, is the *body*. Body of man and Nature — nothing more. When that body disappears, even though the other spirit persists, all that *I have* of him is gone. I have no organ for the experience of other mind; by the nature of other-mind, I could have none.

I would press the logic of this situation, if I were able, until we should cry out that it is a lie, whether or not we see *how* it is false; and that any philosophy which ends in such a situation is impossible. Human communications must be at bottom as real as we think them to be — no intricate, successful, solitary *pantomime* of each with himself and Body.

And then I would urge that we are not quit of this logic by crying out against it; and resolving for our part to treat our world *as if* we were in direct conscious relations with our fellows. For that attitude of common-sense-resolve is precisely the subjective, solipsistic sort of philosophy which we have just denounced. Logic here is the sole remaining bond of genuine mutuality among men; and if we will not patiently earn our conscious right to our fellows, we must likewise forgo our conscious right to God. We cannot dispense with either.

The problem of our social consciousness is as old as Berkeley's idealism (old in fact as Leibniz or Descartes, but not felt before Berkeley as a primary demand on thinking); and since his time thinkers have not been allowed to forget it. It has become a stock spectre, especially for idealistic theories, to show that their logic must end in solipsism. Several ways to escape the logic of separate personality have been devised. We shall examine the most important of them.

One may seek to discover and formulate *infallible criteria* or signs, by which we may certainly know that we have before us another conscious being. This way out has its plausibility; for is it not the sight of other *bodies* and *expressive movements* like or analogous to our own which actually compels our judgment that another mind is here? Or, if we learn (as from Royce and Baldwin) that we rather interpret our own bodies by those of others, than the reverse ; and if we find (by first steps in comparative psychology) that analogies soon fail as we try to test the consciousness of animals and plants ; if we abandon, as we must, the whole argument from analogy as hopeless, certainly the psychology of our impulsive social *reactions* will reveal some reliable *stimuli*, whose presence infallibly indicates other mind. Are there not as Wundt suggests "manifestations of animal life which cannot be explained without the introduction of the mental factor?" Unfortunately there are none such; every physical change must and may be referred to a physical cause. There is no reason why "educability" itself may not be a property of matter.[1] Are there not in certain groupings of actions unmistakable "signs of choice"; or as James better states it, can we not recognize "the pursuit of ends with the choice of means?" Certainly all such signs as these do guide our social judgments. Even more than by strict planfulness ("pursuit of ends with choice of means") are we guided by a certain *playfulness* or superabundance in the apparent government of movements: signs of fluidity, eagerness, emotionality are more immediately compelling than signs of intelligent end-seeking. But after all, these are nothing but signs, physical signs ; and explicit language which rises out of this aboriginal expressiveness is but a further set of physical signs, which nowhere rests on a veritable experience of other mind. If somewhere we could *begin* with an actual consciousness of the social object,

[1] And herewith we exclude Binet, Bunge, Moebius, etc., as well as Schneider who appeals to "irregular muscular action."

all these criteria would help us amazingly to continue and subdivide our intercourse: it is always easier to determine what state of mind belongs with what set of actions than to determine whether there be any state of mind there or no. (Writhings of earthworm on fish-hook express discomfort, if they express *any* consciousness at all, which may be doubted.) Even if infallible criteria could be got — which is impossible — they would still do nothing to bring us nearer the other mind itself: for all such criteria are themselves physical.

A much more adequate way is that proposed by Professor Royce; his criteria are not physical, and do undoubtedly bring us near to an original experience of the other mind. "Our fellows are known to be real" says Royce, "because they are for each of us the endless treasury of more ideas. . . . (They) furnish us with the constantly needed supplement to our own fragmentary meanings."[1] To anything that appears in our life with the character of a *response*, we instinctively attribute outer personality. Not thunder in general, but thunder at a critical moment in our thinking, means that Jove has spoken. If a distant signal moves in direct answer to our own signalings, we need see no human form to infer the presence of an outer consciousness. What infallibly convinces us is the experience that our own thought is carried on to further development (and without our own equivalent effort). The more completely and deeply the answering and supplementing idea caps and enters into our own train of development, the more inevitable the acknowledgment. And so we may build a series all the way from the

[1] The World and the Individual, ii, 168–174.

opportune clap of thunder to the continuous successful intercourse with our fellow men, a series of increasing conviction of the reality of our social experience. When we have reached the stage of voluntarily *putting questions* to our environment, and expecting and receiving conceptual answers, our faith is complete. God is doubtless most real to that person who finds his prayers somehow responded to; for, to paraphrase Royce's criterion, *response* is our best ground for believing the social object real.

Upon this way of reaching the Other Mind, we must make the following comment. That we are still left with only an inference of that Other; a faith and not a knowledge in experience. Even though we say, with Royce, that reality is nothing else than response (or fulfilling of meaning), we have not so far as this criterion goes, found that reality personal save by probability of high order. We can still speak only of "the source of our *belief* in the reality of our fellow men,"[1] not of an experience of that reality itself. The relative passivity of our reception of idea from without is no invincible proof that it does come from another mind: men have been known to dream conversations which add to their knowledge; thinking itself often takes conversational shape, ourself being recipient; in all thinking the new comes to one as if from another. We shall have a difficult distinction to make between such inner development of our own meanings, and that development which we shall regard as hailing from a veritable Other Mind. But no type of inference, however direct and simple, can quite meet our requirement; for that which

[1] P. 169 of work cited; italics mine.

we must first *infer* is one step away from immediate experience.

Are we not driven, then, to a view which closely resembles that first supposition of ours that social experience is a *practical* certainty: that view namely which interprets the social experience as a moral affirmation, an *acknowledgment* which we *ought* to make, something of which no scientific or empirical knowledge is either possible or conceivable. As Professor Münsterberg puts it in his powerful chapter on "Die reine Erfahrung,"[1] — we do experience our fellow men, but even so as we immediately experience all reality, by acknowledging them real. I cannot doubt that the last mystery of mutual contact is contained in the will, rather than in the intellect; a thesis which we shall have later to consider.[2] But all will makes use of knowledge, prior or simultaneous. There is no human will that does not contain a nucleus of *knowledge* which is not our own act; and it is this that we wish to separate out.

All of these ways — by physical criterion, by response, and by acknowledgment — have a common presupposition. They all suppose the mind to be furnished in advance with an *idea* of an Other Mind. We are able to read our signs as we do, because we already expect them to mean something, we have already framed somehow the conception of another mind. Our world responds only in so far as we have our net hung out, confident that Other Mind will fill it with usable furtherings of our own thought: apart from this Other-Mind-meaning of ours, no event could take on the

[1] Grundzüge der Psychologie, pp. 44–55.

[2] Under the general topic of "Mysticism," Part V.

character of response. So also, if we are to *will*, or *postulate, or acknowledge*, the fellow-man, it is to be asked how, apart from previous idea, we know *what* to acknowledge. The conception of the fellow-man, somehow obtained, is necessary before my duty of acknowledging him can be performed, or understood. Beside which, there remains an ulterior question, — to Whom or to What do I owe this duty? I am inclined to think that *obligation* implies a known Other: and that while duty and social experience are doubtless inseparable, it is duty that depends on social experience, not social experience on duty.

It is because all of these theories really accept the doubt of an immediate experience of Other Mind, that they must thus assume the idea of Other Mind to be there, — innate or unaccounted-for. It is for this reason that we cannot adopt any of them as final; though none of them fails to throw much important light on the actual working of our social consciousness.

The ultimate difficulty in this matter is due, as I have come to think, to our over-dogmatic ideals of knowledge, and to the explanations we adopt of the knowing process. We take our knowledge of physical things as the type and ideal of all satisfactory knowledge, — and we find naturally enough that we have no such physical knowledge of fellow minds. We explain our knowing of any object by a relation between object and subject, in which the object presumably produces some effect on the subject, — and we find naturally enough that anything which is intrinsically *subject* cannot become such an object.

But if such were the true ideal and explanation of knowledge, we could not, of course, know ourselves any more than we could know others. For we can have no physical knowledge of our own mind, nor can our own mind cease to be subject in order to become an object. And conversely, by whatever understanding of the matter we can account for self-knowledge, by that same understanding we may probably account for knowledge of other subjects.[1] When Locke suggested his inner *sense*, after the analogy of outer sense, he probably used a misleading figure; intending doubtless only to outline the fact of self-knowledge as a thing distinct from knowledge of physical sense: of special organ there seems to be none for self-knowledge, any more than for knowledge of other minds. In truth, all three classes of objects of experience stand on the same precarious footing: and of these three classes, the knowledge of other mind is the latest to be declared impossible. Each of the other types of knowledge, knowledge of nature or of self, had been shown impossible, by one theory of knowledge or another, before social knowledge had been drawn into technical question. We have only to adopt the proper axiom, and any group of objects we please becomes subject to skepticism, thus:

I. Knowledge of self is impossible. Because the thing known is always other than the self that knows it.

[1] More technically stated: we err in assuming to explain knowing by a *dyadic* relation between subject and object (say S : O). This explanation bears its own condemnation on its face; for if knowing were of the form S : O, S (in every act of knowing) would remain unknown, and the relation S : O must be unknown likewise. If knowledge is to be *explained*, that is, put in terms of something else than knowledge, our dyad must broaden out, — as I think and shall try to show, — into a triad.

On this axiom it might be possible to know Nature, or to know Other Selves,— only not *the Self*. The epistemological subject is unknown (Rickert). Psychological introspection is understood to reveal, not the self, but quasi-physical objects; we find never the *genuine* self.

II. Knowledge of physical objects is impossible. Because consciousness can contain nothing but experience-stuff. When I say of any object "I know it"; I have already made it a part of my experience: when I think of it, I think of it always as contained in experience,— if not my own, then another's. On this axiom, it might be possible to know Self, or even Other Selves,— only not physical things as independent substances. A quasi-physical world of orderly experience we of course have; we never find the *genuine* physical world.

III. Knowledge of social objects is impossible. This is proved by sharpening either axiom above. We may say that the object of knowledge is always other than *any* subject. Or we may say that the object of knowledge is always *my* object, belonging to *my* experience, known as such, thought of as such. In either case social experience is impossible. Quasi-social experience one does not question; it is only the *genuine* Other that we fail to find.

I am inclined to think that the three cases are alike. We have a trilemma, each horn of which is as valid as the rest. We could set up another triad, if we chose, beginning thus: Self is the one object perfectly knowable; Nature is the one object perfectly knowable; the Other Mind is the one object perfectly and ideally knowable. The last of these propositions would be as tenable as the first, and as little tenable.

It is not useless, I think, thus to point out that all types of knowledge are liable to the same type of predicament; and that all such predicaments may be traced to axioms expressing some ideal of knowledge too hastily assumed as exclusive. There is a sense in which we can know *ourselves* better than we can know any other thing, whether of nature or of mind beyond ourselves. There is a sense in which *the physical world* is more thoroughly knowable and satisfactorily holdable in knowledge than any other type of object. There is also a sense in which the primary object of acquaintance for any finite knower is his environment of *Other Mind*.

The alienness and inaccessibility which we are compelled to ascertain from time to time, not more in the Other Mind than in Nature or in Self, may well be only such alienness as we must intend them to have, meaning what they do, if we were to picture to ourselves their most ideal knowableness. May it not be, for example, that if we should become clear what kind of knowledge of Other Mind we should desire, as the most perfect possible knowledge of Other Mind, this ideal knowledge would not differ in principle from the knowledge which we actually have. I propose to try this as the next stage in our search for the actual social experience; enquiring particularly whether we could desire to know Other Mind apart from just such physical mesh as has in this present chapter seemed the chief barrier to that knowledge.

CHAPTER XVIII

SUCH KNOWLEDGE AS WE COULD DESIRE

WHAT is the object which we desire to know? An other mind: but certainly in no case an empty mind. It is a mind which has its own objects, and is at work upon them. There is no principle of attraction between empty minds, i.e., between minds, pure and simple: there is no gravitation between minds as between bodies.

Regarded as pure spirits, minds are very much alike; individuality begins to appear, and our interest there-with, only in so far as the mind engages in struggle with its experience. In truth, minds must be occupied with matter in order to be of interest to one another; whence it may appear that matter supplies the principle of attraction between spirits, as well as between bodies — the principle at once of attraction and separation. Character comes out chiefly in dealing with Nature[1] and what engages us in any person is an individual quality which must be described in terms of his encounter with physical conditions, and the encounter of the race with those same conditions. Every character is some epitome of the economic and artisan labors of the race. Power over nature, clearly seen or dimly divined in another, is what compels us to him. This power is first seen in the body itself, wherein wayward

[1] See above, p. 190.

materials and energies are subdued under an immediate capital command, prophetical of much further mastery; and beauty of body signifies to us an ease of mastery, which finishing its task returns with abundance to control itself. Apart, then, from a world of things which resists desire and so forms the text and context of a temporal career, there is nothing in mind personal and distinctive, exciting to knowledge. These elementary strains and stresses make up our simplest thought of the man. It is the other mind as knowing and mastering Nature that we first care about.

The mind to be known is, we say, a concrete being; worthless even to itself apart from the material in which it operates. It is the Mind-in-union-with-Nature that we want to know. But the mind is still *that which* deals with this material; and we concern ourselves with the material only for the sake of that which it manifests. I make boots; but still, it is no part of my self that I make just boots — I could have found my character as well in making books or laws or music. Would it not be possible, if knowing were ideal, to take the burden of nature-stuff for granted and see that character in itself, becoming conscious of its *thinking* apart from the irrelevant stimuli of its thought?

The notion of telepathic communication seems to propose some such ideal; that of reading thoughts without taking cognizance of sensations. Since we are speaking of ideals not of facts, and telepathy has usually been regarded, whether by believers or by nonbelievers, as an ideal improvement in mutual knowledge, we must look into the meaning of its proposal.

Telepathy would save, presumably, the trouble of expression; it would save the detour of thought, by which it must journey down into language and back into thought again. It would connect the two termini directly, without the complex series of irrelevant means.

Examine this proposal of telepathy. Consider ourselves in the act of knowing the thought of another mind in the direct manner suggested. This must mean one of two things. Either we find ourselves imagining the other person, and in imagination hearing him speak, or seeing him make well-known signs, or otherwise reinvesting himself in fancy with his usual physical media of communication. Or else, we find our own thoughts moving under some "strong impression" that this development hails from a given absent person. In either case, the value of the experience would lie in the possibility of verifying it, by communicating with the person "face to face." If such possibility of verifying were cut off, we should speedily be disabused of our preference for this sort of relation with our friends; what more unsatisfactory intercourse could be imagined than a series of "strong impressions" which had no prior nor further history? Even to the telepathic fancy, the physical presence and vocal evidence of the other's thought remains *the standard experience*, to which all other points as its ideal, however useful (telephone-wise or wireless-wise) in exceptional circumstances. Telepathy, I think, has little to offer toward defining a better way of knowing Other Mind.

The plausibility of the thought-reading ideal comes in part from the very perfection of our ordinary modes of intercourse; through their silent efficiency the physical bearers of our meaning drop out of sight, and it is to us as if we were dealing with meanings purely, without any need of sights and sounds. Our social experience is the pre-eminently developable side of human experience: as we have perfected it, it is of peculiar richness, elasticity, and depth. It is with some effort of abstraction that we look away from those regions where, with amazing technique, the play of our passing thought-exchange takes place, to the simple physical groundwork of it all. We think we might dispense with *that*, only because it serves us so perfectly.

There is another reason for the appeal of the proposal that thoughts may be known without reference to Nature. It is the assumption that men first have thoughts and then later express them. This is less than a half-truth; for the expression of a thought is an integral part of taking possession of that thought. The one quickest way to put stupidity on a par with genius would be to make stupidity owner of all these ideas which it *has*, but is not yet able to express. In truth, it is no hardship that friends must "descend to meet"—as Emerson has it: for such descent into physical expression is a progress into valid and active existence.

An idea shares the history of the body; it needs to ripen and mature; it must find its way by gradual processes to the surface, where it will show itself in language and in action. Hastening this birth involves loss of stamina and quality in the product. The resistance of Nature to the expression of a thought is not the resistance of a wholly hostile medium; detention is a spiritual condition for health and viability, not a physical condition solely. It seems fair to say that the more significant the idea, the more it needs to be lived with before it is uttered. Idea as well as Matter must be "mixed with labor" before it can become *property*. And perhaps also there are no ideas which are mature at birth; but they, like the young of higher species, must pass a certain time in the open under friendly protection, before they can pass current among other ideas, the tools and properties of all men.

It thus requires time and Nature in order that a mind shall *exist*; must it not also require time and Nature in order that a mind shall be *known?* We do not wish to know the mind other than as it is; we cannot wish to know it, then, except in terms of its own traffic with Nature, both in acting and in thinking; in possessing its own character, and in possessing its own ideas.

It is no accident, therefore, that we begin our acquaintances with fellow-men *at their periphery*—at the point of their visible encounter with Nature, with weather and the common physical conditions of existence. It is indeed an accident (relatively speaking) whether a man work out his special career in shoe-leather or in medicine or in ink: it is no accident whether he meet the four elements and make up accounts with *them*. And however far acquaintance progresses, we cannot omit from our concept of the man those items, even trivial, of physical behavior into which we learn to condense the significance of large vistas of his spiritual quality,—the shrug, the still glance, the nervous step, the grasp of the hand. And there is some ground for thinking that we know no man completely until we have been with him in the wild, and have shared with him some first hand measurement of idea against the old elemental human obstacles.

But Nature has other properties beside obstinacy that belong inseparably to the knowledge of souls. What we wish to know of a man is doubtless his Idea (or, as Chesterton says, his philosophy), and therewith *himself:* but we can know an idea only by knowing whatever that idea contains and *aims at.* Contents, we have considered : an idea is always an idea *of* something, and the all-available first something is physical stuff, whatever else it may be. As for the aim of ideas, we thought that all ideas aim at a lodgment in Substance,[1] doubtless first seen *behind Nature ;* if so, no man can be known without knowing that object. The *identity* of personality, we thought, was bound up with some changelessness in its ultimate object; and the *unity* of personality in some unity to be found there in the world beyond : [2] but I venture to say that unless changelessness and unity were discoverable in some character of physical experience, any other object would work against great odds to maintain them. For reality cannot detach itself from the experience of Nature: sensation has some of the characters and dimensions of reality not elsewhere found. Sensation lends to experience its *pungency*, its *vividness*, its *particularity.* The definite separation of parts in Nature, the clear difference between position and position in space — no point confused with any other — make the world of sense the place where all *definiteness* is set up, where

[1] See above, p. 119. [2] See above, pp. 187.

all desire for clarity and differentiation seeks its home. If it is true, then, that we cannot know a definite idea or being save as that being has a definite object; that we cannot know a vivid being, save as having a vivid object; that we cannot individualize that being, save as that being has objects with definite differences; that we cannot measure or estimate any being, save as that being has objects themselves measurable, quantitative: — if this is true, we see that in ways affecting the very foundations of personality, the knowledge of Nature, of Nature pungent and intense with sensation, is an integral part of the knowledge of another mind. These values (vividness, etc.) of physical experience are not *like* the corresponding values of social experience, — they are, so far as they go, *identical* with social values: *they are properties of mind and matter at the same time.*

I do not say that knowing thus the objects of another mind is equivalent to knowing that mind; I say that such knowledge of the objects is a necessary, an integral part of social consciousness, even of ideal social consciousness.

It is not indeed sufficient to know the objects; we should have further to know those objects as *being known by* the Other Mind; we must find the idea at work; we must verify in experience our simplest definition of the Other Mind — an Other-knower-of-physical-Nature. We want the center as well as the periphery; and Nature certainly cannot give the center of personality, the idea itself. But Nature can give a symbol of the center.

We have so far had little to say of the *body* with which we so closely identify the Other Mind; for this identification is all-too-absorbing — we forget that our knowledge of men comes as much from observing their environment as from observing their bodies. But the body is after all *that with which* Nature is handled; as the idea is *that with which* Nature is thought. The body is a symbol of the idea: it stands as subject to the environment as object. In its relation to its physical surroundings, it presents a physical picture of the knowing-process.[1] But the body is more than a symbol.

The body is an incredibly intricate and exact *metaphor* of every inner movement of that Other Mind. To every shade of thought and motive, there corresponds some change in the body, reflecting in its own different sphere each type of variation to which the inner state is subject. Man still "looketh on the outward appearance" only, even though he were able to examine the living brain; but remarkable it is that there is nothing in "the heart" not faithfully displayed in this appearance, and at the moment of its occurrence.

With all our inability to gain the exact key to the cipher;[2] and with all our inadequacy in observing these

[1] And this picture is so significant that in our theories of knowledge, we can hardly escape it. It is the inveterate source of that dualistic theory of knowledge which we have condemned. We forget that We who thus see the Other's knowing, in picture, from the outside, should be included in the picture to give the whole truth, even in symbol.

[2] It is not inconceivable that the key might be accurately defined, to some degree. Such a reading of the metaphor as that proposed by Münsterberg, may offer a conception of a solution. *Quality* of sensation, says Münsterberg, is represented in the brain by the *place of excitation*; *intensity* by *energy of excitation*; *vividness* by *energy of discharge*; *value-tone* by *place of discharge*. A somewhat different suggestion, differing espe-

subtle physical changes; it remains true that the body, if we will take it so, is little else than the soul made visible. If we should say that the body has no independent reality, but only exists as a bulletin of an inner process; being but that process itself, *reporting itself* to us in such terms as we can physically apprehend: — if we should conceive of the body in this way, we should hardly over-state the immediacy with which it presents externally what the mind internally is, and not in its passing phases alone, but in its most rooted habits, its oldest memories, its most permanent wills and purposes. The body is a complete metaphor of the idea.[1]

But, further, the body is more than a metaphor. In some phases, it shows what that Other's experience literally is. Thus *time* is the same for both body and mind; the time of the brain process is identical with the time of the psychosis it represents. For us who look on, the *date* of those processes — if we know what they are — may be said to be a matter of direct experience, — through the body. Also, from the position which the body occupies in space, a particular and exclusive perspective view of the visible world is determined; and we

cially with regard to value-tone, will be found in an appended essay, page 546: but it will be seen from either that the work of key-finding is the main concern of psycho-physics, — a science of definite standing, with legitimate and infinite problem.

[1] The body is the manifestation in spatial metaphor of the will-to-live as inborn and as modified by experience and choice. I do not mean that this metaphor can be read by simple inspection; for in the body other records are composed with the record of the will: the will of the world beyond, as it attacks the inner will and impinges on it, leaves its trace here also. The surface of the body is the shore-line where outgoing and incoming purposes meet, conflict and cross; and one tale confuses the clarity of the other, — yet adds the data without which the other were less than true.

who look on, can through our own physical experience know something of the *spatial experience* of that Other. Moreover, as the place of that body alters from point to point continuously, a like continuous change takes place in the physical experience of that other; the two continuities are identical, and we observe that *continuity*. And this continuous history, which cannot be duplicated by any other mind, is taken together with its view of the Changeless, to form the ground-work of its *individual identity*,—of which, thus, through our experience of that body, we get some literal glimpse.

It is for this reason that our conceptions of disembodied spirit, or of an Other whose body we cannot locate or imagine, tend to lose just these qualities of individuality and particularity (as early survival theories and spiritism sufficiently show); we find ourselves impelled to assign them deliberately a place or *seat* in Nature, or else in some other nature accessible to us in imagination, in order to save their personality from obliteration before our minds. How little, then, from our ideal of social experience can we dismiss the experience of body.

I trust I may be pardoned for dwelling thus long on considerations that are familiar. I confess that this extraordinary device by which the Other Mind presents itself in the guise of a body in the midst of Nature seems to me each time I think of it more wonderful than before. The inseparable union of two things so disparate as social experience and experience of Nature seem to be: is there not a perpetual amazement in this? It would be less amazing, perhaps, if it were all pure metaphor, or symbol, or the mere outside of what is within; but we have noted points at which the material world, as we call it, ceases to be a metaphor and shows us, as it were, a literal edge of the Other Spirit shimmering through its physical encasements. Surely there can be no accident, or superfluous illusion, or arbitrary unnecessary sundering of mind from mind in such a union. Nature and the natural body must *belong with* the experience of Other Mind, even in its ideal condition. Of myself, I seem to have only mind; of the Other, only body: and yet, as I think it through, there seems to be nothing about that body which conceals the spirit — body seems to do no more in separating than to fix and define the simple other-ness of that Other from myself; in all other respects it does but give me that Other Mind in more tangible form than by experience of its inner life on its own grounds alone, I could have it.

Let me pursue my reflection a step further. I have sometimes sat looking at a comrade, speculating on this mysterious isolation of self from self. Why are we so made that I gaze and see of thee only thy Wall, and never Thee? This Wall of thee is but a movable part of the Wall of my world; and I also am a Wall to thee: we look out at one another from behind masks. How would it seem if my mind could but once be *within* thine; and we could meet and without barrier be with each other? And then it has fallen upon me like a shock — as when one thinking himself alone has felt a presence — But I *am* in thy soul. These things around me are in thy experience. They are thy own; when I touch them and move them I change *thee*. When

I look on them I see what thou seest; when I listen, I hear what thou hearest. I am in the great Room of thy soul; and I experience thy very experience. For *where art thou?* Not there, behind those eyes, within that head, in darkness, fraternizing with chemical processes. Of these, in my own case, I know nothing, and will know nothing; for my existence is spent not behind my Wall, but in front of it. I am there, where I have treasures. And there art thou, also. This world in which I live, is the world of thy soul: and being within that, I am within thee. I can imagine no contact more real and thrilling than this; that we should meet and share identity, not through ineffable inner depths (alone), but here through the foregrounds of common experience; and that thou shouldst be—not behind that mask—but *here*, pressing with all thy consciousness upon me, *containing* me, and these things of mine. This is reality: and having seen it thus, I can never again be frightened into monadism by reflections which have strayed from their guiding insight.

Any connecting medium is apt to appear as an obstacle to direct relationship; on the other hand any obstacle may discover itself to be a mediator, sign of unbroken continuity. The sea separates,—or the sea connects; it cannot do one without doing the other also. So Nature *may be* interpreted in its relation to social consciousness, as the visible pledge and immediate evidence of our living contact. If there be any social consciousness, it must include within itself just such physical appearances as we have been reviewing, even in its ideal perfection.

We have pictured such ideal knowledge of the Other; we have faith in it—but we have not verified it. We have still to seek experience of the center, the knowledge of that which knows

CHAPTER XIX

THAT KNOWLEDGE WE HAVE

ANY experience of an Other Mind which I could either wish or fancy must contain in it, we have thought, a World, full of sense and variety, full of obstinacy, and with substance at the back of it—like this present world. In a truly social experience, such a world would be known *as being the world of the Other Mind.* That world would be known by me; but as it were through the eyes of the Other Mind. It would be in some sense a world common to both of us; known by both at once.

And though it would be perhaps conceivable that we might carry on mutual relations, each of us having his own separate world (as, for example, I might imagine myself in dream conversing with some resident of heaven or hell, having at the same time a vision of that spirit's world and reaching some understanding of him thereby): yet all real understanding and mutual measurement, mutual judgment, appreciation of character and so even of self-knowledge, must come through having the same world with him throughout. A perfect social experience would require that this present world of Nature should be known as being the World of the Other, precisely as it is my World.

And here begins our final enquiry. For as it seems to me, this present World of Nature *is* known by me as being, in just this sense, a common World: it seems to me, indeed, that it is *not otherwise known* — that is, that a knowledge of Other Knower is an integral part of the simplest knowledge of Nature itself.

It is more readily granted that social consciousness involves nature-consciousness, than that nature-consciousness involves social consciousness. If for no other reason, at least for this: that our experience of Nature is constant; whereas our social experience is, at best, *intermittent* — we can and often do experience Nature by itself. It is enough if we can find a genuine social experience now and then — we have not yet done so much as this — but to make such experience an organic part of nature-experience would be to make it perpetual.

Yet I confess that I cannot find a genuine social experience at all, except as a continuous experience. It appears to me that all three types of object are intermittent in the same sense, and continuous in the same sense. Intermittent enough is self-consciousness; yet self-consciousness is always with us. Intermittent is also the consciousness of Nature, as an object of direct attention; yet the undertone of Nature's presence never deserts me, even in deep sleep. In a way closely similar to that persistent awareness of my Self, which is compatible with the most fitful movements of attention to Self, is the awareness of Other Mind persistently present in experience, though doubtless less readily discoverable than any other. Inseparably bound up as I think with the continuous experience of Nature. And such continuous experience is the foundation of all the rest. I shall attempt, first of all, to make clear that *there must be such continuity, if there is to be any social experience at all.*

The chief elements of intermittency in social experience are removed when we look away from the body of the Other and regard his environing world of objects. It is in these, we have said, that we know him, quite as much as in his body. His body appears and disappears to our sight; but his environment does not disappear. It is true that these immediate objects of mine do cease, when he is gone, to occupy his consciousness, and can no longer be counted in his environment. But his experience of Nature was not limited to immediate objects, and never is so limited. Any idea of a thing, is an idea of that thing *placed* in a world of space and energy which remains a constant object. Our Space does not move as we move about in it, nor does our idea of it alter; our placings are successful, coherent, unconfused, and for any moment absolute, only because our ideas reach an unvarying field for these varying locations. If, therefore, at any time I have known an Other; and in knowing him have known Nature as his object; then this same Nature,—with its Space-field, Force-field, and the like—does not cease to be *his Object* when he disappears.

As my own physical world is not bounded, at any time, by the partition or forest or hill that happens to limit my vision, but extends with my Space in all directions indefinitely,—so does his physical world indefinitely extend, wherever he may be—reaches throughout my Space, reaches me and my place, reaches Substance—that same Substance which I also reach as my ultimate object. If I have once got into his world, I cannot get out of it while he endures,—any more than he can get out of my world, so long as I can mean him; and these fundamental objects of mine, which I sum up in the word Nature, if they have ever been common objects, common to him and me, can never thereafter cease to be common objects. If my own continuous experience of Nature has ever been a *social* experience it can never thereafter lose its social reference.

But I seem to imply that there can be a *beginning* of social experience, and so a time when it was not—a time when my experience of Nature was mine alone. What I am required to show is that social experience *has no beginning*, except with physical experience itself: that my knowledge of Nature and of Other Mind are in their whole history interlocked, and inseparable. If Nature is ever common object, it *has always been* common object.

Let us consider how a social experience might be supposed to begin, as at times it does appear to begin, even abruptly. I think myself alone, for example, and with uncomfortable surprise find myself observed. It seems to me that I experience a jarring change of scene: my various objects have now to be connected up, in swift series, with the intruder's eyes. They have been exclusive objects; they have suddenly and perforce become common. They are all seared with this new relationship, as with a running breath of flame, and delivered over to joint ownership. Such readjustments often take perceptible *time* to effect. Have we not here a sufficient contrast between solitude and society, showing that social experience may *begin* — being imposed as an addition upon an experience not social?

What such a transition does unmistakably show is that exclusive property in the contents of experience is possible and may have distinct value attached to it. Such exclusive property is made possible by sensible barriers, such as opaqueness and distance. When I say, "I am entirely alone and unobserved," I am putting my trust in these barriers. But when I resort to a barrier, I confess that the objects which I thereby seek to monopolize or conceal are in some danger of being known by Others. They are already thought of by me as being sharable. And if they are sharable, it is because they are already in the World of an Other Mind; there are continuous lines through space between him and me; our world of Nature is already common. Is it not clear that when I suppose myself alone, and regard my solitude as an achievement, I am in that very thought acknowledging my world of Space and Nature to be a world common to me and Others? My negative sociability has a very positive social consciousness at its basis.

What such experiences imply and illustrate may be more compactly stated in terms of the logic of communication, as follows: *In order that any two beings should establish communication, they must already have something in common.* For when I consider the two beings, prior to their communication, as apart from one another, I must consider at the same time the field through which they must pass to approach each other: and this field is already a common field. Two beings wholly independent, having no common region to measure their distance from one another, having between them no continuity through which to travel *toward* each other, are lacking in any "toward" — are unable therefore to *approach* each other, cannot come together. All actual approach implies a deeper-going *presence* as an accomplished fact.

Given a minimal core of communication, and further communication may spin itself out upon that core, may grow intense and varied, develop its ups and downs, its relative presences and absences. But given nothing at all — nothing at all can happen. If then, experience ever becomes actually social, it has, in more rarefied condition, always been so; and hence is, in the same fundamental sense, continuously so.[1]

There is some satisfaction in reducing our question to this alternative: that social experience is either always present or never present. If now we can show that we have at any time a veritable experience of

[1] There is indeed no sufficient reason for supposing that the sociality of my nature-experience continues to exist after my fellow has gone in any different sense than before he appeared. The episode of his coming and going does not change the physical aspect of my world ; those objects of Nature seem intrinsically *ready to be observed* by an Other Mind, to be essentially public in their constitution. If I were actually alone in this same cosmos, it is difficult to think that I should be without the idea of possible Others, conceived of as sharing it with me ; it is difficult to believe that Nature could be experienced as simply *meine Vorstellung* — for the physical object itself, the common *thing*, seems to present itself as numerously knowable, having many unused knowable aspects or valencies which I with my single point of view can never exhaust. Nature seems *structurally* common, or let us say *commune ;* made up with reference to many co-experiencing minds. My thought of Nature suffers no jar as men come and go, for soci-ability is its element. In experiencing it, I am potentially experiencing the Other, and continuously.

Other Mind, we show that we have such experience continually. I believe that this can be shown.

For suppose that experience is never social. In making this supposition, we mean to contrast the supposed non-social experience with a supposed social experience. In imagining my experience to be confined to myself and my objects, I admit or assume that I have an Idea of my experience not-so-confined; that I know what a social experience would be like. Now I submit that *this Idea of a social experience would not be possible, unless such an experience were actual.* Otherwise stated,—In any sense in which I can imagine, or think, or conceive an experience of Other mind, in that same sense I *have* an experience of Other Mind, apart from which I should have no such Idea.

For every supposition we may make to the effect that our idea of Other Mind is a "mere idea" to which no real experience corresponds,—that our supposed social experience is, in reality, subjective,—implies that we have in mind a type of experience in comparison with which we can condemn our supposed social experience as merely subjective. But the only type of experience in comparison with which any experience can be judged as merely subjective, is a non-subjective experience. *The only point of view from which our supposed social experience can be criticized as incomplete is the point of view of social experience itself.* The only ground upon which this idea can be judged a "mere idea" is the ground of this same idea as *not mere*, namely, as actually bringing me into presence of Mind which is not my own.

Leibniz, for example, judges that all experience is

monadic, and that monads do not in actuality experience each other, though to themselves they seem to do so. In making this hypothesis, Leibniz presents to himself the world of monads, and *he* knows their relations to be other than they seem: *he* at any rate occupies a non-monadic position, is for the time being an inter-monadic Mind. And any one who judges that he — and God — know the actual reach of ideas to fall short of their apparent reach, does thereby assert that *his* idea has not thus fallen short. There is no degree of outwardness of which we can think; no degree of reality which we incline to *deny* to idea; but in that thought we have claimed it for our idea. Let me represent to myself the Other Subject, his living center, as inaccessible to my experience; then either I deny myself nothing conceivable, or else I have that which I deny.

An objection (or, let me say, *the* objection): may not this idea of a genuine social experience, which you say guarantees the experience, be an *ideal*, i.e., a conception of something we may desire and think of, which we may well use to criticize what we have, admitting that we have it *not?* Surely, not every ideal implies the experience, but rather the contrary.

Answer: An ideal is either an extension of experience as given, or an innate standard.

The idea of a genuine experience of Other Mind is not an extension of other types of experience. Imagination has its ways of building improvements on experience by combining, enlarging, extending what is given, according to known types of relation. But if the idea of Other Mind were not already given, it could not be built up in this way. Certainly not by any arrangement of physical ideas in physical relations; nor yet by any arrangement of psychical ideas in psychical relations; nor by any union of physical and psychical. To reach the idea from these, we must use the special relation of Other-self-hood, which is the idea itself. Since my idea of social experience is uniquely different from all such constructions within the physical and psychical worlds, it is not an ideal based on them. It is not an ideal by construction at all; what we seek is simply the thing, social experience, in its unique difference from all immanent variations of other fields of experience. If this unique difference is an ideal merely, it is not an ideal by imaginative construction, — it must be innate.

To say that an idea is innate, in Cartesian fashion, may mean simply that it is once for all there, and there is nothing more to be said about it. Or it may mean that the idea is due ultimately to some outer source (ancestral or divine); whereby we only reinvest in that Outer Source the difficulty of the idea in question — namely, how my ideas can reach that which is not-myself. Or, it may mean, in Kantian fashion, that the idea is a native and necessary form by which the Self orders the material of its experience, as otherwise given. Of these, the Kantian form is doubtless the strongest: and our social experience does most closely resemble, as we have noticed, a form of interpretation, a successful hypothesis clothing our manifold experience-stuff — ultimately sensation — with social meaning.

As an hypothesis our idea of Other Mind has certain interesting peculiarities. That it is not framed imaginatively of materials taken elsewhere from experience, we have observed. But further, there is no way in which it could be proved false, or even brought to other test than its use. There are various ways in which my social judgments may err, and suffer correction in experience. Thus I may impute to a friend a false motive, accepting his statement that I am in error. This judgment clearly relies on the more authentic social experience for correction. So with other errors, as by mistaking the identity of a person, or by mistaking a post for a man; these are corrected with reference to a better social experience. There is no type of error to which social experience is subject which can refer me away from social experience for correction, — none which can send me back into myself for final court of appeal. As an hypothesis, the idea of Other Mind cannot be tested, — nor can it be withdrawn.

But now, when we suppose that this idea of ours is an hypothesis *only*, what more than hypothesis do we think it might be? We think, do we not, that it might be a genuine social experience, and no mere hypothesis? But "genuine social experience" is the hypothesis itself, if it is such. And the contrast between real and apparent in social experience is only such contrast as social experience has already furnished us with. My idea of social experience is then, of social experience *as it is*: my ideal and my idea are the same, — they refer me to what I have.

But let me make clear that in referring our idea of Other Mind to experience, I do not mean that it is derived, in Humian fashion, as a copy from a *previous impression*. It would be as little to the point to suggest that my idea of myself is derived from a previous impression of myself. My idea of myself is *at the same time* an experience of myself (unless my idea flies wild). So, unless as frequently happens I use some paper currency in referring to Other Mind, *my idea of Other Mind is at the same time an experience of Other Mind.* Let me but think what I mean by the Other Mind, and there, as I find my Self, I find the Other also. As an idea of a fundamental and constant experience, bound up with my equally permanent experiences of Self and Nature, this idea is not *prior* to experience; but is indeed prior to all *further* social experience, to all such as is intermittent and subject to error. This fundamental experience, and its idea, deserve, from their position in knowledge, to be called a *concrete a priori* knowledge.

Of the logic of this proof that we have actual experience of Other Mind I shall have more to say in a later chapter. It stands before us now somewhat barely. Unconvincingly, too, unless we can clothe with some living sense that strange assertion that Nature is always present to experience *as known* by an Other. That we cannot genuinely conceive ourselves as mentally alone in this cosmos, though we can well imagine ourselves bodily alone. That the inherent publicity of Nature, the fitness of all its objects to be communally experienced, is no empty potentiality, but a potentiality, founded (like other potentialities) on some actuality. We must now try to bring that experience more vividly before us; for we can hardly believe in an experience which we are yet unable to disentangle, or verify in ourselves. But let this conviction stand as a firm ground in our further search: that we should have no idea of an Other Mind or of a social experience unless we had the experience itself. That in whatever sense we can think, or imagine, or even *deny*, the reality of that experience, — in that same sense it must be and is real to us.

There are, I think, three natural difficulties in the way of distinguishing the undertone of social experience amid the general rumble of the ground-levels of experience. First, that we cannot identify that constant Other with any *particular* individual, yet an Other must be an individual. Second, we cannot help regarding the experience of Nature as sufficient in itself, the presence of Others in the world being additional and wholly separable fact — that the experience of Nature *may* be at the same time a social experience we can more readily believe than that it must be. Third, that we cannot verify the social experience *socially*, in the same way that we verify the facts of Nature. I shall consider these three, beginning with the last named, — reserving the others to the following chapter.

An object of knowledge or experience is, for the most part, a thing which you and I can verify together. I assert that something is true, in history, in physics, in mathematics; and when I make such statements *to you*, I mean that you also can go to the same facts and experiences and find the same thing that I have found. The truth of my assertion means that it is valid for you and other real persons in the same way that it is valid for me. This association of minds which we call "we," accustomed as it is to sit in united judgment upon facts external to itself, cannot in like fashion sit in judgment upon itself. If we doubt "we," we know not to whom to appeal. We can hardly find our fundamental sociality, because we can hardly get so far away from it as to doubt it.

Nature is pre-eminently the world of socially verifiable things, the world of scientific research — which is general human collaboration on a common object. We look at Nature through the eyes of a social world. As we look at physical things through two eyes at once, and our prospect thereby acquires something in solidity and depth; so in quite similar fashion we see objects and truths in general through two *pairs* of eyes, through indefinite multitudes of eyes, and thereby acquire that deepest solidity of judgment which we call "universality." Universality is a social habit; the necessary habit of looking at any truth as if not I alone but the whole conscious universe were looking at it with me. The simplest judgment of physical things is universal in this sense; the most particular matter of fact, as I place it in my world of Nature, is so placed by help of this deep sense of the "cloud of witnesses" to whom this fact belongs, as well as to myself. Without this habitual democracy of judgment, this habitual loss of my life in the universal judgment, I can have no life at all in Nature or in the world of truth.

And just because my social consciousness is *that with which* I am thinking my world, I am not at the same time and in the same way thinking *of* it, — as one does not see his own eyes in the usual processes of seeing things. When we speak of *experience*, what is called to mind is usually experience with the experiencers left out; experience just so far as it can easily be common object and no farther. Hume, in his examination of experience, found no Self ; he had gone out of his house, as one noted rejoinder had it, and looking in at the window was unable to find himself at home. In truth it is not I alone, but *we* who go out, and cannot be discovered by ourselves in that house. And that same reflexive turn of consciousness which takes notice of Self, as of something always present, must, if we are right, discover the Other also, my other I, perpetual sustainer of universality in my judgments of experience.

When, then, we think of "experience" as something solitary and subjective, we are cutting it off from ourselves, and calling upon the Other Mind to view it so, together with us. Holding it thus, at arm's length, we criticize it, and as we thought, by means of an idea of something better: we criticize our solitary experience by the standard of a conceived social experience which would be more comprehensive. And this idea of a better, we thought, confessed the reality of that better. In truth, we should read the situation the other way. That experience, thus held off at arm's length and criticized, is not the Real Experience, judged by standard of an Idea of a better. That criticized experience is but a conceptual part of reality, abstracted from its context, and criticized not by idea (alone) but by the reality itself. The real and the conceptual have changed places. It is through my present inseparable community with The Other that I know that abstracted "experience" to be incomplete.

CHAPTER XX

OUR NATURAL REALISM AND REALISM ABSOLUTE

OUR second difficulty in finding social experience is that the experience of Nature, though admitting social experience as an appendage, still seems to be something else than social experience, separable from it, sufficient in itself. Any particular person may come and go, making no difference to my experience of Nature. Come and go, not only from my eye-sight, but from this World of Time itself. Any particular person, Nature is independent of; and if of any, then, we reason, of all. The soci-ability of Nature is an extraneous circumstance. Nature first *is*, and then is experienced by us; Nature first *is*, and then is mine — and yours — and theirs. This is our besetting natural Realism; and it is the most persistent difficulty in the way of finding social experience.

It is fair to recall, at first, that *if this natural Realism is right, there is no such thing as social experience.* If every mind may come and take its own view of Nature without making any difference to Nature, hence without weaving into the nature-experience of an Other any necessary reference to itself, then a solitary experience of Nature is possible. But if a pure solitude is possible, it is perpetual. Experience is always and necessarily social, or never, — these are our alternatives.

But we wish, if possible, to meet our natural Realism

on its own ground, rather than on our own, and satisfy it. Its own ground is, that Nature becomes a medium for social intercourse as it were accidentally and externally, as one picks up a stone which chance has shaped to the hand. Nature-experience becomes associated with social consciousness; but is itself to be defined independently, or as *That Which* serves social consciousness. In knowing Nature I am indeed always dimly conscious of its fortunate publicity. I know myself as merging, on this side of my experience, with whatever Other Minds may happen to be extant. But all this social reference is indeterminate, and adventitious; it rides on the outside of Nature. Nature is hospitable; offers infinite and permanent possibilities of sociality; caring not, however, whether many points of view are occupied, or all, or none. Nature-drama goes on, careless of the seating of the house, or of the gossip there. This is our natural Realism, so far as it has bearing on social experience.

Now all this is report of truth. I find Nature ready made, and so do you. This world, in its constitution, is not my doing; nor is it the doing of any one else situated as I am, nor of any assemblage of such. Nature is object of our knowledge; and knowledge is co-extensive with *empiricism*, — that is, with the attitude of taking what is given, in obedience (not, of course, without activity, nor without hope). Have we not contended, at some length, that the ultimate object of knowledge has its independence of us; its perfect priority, to which we who wish to live submit? It is true that any Mind depends on Nature as Nature does not depend on that Mind. I would not seek to minimize this independent priority, even obstinacy, of Nature. For it is just in this character of ultimate opposition to me and my wishes, of high superiority to any doings or thinkings of mine, that Nature begins to assume for me the unmistakable aspect of Other Mind. We must dwell for a time on this point.

So long as our attention is given to a physical object for its own sake, or for the sake of further physical ends, the independence of the object seems exhausted in that mysterious obstinacy which demands our submissive attention, our empirical attitude. But that obstinacy does not fail to call forth enquiry; it does appear as a "mystery." We cannot accept the simple There-ness of Nature as final truth (any more than we could accept pain as the last word of pain). We require to know *why* it is there, and by what principle we are made dependent upon it.

The "objectivity" of Nature requires to be explained: it admits explanation. This is the critical feature of the case. For in so far as we are able to conceive the obstinacy of Nature as explained by, or dependent upon, some further source of strength, we approach the discovery of a more fundamental object. We shall find, I think, that physical experience, taken as a solitary experience, has no very perfect independence of my Self; is not so external but that it can at any moment be conceived internal to me—and does actually roll away from sensation into memory (which exists only in me) instantaneously (as in a rolling wheel the point of contact instantly leaves the ground) and without substantial change:—on all these things idealism has sufficiently enlarged (and the force of this idealistic motive comes from conceiving Nature-experience as solitary). We shall find that that which is most completely independent of me, external to me, is not physical experience *per se*, but Other Self. The independence of Nature hangs from this more fundamental independence, and not vice versa. The objectivity of the physical object is derivative: it shines by reflected light, not by its own.

Let us present experience to ourselves in simple terms, as an interplay between an active Self and an active External Reality. Grant, tentatively, a degree of independent activity to each. My own independent activity in making experience what it is may be fairly estimated by that force of expectant imagination with which I meet and place the materials that sensation offers me. The mass of idea which I call my Self, my "apperceptive mass," carries on a spontaneous self-projection, running-ahead in anticipation of experience: and no experience can come to me which is not an answer to certain organic *questionings* set out to receive events. Though I do not determine *what* the detail and particularity of experience may be, yet I do *expect detail and particularity*. This scouting-wave of my idea-system thus defines a complete physical world, — in all but the last touch of answer-to-question. My present moment *expects* the next, in all but the last touch of change which sensation must give. Large world-making powers must, on such showing, be credited to the Self. Cut off suddenly that relation to External Reality in sensation; and this world-expecting, world-forecasting, world-spinning activity does not cease

— physical worlds still exist for me in imagination, or in dream. Here is a complete dream-Space, dream-Nature and nature-processes, dream-social-conditions too, and all filled in with sufficient dream-detail and particularity, on whose development I expectantly wait with all appearance of passive, empirical attitude — though it is *my own world.*

There is large creative power here; yet such, we think, as a touch of *sensation* would shatter like a house of cards. That same own-made-world is doubtless permanently present to me; but as the stars in daylight, quantitatively annihilated. What vividness and definiteness I now seem to possess comes, we must still think, chiefly through this flood of sense which irrupts upon my anticipative out-goings. Cut me off in earnest from my experience of Nature, and I tend to become vague, indefinite, uncertain of myself. Let me lose a little in sight or hearing; and I find how much not only self but sense has been concerned in that influx. However vigorous the impetus of advance-weaving on the part of my ideas — vigorous enough at times to falsify experience, displacing feebler sensation — my own activity always accepts the irruptive material as its own authority and completion. Toward that Outer Reality I hold myself as toward that which sustains me from moment to moment in my present being.

Is not that outer activity then essentially *creative* in its constant action (as probably also in its original action) — creative of *me?* My dependence upon Nature, my momentary submission to its independent, obstinate, objective decision of what Fact and Truth shall be, both in principle and in detail: — is not this a finding of my own mind? It is here, in this momentary (as well as permanent) creation of my Self that I begin, I say, to find Nature taking on the aspect of an Other Mind.

For if the full-fledged otherness of that which is thus over against me cannot be doubted, neither can it be doubted that this which so immediately becomes Self, makes Self, is already a Self even in its otherness, — namely, an Other Self. We find the weakness of natural Realism when we consider whether a physical experience so organically and actively concerned in mind-existence and mind-process could exist also, and fully itself, apart from such active relations. If only I were independent of Nature, I might think Nature independent of Self. But since Nature *obstinate* is Nature *creative*, and creative of mind; since my deepest roots and those of all co-experiencing mind are in her deepest objectivity, I cannot clear Nature of *selfhood*, though I can well clear her of my own self or of any other particular self.

Space, here, is my space, — also everybody's space; and is known as such. Energy is everybody's energy: Nature as a whole is everybody's Nature. Even now, space, and the rest, are integral parts of everybody's mind — *are idea and experience at the same time;* are the activity of each finite thinker, — but an activity held empirically in place by the active decisiveness of Outer Reality. You and I vanish, and leave space behind — leave thereby so much of our mind behind, and more. Leave behind necessary elements in our continuity, individuality, unity, even character. Leave them behind in what condition? In the same condition in which we have always known them: as something communicated by an Other Mind, and meant by an Other Mind. For in immediately experiencing my Self as limited and determined (in the ways described) by an Absolute Other, I am experiencing that Other as Other Mind. As space is found limited by no other than *more space*, so Self is found limited and individualized by no other than Other Selfhood.

This is our fundamental social experience. And I wish to make it clear that this experience is not an inference, but an immediate experience. As simply as Nature presents itself as objective, just so simply and directly is the Other Mind present to me in that objectivity, as its actual meaning. I do not first know my physical world as a world of *objects* and then as a world of *shared* objects: it is through a prior recognition of the presence of Other Mind that my physical experience acquires objectivity at all.[1] The objectivity of Nature

[1] Nothing is gained in differentiating physical objects from psychical objects by pointing out (as is commonly attempted) that the psychical objects are for one only, whereas the physical objects are *also* objects for another. This simply doubles the mystery. I have now to understand how these physical things can be objects for both of us at once, obstinate to both of us, and not to one only: the nature of objectivity itself with its capacity of being equally objective to two souls, or even to an infinite number, is not in the least illumined. There is rather the additional mystery how I know (as it seems I do immediately know by considering the physical object alone) that it can be objective to others as well as to myself. Are these objects, then, labelled "common," while the others are without such labels? have they about them some physical mark which points the mind to an other knower? Hardly this. The only way in which I can know an object to be common is by catching it in the act of being common, that is, by knowing it as known by other mind. The social experience must have a prior and original recognizableness. And this recognition of other mind than my own is a simultaneous recognition of those aspects of experience which such mind needs for the maintenance of its intercourse with me, without loss of its own separateness of career.

is its community, not two facts but one: but the *whole* truth of this one fact (which whole I do not see unless I note what I am thinking *with*) — the whole of this fact is *community*.

Here then is the point in which natural Realism is both right and wrong. That which limits and opposes the Self, setting bounds to our expectations, offering instead of our desire its *I am*, is indeed Not-self. That outer individuality is first — our own follows. That outer world asserts itself upon me, and creates me; even my "forms of apperception," my space, my time, I accept from it and reissue — even here I am empirical first and creative afterward. In so far natural Realism is right. But it is just because the empirical factors of experience extend thus through my whole selfhood that this Not-myself is known in positive terms as Other-self.

In failing to penetrate through the blank otherness of Nature to the spirit that is its support, natural Realism falls short of the truth.[1] Idealism corrects this

[1] In the physical experience of outer reality Kant descried the point at which subjective idealism is broken: in Wahrnehmung (physical perception) he found the active effect of the unknown Thing-in-itself. At this point he thought that experience reaches an unusual pitch of outwardness — reaching, indeed, beyond the Self, achieving the impossible. What is the evidence of this feat? It is that the self here discovers itself in process of being made; finds the source of those individual characters of itself, which since they define itself cannot be *from* itself. But Kant did not note that in thus viewing itself as a particular Self, the Ego is accomplishing the standpoint of another (and universal) Self; and that this standpoint is a permanent part of its own being. Hence he misread the relation between the active non-ego and the ego in the process of physical experience. For *causality* (on his own showing) it is not; but *communication* it may well be, — and self-communication, which is *creation*.

For more explicit discussion of this matter, see the explanatory essay, "The Knowledge of Independent Reality."

error; and in correcting this error, falls as a rule into another — it refers the experience of nature to a spirit, which turns out to be only the solitary finite self. The logic even of 'absolute idealism' usually fails here, as Professor Howison has well shown.[1] The corrective of both this natural realism and this solitary idealism must be found, not by changing the venue of the question to the moral consciousness, but by an appeal from natural realism to a *realism of social experience.*

If, then, I wish in simplest fashion to find my fundamental social experience, let me consider that feature of experience which I call the independence, or objectivity, of the physical world about me. Let me consider that until it is disabused of its finality, and seen to be open to challenge; let me consider it until I see that in this knowledge (that the objectivity there has a further account to give) I am already in present experience of that Other Mind which in Nature communicates itself to me. The only way to a *realism of social experience* is through a Non-realism in regard to the surface of Nature. What we reach is a super-natural Realism, or a Social Realism, or more truly a Realism of the Absolute — not far removed from Absolute Idealism.

[1] The Conception of God, Royce, Le Conte, Howison, Mezes, page 104, etc.

CHAPTER XXI

THE GOD OF NATURE AND THE KNOWLEDGE OF MAN

BUT finally, who and what is this Subject, to which we have been referring in such vague terms as the Other, the fundamental social object?

It cannot be identified with any particular other personality such as these with whom I enter into conversation and reach various stages of acquaintance and concrete intercourse. For I recognize them as being co-dependent with me upon this same Other Mind revealed in Nature. In this intercourse with them there are beginnings and endings; and the entrance of any one of them into my life is relatively speaking an accident, making unquestionable historical difference in that general fund of idea with which I regard Nature, but not determining the character of any fact of Nature such as he and I might be called upon to give common witness to.

Further, my knowledge of any such individual person is uncertain, with varying grades of uncertainty. I am liable to mistake at many points in interpreting his thoughts and experiences; I may be mistaken in his identity; I may even be mistaken in judgment whether a conscious subject is there — whether any given physical object is a body to an Other Mind. I never know how much of my physical world is at any time officiating as *body*, and how much is only *environment*. I have no absolute assurance of these minds severally. It is true that on occasion I may be surer of the reality of a given fellow man than I am of my own: I may call upon my friend to assure me of my own sanity, by acknowledging as real for him also an object of mine which I fear may be an hallucination. But I am more likely to judge *his* sanity by his assent to the reality of objects which apart from him I regard as unquestionably real. I am not sure of these fellow minds severally.

But the doubts to which my experience of individual persons is liable must diminish when I consider them not separately but together. The reality which I can question in the detached person becomes substantial in groups of persons, in my total historical context, in collective humanity. The uncertainty which holds against any one, can hardly hold against the whole. May not this fundamental Other Mind of which we are in search be simply my total world of Others in its collective bearing upon me?

Such a world of other spirits does not come and go; it was before me, and shall be after me. Out of such fellow beings and the world which they have built up, I come; my creation is theirs; and to such, having myself shared in creation, I hand on the same world to be perpetuated as humanity's world. Might not Nature itself be conceived as an expression of the common will of such an over-individual or composite entity? Through this physical community our developing intercourse is built up; through it, humanity persists in its own being, and communicates being, from generation to generation. Is it not this common will of mankind, or of collective spirit generally, of which in Nature I become aware?

There are not wanting observable facts of our social consciousness which support such a conjecture. Frequent intercourse with fellow men does much to determine the stability of physical experience in comparison with the world of imagination. The hermit, the lonely sheep-driver, is likely to succumb to his illusions, living with them in preference to the world which we of the majority call real.

The explorer, the polar traveller, the man in solitary confinement, find the feeling of unreality a more common visitor than we do and threatening to become a permanent companion. The "established character" of Nature is sharpest where men are thickest, is clearly some function of the volume of our empirical conversation: it gives the impression of being a consensus effect.

But there are several reasons why we cannot accept this theory of the Other. One is that any such consensus implies a prior unity; we communicate because we are already one, — a proposition which is as valid for an indefinite number of communicators as it is for any two, and as valid for present humanity and past humanity as for any two contemporaries. The entire individuality and permanence of Nature implies a corresponding individual permanence in the Subject whose communicated being this Nature is. Upon such ultimate unity of substance the unity of each finite self is based.

Further, that is no genuine social experience which is not *known as such* by the participants. Two beings, we have said, can come into communication only if they already have some point in common: but if the beings are *conscious* beings, and their communication is to be conscious communication, we may specify our proposition thus, That two conscious beings can communicate only if they already have some *known* point in common, some object known by each as object to both. If I have any genuine social experience at all, then at some point I do actually know the Other Mind *in its knowing* — beyond any doubt or shifting of identity; beyond any possibility of error in the intentional character of the experience — that is, in the address of the communication *to me.* This seems a great deal to claim of the experience of Other Mind in Nature; but I cannot escape these conclusions. And I see clearly that there is in no assembly of fellow minds any conscious reference of Nature to me; as I see that I have no conscious part in presenting my world of objects to them. It is useless to appeal to subconscious activity, for an activity that is unintended is not my own.

In short, we are all, whether singly or collectively, *empirical* knowers of Nature. But if there are none but empirical knowers in the world there is no social experience. I am only in presence of an Other Mind when I have pressed through the region of my passivity, and turning its corner, have come upon that which is there actively and intentionally creating me.

Even were there, in addition to all visible passive knowers in the world, one all-comprehensive passive knower, we should be no nearer a conscious unity. For unless he too could pierce the obstinacy and self-assertiveness of the world confronting him, he would still be, so far as his consciousness is concerned, a self-enclosed being, and would be obliged as we are to work through the problem of that dependence to a knowledge of that Other on which he depends. There is no sociality for any knower, so we now discover, until the objectivity of Nature wins its further meaning, and is found as an intentional communication of a Self *wholly active.*

It may be that the more we press the conclusions of our position, the less we shall be able to recognize in any concrete characters of our own experience, the experience here described. We have made all social experience depend upon a conscious knowledge in experience of a being, who in scope and power might well be identified with God. We have been led by the successive requirements of our logic to the position that our first and fundamental social experience is an experience of God. Where in our continuous current consciousness do we recognize any such element as this?

Conspicuous in experience such knowledge certainly is not; and as permanent knowledge, with which we forever begin, and *with* which we forever think our world, we shall not expect it to be conspicuous. It will be present for the most part in no other form than as the abiding sense of what stability and certainty we have, as we move about among men and things; it will be present for the most part just as our own force of self-assertion and *self-confidence* is present, that force by which we individually will "to maintain ourselves in being" in a world known, by what assurance we do not ordinarily enquire, to be no hostile, nor ultimately alien, thing. It will be present chiefly in my persistent *sense of reality* in that with which I am dealing, and in those fellow minds with whom I converse. It will be present in that sense of reality also in its active aspect; in my own degree of what we have called "objectivity of mind," my disposition to take experience with full *empirical openness*, breast-forwardly, oriented by the universal or common eye which the fundamental God-consciousness gives me. In whatever rigid scientific acceptance of fact I may accomplish, I detect the degree of this experience. And whatever consciousness I may have of *responsibility* and *dependence* are workings of the same thing: if I am conscious of obligation closely conjoined with the simple fact of my existence; if I know that what creativity I have and must have is built upon a continuous docility; in thus knowing I am conscious though but indistinctly of my Absolute Other.

Inseparable from self-consciousness is this experience, and discernible in all the dimensions and assertions of self-consciousness. God is known as that of which I am primarily certain; and being certain, am certain of self and of my world of men and men's objects. I shall always be more certain *that* God is, than *what* he is: it is the age-long problem of religion to bring to light the deeper characters of this fundamental experience. But the starting point of this development (which we shall have occasion to trace in some rough way) is no mere That Which, without predicates. Substance is known as Subject: reality from the beginning is known as God. The idea of God is not an attribute which in the course of experience I come to attach to my original whole-idea: the unity of my world which makes it from the beginning a whole, knowable in simplicity, is the unity of other Selfhood.

God then is immediately known, and permanently known, as the Other Mind which in creating Nature is also creating me. Of this knowledge nothing can despoil us; this knowledge has never been wanting to the self-knowing mind of man.

Given this original certainty in social experience, the uncertainty and experimentation in the knowledge of Other Minds generally can be faced with some confidence; no failures here can require a "retreat into the subject"; I can never whether by the logic of my own defective social practice or reflection be shut in to myself alone, a monad without windows. But how do I find my fellow men at all? I have God; them I have not.

I answer that here those criteria of the presence of other minds which at first we thought could not give us what we required, because they presupposed the *idea* of an Other Mind, now have conferred on them the breath of life. The idea is in our possession; with this key all metaphors of mind and mind-relations in Nature become a living language. I am in possession of the net which being hung out in experience will gather in what "supplementation of my own fragmentary meanings," what response to my questions, may be discoverable there. I have what Fichte calls the concept of a concept in its outward appearance. My current social experience, the finding of any fellow finite mind, is *an application* of my prior idea of an Other; in a sense, an application of my idea of God. *It is through the knowledge of God that I am able to know men;*

not first through the knowledge of men that I am able to know or imagine God.

And further, in them I find something which I require in order to make that consciousness of companionship wholly actual to me. I have some need to reproduce the relation to God in a visible relationship *within* God's world. Why I must try to make that central companionship more tangible and physical I do not here enquire; but in that need, whatever it is, I may find an inkling of God's own motive in creating just such a sphere of things as this visible Nature-field, in which spirits wander as shapes embedded.

Nor is this applying of the God-idea to these shapes wholly unliteral. For God is not apart from what he has created. We have found God only in the relation of otherness and objectivity. God is other-than-me; also other-than-my-fellow-Others. We have deliberately dwelt upon the absolute objectivity of God; or rather, have chosen to come to the recognition of God in the absolute object of knowledge. But we have not been unmindful of the truth that Self includes, and is with, its objects, in so far as it comprehends them, or is creating them. God, then, does actually include me, in so far as I am dependent upon him; does likewise include those fellow Others, in so far as they also are his created work.

Nature is not, as I experience it, a consensus effect, due to the wills of my fellow finite spirits, conscious or sub-conscious: but I dare not say that their presence has no part in making Nature what it is, even to my experience. For Nature, we may say, is the region where this system of minds does actually *coalesce.*

Space does not reside in me, nor in any mind; but in all minds at once. In space and time and their contents we have not merely common *objects*, we have a region of literal common Mind. It is not that we are each so constructed after a common pattern called Human Nature, with certain a priori ideas or forms of arranging experience, that given certain stimuli at our nerve ends we all do, as a fact, turn out the same world, each in his own private copy. I do not in my growth make up a new space and a new causal system for myself. I *adopt* them. Space and Nature are numerically one, and I by my community with Other Mind, am born inheritor of that one identical object. In my experience of Space and Nature I am experiencing identically all that Other Mind which is contemplating that same object; in so far, I have an infallible element in my knowledge of my finite comrades, as well as in my knowledge of God.

Existence of conscious beings begins, then, if we are right, with intimate sociality and dependence; growth gives to each conscious being powers of independent world-building and creativity generally. This present existence, we say, is an apprenticeship in creativity. At the same time (and as part of the same fact) we acquire the power of solitude, jutting out into the alone — alone perhaps even with reference to God. Such a monism as this of ours is rather more favorable to personal freedom and enterprise than such pluralisms as have usually been defined. For *we do not begin as solitary beings and then acquire community: we begin as social products, and acquire the arts of solitude* —

a direction of progress more hopeful for variety and origination than a progress in the reverse direction.

In applying the name of God to the Other Mind which in sustaining physical experience does continually create and communicate itself to us, we have gone indeed beyond our warrant. We have not here the conception of God in its fulness. But we have its groundwork. We have what must justify the animism of our ancestors, — the inevitable animism of all mankind; for the finding of spirit in Nature is but the finding of the truth as continuously experienced.

If the difficult problem, what parts of Nature are to be regarded as body of Spirit, and what only as environment, is not early solved; if the idea of Other Mind at first is applied too indiscriminately; that is all such work as experience may well take time to perfect. Nature, we find, is the mediator of God, par excellence. As for our fellow beings, they are first vessels, recipient of the meaning already established; and then secondarily mediators, as through them the idea of God receives further definition and content. Meager as the glimpse of Deity may be which is opened through the humble channel of the experience of physical Nature, even through sensation, it is sufficient to initiate that long course of the knowledge of God in which mankind has found its highest ambition. But before glancing at the outline of that growing knowledge I shall ask in the next chapter to dwell still longer among these severe questions of truth and experience, enquiring by what other ways men have tried to secure conscious certainty of the existence (if not of the presence) of their God.

CHAPTER XXII

THE ONTOLOGICAL ARGUMENT FOR THE EXISTENCE OF GOD

IN our search for other Mind we came upon the experience of God, as by surprise. We were looking for man, and we found God. We discovered that our fellow Mind can not be touched, except through first touching God; that the one point in which we do break through to unmistakable knowledge of spirit not ourself is here, in the presence to experience of the Absolute as Other Mind. Which one point being given, all the rest of social experience with its endless experimentation, trial, error, and infinite acquired skill, can follow.

We have first found God as a God of physical Nature, a God through Nature creating ourselves. And herein lies that *literalness* of the God-idea which we have thought necessary for religion. For Nature is the home of literalness. To be literal means to be real in the same definite and particular fashion that we surmise in sensation, and realize in the precise work of physical science. Sensation embodies for us much of what we conceive all reality ought to be in definiteness and vivid individuality. Nature has its decisive yea or nay for every question that can be put to it. We would not lose these qualities from our religious consciousness. And we do not lose them if we can interpret the whole individuality of Nature as one with the individuality of God in its communicated form.

Doubtless we feel in this conception at once the defects of literalness also, — a certain obnoxious and humdrum levelling of religion to the status of fact. This is a fault of emphasis: it is the literal that has been by necessity uppermost in our discussion, but literalness, of course, does not tell the whole story of any spirit's existence. It is merely an attribute which, among the rest, we should sorely miss if it were absent. It is not customary, I know, to seek for God at the level of sensation: that is one reason why it has seemed to me important to have found him there. Sensation may supply, as it were, a missing dimension to our thought of God. God must now be to us not less real and present than Nature, not less definitively here and now than these impressive objective Facts.

We have no reason to think slightingly of sensation, or to refer to it as the lowest level of our being. It marks, in many ways, the line of *our* limitation; line of our passivity and dependence; line oftentimes of intellectual and moral defeat; a region which self and idea fail to penetrate; but by that same sign containing the soil and air of the future. The line of our limitation may be, if we will, the line where we meet God. Where should we more expect to meet him?

We have not been expressly undertaking a proof of the existence of God. But in finding God as a necessary object of experience, have we not, in a way sufficient and decisive, proved his existence? What other final proof can we have that any being exists than to find, or *demonstrate*, that Being in experience? For my power of recognizing existence is summed up in the word experience.

Still, this again has not been the usual procedure of those who have tried to reach conscious assurance that there is a God. Proving God has usually meant reasoning *away* to God, by making speculative connections between the world that now is and its unseen author or destiny. And if we believe with Kant, and with many another, that God is not to be found in experience, there are none but such speculative connections to be made. We have thought, however, that experience is essentially metaphysical, — the place in which we meet Reality; in experience we are "taught," our errors are corrected, our true ideas confirmed, by what else than by Reality? In common action we are dealing with the passing, — and with the Absolute: and it is for us to recognize that Absolute as Spirit. The course of discovery which leads to that recognition — this will be our interpretation of the process of "proof" of God's existence.

Such proof is but a clearing of the mind, so that experience may be recognized for what it is: it is a banishing of illusions, a consideration of what we may expect to find, and could wish to find; and a noting that this wish of ours corresponds to experience as we have it. Proof, in this sense, does but follow the route of prayer, — which also is a "lifting of the mind to God"; not in any sense equivalent to prayer, but making evident that filament of wholly objective relatedness between man and God which (as a minimal core of community) must lie at the center of all ventures toward further and moral relationship.

What such proof assumes is simply that God and the world do stand in permanent organic relationship, and that the traces of this relationship cannot be lacking in experience. Proof, in this sense, is a necessary concern of religion; whose function is to make the way to God plain to all men, to escape from the accidental and the fortuitous, to establish universal and conscious intercourse between the human and the divine. Proof in set terms has never been the work of religion; for religion knows how to convey proof, or demonstration, in the form of deeds. Religion practically and personally points men to God; let philosophy give men the conscious possession and certainty of this which religion has in deed established. The proof of God, we may say, is the *good faith* of man with regard to religion. It is not a thing with which religion can dispense; nor has religion ever been willing to forgo it.

If proof, then, is the finding of the way to God from where one at any time consciously stands, the proofs may be as many as the standpoints are many. But in so far as we can describe in general terms the conscious situation of all men, there is but one way to God, and one proof. We shall attempt to make clear in this chapter the nature of that proof in the barest possible sketch,—and after all is there not some keen and proper satisfaction in the utmost bareness of statement, when a truth has once been grasped as truth?

Nature appears to men as their most general bond of community. Nature also appears as existence *par excellence.* When we lose sight of God, Nature becomes our standard of reality. If we have a God we should like to make his existence as sure as *that!* Hence it is that most attempts at proof of God have begun with Nature, and have tried to make his existence secure by showing him in some valid connection with this world, such as that of cause to the world as effect. God as cause of the world would be real even as the world is real. The so-called cosmological argument follows this line of connection, and finds that the world has a single conscious cause, itself uncaused, who is God.

If we wish to be assured that this cause is not only a voluntary cause but a benevolent one as well, we make a premise of the *good* which as experienced in the world is our natural type of goodness; and we find that the intender of this is good even as the result is good.

But by these means we do not find God. If we could prove a first and conscious cause, still we could prove only such cause as is equivalent to his effect; we could prove only such goodness as is equivalent to this mixture of goodness and evil that we here find. A very limited Being would this be, a God who is only as great as his world, only as good, and finally *only as real.*

By such ways we can only reach a being in whom the qualities of experience are refunded, without change or heightening. But in such case, we may as well believe in the world as we find it; and proceed with our work of mastering it, without reference to God.

Such proofs are not wholly true to the spirit of religion; for historically men have lifted their minds to God rather because the world is unsatisfactory, than because it satisfies. We wish a God who is greater than the world, also better than the world as found, and also more real.

And such more perfect being is what these proofs have in spirit sought: for in referring the world to a conscious Will, they have meant to imply that Will is greater than Nature; and in making the world dependent upon a divine Purpose they have intended to show that the Good is more real than the evil, and will vindicate itself. But clearly no such results can be gained by taking Nature as a standard and moving toward God by relations of causality or purpose: these relations can rise no higher than their source. It is the denial of that assumed starting-point that is the intellectual heart of religion.

On the other hand, we cannot dispense with the world as a point of beginning for the reasons given. What other way, then, can be found of relating this world to God? Follow the history of religion. Observe the Mind dissatisfied with its world. Note the criticism which it makes of Nature, as less than self-sufficient, less than all-good, less than real. And note that of a sudden it has claimed to possess the self-sufficient, the good, the real. What has occurred to the mind of man?

It may seem as though that with which man had been criticizing his experience, namely, his idea of a better and more real, had in a moment taken on objective shape to him. His dissatisfaction with his world has implied a conception of a world not thus defective, and this conception has been set up as substantial fact, in his idea of God. He has turned his idea into a reality; or he has instinctively assigned a reality to his idea, yet without blurring the features of his actual world. It is *some leap from idea to reality* that constitutes the essential historic movement of the mind to God.

Now it is just this leap from idea to reality that distinguishes an ancient proof of God's existence; a proof which has become known as the "ontological argument," the argument which assigns a real or ontological value to an idea. I have an idea of God: therefore God exists.

In general, the circumstance that I have an idea of an object is the emptiest of reasons for supposing that object to exist. Whatever force such reasoning can have must depend on some peculiarities of the idea of God, not found in ideas or ideals generally. It must be shown, as we tried to show of the idea of Other Mind, that this idea has something unique about it which forbids the supposition that it is a "mere idea." This, with various degrees of success, have the thinkers who resort to the ontological argument — from Augustine and Anselm to Hegel and Royce — tried to do. It is always with some incredulity that we meet the assertion that any idea of ours carries with it its own guarantee of reality. Yet this same ontological argument is the only one which is wholly faithful to the history, the anthropology, of religion. It is the only proof of God.

Although an idea which should carry on its face an assurance of reality must have something unique about it, we are not without analogies which may help to interpret this extraordinary type of argument. The idea of God is not the only one of our ideas which seems to convey an assurance of objectivity. My idea of *space*, for example, I incline to regard as real. Of my idea of *causality*, I can hardly think that it is an idea only, a form of relating events without an objective counterpart. So also with the beauty of things, or their goodness; I know that these are ideas of mine, and yet as I regard these qualities valid for other viewers of the same objects, I attribute these qualities to the objects. Instinctively also we project beyond ourselves, or repudiate in some way as not our own, whatever in idea is new, whatever is sublime and holy, whatever is obligatory, whatever strikes me with a consciousness of my self as a lesser thing. Even self-consciousness seems to come, at times, as a revelation from beyond myself. It is not without precedent, then, that an idea should convey with itself some apparent title to reality: it is not impossible that some idea, as perchance the idea of God, should be able to make this title good.

Let us examine this movement of thought more nearly. Nature must early have appeared to man as somewhat less than real — else those early speculations with regard to a creator or maker would hardly have occurred to him. At the root of all these awkward conceptions regarding clay-shaping or egg-laying or spewing or magic-word-pronouncing deities lies an uneasy persuasion that the things of physical existence are subject to something; and to something of the quality of human spirit. If Nature ever wore to early man that aspect which seems primary to us — the aspect of *self-sufficiency*, it must have gone hand in hand with a quite contrary aspect — that of being *illusory*, also possible to us, though with some effort.

We may find that illusory aspect by such considerations as these: The appearance of self-sufficiency belongs not more to Nature as a whole than to each thing in Nature. By that same view which shows us Nature as *there* in its own right, is also each thing there in its own right. But with regard to the several things in Nature we know that this appearance is not true. The apparent self-sufficiency of single things if real would make the World an aggregate in which every thing went its own way without regard to another: self-sufficiency of the parts is equivalent to *accidentality*. Each thing is in reality infinitely dependent on all the rest. But with the banishment of self-sufficiency in the parts, there is no retaining of it in the Whole: there is nothing in which this infinite dependence of part on part comes to rest, unless I conceive the whole thing as *dependent on my Self*, dream-fashion,—deriving its reality, so to speak, from the center outward, rather than from inaccessible infinitely distant world-borders and beginnings inward. The world is real I now say simply *as my experience*—a not-unheard-of point of view. The self-sufficient world of Nature has suddenly become an *illusion*.

Yet I cannot rest here; because I know that I am not the source of the reality of Nature. True, if I am not real, nothing is real: something in my conception of reality starts from me; and all my objects become real, as by infection from that. But true it is, likewise, that unless Nature is real, nothing is real: something in my conception of reality is borne in upon me from beyond. I am real, in part, by virtue of what is not-myself. The real must partake of the qualities of myself and of Nature; and must be other than either.

Through this experience of cognitive restlessness (or "dialectic") early man, to whom the illusory side of

Nature was more familiar probably than to us, may have passed in his own readier way; he finds as his resting place the real as Creative Spirit. Nature settles into its third stage of regard: it is neither self-sufficient nor illusory; it has *derivative* reality. As over against me, it is real; as over against the Creative Spirit, it is not real. But how is this conception hit upon? May it be that this thought of Nature as dependent on Spirit is some quick embodiment of an elusive but genuine experience? This idea of a creator does indeed quickly float away from any experience it may have sprung from; becoming promptly materialized and set in the sky as part of the world-created — removed from that World, yet all too much involved in it. Yet may it be that *this idea* is one which must have reality?

Must it not be so? For one thing I cannot by any means escape: namely, that reality itself is present to me in experience; and all of this process of judging this and that thing to be unreal or less than real is made possible simply by the grasp of that reality which at any moment I have. My negations are made possible by my one secure position; and as my hold on reality is variable, so my ability to see through the various pretenders-to-reality to reality itself will vary. Nature can only appear to me as illusory in some moment of unusual clearness of perception; for ordinarily the pretence of nature to be self-sufficient is a harmless and even useful simplification of my view. So if my own existence is recognized by me in some moment as a partial and dependent existence, that recognition is a moment of "illumination," in which the relation of my self to what is beyond my self becomes presently distinct: and in grasping this relation, I am catching some fleeting glimpse of the *terms* between which the relation exists. I am experiencing that which is beyond myself in no wise differently than in that moment I am experiencing myself: and my judgment of dependence is made possible by a positive and present knowledge of that upon which I depend.

If, then, I discover that my world of nature and self, taken severally or together, falls short of reality, this discovery is due to what I know of reality — not abstractly, but in experience. If I judge this system of nature-and-self to be non-self-sufficient, it is by a knowledge of the self-sufficient; if I condemn, it is by virtue of something in my possession not subject to condemnation; if I criticize and correct, it is by comparison with or reference to some present object not subject to criticism and correction. When I perceive myself in this curious relation to the world of physical facts — superior and not superior, creative and unable to create — that play of unrest is due to, and is defining, a simultaneous perception of the object to which this unrest does not apply. The positive content which I give to that absolute object is a report of experience; whatever idea I make of it is an idea derived nowhere but from that experience. If I am able to frame a tenable conception of nature in dependence upon a creative spirit not myself, that conception is true; for my idea can set me outside of nature only as in experience I have already broken away from the spell of the natural world. In whatever sense, then, I am able to conceive nature as dependent upon spirit, in that sense nature is dependent upon spirit. This idea carries its reality with it.

It is impossible that my idea should be a "mere" idea, for it is only possible for me to take this standpoint, external to nature and myself, in idea in so far as I do at the same time take it in experience also. And that this experience of a more valid reality than that of nature is truly described as an experience of other mind, we have in our previous chapter sufficiently dwelt upon. The ontological argument may be regarded as a logical epitome of what we there, in our own independent research, came upon.[1] The ontological argument, in its true form, is a report of experience.

If we wished, in briefest compass, to state the antithesis between the ontological argument and other arguments for the existence of a God, we might put the situation thus:

These other arguments reason that *because the world is, God is.* The ontological argument reasons that *because the world is not, God is.* It is not from the world as a stable premise that we can proceed to God as a conclusion: it is rather when the world ceases to satisfy us as a premise, and appears as a conclusion from something more substantial, that we find God — proceeding then from the world as a conclusion to God as a premise. We have no other premise to begin with: no proof of God can be deductive. It is because neither my world nor myself can serve as a foundation for thought and action that I must grope for a deeper foundation.

[1] Here the abstract argument of a former part of the book (ch. xii) maintaining the need of religion for basis in an independent reality, begins to receive its concrete filling. I may again refer the reader for further illustration of this logical situation to the appended essay on "The Knowledge of Independent Reality."

And what I learn in this groping is, that my consciousness of those defects will reveal, though in faintest degree, the positive object which is free therefrom. It is because we cannot infer from nature to God along causal or other natural lines, and only because of this, that the idea of God implies existence.

It is not every historical form of the ontological argument that has expressed this experience: and not every form of it appears to me valid. It does not seem to me that any abstract idea of an "all-perfect being" must necessarily be real. Nor does it seem to me that we are justified in inferring from any idea to its reality unless that reality can be present to the idea in experience. No form of the argument can be valid which finds God at the level of thought only, and not at the level of sensation. We are only justified in attributing reality to an idea if reality is already present in the discovery of the idea. When in our search for reality we fix attention upon Nature, it is because we already know that whatever reality is, it cannot be out of connection with that world of Nature-experience: and when we judge Nature unreal, it is only as we discover at the same time in concrete way how Nature is related to the Real. I can infer from that idea by which I criticize Nature to the reality of that idea only because I know Nature (and Self) to contain some characters of reality that cannot be omitted, or left behind. My real must already be given, in order that my idea may be found real. The true idea of God is not one which can leave out either Nature or myself; if my idea of God is real, it is real in experience. Hence I have preferred to state the argument not thus: I have an idea of God, therefore God exists. But rather thus: I have an idea of God, therefore I have an experience of God.

Reality can only be proved by the ontological argument; and conversely, the ontological argument can only be applied to reality. But in so far as reality dwells in Self, or Other Mind, or Nature, an ontological argument may be stated in proof of their existence. Thus, the Cartesian certitude may with greater validity be put into this form:

I think myself, therefore I exist; or

I have an idea of Self, Self exists.

For in thinking myself I find myself in experience and thus in living relation to that reality which experience presents. So may it be with Nature:

I have an idea of physical Nature, Nature exists.

That is, in whatever sense I conceive Nature, in that sense physical nature is real. Idealism has wavered much in its judgment regarding the reality of Nature, and of "material substance." It has said that we have no idea of matter; and again it has said that matter does not exist, which implies that we have an idea of it. Some meaning, however, we do attribute to the word matter; and without enquiring what that definable meaning may be, we may say in advance that whatever idea is framable corresponds to reality as experienced. We need not fear that this realism of Nature will detach Nature from God; though if we could think it so detached it would doubtless so exist. For of independence also, in whatever sense I can think the independence of beings, in that sense independence obtains between them. That which is most independent of me, namely the Other Mind, has been the first object of our ontological findings. The object of certain knowledge has this threefold structure, Self, Nature, and Other Mind; and God, the appropriate object of ontological proof, includes these three.

And is not, after all, this same ancient ontological argument the great and timely necessity for man in all his thinking? That which permanently threatens all our thinking is the damning commentary, "mere thought"—our own commentary on our own work, especially upon our own religion. Escape from illusion is what we require, whether in dealing with God or man or nature; escape from phantasmal intercourse, from subjective prisons from whose walls words and prayers rebound without outer effect. *Idea* we must have if we think; but an adequate realism for our idea we must also have. We shall never be too fully assured that our idea has reached beyond ourself, and has its ground in that which is not ourself.

Any reflection that can infallibly break the walls of the Self, opens up at once an infinite World-field. Set a second to my One, and I have given all the numbers. A single point outside the circle of "*Bewusstseins-immanenz*," and I am free to open myself to all reality and to all men. It is this point that the ontological argument aims to put into our possession; the reflection which this argument embodies is the only, and wholly simple, defence against our besetting subjectivity. "Bethink thyself of the ground whereon thou standest. *By what idea* hast thou judged thy thought to be illusion, and mere subjectivity? Is it not by an idea of something wholly actual and immediate? Is not that Reality thy own present possession?"

This present actuality of experience, "pure experience," finds me in living relation with that which is most utterly not-myself. Here, in the immediate, is my absolute escape from immediacy. Here in the given present is my escape from myself, my window opening upon infinity, my exit into God. Religion thus becomes the concrete bond between men; for he who has consciously found his way to God, has found his way to man also.

Thus it is that idea may give back the reality of which idea is forever robbing us; for while idea is the greatest enemy of the actual, it is only through idea that idea can be held firmly to its compelling and controlling object, the real as found in experience.

CHAPTER XXIII

DEVELOPMENT OF THE KNOWLEDGE OF GOD

MAN knows well that he is not alone: he does not so well know in what companionship he is. The knowledge of the presence of spirit beyond self is no conjecture; nor does this social experience ever *arise*. Man's world is from the first a living world, even a divine world; and primitive animism is in so far no mere theory, but a report of certain and intimate experience. There are no dead things in that early world of swarming spirits.

But this, we think, is at once its glory and its chief defect. The idea of Other Mind is applied too indiscriminately, and in too petty a fashion. The conception of the inanimate is one we have had to work for. The growth of social intelligence is in the direction of *clearing away* the exuberance of *animæ*, of charting certain large tracts of Nature which we may regard as uninhabited, and hence subject to unlimited remorseless exploitation. We require — not so much for free movement as for free-hearted movement — a *belief in the dead:* we need to know Nature as very largely *environment*, and very little body-of-Mind; we need to regard the phenomena of physical fact for the most part as essentially the world of objects, of things intended rather than of intentions, mine of meanings to be dug out, veil of osmosis between humanity and Creative Spirit generally—having no intrinsic claim on deference for its own sake.

We find it even now hard enough to decide, as we pass down the scale of organisms and therefrom into the inorganic world, where animation ceases—or whether it ceases. Even of such conquests as we have made, our sense of continuity—and doctrines of panpsychism—are willing to deprive us. It is hard to conceive that the livingness of micro-organisms is to be traced backward, not to the atoms and molecules which have been synthesized in their protoplasm,[1] but to the whole living world itself. Yet this way lies progress. Not all the world is body; not every unit our fancy outlines as One Thing is the metaphor of an individual spirit. Our animistic world must be clarified, and its life concentrated in more definite foci; gaining at once in meaning and in character.

This is, I suppose, the sense of the advance by which man gets himself *gods* in place of spirits only. Spirits are mere flashes of divine life breaking out here and there, spot-wise, in Nature and in human event, as we have seen. They float with the stream of event, pass with the event, are numerous as the events are numerous, have no persistent individuality, are remembered only as a shock or an excitement is remembered, take altogether the character of the historic medium in which they are found. There are no *gods* here. Nor can there be gods until man in some way begins to think. He must get his world into more general unities by classifying and speculating: he must see *similarities* in the forces of light and storm and sea, in the life-producing

[1] See for example Verworn, *Protistenstudien.*

agencies of plant and animal and man; and, perhaps with the division of labor in his own societies, he must conceive the *functions* of the spirits, and assign a recurring though intermittent function (healing, or luck of chase, or boundary-protection, or sending of sons) to a special, or at least continuous, spiritual agency. Thus arise functional deities, and causal deities, and deities presiding over the three or four great spheres of Nature, heaven, earth, sky, water; and even deities of *species*—as of tree-life in general or of fox-life or of eagle-life, deities which pass from one fox or eagle to another on the death or sacrifice of the one, from the whole of a field to its last sheaf as the harvesting progresses, and then—reappear next year in the next crop. All these take the place of the fitful spirits of particular objects and events, not without aid from all the agencies of man's growing culture which are fostering this thinking process; and man finds himself supplied with *gods*.

But there is one other character of a god, lacking to spirits, beside these of continuous individuality, wide scope, and definite function or group of functions. The god is *addressed:* men use toward the god the vocative case; use "Thou" and not only "It" or "He." The god having a continuous character may also support a definite relationship, even an institution of intercourse In gaining a more general scope, the god has loosened his attachment to particular physical objects; but he never completely detaches himself from the tangible: he resides, perhaps voluntarily, in some special place or thing—and this relic and clue to the god, seems to serve as the means of approach, physical and mental.

Through his holy place, his temple, his pillar, his image, his altar, his ark, the spirit becomes an *historic god*, worshipable by an historic people in definite institutional ways.

Herewith the way is opened for a new *method* of progress in divine knowledge,—the method of experiment: the god's dealings with his worshippers become matter of record in tradition: and slow as men are to learn new things about deity, or to give up old ones, there is a wholly verifiable process of elimination and survival of ideas about God, predicates of God, in religions which have attained the historic stage. With the acquisition of a god in place of a spirit, the knowledge of God becomes a matter of tribal, national, racial experience.

It is not my intention here to follow the history of the growth of the idea of God, even if that were possible. I wish to consider only some of the *principles* involved in this growth and a few of its *directions*.

It is a curious paradox that this most original and constant knowledge should be the one most and longest subject to change, the most ancient subject of human experimentation, the most encumbered with rubbish and error. We understand in part the reasons for these errors. We understand that it is not natural for man to reflect, becoming fully aware of that *with which* he is thinking. We understand that we have little or no native power of recognizing either self or God apart from mediators: so that in the conceptions we make of God there must always be an overburden and over-influence of the *medium*, physical or personal, wherein God is thought.

Still, we have not to read the development of religious thought as a progress from error to truth. We must read it as a progress of growing acquaintance, adding to ideas which from the first have been true within their own intention. Early man thinks of God, no doubt, more truly than he is able to say or hand down in language; and we cannot forget that it is his infallible identification of God in experience which enables him from time to time to correct his straying conceptions. After all, there is no other essential error in thinking of God than this: that God becomes an object among other objects, natural or psychical. And this is *not all error*. For not only do these over-materialized conceptions hold fast the genuine objectivity of God (which all-important character is usually weakened by attempts to think of God as pure spirit); but further, there is indispensable truth in the tendency to incarnate God in his works, and to think of him as there where his activity is, and where his objects are. I would rather have a worshipper of a thousand idols than a worshipper of a subjective deity or of an abstraction.

What a man begins with in knowing God is *truth*. He adds to this, further truth and an admixture of error and earth. The elimination of this error by further experience does at the same time develop the truth still farther. The growth in the knowledge of God is a growth of *predicates*. Every mediator gives some quality or predicate to the experience of God. The early mediation of God-knowledge is fragmentary and occasional, albeit cumulative: but with progress further aspects of experience, social, political, moral, concerns of theory and art, acquire reference to the consciousness of God, until it becomes a postulate of religion that God is to be seen in everything, even in evil. As many mediators, so many predicates; and doubtless so many problems also. For a predicate is, in general, nearly as false as it is true; and the accumulation of religious knowledge is no simple sum of positive contributions. Yet given the infallible identity of the subject-matter, the growth of this knowledge is not in principle unlike that of all knowledge.

There is one peculiarity, however, that deserves mention. I have said that these predicates of God are, each one of them, nearly as false as true; always in need of being balanced by a predicate of opposite or contrasting name.[1] God is person and no-person; lov-

[1] Among the psychological reasons for the inadequacy of any given predicate is this : that as such predicates arise in experience their most emphatic elements are their negations. They are surer of what they deny than of what they affirm; and should be read in the light of these denials. Those occasions which early excite the specifically religious turn of reflection are occasions, as we can now see, when some *incongruity* is felt in applying the usual habits of thought. Thus in the event of a birth. The insistent naturalism of the birth process clashes hard against man's pride and spiritual self-consciousness. There is unfailingly roused some doubt of Nature, some wonder ending in a denial in which flesh is reduced from a finality to a symbol. The reality of the birth, so we assert, is something other and more than its physiology; and this something other is able to confer dignity and awe on that event. All this, which here takes the form of an inference, is in fact a direct report of the feelings that here, though with greater struggle than usual, the spirit alone is real and essential, not deserting nor despising but interpreting the material. So with other propitious and unpropitious aspects of experience, with disease, and death, and marriage, and wherever the course of events most surely and elementally strikes religious fire : the same sense of incongruity and conflict will be found. And in all this man is naturally more aware of the checkage, the emotion, the disturbance in self-consciousness, than he can be of *that by which* the habits of his thought are being checked (on the one hand) and maintained (on the other), — his

ing and non-loving; fighter and no fighter; just and yet alike to all; merciful and unbending. The positive and tenable value of any predicate, subject to such subtractions, is problematic. God appears as a being in whom opposite traits are strangely united: but the nature of the center in which such oppositions agree, or are neutralized, is not picturable — is known, if at all, only to immediate experience. As an object in the world of objects, God is *next to nothing;* so the mystics have always truly said. Hence atheism is truer than many a florid religiosity whose God is but a surfeited agglomerate of laudatory epithets. Atheism is the proper purgative for this kind of religion; and has been historically an indispensable agency in deepening and keeping sound the knowledge of God.

But atheism discards the one hopeful element in the situation, — namely, that God may actually furnish the solution of these dilemmas; which are never problems about God alone, but are at the same time threatened splittings in the world of human idea and ideal. For man, as a thing of Nature, is a being of opposing instincts, whose balance becomes increasingly fine; and only in the increasing security of hold upon some Absolute, such as sanctions both the one and the other of the divergent ideals, can his tottering balance be kept. With his God, as a god of opposing predicates, this growing instability of human nature becomes a condition of

ultimate consciousness of God. He is moved, but he does not see clearly of what idea his feeling is the work. He reports his experience, therefore, in the form of dogma; adopting such positive objects as he can distinguish and judge appropriate to his feeling. Hence his dogma is permanently subject to the elimination of whatever is extraneous in the assumed objects.

speed in his forward movement. Thus, in more senses than one, is God the pledge of the unity of human nature. It is by holding vigorously to the identity of the ultimate Object of experience that the antitheses in the judgments *about* God (and about man) do in time get their positive solution. But let us consider some of these antitheses.

One elementary antithesis in the thought of God is that between the one and the many; between polytheism and monotheism. This is a primitive antithesis, but also a permanent one: for every other antithesis has some bearing on this one,—as, for example, that between the personal and the impersonal. God as personal inclines to be *many,* since the personal being seems to have outline, and to need external relations to other persons: even in Christianity the persons of God are three, whereas the Godhead which is one is relatively neuter.

The development of religion has been, in the main, in the direction of unifying the heavens, a continuation of the movement from spirit to the god. But there is a current in the opposite direction also. The god-*meaning* has always been single; that is, spirits have always been known as belonging to the genus *divine,* supernatural. And this belonging to the one genus has frequently meant, even for very primitive thinkers, a participation in one pervasive *world-energy.*[1] Behind the numerous gods we can usually discover a more general divinity, vaguer but also more exalted, and

[1] See Arthur O. Lovejoy. The Fundamental Concept of the Primitive Philosophy.

often more ancient than the rest. Man has never been in doubt that the qualities of God are such as can belong only to one; and even when he has many deities, they are addressed in turn (for the most part) as the all-powerful, the Lord of lords. A polytheism that is not in some sense a *henotheism* is yet to be discovered. The many gods have had their birth one by one, each one in turn a god, — or rather an *attempt* at God. The gods must grow in number because the first god-shapes are too poor. Each god satisfies within the region of his own group of events; seems hero and superlative enough in his own province. But another province requires another figure of God. Hence we may say that polytheisms are galleries of aborted monotheisms; collections of god-figures each of which well intends to be all, but is incompetent. There is no such thing in history as a primitive monotheism; but there is a permanent singleness in the thought of deity which man forever departs from, through loyalty to the variety of deity's manifestations.

Polytheism then has its right; its richness; its acknowledgment of the omnipresence of deity. It is truer than many a monotheism. Premature monotheisms have invariably been too poor. Witness the sad-fated monotheistic moment of Egypt; the sun-disk god of Amenophis IV. Witness those other royal monotheisms in Peru and Mexico. There was memorable reasoning in that speech of the Inca in religious conclave, worthy of being transmitted from times long prior to the Spanish discovery: "We are told, he said, that the Sun has made all things. But this cannot be; for many things happen when he is absent. He behaves neither like a living thing, — for he never tires; nor like a free thing, — for he never varies his path. Therefore the sun must have his master, greater than he; which greater god we ought to worship." Yet it was not the destiny of this greater god, nor of the greater gods of Persia nor of India to attain sway over the religious sense of man. *Pantheism* goes farther, is able to dissolve and absorb the many partial deities; but pantheism also is a unity still too poor and quantitative, breaking out everywhere in assertions wholly polytheistic, "This thing is god, — and that, and that." It is long before monotheism can be true for man's conception. It cannot be true until after much free growth of the God-idea (in which each new element in the conception of God may appear as the birth of a new deity), God can be known in experience as *the one of* all these many.

Another antithesis is that between God as near and God as remote; an antithesis which has taken technical shape as that between the transcendence and the immanence of God. This also is associated with the contrast between the personal and the impersonal. For the god who is near is apt to be thought of as sympathetic, and so far like mankind; the remote god is thought of for the most part as unlike and impersonal. In the logic of the Inca reformer above quoted, the deity in becoming one became at the same time more remote and less personal: his temple near Callao held no images, and witnessed no sacrifices.

Here again the direction of religious progress is not single, but twofold. We have heard much in recent years of the advantages of the immanent God; and I have nothing to say in doubt of these advantages — they are the modern form of the more omnipresent and polytheistic aspects of religion. But they are fatal advantages if they lose from sight that other direction of progress, notable from the earliest, the *retreat of God*. Religion may be too romantic, too much interested in what is *not here* but beyond somewhere in the ineffable; yet religion if it lives chiefly in the next things will turn out to be no religion at all. In proportion as the religious horizon is drawn close, the gamut of religious experience becomes trivial.

Early gods are like man and near him. But still, they were *as unlike and as remote as he could imagine them*. The differences between spirits and men, the gulf fixed between the natural and the supernatural — gulf leaped in death — the exaggerations and superlatives, these are as important parts of the conception as are the likenesses and the simplicities of intercourse. When man can *think* beyond the sun, and beyond the sky, — there God goes, and probably first goes. For the God-idea, as the limiting idea of man, is also his explorative idea: by dwelling in speculative fancy on that which is beyond what he has yet thought, man prepares the next conceptual conquests — wins at length one more idea of which he must say, God is *not that*. We need not fear that God will be thrust out of consciousness by this effort to assign him ultimate otherness; for God-thinking can not well expel God from thought. On the contrary the work done, and the potential acquired, by dint of such endless series of negations, is a most practical measure of the worth of that conception for the lives of the thinkers.

For we do not find that the greatness of man and the importance of human business are in proportion to the restriction of man's outlook, but the reverse. The present day has its supreme worth, every present moment is the measure of all the rest: but this is so, in the main, because every present day is "the conflux of two eternities," which eternities being eliminated the worth disappears also. We have outgrown the days when we make the citizen great by making the government small; we shall outgrow the days when we make man great by making God small and *useful*.

The apostle of the present moment depends for his persuasiveness upon his skilful use of the remote. The charm of Omar is wholly dependent upon his vision of the long reaches of destiny in which that moment is framed, and which none knows how to invoke more finely than Omar himself. It is the thought of the Seven Seas which makes the plash of the pebble a melancholy marvel: and it is the vista of the long human caravan, with a delicate loyalty to its shadowy figures as they vanish, which lifts Omar's own moment from the level of the sensual into the atmosphere of alluring poetic worth. It is that remote thing *with which* we think the present that gives value to the present. And in this same way, and quite unconsciously for the most part, the remote God-thought of the Orient (where the sublimity and romance of religion are native-air) has served through centuries to preserve from utter desolation the value-element in millions of careers which to our eyes are inconceivably monotonous and intolerable.

The near-by deity of a religion that betones immanence proves in experience to be a baffling object of worship. Paradoxically enough he is not so accessible as the unreachable God. If we look through the history of religion for instances of genuine intimacy between the worshipper and his god, we do not light upon sorcerers generally and their "familiar" spirits, nor upon the relation between the human Greek and his human Zeus. There could be no intimacy here, simply because this Zeus was all too near and all too human. Such deities have descended too far into the current of the world in which all things and all spirits are insulated one from another. We might more probably think of the Persian Mazdeans, between whom and their Ahura there was a tie of remarkable intensity: and yet Ahura Mazda even more than the god of the Jews was a being of remote and transcendent nature. The explanation of the paradox seems to be this: that the effort to think God must first differentiate God from our other objects. But *we also* are in a different world from that of any of our World-objects: something in us is foreign and transcendent to all that we view. There could be no absolute rapprochement between the heart of this alien-within-the-world which we call Self and its God, unless that God were also in some way alien to that same realm. Worship must be always in some measure, as Plotinus puts it, a flight of the Alone to the Alone.

The religion of Brahm is the historic demonstration of this truth, in the abstract. For these Brahman pietists who most clearly recognized and defined the otherness of God from all things phenomenal and even conceivable were the ones who first asserted (so far as history knows) the immediate unity between the ineffable without and the ineffable within.

Upon this point of the remoteness of God as object we have much to relearn that the Orient has never forgotten. We have God the Son, as they had not: there is little danger that we shall lose the perception of the divinity of the Life within Nature and Man and Present Affairs. But while God the Son may now have become our necessary way to practical union with the Father, yet the Father must first be known before the Son is recognized as God. Without the Father, the Son is a mere man: for the incarnate is always bound and infected by the finite thing it touches. Until the human spirit knows the self that is more at home in the infinite than here among Things, it has not yet found its Self nor its God. Only the transcendent God can be truly immanent. This also is a matter of experience.

One of the most striking stages in the development of religion is the epoch when religion adopts morals as its own province, and when the gods of religion take on ethical character. This is so distinctive an advance from earlier *amoral* thoughts of God, which present him simply in terms of nature-powers, quite as likely to be evil as good, that most classifications of historic religions (Tiele's especially) mark off in some way the "ethical religions" from the earlier as merely "naturalistic" or "objective." How do the judgments arise that God is good, or that he is moral? Is it not rather that he is found favoring the good of men and the right of men, than that he is himself good or moral in any sense in which we attribute these terms to each other? Immoral or malevolent, God cannot be; but there is a struggle in our thought of God between the

God that is described by our ideal predicates, and that God who rejects all these as something less and other than the truth. And here again, we can see at once that the problem of personality and impersonality is involved.

It is pertinent to call attention to the fact that the God who merely *is*, as our Absolute Other, is by that fact both promotive of our weal and of our morality. This has been one of our cardinal doctrines. In our discussion of the need of God we showed in some detail how the mere presence of a companion Mind, standing outside the arena of human effort with its contrasts of good and evil, may be found, in experience, to transmute evil into good; that while, by this very experience, the companion would deserve the attribute of goodness, yet this standing outside the arena itself is a necessary condition of his being found all-powerful in this transmuting work. It is not otherwise with the morality of God. Did not Jesus of Nazareth preach that new conception of God's justice which so strongly resembles an indifferent treatment of the righteous and the unrighteous? If God merely *is*, that existence of God is a promotive of human morality. For what is the essential morality of man if not this, that he make himself universal, escaping in thought and act from his self-enclosedness? If God were but a *point* external to man's consciousness, and if man could reach that point, his feat in doing so would be at least the beginning of morality. The moral importance of God in history has been chiefly dependent on the *relations* which man has sustained to his gods: loyalty to a god is a moral relation; and when through loyal obedience to a common god men become loyal to fellow-tribesmen and their customs, that god is favoring morality among men, quite apart from any mythical reputation he may have. In finding God as simply existent we find him, I say, both good and righteous in his activity; and the condition for so finding him is that he himself remain above the contrasts of good and evil.

There are then, we believe, no pre-ethical stages of religion, though there are indeed pre-legalistic stages; there is no moment at which God in his totality begins to be thought of as good, though there are great moments in religious development when specific characters of God's goodness become clear, as of "mercy" and "loving-kindness"; and finally, there are no such specific predicates of good that do not stand in need, as we think of them, of being tempered with contrasting qualities, such as justice and universality. The God-idea must advance at times from the moral to the *amoral*, as well as in the reverse direction. But herewith the question of the moral attributes of God debouches wholly into the question of God's personality. This question we have variously encountered, and shall now briefly touch upon for itself.

We have found God in the first place as an Other Mind, an individual Subject, wholly active: and no war of predicates can invade this certainty. But so large are the differences between this Other Mind and those with whom we commonly converse, that we do continually recur to the query, How shall we think of Him? We are baffled and not foolishly by the absence of a body that we can attribute to God; for here the perfect metaphor of Nature seems to break — there is no point of view which is God's in particular, and the being that has *every* point of view loses to us all semblance of individuality. "O that I knew where I might find Him."

It is something to note that our body is the sign of our limitation, and of our dependence. Our body is that through which we are *acted upon* as well as that through which we act. But our body is also that through which we are found and become personally present to other persons. The abolition of body is the abolition of the recognizable and the understandable in all personal relations.

And we see, too, that the advance of religion has been very largely from personality to impersonality. For most like ourselves are those early *souls*, doubles, shadows, which people the other world. Religion must lose that literally human heaven, and its human gods, and therewith vanish from grasp and from interest. The alternative to the thought of God as person is the thought of him as Substance, as Energy, and chiefly as Law. Brahmanism, we may say, finds God as Substance, the great *That Which.* Buddhism, often accused of having no supreme god, sometimes described as the godless religion, has also its Absolute: but its god is the Law, the law of Karma, the fixed principle of justice in the heart of all change. Karma is, as nearly as possible, a "Moral Order of the Universe," in which terms — though with quite other meaning — Fichte described *his* deity. Emerson's "Spiritual Laws" which are alive and which execute themselves, which are another name for his Over-soul, are a deity of not unlike character. The Greek Fate and Chaos, the Stoic material Reason, the Chinese Tao: all such conceptions of God, are they not the enlightened thoughts of men about deity? Have we not said but lately that the remote God is the primary necessity of religion?

We have said this; and noted at that time that man is not made great by diminishing the majesty of his world. In the same spirit we may now say that man is not aggrandized nor freed by *weakening the type* of his world's unity. Just as we could not enhance our own definiteness by blurring the definiteness of Nature, but the contrary: so we should detract from our own concreteness in any detraction from the concreteness of our world-unity, and in our thought of it. There is neither merit nor truth in rarefying the thought of God; nor in presenting him to our conceptions in terms of some thinner and weaker sort of world-unity easier to image and believe in than a personal world-unity.

It is God in external relation to me, as my Other, that seems the personal God; it is God as the Whole, including me within himself, that seems impersonal: and the true God is the Whole, as in Christian doctrine God is the One of the three persons. But we may discern in the world generally a principle to the effect that *inner relations assimilate themselves to outer relations*, and conversely. Thus, of organisms, the whole cares for the parts in the same sense that the parts may be said to care for each other: and the several organs of an organism do tend to reproduce in themselves the features of that whole, becoming in themselves organisms with internal relations resembling their own outward relations. Of State and citizen the same holds: and whatever the character of the State in its international relations, that same character (be it of Athenian greed, or of Machiavellian expediency, or of better sorts) will reproduce itself in the character of the members of the State. Now the State is in some measure an artificial body, and its moral quality lags behind the qualities of its members. But the World is not artificial: the character of the World is first, — that of its members derivative. We may find our thought of God following in arrear of the best conception we have of ourselves; but it is only because we know that whatever selfhood we have is an involution of the selfhood of the Whole, and that our external relations to our fellows do but follow and reproduce in their own more distant fashion the relation of God to us which from his view is internal. Hence the remark that "Man is never long content to worship gods of moral character greatly inferior to his own" [1] may be accepted, with its sting drawn, because of what we know of our relation to the Whole of which we are natural parts.

The conception of God as Law has its right in destroying the *poverty* of my thought of personality. I confess that this word "person" has for me a harsh and rigid sound, smacking of the Roman Code. I do not love the word personality. I want whatever is accidental and arbitrary and atomic and limited and case-hardened about that conception to be persistently beaten and broken by whatever of God I can see in the living law and order of this Universe until it also has all such totality and warmth.

But I see that personality is a stronger idea than law;

[1] McDougall. Social Psychology, p. 311. 2d edition.

and has promise of mutuality and intercourse that laws, even if living, cannot afford. I see further that personality *can include law*, as law cannot include personality. And I see, finally, that this deepening conception of personality is not more an ideal than an experience. For God is not falsely judged in experience to be *both the one and the other*. The negation of any one such attribute by the other is only for the enlargement of the first, not for its destruction. Until I can perfectly conceive personality, God must be for me alternately person and law; with the knowledge that these two attributes of one being are not, in truth, inconsistent, and that their mode of union is also something that I shall verify in some moment of present knowledge, as by anticipation of an ultimate attainment. Not only is God to be found in experience, but whatever attributes are genuinely predicated of him are to be found there also.

God is the Eternal Substance, and is known as such; God is also the Eternal Order of things: but God is That Which does whatever Substance is found to do. If it is the knowledge of God that first gives us our human comradeship and its varied and satisfying responsiveness, the God who is the bearer of that responsiveness is not himself without response. These comrades are in a measure God's organs of response, even as Nature is God's announcement of his presence and individuality: but God has also a responsiveness of his own, and herein lies the immediate experience of the personality of God. The relations between man and God have, in the course of religious history, become more deeply personal and passionate, with the deepening sense of evil and spiritual distress. The soul finds at length its divine companion.

But as religion enters into these deeper and more fertile strata of the knowledge of God, it becomes evident that the development of religion falls increasingly upon the shoulders of individual men, whose experience of God and its cognitive content becomes authoritative for others. We find that religion becomes universal at the same time that it becomes most peculiarly personal, and takes its impetus and name from individual founders and prophets. Buddhism and Christianity and Islam are religions of redemption and of universal propagandism; and it is they, chiefly, that willingly refer their character and revelation of God to one person. Our understanding of the higher stages of the knowledge of God, so far as man has yet progressed in this knowledge, will best be pursued in a closer study of mysticism and worship.

PART V

WORSHIP AND THE MYSTICS

CHAPTER XXIV

THOUGHT AND WORSHIP

WORSHIP, or prayer, is the especial sphere of the will in religion. It is an act of approach to God: and while this act involves a lifting of thought to God, it is more than an act of thought — it intends to institute some communication or transaction with God wherein will answers will.

What this transaction may signify it is not easy to understand. Prayer is instinctive; and as with all instinctive actions its motive lies deeper than any obvious utility: our attempts at explanation are likely to leave its ultimate meaning uncaught. The motive of worship may seem to be *moral* — an impulse of deference to the great and holy and a desire to share in that holiness; or we may think to discern an end more deliberately *practical*, as when prayer takes the form of propitiation or petition: yet all such moral and practical motives are but appurtenances of the primary motive, which as yet we must simply call *religious* — allowing its rightful uniqueness and problematic character. Worship, we may say, is governed by the "love of God" — whatever this mysterious phrase may mean. In so far as love seeks knowledge of its object, worship resembles thinking: yet love seeks its knowledge by its own way and method, characteristically different from the way of reflection: it is these differences which are now important to us.

For philosophy, in its rightful and necessary effort to do justice to the religious idea in contrast to a religion of feeling, is inclined to halt in the world of thought, unable to see what more than thinking may be involved in the act of prayer. Recognizing that idea is necessary, it assumes that deliberate reflection is sufficient. It identifies Gottesdienst with Denken, and thereby impoverishes the meaning of worship.

Worship is indeed a reasonable act, even when instinctive and momentary: it is informed of God; it uses and contains all available knowledge of the being whom it addresses. But in worship the universality of thought is overcome; and God is appropriated uniquely to the individual self. Worship brings the experience of God to pass in self-consciousness with a searching valency not obligatory upon the pure thinker: in some way it *enacts* the presence of God, sets God into the will to work there. In the nature of the case, the aspect of deity which reason discovers is an unconditional, inevitable, universal presence: from such a presence there can be no escape—and so no drawing near—save by the movements of deliberate attention. But the drawing-near of worship is more than a movement of attention.

Our philosophical thought finds God as an object—in the third person, not in the second. Thinking comes upon God in a contemplation which the sound of the word "Thou" would break and startle. There is here some spell of distance, some veil of insulation, from which natural religion does not suffer. In worship, not alone the universality, but also the objectivity proper to deliberate thought must be accepted—and overcome.

Our moral freedom consists in this, that in knowing God we maintain a moment of reserve; the further relation requires a further *consent*. And in the consent which distinguishes the act of worship, objectivity, the otherness of God and man, ceases to be the whole truth of that relationship.

What this further element may be, we shall for the present simply illustrate. We are well acquainted with the difference between the observer of life and the sharer of it. We know the man to whom nature, for instance, is a foreign and independent spectacle, and the man who in the presence of nature readily becomes a part of all that is around him. We know the man who in all social situations maintains some fine insulation, some predominance of the self-preserving instinct; and we know the man whose self spontaneously diffuses and mingles with each situation by some natural osmosis between him and his object. And we know further that while the former temper has a certain advantage in discoursing about its world, the latter temper though less fluent in speech does win a kind of knowledge of its world which the less adventurous and more objective temper may wholly fail to understand. We experience these varieties of temper in ourselves, and know well that while this consent is sometimes in our power, at other times even this touch of freedom which makes us one with our object seems to have drifted beyond our present grasp. And though this difference has cognitive consequences, we are inclined to refer it at last to an attitude of will, to a moral difference which in its beginnings is under voluntary control. In any case we recognize here an other-than-theoretical relation to our object, a relation which surmounts objectivity without destroying it, and which is seen quite simply in that transition in consciousness from "he" to "thou," and from "thou" to "we."

These two aspects of our living belong together. As we have just now compared the two tempers — of isolation from our objects and of fusion with them — we recognize that neither would be significant without the other. Distance without fusion becomes individualistic and sterile; fusion without distance is formless, sentimental, and oppressive. We want our living to add to its objectivity this unifying consent; but we want no consent save of one who in thought has made himself free. Consent, and that union with the object so curiously uncommandable by direct effort, flows through and around all our deliberate thought-work, lifting and floating it on the tide of a more central relationship with our world. Reflective thought, it appears, is too purposive, active, self-distinguishing, self-preserving, and at the same time too unindividual and unfree in its result, to do justice to the meaning of worship.

The discrepancy between these two processes appears most vividly when we consider their historical aspect. If we identify the essence of worship with thinking, then whatever else has been historically associated with worship by way of external action, ceremonial form, and the like, is set aside as accidental, as something with which the man of thought may dispense, as something with which civilization itself will dispense in time. From this point of view, historical worship has two elements: reflection (which is important) and *rite* (which is relatively unimportant), the merely practical aspect of religion, making use of the knowledge of God but adding nothing to it. These practices, as we now see, are not only untheoretical—they are even peculiarly unpractical: here is a great accretion of activities, not turned outward into the world, but directed upward and disappearing in their energies, like the fire of sacrifice, in an unanswered gesture of aspiration—unanswered, unexplained, though seemingly undiscouraged. This external part of worship is the exclamatory or demonstrative side of religion; it is religion vaunting itself, celebrating itself, decorating itself,—and in the process of time these externalities, once pedagogically or socially useful, become unnecessary.

But our historic conscience has been making us aware that this line of cleavage between the important and the unimportant in religion is badly drawn. It produces a conception of religion which is in much danger of omitting religion itself. For religion has always assumed that there is something in particular to be *done* about God; and has identified itself with the work of doing it. It has assembled religious practices into institutions—systems of just such special activities; it has spent itself in perfecting and establishing them; and what a spectacle do these structures constitute as they heap themselves in history. What will our philosophies make of this rank growth of deed, ceremony, orgy, assembly, ritual, sacrifice, sacrament, observances public and private of a thousand sorts? Is all this to be left as an alien mass? are these performances and experiences to be turned over chiefly to the student of abnormal psychology? If in the presence of these phenomena of religious practice our most lively sense is a sense of the erratic, do we not thereby measure the inadequacy of our understanding? Must not the mere bulk and persistence of this aspect of religion convey some impression of importance; and still more so, the intensity of spirit with which it has been carried on? Our eliminations of the unimportant in religion must mightily reduce this mass, no doubt; but it will not all be cut away from religion. Something which is other than reflective thought will appear as an essential ingredient of worship. And perhaps a rapid survey of these historic phenomena may suggest what this essential ingredient is. We shall find religion, perhaps, making its own selection.

There is no moment in the early history of religion when this active, vocative side of worship is without its own distinct importance, real or supposed. If man's religion is first embodied in his exclamations, these exclamations were at once cognitions and prayers, incipient transactions. God-friendly and God-unfriendly are distinguishable even here; and God-unfriendly can be made God-friendly. What consequences may hang from this practical issue of the friendliness of God is not clear — early theories are no better than our own: the imagination exhausts itself in picturing the divine rewards and punishments; but behind all these pictures there is, even from the beginning, a residual importance in being right with deity which we might call an *ontological importance*, i.e., affecting somehow the substance of one's self, the soul and its destiny, opening up some bottomless depths of being such as the eye is hardly fitted to gaze into. The amount of power that can be released when the religious nerve is pressed is quite out of proportion to the belief in the more definable pleasures and pains. Let political and legal needs make the most of this superstitious potency while it lasts. To keep God friendly there are few efforts that men will not make, few privations that they will not undergo. It is but a trifling symbol of such efforts and privations that the god requires a deliberate and methodical approach in sacrifices and prayer; whatever importance religion has begins to concentrate in the special act of worship.

But these necessary moments of approach have their own terrors, when some one must take it upon himself to break through the habitual taboo of Holiness; a cloud of oppressive gravity deepens over the event, supportable only by fierce resolution, wrapped probably in mutilation and blood. And when the act is accomplished in safety, an exultancy equally fierce floods the brain; exhibitions of savage gaiety, the license of supermen, can alone satisfy the spirit. We are strangers now to this vehemence, whether for better or for worse; but we can still catch from afar the pulse of this ancient ocean, its terrors and its glorious liberations. We can understand how this strange sense of ontological importance must condense in any phase of human experience in which the actual remoteness of deity seemed overcome. We shall expect it to set excessive value upon those states of enthusiasm, ecstasy, intoxication, in which heaven and earth were felt to flow together; and to raise into prominence persons specially apt in the arts of worship, quite apart from any other human capacity that these persons might have or lack.

Thus the system of worship develops its adepts,—its *mystics.*

Judging externally, from the qualities of dervishdom, yoginism, devoteeship and sainthood generally, all these special achievements of approach to God might be regarded as the luxury or extravagance of the religious consciousness, were it not that they have been regarded by religion as in some form and degree its chief necessity. Religion (which in any given people lives more or less as a single body) seems to breathe chiefly through the experience of individuals who carry to its highest the art of personal worship: the Brahmin becomes holy because the act of prayer (Brahman) is holy. The value of the saint, to all appearances, must lie in the simple fact that he knows how to communicate with God; this simple fact gives to his look, his gait, his way of judging events, the sentences that fall from his lips, an unaccountable weight. Of substantial result not much more can be extracted from these persons; not much more has been demanded of them. Their art of dealing with the god has been a matter of wonder not to the people only, but to themselves as well; they have difficulty in communicating either that art or its significant fruits to the religious public. They do not mix well, these mystics: they must live as objects to the crowd, solitary often, often in exclusive groups of like-minded spirits, willing and able to accept from each other large meanings on small suggestions, leaping to some substance through a swirl of dizzy symbol. It is this difficulty of communication, this separation from the mass in thought and habit, this embarrassment of speech, which has embodied itself in the word *mysticism.*

The suspicion of unreality and of pious distemper which this name must always bear is a monument, not all unjust, to the vanity of those who first adopted it, as if their esoteric knowledge and privilege with deity, this circumstance of separation from the rest of men, were the essence of their art, and wholly a matter for congratulation. But it matters not to us if some or even most prophets have been vain or false, *if there are any true prophets.* In this, as in other great matters, nature makes a thousand failures to bring forth one consummate product. The existence of the genuine mystic — Bernard, Mohammed, Lao Tze, Plotinus, Eckhart, John of the Cross — however seldom he is found, is the momentous thing; sufficient to command respect for the tradition of mysticism, sufficient to justify the attention which through religious history has been focussed upon these individuals.

For the mysteries and the mystics have in the course of time distilled into their own tradition the essence of religious practice. They know, if any know, how it is that the knowledge of God can be the most universal of perceptions, and at the same time the most rare and difficult. They know wherein the act of prayer differs from an act of reflective thought. A philosophy of mysticism would be a philosophy of worship.

NOTE ON THE MEANING OF MYSTICISM[1]

WHEN we speak of mysticism we have now before our mind a great historic phenomenon, found everywhere that religion is found: for as there is no religion without worship, so there is no religion without its specialists in worship. And a survey of the modes of approach to God practised by the mystics in all ages seems to confirm our distinction between worship and the usual processes of thought. In these strange courtings of frenzy, ecstasy, intoxication; in these traps set for the inspiring deity, preparations elaborate, demonstrative, fantastic, inhuman at times, we see little external resemblance to the quieter processes of reflection.

Yet, as the methods of devotion clarify; as excitement learns its own due channels, finding assuagement in art and ceremonial dignity; and especially as worship recovers a right to private as well as to public pursuit; worship approximates meditation, even externally. Worship takes on the aspect of a more deliberate, intense, and thorough thinking. In thought as in worship, I must to some extent remove myself from the current of experience, from "appearances"; I must stop the intrusions of sense, and check the prepossessions of habitual idea. Further, in thought as in worship, I must yield myself to my object and identify my being for the time with its own. Worship, then, is but the completion, is it not, of these partial works of common thought? and true worship will issue in true knowledge, as its essential result and aim. What

[1] Readers whose eye may have fallen upon an article in Mind, January 1912, on "The meaning of mysticism as seen through its psychology," will perhaps recognize in this note and in some of the following chapters *disjecta membra* of that article, much revised.

this knowledge is, the mystics will report as their peculiar discovery.

Thus some of the greater mystics and schools of mysticism have actually reduced worship back again to thinking, contemplation, reflection; and have represented the end of worship as a personal knowledge of God, or even as a doctrine about God. To the Vedantist, thought becomes the true sacrifice, equivalent to and replacing all other sacrifices. The only art of the mystic is after all an art of knowing, difficult perhaps, but not different in character from other thought. Naturally, then, we might expect the doctrines of the mystics to approach a common type; and we might better identify mysticism with its cognitive result than with any peculiar act of will deserving the special name of worship. Such has been, in fact, the fortune of mysticism: in so far as the mystics have presented their results systematically they have tended to a common type of metaphysical theory; and the name mysticism has become attached to a well-known and well-refuted doctrine about the nature of God, or of Reality. In the refutation of that doctrine the excuse for worship as a peculiar esoteric art of thinking disappears, and practical religion merges itself with philosophical thought.

Thus, when Royce writes of mysticism he treats it as one of the four leading types of metaphysical system, identified with the doctrine that reality is pure unity, the negation of all appearances and pluralities, immediate therefore and ineffable. Of this doctrine Royce exhibits the emptiness in wholly conclusive argument: speculative mysticism needs no more refutation, and shall have none here. And we may the more willingly refrain from further criticism since our own view of reality which excludes that one is already before us.

But unquestionably we restrict our view of historical mysticism in identifying it with this result: mysticism has been a much broader thing than this type of metaphysics. Not all mystics have been independent speculators; and not all speculators among the mystics have conformed to this type. If mysticism is found in all religions, it must be found avowing every conceivable variety of metaphysics; every variety, that is, consistent with its one necessary postulate, that reality may be, and ought to be, approached in worship. Christianity, for instance, is the home of much mysticism, even of the best; yet Christianity does not profess the "negative metaphysics"; it is the express foe of the "abstract universal," for its God has once for all sanctioned the world of appearances by becoming flesh and dwelling among us. Nor have the Christian mystics as a body been at war with their creed. It is to be presumed that the meaning of the mystics is compatible with *truth*, whatever that may be; and is itself therefore independent of any passing theory of it. We cannot then predetermine the meaning and fate of mysticism by identifying it with a doomed metaphysics. We shall judge mysticism first by the mystics, not by the theories of a few: and the agreement of the mystics lies in that fact, prior to doctrine, and wholly coextensive with religion, the practice of union with God in a special act of worship.

While we cannot attach the meaning of historic mysticism to any one result of thought, it remains true that the art of the mystic is closely allied with the art of thinking. We cannot fairly explain worship as a developed and extended process of reflection; but we may yet find that thinking is definable as a partial worship. Worship has its own way of reaching wisdom, and must certainly make for truth rather than for error. But if this is the case, how can we account for the undoubted tendency of various important schools of mysticism to converge upon that falsely abstract metaphysics?

This seems to me to be the explanation: that the mystic in reporting what he has experienced has attributed to the objects of his experience some qualities which belong rather to his own inner state. To distinguish between what is subjective and what is objective about our experience is frequently difficult, even in physical observation; but especially in the experience of the mystic, the objects are difficult to grasp, while the inner event is comparatively tangible. It would be strange if there were not a general tendency to mistake one for the other. Let me enlarge a little upon this point.

The mystic prays; and wins, if he is right, some answer to his prayer which is significant to him. He has won knowledge, and such knowledge as he thinks reflection could hardly have brought him; but he cannot say exactly what it is. Nothing is more notorious about the mystic's knowledge than its inarticulateness. The mystic himself knows that his insight is unfinished and unsatisfactory, even while he declares his experience to be one of perfect satisfaction. "The soul knows not what that God is she feels," says Corderius. Curiously helpless and plastic is this knowledge: able to live under various theological systems just because it needs some help from the environment to determine what it is.[1] It is not without an independent force of reaction upon the conceptions it uses; but without these conceptions to give it voice, it could scarcely win strength to react on them. And as the mystic has been hard put to it to tell what it is that he knows, he has in our later and Western world had increasing recourse to reporting the *psychology* of his experience, in lieu of its cognitive contents. Indeed, he has not only used psychology, but has made it for his own purposes.

And unquestionably the reputation of mysticism in this world would have suffered less if our mystics could earlier and more completely have commanded this psychological mode of expression. Objective-mindedness is the great merit of all original religion; but the long-standing inability to distinguish between the characters of an experience as a temporal inner state and the characters of its object has cost religion much. Is it not more than probable that those words "one, immediate, ineffable" which describe the Reality of the "negative metaphysics," are in their first intention descriptions of the mystic's inner experience? May it not be that those negations which

[1] See Höffding. Philosophy of Religion, p. 178 ff.

have passed for metaphysical definitions are in their original meaning rather confessions of mental obstruction and difficulty than assertions about the Absolute? There is a wide difference between saying, "My experience of Reality is ineffable" (passing my present powers of expression) and saying "Reality is ineffable" (without predicates). As a report of procedure and experience Reality may be that which one realizes when he cuts *himself* off from "appearances," closes as far as may be the avenues of sense, silences the cataract of ideas, and withdraws his mind into its deepest cave: in such manner it may be that the central unity of the soul meets the central unity of the world, and knows it to be one with itself. And yet, this report of experience is not to be forthwith translated as a complete account of Reality. I must abstract myself also to think; but what I think is not therefore an abstraction.

Something of the character of that experience must indeed belong to its object. If there were no contrast in reality between the one and the many, between the substance and its appearances, between its indescribable and its describable aspects, then an experience which was "one, immediate, and ineffable" would find simply nothing in the world to light upon. But he who would deny that such an experience can discover anything real must be prepared to abolish the reality of substance. The mystic cannot find the whole of reality, but he may find its center; he may find the only handle by which the whole can be held as a unity.

And this is the advantage of psychology in dealing with mysticism, that it is non-committal in regard to the cognitive or other possible importance of an experience, and may yet furnish the clue to such meaning. For where self-expression falters the signs of meaning may still be read in causes and effects. The immediacy of any experience must submit to interpretation by what is outside it and related to it. The logic and the psychology of our experiences are so adjusted that what becomes invisible to one becomes visible to the other

It is possible that the thread of meaning, lost though it may be to the mystic himself in his ecstatic moment, may at that very moment appear, so to speak, on the reverse of the cloth, as something then and there happening to the substance of the mystic himself; justifying his sense of the "ontological importance" of that event.

This implies, of course, that the "immediacy" of the mystic experience has its external relations; and this implication I fully accept and shall try to justify. Some part of the meaning of this experience is to be discovered in its external career. For which reason, not only the psychologist, but such other scientists as like him see mysticism in its outer bearings, the historian, the sociologist, have been quicker than the metaphysician to recognize its vital importance in religion.

Mysticism, then, we shall define not by its doctrine but by its deed, the deed of worship in its fully developed form. Nothing concerns us more than to know what that experience means, and what it may add to our knowledge of God: but we shall not foreclose these questions by taking a finished speculative system into our definition of mysticism. Mysticism is a way of dealing with God, having cognitive and other fruit, affecting first the mystic's being and then his thinking, affording him thereby answers to prayer which he can distinguish from the results of his own reflection. Since the Pseudo-Dionysius, "mystical theology" has not meant a rival theology, but rather an "experimental wisdom," having its own methods and its own audacious intention of meeting deity face to face.

CHAPTER XXV

PRELIMINARY DOUBTS OF THE WORTH OF WORSHIP

BUT can we find anything in ourselves to corroborate that sense of "ontological importance" which formerly attended the processes of worship? To attain union with God in a mystical experience, other than in thoughtful attention to the mysteries of self-consciousness and existence: we can no longer take it for granted that there is any superior worth in this, or indeed any worth at all. To our present ethical and immanental mind, it is necessary to show cause why any distinctive practices for religion should exist. To find God in personal intercourse and business is enough, is it not? — the religion of daily life and duty is the important thing. Let us approach God through these many mediators — convenient mediators, requiring no deviation from our reasonable plans. Further, is there not something displeasing not alone about the historic forms of mysticism but even about the notion of direct unmediated union with deity? If we avoid the vocative case oftentime in dealing with our own great; how much more in thinking of God. The pretence of the mystic stands on no secure footing in this modest and third-personal generation.

Only, let us be thoroughgoing. Let us be clear that mysticism and common worship do stand or fall together.

Are we prepared to make away with all religious observance, with "church," and all that goes with church? If not, then recognize here some muffled remonstrance against the total vanishing of the art of the mystics. Is any religious practice or institution, prayer or prayer-posturing, solemnity, sacrament, or consecration, or priestly-office in any form, of lingering significance to us, even instinctive and irrational? Then, in heaven's name, let us do what we can to isolate this element, valued by many in dumbness and dilution, and make an issue of its intrinsic worth.

Further, let us be clear that wherever *mediated* and indirect relations are possible and valuable, there presumably *immediate* relations are possible and valuable as well. Greenbacks and reflected light are on the whole more widely useful than gold and direct sunshine; men have tried to get on without the originals here also, but not so far successfully. And when we consider, is not our doubt of worship even now directed rather against the special mediators which worship has been using than against the thing itself? We do not quite know what to do with our Holy Writ, our Christ, our Priests and Saints, and our church institution. We are trying to shift our mediators from these special ones to some of more universal character. But just because of this uncertainty of mediation, the element of unmediated dealing with God which is at the heart of all mediated dealing must assume greater importance. Could we regain the secret of the worth of worship, it might well become clear to us what place in God's world and humanity's world is to be taken by bibles, priests, and redeemers. A true understanding of mysticism, I venture to say, must either cleanly emancipate us from the whole of special religious trapping and performance, or else reanimate in some vital fashion our historic system of mediation.

Thus, though the art of worship as interpreted by the mystic is foreign to many of our prejudices, a definite self-understanding may still show that a clear rejection is too indiscriminate: it may be one of those things which we can hardly live with, nor yet live without. The effort to dispense with it is the best way to realize its vitality.[1] And it may be possible, as a preliminary to our detailed study of mysticism, to verify — even in a superficial review of our own current consciousness — certain of those motives which have led men in the past to approach their god thus directly and individually. I doubt much whether that ancient sense of "ontological importance" is yet dead. The instinctive nature of prayer is some guarantee of its survival; and it is fair to assume that every fundamental instinct can present intelligible grounds for its existence. The expressions of prayer are sensitive to all the advances of self-consciousness; hence there is little outward resemblance between our own reserved devotions and those enthusiastic orgies, incantations, and slaughter-feasts — we can put ourselves to worship more handily than did our forefathers and with less noise. But in

[1] Worship is an art which is perhaps being lost rather from over-practice and dilution of its proper instinct than from actual loss of the secret. We think that we know what it is all about; we find that we get on perfectly well without it; we learn with some surprise that we can give no tenable reason for pursuing it; we end by judging that it is not for us, who are now able to follow our religion by the pervasive and unobtrusive processes of thought and moral action.

some way, if I mistake not, we can still recognize in ourselves traces of that impulse which in the religious tongue is called the "love of God," some form of that same ancient demand for more direct touch with our Absolute than the usual processes of thought afford.

In the first place, no one wholly escapes the sway of a certain spiritual ambition, which is unwilling — if there be in the universe any supreme consciousness — to remain apart, or in any relation to that consciousness which is relatively external and distant. If there is in the world any such being as God is supposed to be, a career is set for every soul : there is an inevitable trend of all finite spirits to a consciously understood footing with that being. In structure this is a well-known principle of human action. It is akin to the necessity whereby every Christopher must serve his Strongest : because, namely, it is not good, and in the long run insupportable, that two great, self-conscious, self-appreciating powers should exist in simple pluralism or disunion, unperceptive of each other, unmeasured against each other. The strong man who values his strength is restless until he finds that situation in the world where his strength is *placed*. There is a necessity imposed upon every self-knowing thing to seek the most self-knowing and the most excellent as that in whose presence it finds itself finally known and judged.[1]

[1] Doubtless I am attributing to the lovers of God a greater sense of their own merits than at once appears to their own overt consciousness. But in all these matters we are seeking an interpretation that is not yet found : and we must assume the privilege of knowing the soul of the mystic, if not better than it knows itself, at least more analytically, appealing to our own self-scrutiny above all traditional descriptions of the worshipful temper.

There is an impulse here like that by which men flock to cities and to great occasions, seeking centers where there is adequate knowledge, measurement, and placing of men. A fundamental and holy presumption of worth there is in this love of God, such as no soul can dissemble. However retiring the spirit may be with regard to the highly-conscious regions of this historic world, to be retiring with regard to God is unmeaning and impossible. A sheer hunger there is in all of us for self-consciousness more nearly absolute than we yet have: in some form and degree this motive is felt and appreciated by all men.

And what we can thus appreciate in diffusion, we must allow to come to legitimate dominance in specialization (quite another thing from extravagance or exaggeration). In some souls this ambition may still become a ruling passion, and in them we may best see the meaning of what is vague and truncated in ourselves. To such minds the simple fact of the existence of a god is an imperative profound and practical: prayer with them becomes a clarified and persistent purpose which strikes out at once upon an unrecalled journey of devotion. This impulse is seen at its height in those precocious mystics who even in childhood (as Teresa and Guyon) could not hear of martyrdom without a surge of envy, and resolves to become martyrs likewise. Here is a spiritual exquisiteness which may easily become a spiritual avarice: but it is obviously in this sense a disinterested love, that it takes precedence of all other interests, and requires no recompense in their terms. These are the mystics by birth,—they who "desire to leave all in order to be with God."

But note well that while the mystic of genius is a natural product, the mystic impulse is not a matter of special temperament. For there are mystics in all temperaments. This incentive is deep enough in human nature to take various forms according to the disposition of the mind. There are fierce mystics as well as tender ones; men who scorn to live in a world where they are uncertain of their own souls; who storm the gates of the heavenly city till they wrest from God the pledge of their security — the Jacobs, Brunos, Luthers. Under all such saintly bluster and Teufelsdröckian defiance we can still recognize the love of God, the ontological ambition, the need of an unyielding origin for the thrusts of the will. There are practical and world-moving mystics as well as dreamy ones, — the Mohammeds, Bernards, Loyolas, Wesleys.[1] The love of God, also, will be coloured by every defect of the lover: there will be sentimental mystics, and cowardly mystics, and lazy mystics, and many another sort. It is the property of mysticism to set all such elements of personality into high relief — not a disadvantage, if one demands self-knowledge. We have no present interest in these peculiarities save to show that the spiritual ambition of the mystic is the prerogative of no one peculiar type of human nature.

The love of God, I have said, desires the assured presence of God and the drastic self-knowledge which that presence brings, as an immediate insight. But

[1] Wesley and Luther were mystics within our definition, though both were hostile to certain types of mysticism which came uncomfortably near to their own positions, so that verbally they are known rather as opponents of mysticism than as mystics.

there is another aspect of this same spiritual ambition; for worship seems to contain a demand for knowledge of truth about the world, as well as about self. The mystic reports that he now knows something about the meaning of life and death, and of the other grave things that concern mankind. This is such knowledge as each individual soul of man has need of, and such as one can hardly accept either on hearsay or on inference, if it can be obtained in one's own immediate perception.

Fear of the unknown, the primitive human fear, though it has become much socialized, is not to be banished. Our own personal destiny we may now, in the midst of a worthful social order, more readily and honorably forget than could our ancestors: and to affect an unconcern regarding death and the future has become in some eyes a stock virtue. But these things cannot always be forgotten, nor ever rightfully forgotten, until we have once cleared our minds with regard to them. The need to make immediately sure the foundations of life is not an impulse that can grow antiquated or improper. No motive to prayer is more fundamental than this, which in presence of such a limit of insight as makes the soul a subordinate in the universe requires of existence the power to surmount it. And on no point are the mystics more agreed than on this, that worship brings "revelation." The "noetic" character of mystic experience is so general that James includes it in his definition of mysticism. *How*, in the presence of God who knows these things, the worshipper also gains some insight into them I do not here enquire; but it seems evident that the impulse of prayer has in it as one ingredient a desire for such insight as this; and that some of the mystics think themselves to have gained it.

The mystic's remarkable inability to speak out may be no discredit to either the value or the universality of what he so mysteriously knows. It is a principle observable elsewhere that the more heavily we are impressed by a truth, the more difficult it is to put its significance at once into words. He who knows in any intense and profound fashion may labor, as poets have sometimes done, for years with the burden of his meaning. It is quite possible to win an insight suddenly, and to know that one has it; and yet to find that knowledge standing forth in the midst of the soul like a body at once powerfully charged and powerfully insulated, sputtering with sparks and fringes and penumbræ, but accomplishing no relieving strokes. The circumstance which gives credit to the mystic's assertion is that he has held himself responsible for his alleged revelation. He has labored to make it public, notwithstanding its difficulty. Boehme spends twelve years, so he tells us, in bringing to birth the truth with which two such experiences had burdened him. In spite of what James tells us, that the mystic's knowledge is not binding on any but himself, it is obvious that the mystic is under some radical necessity of propagating his truth: is he not the most vehement propagandist of history? And have not men, on the whole, benefitted by his announcements? Some knowledge of universal truth, it seems, may come to men through worship.

And our judgment of the worth of worship must also take into account, as I surmise, the worth of *novelty* in knowledge and in life generally. In the worship of the gods, the force of all habits is for the moment destroyed, habits of mind and of action. In tribal life, the customary taboos are suspended; the moment of worship is an antinomian moment, and what is deposited out of it may be different from what was dissolved into it. From their mystics the people are ready at this time to hear things and to receive commands which would previously have been blasphemy. Mystical practices may themselves become habitual, and have their acknowledged place in the system of things; oracles and prophecies have their established modes and places: but these are habitual ways of receiving the destruction of habit; they are the point of fixity which renders all other fixities relative and unnecessary. Worship is the provision which the spiritual constitution has made for its own perpetual amendment.

In the increasing solidification of tribal life, and the submergence of personality in the "cake of custom," the god-consulting process is the one spot which remains fluent and *strange* to the tribe itself. Hence doubtless the uncouth forms in which mystical practices have clothed themselves; the strange spot in the life of a strange people may well seem alien to our own habits (unless, indeed, we find it the one spot in which that weird social machinery becomes wholly human and universal). But however tamed worship may become, it has always this same function in the life of people or of individual: it involves the external criticism of all habit, and a radical openness to novelty. Within the motive of worship there is to be discerned, I believe, a weariness of the old, the habitual, the established, — a hunger for what is radically new and untried. This is, in part, the significance of that deliberate undoing of all bonds and attachments, of all received knowledges and properties, which is part of the preparation for the mystical experience in all ages. If it were possible for the soul to become aware of all its attachments and habits, how could it be better disposed for originality? The scientific discipline of the mind is of the same effect in its own sphere: to disaffect oneself as far as may be of prepossessions, to recognize and allow for the biases of the person, the body, and the age. It is not improbable, then, that worship may include this value of preparing the soul for the reception of novelty with its primary value of uniting the worshipper with his God.

Worship may be regarded as an attempt to detach oneself from everything else in uniting with God. It seeks God first as an object, that Other of all worldly objects; and it seeks to join itself to that absolute Other. The mystic proceeds by negation; this and that, he says, are not God: it is not these that I seek. The effort of worship measures the soul's *power of detachment*. And my power of detachment measures the whole of my freedom, the whole of my possibility of happiness, the whole of my possible originality, the whole depth and reach of my morality and of my human contribution. What the mystic reaches is, in terms of his world-conceptions, a zero: not indeed the Whole of reality, but Substance, the heart of God. It is just such a zero as one encounters when he seeks his own soul behind the shifting content of his experience, or when he seeks the soul of another, in distinction from that other's various external expressions. This zero is not a place to stay in; but it may be pre-eminently a place to return to, and *to depart from.* In worship one touches the bottom of that bottomless pit of Self and perceives at hand the real Origin of things; gaining not the whole of any knowledge, but the beginning and measure of all knowledge. May not worship be described as the will to become, for a moment and within one's own measure, what existence is; or more simply, as the act of recalling oneself to *being?*

If these suggestions have truth in them, the act of worship may begin to justify itself, even from the standpoint of use in experience. It might be described as a spontaneous impulse for spiritual self-preservation; for self-placing, for the ultimate judgment of life, and for the perpetual renewal of the worth of life. And in thus returning to the sources of being we may still more dimly discern, it may be, a self-preservation of farther scope, such as immortality may hang on; a glint of ontological bearing of unlimited importance.

It is true that the "love of God" does not explicitly seek these things: it is the wholly simple impulse of which these strands are but artificially severed elements. The worth of God's presence to the genuine mystic is a sufficient and absolute good; and he often expresses himself as if the ecstasy of his moment were its own justification. But every immediate value must be sanctioned by its bearings in the system of all values, must have a meaning which can give account of itself in the form of knowledges such as we have suggested. Worship must not be an intoxication which alienates the soul from the duller interests of experience; and hence, as mysticism has learned its own meaning, it has realized that subjective delight recommends nothing, and that the supremacy of the moment of its experience must be judged by the staying powers of its insight.

We must not hesitate, therefore, to explain the love of God by what it is not, — the one by the many, the disinterested by the interested, the self-abandoning by the self-seeking. We must assert that there is no love of God which is not at the same time an unlimited self-valuation; that there is always something self-seeking about worship and mysticism generally. Something forever dissatisfied with what mankind, in its habit, philosophy, art, and formulæ generally have to offer this individual soul for its safety and comfort and occupation and enjoyment and loyalty. Not good enough is all this for my personal particular spirit, says the mystic; nothing in the world is good enough for me. But because of this personal dissatisfaction, and demand, and further seeking for self, something creative might well come of worship, we think. And something not un-social in its result. Perhaps this spark of ontological ambition which creative nature has deposited in the single self, is nature's own way of bringing the new to pass for the good of all creation. It is indeed the noblest and truest of all self-seeking tempers, the utmost measure of character and worth. The love wherewith God loves the individual may reappear, perchance, in that love wherewith the individual loves God, — and himself, — and all men.

So much, then, for preliminary conjectures as to the

possible permanent worth of worship, the meaning of the mystical love of God. We may now put ourselves, I trust with greater patience, to an examination of the facts in the case.

CHAPTER XXVI

THE MYSTIC'S PREPARATION: THE NEGATIVE PATH

WHAT worship is, and how it differs from thinking, the mystics themselves have made copious efforts to explain. Whatever the distinctive nature of worship may be, something of it should appear in a study of the ways used by the mystics in approaching their god, and in the directions which they have given to other souls who would win the same certainty.

In undertaking such a study, we shall not do well to impose at first our own language upon the mystics. We must give ourselves over for the time to their guidance, to their own modes of expression, and even—so far as we can—to their sentiments; realizing that they are laboring with conceptions not wholly literalized, and that we shall be able in due course to win our own freedom and our own interpretation.

But as the mystics have been pioneers in psychological analysis we shall not be at any moment free from the necessity of looking behind their language. In trying to give explicit guidance, our spiritual directors have been only too careful, too profuse, too minute in their distinctions; and one must perforce ride over the distinctions somewhat roughly. And further, we must expect much of the figurative and even cryptic in their speech. There seems to be some intrinsic difficulty about explaining worship in literal terms, or without presupposing that the hearer already knows what is meant. The Book itself nowhere explains, but simply assumes that we understand what is implied in "lifting up our eyes unto the hills," and in all similar figures.[1]

Indeed, there is a strong disposition in the mystic, even when he acts as guide, to give up the effort of describing what is distinctive of worship : he is inclined to summarize whatever is unique about the process, and especially whatever distinguishes it from thinking, by invoking a *special faculty* of the mind — this we have already noticed. Nothing could more strongly express his conviction that worship and thought are diverse; but of course all such appeals to a special faculty throw the burden of understanding back upon the hearer. The names which the mystics have invented for this special faculty are curious and wonderful, yet not without power of suggestion. We found Tauler, in the

[1] As power of psychological analysis grows, our mystic advisers are able to meet the soul more nearly on its own ground ; yet the results of this progress for the most part make not less demand, but rather more, upon our native understanding. This passage from Tauler is not more cryptic than many another : "Only to those is this great Good, Light, and Comfort revealed who are outwardly pure and inwardly enlightened, and who know how to dwell within themselves. . . . When the Nameless in the soul turns itself wholly inward toward God, there follows and turns with it everything which in man hath a name. And this turning attaches itself always to that in God which is likewise Nameless. . . . Then in such a man God announces his true peace." Such words as these are surely addressed rather to those who already know than to those who from the standpoint of ignorance enquire, and Tauler is not unconscious of this. "Now I will tell you something further of this search . . . and in plain German words, too ; yet I fear that you will not all understand them. But those of you who have already experienced something of such sacred things, and in whom such light has once inwardly shined, may well understand something of what I say." (Predigten, ii. 307, Ausg. 1841.)

passage quoted, referring to this faculty as "the Nameless in the soul"; and Tauler is exceptionally fertile in just such names for this Nameless. It is called the Spark of the soul (Fünklein, Eckhart; Scintilla, Bonaventura), the Apex of the soul, also the Ground of the soul, further, its Groundless Nothing, its Right Eye, its Eternal Eye, its Upward Face, its Innermost, and the like. He that hath ears to hear, let him hear. We understand these expressions, more or less dimly, just as we understand what "The Subconscious" is — our modern Great Fetich of a special faculty: we understand them in so far as we find within our own experience something which may serve as key to the riddle. We have, indeed, no reason to reject as meaningless these appeals to a special faculty: we are no longer in danger of picturing our mind in insulated compartments: we may use these names as indicating *the process of worship in its totality*, and vaguely characterizing its difference from other activities.[1] They are summary names for our problem, and as such they are useful and true: but they are the beginning of our analysis, not the end of it.

I

Various as the ways are which mystics in different ages have used in approaching their god, their resem-

[1] We know that one "faculty" is distinguished from another only (a) by difference in the objects with which it deals, and (b) by a difference in the procedure by which these objects are found. The faculty of religious knowledge is thus to be defined (a) by the fact that it considers God as its object, and (b) by the fact that we have distinctive things to do in order to approach God. The faculty itself is but a name for these actions taken as one.

blances run deep. In all of them there are efforts of the mind fairly described in the mediæval terms, purgation and meditation. And in all of them these active efforts are brought to a close by a voluntary passivity.

Let me note in passing that in all acts of will, the body plays its part; and it is the physical side of all mental acts, whether one sets himself about thinking, or enjoying, or praying, which is most directly controllable. In proportion as the inner process is subtle and evanescent, the physical preliminaries must be extensive. The most delicate instruments of precision require the heaviest of foundations. If attention is preparing for some especially fine discrimination, as in listening for faint sounds, the larger muscles will be called into play as a frame to the smaller ones. Thus in worship also, or rather, especially in worship, the physical basis must be cared for: the first preparation of the mystic has always been a physical preparation, more or less elaborate — of cleansing, fasting, continence, ascetic practices generally, solitude, darkness, kneeling or other special disposition of the body. We have no need to go into the details of these performances, which are at bottom quite as instinctive as are the physical efforts of thought and emotion; we have simply to note their necessary presence. Worship is too spiritual a process to dispense with the material. It is only by the enlistment of the body, in some fashion, that the body can be held in leash during the difficult flight of the soul.

Now of the inner preparation itself which accompanies this external activity, it is predominantly negative; and we may begin by considering the mystic's self-denial, or "purgation."

The mystic's effort is largely given to suppressing the various natural momenta both of the mind and of the desires, — an essay, as we have said, in detachment. It is a summary exercise of one's power both of abstraction and of renunciation. "Into this house (of his innermost self) must man now go, and completely desist from and abandon his sensations, and all sensible things, such as are brought into the soul and perceived by the senses and the imagination. And he must also put away all ideas and forms, even the conceptions of reason, and all activity of his own reason."[1] "A man must begin by denying himself, and willingly forsaking all things for God's sake, and must give up his own will, and all his natural inclinations, and separate and cleanse himself thoroughly from all sins and evil ways . . . And when a man hath thus broken loose from and outleaped all temporal things and creatures, he may afterward become perfect," etc. "No one can be enlightened unless he be first cleansed or purified and stripped. So also, no one can be united with God unless he be first enlightened. Thus there are three stages: first, the purification (or purgation); secondly, the enlightening; thirdly, the union."[2]

In this sort of mental and moral self-suppression, there is much room for casuistry. The attempt to deny self completely brings Oriental mystic and Western mystic into the same familiar paradoxes of self-consciousness. From what self, and from what desires must I detach myself? or from all? And if from all, for what motive?

[1] Tauler. 3. Predigt auf den 3. Sonnt. nach Trin.

[2] Theologia Germanica, trans. Winkworth, chs. xiii and xiv.

Here the philosophies part the mystics. The more roundly God is divided off from the world, the more unrelenting is the antithesis between all heavenly and all earthly affections. If we can draw a clear line between the eternal and the temporal the task of repudiating the temporal becomes a deadly affair. If it is once fairly accomplished, the mystic has destroyed all reason for return. "If our inward man were to make a leap and spring into the Perfect, we should find and taste how that the Perfect is without measure . . . better and nobler than all which is imperfect and in part, and the Eternal above the temporal or perishable, and the fountain and source above all that floweth or can ever flow from it. Thus that which is imperfect and in part would become tasteless and be as nothing to us."[1] Such a soul has become a citizen of another country; it resumes its loves, if at all, with a gleam of absence—the mystic has become spoiled for living.[2]

It is one of the most extraordinary facts about human nature that it is capable, under the spell of religious ambition, of such superhuman heart-steeling. A large part of the fame of mysticism in history is due to its achievements in indifference. And though the giants of self-mutilation may have been the victims of mistaken theories, I find in their willingness to pay the extreme price something heroic to which I cannot but do reverence. He who believes that "if God is to come in, the creatures must go out" must make his drastic choice.

[1] Theologia Germanica, ch. vi.

[2] "And if our Lord did not now and then suffer these visions to be forgotten, though they recur again and again to memory, I know not how life could be borne." Teresa, Life, ch. xxxviii (tr. Lewis).

But human nature has also its own quiet refutations: these holy ones do often grow less zealous when separated from their influence and fame. Can it be that all this violence has but driven worldly interest to more subtle attachments? For the most part, yes: the love of life has been dispersed and transformed, not destroyed. It has been, in part, the good-fortune of mysticism that self-scrutiny has its limits; that many a wider human affection may exist without being observed and hunted to death. If St. Catherine of Siena has become the "bride of Christ" she cannot, of course, be the bride of any mortal: but she is set free to love many a mortal as no other woman dare. Fortunate St. Catherine, whose self-searching has its limit. Unfortunate Meister Eckhart and many another who can think out such demands as this: "So long as ye desire to fulfil the will of God and have any desire, even after eternity and God, so long are ye not truly poor. He alone hath true spiritual poverty who wills nothing, knows nothing, desires nothing."[1] Here mysticism groans on the rack of its own logic; and must continue to do so, until after untold spiritual agony it discovers the meaning of its negations. This radical self-annihilation must give way: the negation of opposition must become a negation of priority. For the sounder mystics the love of God remains at the heart of their plural other loves: and if the fires of these

[1] In justice to Eckhart I should say that he is not always so nihilistic. The following fragment of a saying (italics mine) may more fairly express what he means: "was ist luterkeit? das ist das sich der mensche gekeret habe von allen creaturen vnt sin herce so gar uf gerichtet habe gen dem lutern guot, das ime kein creature trœstlichen si, vnt ir ouch nit begere *denne als uil als si das luter guot, das got ist, darinne begriffen mag.*" Wackernagel, Altd. Leseb., col. 681.

become invisible during the moment of sacred passion, it is not the invisibility of death. They have joined their tongues in one upleaping flame, to return without break to the severalty of their individual altars.

Changing conceptions admit some union of the infinite with the finite; nevertheless the active part of worship still remains a path of negation. For the god whom the mystic seeks is in fact something other than any given natural object of pursuit; and since we are always better aware of what our absolute is not than of what it is, the note of negation must remain predominant. But meanwhile, worship has its positive side also; the mystic has always in some way recognized the fact that passion can be cast out only by some greater passion. We may now consider what these positive elements are.

II

In turning away from the world, the mystic has always needed something to turn toward; in all of his purgation there has been an element of "meditation." He has done what he can to find his own positive ultimate will, to make real to himself what it is that he most deeply cares for. He has tried to *remind himself* of his absolute good.

A great part of what we commonly know as prayer is, in effect, just such a process of self-reminding. The simplest rational account of prayer would probably be this: a voluntary recollection of those deepest principles of will, or preference, which the activities of living tend to obscure. In essence, this is not different from the practice developed chiefly by the Roman

Stoics, who found it useful as a matter of self-discipline to recall, in this or that trying situation, what is truly to be desired and valued, and what is a mere illusion of value. "Straightway practise saying to every harsh appearance, you are an appearance, and in no wise what you pretend to be. . . . Never say about anything, I have lost it; but say, I have restored it. . . . Is the oil spilled? Say, on the occasion, At such a price is sold freedom from perturbation. . . . In every circumstance, hold these reflections ready:

> Lead me, O Zeus, and thou, O Destiny,
> The way I am bid by you to go:
> To follow I am ready. If I choose not,
> I make myself a wretch — and still must follow."

Thus the practice of bethinking oneself of one's first principles of value shades with Epictetus insensibly into prayer.

But in the prayers of the typical mystics, the act of self-reminding is less frequently concerned with such explicit truths or principles: it is more often a meditation upon some object in which values are rather embodied than expressed. Objects of familiar pious reflection are chosen as means of recovering the mystic strand of consciousness, and of bringing into abstract preference the quality of conviction. A concrete object, moreover, is less confining than a formula: it has its truth as the formula has, but in infinite concentration. Especially if this object is a person, or an event of religious history, the soul may find in it an all but adequate embodiment of the absolute good, bearing at once on all circumstances of life, and not on some only.

But neither the formula nor the concrete object is wholly satisfactory as an object of meditation.[1] As the mystic becomes proficient, he recognizes that all such objects have but relative worth.[2] Teresa used at one time to begin her orisons with thoughts of episodes of the Passion: but she writes, "There are many souls who make greater progress by meditation on other subjects; for as there are many mansions in heaven, so there are many roads leading thither. Some persons advance by considering themselves in hell—others in heaven; and these latter are distressed by meditations on hell." Clearly, then, there is no necessity in any of these objects. And further, their office (as objects of deliberate meditation) is transient: they must go, at last, the way of all other objects of thought and desire.

For to all the mystics, whether of East or West, this

[1] In the choice of these objects, the working of experience is evident: any religious tradition lights upon the words and episodes and characters and phrases and hymns which best mediate the mystic consciousness of its own epoch; and as the mental attitude to be reached is one of difficulty, this choice must be sensitive to all the shades of human temper. It is here that questions of taste intrude to dispel religious harmony: acceptable objects for such reflection must vary not alone from age to age, but also from person to person, and from social group to social group. A loss of sympathy here makes the greatest of difficulties in religious understanding, quite apart from questions of creed. We do not now find those objects edifying upon which our mediæval brethren could dwell for pious hours without pall, and which made the themes of their religious art. What we have to do is to penetrate to what is necessary and universal in these objects, fitting to humanity, and not to this or that stage of religious sentiment.

[2] I ignore for the present questions which naturally gave the Christian mystics much trouble, whether in the higher reaches of prayer any consciousness remains of the sacred humanity, the Holy Trinity, etc. See, for instance, Fénelon, Explication des Maximes des Saints, Arts. xxvii, xxviii.

stage of meditation is a mere preliminary; and the function of these objects is at least as thoroughly negative as positive. They have rather to recall the mind from other things than to fix it upon themselves. Their function is chiefly one of neutralizing and sky-clearing: in so far as they leave the mind occupied with particular images, they too must be put away. The Yogi must meditate upon the syllable OM, but only to unify his mind and to prepare for the exclusion of that syllable together with all other objects: it is but a ladder which in mounting he puts beneath him; it is the sand with which the sweeper covers his floor.

The one positive admonition which is most persistent is the vague direction to turn the thoughts *inward.* And even the meaning of this "inward" is rather not-outward than positively introspective.[1] "Introrsum ascendere" is the brief formula for the mystic's self-direction. In all its vagueness this direction has probably served a better purpose than any attempt to be more explicit. For any positive and literal direction is apt to become a misdirection, a danger clearly recognized by many a keen student of human nature among the mystics, and warned against. "Let him not presume to approach that excellent Darkness which is beyond all Light, but rather the darkness of the *not-knowing of God*; and there let him yield himself to God in all simplicity, asking nothing, begging and desiring nothing, but loving and intending only God, and verily such an

[1] In so far as it suggests a subjectivity of interest, we shall find the mystic endeavoring to correct the impression. "To ascend to God," says Hugo of Saint Victor, "is to enter into ourselves; and not only so, but in our inmost selves to transcend ourselves" (ineffabili quodam modo in intimis se ipsum transire).

unknown God. Yea, upon His unknown will let him throw all his affairs and concerns as well as his sins and wickedness as they there occur to him, and this all with genuine love."[1]

Thus the content of the object of meditation tends to reduce to a nothing — so far as picture-content is concerned — but not quite to nothing, unless will is nothing.

III

In the long experimental history of these efforts of purgation and meditation, three things have become clear. First, that the mystic cannot complete his own

[1] I cannot refrain from quoting here at length Tauler's recognition of this difficulty.

"In dieser seiner Erneuerung und Einkehrung erschwinget sich der Geist alsbald ueber sich, gegen die göttliche Finsterniss, viel geschwinder und höher, als ein Adler gegen die Sonne. . . . Hiervon stehet im Buche Hiob also geschrieben : 'Dem Manne ist der Weg verborgen, und Gott hat ihn umgeben mit Finsterniss,' nämlich, mit Finsterniss der Unbegreiflichkeit oder Unerkennlichkeit Gottes, da er weit über alles, dass ihm zugeschrieben werden kann, erhaben, und ganz namen-, form-, und bildlos ist, ja er übertrifft darin alle Weise und alles Wesen. Und dies ist, liebe Christen, die wesentliche Einkehrung, zu der das Stillschweigen der Nacht, samt ihrer Ruhe und Einsamkeit, sehr viel hilft und nützet. Darum rathe ich einem jeden treulich, wenn er vor der Mette gut geschlafen hat, dass er sich allen seinen Sinnen und sinnlichen Kräften gleichsam entziehe, und nach verrichteter Mette mit allen seinen Kräften sich über alle Bilder und Formen versenke, ja, über alle seine Sinne und Kräfte sich erschwinge. Doch solle er wegen seiner Kleinheit und Nichtigkeit nicht gedenken noch sich vornehmen sich der vortrefflichen Finsterniss zu nahen, von welcher ein Lehrer spricht: 'dass Gott eine Finsterniss sei nach allem Licht,' sondern zu der Finsterniss der Nichterkennung Gottes, und da ergebe er sich Gott ganz einfältiglich, frage nichts, bitte und begehre auch nichts, sondern liebe und meine nur Gott, und zwar einen solchen unbekannten Gott; ja, in seinen unbekannten Willen werfe er alle seine Sachen und Geschäfte, auch seine Gebrechen und Sünden, so ihm alsdann einfallen, und dies alles mit wirklicher Liebe." Predigten ii, 553.

purification; second, that there is a clear self-contradiction in trying to expel all desire; third, that when the deepest will attempts to subordinate all partial desires by setting up its own absolute good as an object of meditation, this effort is notably liable to substitute some false god for the true one. Taken together, these three results amount to a practical demonstration that the attempt of worship, in so far as it depends upon the mystic's own active efforts, is impossible.

There must be some way of cutting short these infinite processes of self-preparation, if in order to see God one must in fact accomplish a pure heart. The mystics have not failed to find ways of summarizing all this preparation in a single act. Ruysbroeck, for example, cuts the knot by a stroke of will: we have the necessary humility and love if we will to have them. In the good-will to renounce oneself, the renunciation is, for the purposes of worship, completed. Santa Teresa has another way of concluding the matter: let us once clearly see and acknowledge our defects, and in that knowledge be free from them. "This matter of self-knowledge," she says, "must never be put aside. . . . The knowledge of our sins and of our own selves is the bread which we have to eat with all our meats, however pleasant they may be, in the way of prayer; without this bread life cannot be sustained, though it must be taken with measure. . . . (But) when a soul beholds itself resigned, and clearly understands that there is no goodness in it . . . why should it be necessary for it to waste its time on this subject? From foolish devotions, Lord deliver us." For both Teresa and Ruysbroeck this dismissal of the processes of prolonged self-discipline is made possible by a self-examination which has reduced all their sinful desire to one category, namely, pride: and it is the summary repudiation of this pride, in the one by a magnificent will to be humble, in the other by a clear perception of its nature, that effectually closes the earlier stages of preparation.

But whether in one way or another these efforts are brought to an end, the mystic finds himself at last not trying, but waiting. His last effort is to destroy all effort, and to make himself wholly passive. It seems, indeed, as if the attainment of passivity, of the right kind, were the whole aim of these preparations; the act of worship having rather to clear the way for the assertion of some other power, inner or outer, than to do anything of its own. Just how this passivity is to be brought about, and what it consists in, is not easy for the mystic to define. He uses many a figure to describe it: emptiness (Ledigkeit), silence, permissiveness (Lidekeit, Lidelicheit, lydende Vernunft,—Tauler), poverty, destruction of self, inward stillness (innere Gelassenheit,—Suso), nothingness (in the sense of the "O, to be nothing" hymn), even idleness, or dormancy ("Müssigkeit"),[1] death, extinction. In the ideal of passivity, indeed, we come upon one of those far-reaching discoveries of religious experience which take a thousand shapes and names, and enter in various degrees into all phases of worship. In Quietism, it comes to an especial cultivation: for if one must resort

[1] "Alles das Gott von uns haben will, das ist, dass wir müssig seyen und ihn Werkmeister seyn lassen; wären wir ganz und gar müssig, so wären wir vollkommne Menschen." Tauler, quoted by Karl Schmidt, in "Johannes Tauler," p 120.

to passivity in the end, why not from the first. But in Luther's appeal to grace, rather than to works, his reliance on the forgiveness of sins; in the self-abandonment of conversion; and in many another assertion of the "feeling of absolute dependence"; we see other forms of this same principle of passivity which completes the preparation of the mystic.

However, it is obvious that there can be no question, here, of pure passivity. The state is the precise opposite of a state of drifting, or of psychical indolence. The will to worship remains to distinguish this nothingness from all others. The mind is in a condition of powerfully directed attention. Such as the term "contemplation" suggests.[1] The effect of all these various self-suppressing efforts has been to lop off interfering and distracting movements of attention; whereby all the strength of these inhibited tendencies has been *told over into* a single comprehensive thrust of the mental energies. It is a suppression of body by body; of desire by desire; of activity by activity; in sum, a suppression of self by Self. The loss of self and of self-consciousness of which the mystics often speak, a loss concomitant with the cessation of traffic with things, is essentially a recalling of all subordinate and partial selfhoods into the one master-self of all, a *simplification*, and at the same time an extreme heightening of self-consciousness in its now exclusive relation to its Absolute.[2]

[1] "Contemplation," as used by the mediæval mystic, implies that the effort of "meditation," in which one holds the object before the mind by force of will, gives way to a state in which the object attracts and holds attention without further conscious effort.

[2] "This slumber of the mind resembles at first a negation of existence, but it is the exaltation thereof. Nothing perishes in us but the

Something deeply paradoxical there is about this voluntary passivity of the mystic, like the motionlessness of a rapid wheel or the ease and silence of light. And this paradox the mystics themselves have not failed to observe and study. They have seen that there is an idle passivity which must by all means be ruled out; and they have spared no effort to distinguish between the true passivity and the false. Let me quote a few of their own explanations.

These from Molinos:

"By not speaking, not desiring, not thinking, one arrives at the true and perfect mystical silence wherein God speaks with the soul, communicating himself to it, and in the Abyss of its own Depth teaches it the most perfect and exalted Wisdom. . . . Strive to be resigned in all things with silence, and in so doing, *without saying that thou lovest Him*, thou wilt attain to the most perfect, quiet, effectual, and true love."

"*The very Virtues* which have been acquired and not purified *are a hindrance* to this great gift of the Peace of the Soul, and the more so, the more the soul is dogged by an inordinate desire for sublime gifts, by the wish for spiritual consolations, by sticking to infused graces, entertaining herself with them, and desiring more of them in order to enjoy them: and finally, by a desire of being great."

"It is a vulgar error of those who say that in Internal Recollection or Prayer of Rest the faculties operate not, and the soul is idle and inactive. This is a manifest fallacy, and belongs to those who have little experience, because although the mind operates not by means of memory nor by the second

person, that is to say, the limit. . . . To return to the universal is to enlarge, to become divine, not to abolish and lose oneself." Simon, *École d'Alexandrie*, pp. 156–7, 218.

[1] The Spiritual Guide, tr. R. Y. Lynn (with liberties).

operation of the intellect, which is judgment, nor by the third which is discourse or reasoning, yet it operates by the first and chief operation of the understanding, which is *simple apprehension* enlightened by holy faith, and aided by the divine gifts of the Spirit; *and the will is more apt to continue one act than to multiply many*, so that the act of the understanding as of the will is so simple, imperceptible, and spiritual, that hardly the soul knows it, much less reflects upon it."

These from Teresa:

"In mystical theology, the understanding ceases from its acts because God suspends it. We must neither imagine nor think that we can of ourselves bring about this suspense."

"To have the powers of the mind occupied, and to think that you can keep them at the same time quiet, is folly. There is no great humility in this (trying to be passive), and though it be blameless, it carries a sort of punishment after it, in that it is labor thrown away, and the soul is a little disgusted: it feels like a man who preparing to take a leap is held back—he has used up his strength, and is yet unable to do as he wished."

"What the soul has to do at those seasons is nothing more than to be gentle and without noise. By noise I mean going about with the understanding in search of words and reflections whereby to give God thanks for this grace, and heaping up its sins and imperfections together to show that it does not deserve it. Let the will quietly and wisely understand that it is not by dint of labor on our part that it can converse to any good purpose with God, and that our efforts are only great logs of wood laid on without discretion to quench this little spark."

And these from Fénelon, who had reason to feel the force of the Quietistic discussion, from both sides, and who speaks, if not as mystic, yet as a sympathetic arbiter:

"All passive contemplation reduces itself to something very simple. It is a tissue of acts of faith and love, so simple, so direct, so peaceable, and so uniform, that they do not appear to constitute any action, but a repose of pure union. This is why St. Francis de Sales wished to reject the term 'union' for fear of expressing some uniting *act* on the part of the soul: he would have it called a simple and pure Unity. Hence also it is that this contemplation has been called orison of silence or of quietude; hence finally that it has been called passive. God forbid that it should ever be thus described for sake of excluding the action real, positive, and meritorious of the will, nor acts real and successive which must be reiterated every moment. It is called passive only to exclude the self-interested activity or *empressement* of the mind, when it is inclined to continue some agitation in order to feel and see its own operation, which if it were more simple and unified would be less noticed."

"It is passive as a feather is passive, which when dry responds to every touch of the breeze, but when wet with the dampness of its own heavy desires shows an inertia which is felt as a real object. It is passive as the mirror of the lake is passive, which when its own motion is stilled, is able to return faithfully the objects whose light falls upon it; but when agitated by the breath of its own desires, returns these same rays in a broken, disordered, and so unintelligible condition."

IV

This, then, is the preparation of the mystic: on the whole, a negative path; an activity ending in a voluntary passivity, destined to give way in turn to an *involuntary passivity* when God accepts and lifts to himself the prepared soul. Its history is that of an activity of self-suppression which must itself be suppressed. And what, in the end, does it amount to? Wherein does it differ from the simple act of thought, the "lifting of the mind to God"?

First, I should say, and most obviously, in the moral character of the process, in the ideal of the 'pure heart' which is recognized as the condition of finding God in worship.

Second, in the simplification of consciousness. Instead of spinning connections, the mystic strives to be rid of connections, and to reach an object which is behind and prior to all distinctions. He has practised recollection, and has become *total.* He wishes to be, rather than to think; assuming that there is a distinction between being and thinking.

Third, in the repudiation of effort. What the mystic knows will be empirically known. What the mystic wills, will be willed by necessity. The worshipper has exercised his freedom, perhaps the first and last absolute freedom possessed by the human spirit, to consent to an empirical apparition of the real.[1]

The mystic is prepared: what will happen to him? Will there be an event? Will his voluntary passivity give place to an involuntary passivity; and will he know that he is one with God? The mystic has been knocking at the door of his world, an outsider, preparing himself inwardly and outwardly, doubtless with a certain sense of *magic* and *mummery* about it all; as

[1] Royce's often-quoted phrase which describes the mystic as the "thoroughgoing empiricist" is strikingly true of the mystic's method of knowing. But the mystic's peculiarity is that he applies this method to objects which empiricists generally insist cannot be given in any such immediate, unreasoned manner, namely to totals not to elements; to souls, not to sensations; to resultants (like history, or society) not to factors; and finally, to God himself.

of doing things whose reason he does not see, and which through hidden laws or arbitrary will of the God will have an *effect* if they are well done. Yet the true mystic has known well enough that his experience is no adventitious effect, but wholly a response to his own meaning and within his own unbroken idea. If the effect were magical and external, the mystic would be thwarted, — he would not consciously have been with God at all. What he reports is, that he *has been admitted;* that from being an outsider, knocking at the door of things, he has ceased to be an outsider and a subordinate. He uses the words illumination, union, sometimes deification, to express what has come to him. In some way he is admitted to the council of the maker of this world of things. He has become an understander of the heart of it. And in evidence of his truth he is able to walk about among things and men, — do we say as an alien? — on the contrary, as one for the first time fully present and at home, able to recognize himself and God in whatever declares itself, able to open himself to the whole of experience.

This is what the mystic reports. But having followed the course of the mystic's own volition, and largely in the mystic's own tongue, we must now seek further light, *external* light, such as psychology can furnish, upon the nature of this experience, and its interpretation.

CHAPTER XXVII

THE PSYCHOLOGY OF MYSTICISM

WHAT is the experience of the mystic? And what meaning has that negative path for us of the present day? To the mystic, the whole meaning and logic of worship is personal; and there is no more to be said about it than has been said. He has come consciously into the presence of God, and what is more, into a unity of will with him. He knows nothing of any psycho-physical facts which could make clearer the significance of that event. On the contrary, he seems to find himself — though perhaps only for a brief instant — free from the body, wholly "in the spirit," where neither mortal thought nor mortal psychology can follow him. We must allow the mystic the first word in reporting, and also in interpreting, his experience. But while he dwells upon its unique, superlative, indescribable aspects, psychology helps our understanding of that experience by finding what is *not* unique about it, what analogies it has in more commonplace experiences, undertaking thereby both to describe and to explain it.[1]

[1] The mystic himself, as we have noticed, plays the psychologist so far as the beginnings of description are concerned; and he alone can properly inform us of the inner nature of his experience. But his description offers the clue to concrete analogy; and this in turn to more scientific description and explanation.

There is danger, no doubt, in pursuing analogies of what is essen-

The mystic experience is unique and free, but not in the sense that it has no analogies and no ties in the world of common experience. The fact that these ties exist is to be seen in the simple circumstance that the experience is *transient*.[1] For if union with God were the whole story of mystical experience, there could be no reason why that moment should pass. The mystic himself knows very well that his vision cannot last, so long as he remains a human being.[2] Many a mystic has expressed regret that his joy could not endure, but none (so far as I have found) has expressed surprise. This absence of surprise may show that the immediacy of the experience is never so great as to be wholly free from outer reference, that some consciousness of the worldly self and of its ties remains. The mystic has found himself in a region where the gravitation of earth

tially a religious event. The religiousness of it lies, as the mystic instinctively knows, in what is unique and can be told only in the personal language of religion. The religious element is always lost among its many copies, and degraded. Nevertheless, this is the only way in which the unique can permanently hold us. We must run the risk of this loss; and when analysis is finished try again to recover the original.

[1] It is hardly necessary to recall the familiar description which William James has given to the class of experiences he proposes to call mystical: they are ineffable and noetic, usually also transient and passive (Varieties of religious experience, p. 380 f). In the character of ineffability, the indescribable quality of the experience becomes a point of psychological description; and both this ineffability and the transiency are to be explained, as I shall try to show, on psychological grounds.

[2] "This sublime condition is not of permanent duration. It is only now and then that we can enjoy this elevation (mercifully made possible to us) above the limits of the body and the world. I myself have realized it but three times as yet, and Porphyry not once. All that tends to purify and elevate the mind will assist you in the attainment, and facilitate the approach and recurrence of these happy intervals." Vaughan, Hours with the mystics, vol. i, p. 81. An imaginary letter from Plotinus to a disciple.

operates but slowly; but that it still operates and will claim its own, he seems by this silent confession to be fully aware.

Thus mystic experience comes within the range of law, and probably also within some law of *rhythm*. That is, the mystic's elevation is transient presumably because it is a phase in some natural rise and fall, some organic wave perhaps, in experience. If so, this transiency, external character though it is, will offer the most favorable angle for scientific approach. For any rhythmic movement in experience reveals not only an organic bond, but a law of connection as well, through which the special phase in question is bound in with the before and the afterward, and begins to be interpreted.[1]

[1] The idea of rhythm with its organic relatedness (causal or otherwise), need not be wholly alien to the mystic's inner meaning — not more in regard to the forces that bear him up than in regard to those that hold him down. The logic of the relation between the worshipper and his God is indeed wholly personal and particular — not magical — but the worshipper still relies upon a steadfastness in the being worshipped; he frequently comes to look upon his elevation as a response to a right approach on his part, as some function of the condition of his own heart. He holds a quasi-natural adjustment of attitude to the supernatural. Meister Eckhart says, "I will never ask God to give himself to me: I will ask him to make me pure of heart. For if I am pure, God must of his own nature give himself to me, and flow into me." "Meister eghart sprach: ich wil got niemer gebitten das er sich mir gebe: ich wil in bitten das er mich luter mache: wan were ich luter, got muest sich mir geben von siner eigener nature vnd in mich fliessen" (Wackernagel, Sprüche deutscher Mystiker, in Altdeutsches Lesebuch, col. 681). The Spruch continues: "Wo mit kumet man zuo luterkeit? mit einem steten iamer na dem einigen guot, das got ist. Vnt wo mit kumet man in ein jamer? mit uernichten sich selben vnt mit missevalle allen creaturen." Thus the mystic himself is often disposed to read his experience as a course of interaction between a higher and a lower law — with an element of hnman freedom in the circuit.

This, at any rate, is what has impressed me in mysticism: That the turning away from the world in the negative path of worship (together with the mystic experience itself which marks the limit of the up-swing) and the turning back again constitute a normal rhythm or alternation which has many analogies, and a vital function in the human mind capable of psychological expression. The marked disconnection between the mystic experience and the usual level of life, which obscures both to the mystic and to the observer the presence of any organic bond between these levels, has also a psychological meaning. In the present chapter, I shall do no more than bring forward some of the analogies which help to interpret (1) the rhythm, (2) the disconnection, and (3) the unsociality of the mystic's life circuit. In the next chapter, I shall try to bring its law to definite terms.

1. *Rhythm.*—If there is any rhythm in life which religion, in the observances of worship, follows and cultivates, it is something more than the simple ebb and flow of our "animal spirits." Excitement and depression, high spirits and low spirits, are organic fluctuations which leave their mark on the religious life as on all life. Undoubtedly there is a kind of vision connected with the high places in this vital rhythm, which resembles, and may actually develop into, mystical experience. Variations of this kind do affect most markedly our capacity for fellowship, and the promptness of that "fusion" with our objects which we thought characteristic of the mystic consciousness. I can conceive it possible that the habit of worship

might take possession of some such subtle wave in our organic life; but I cannot think, as do certain writers,[1] that this type of flux brings us very near the mystic's experience, and for the following reasons:

First, quasi-mystical moods of this sort are as likely, perhaps more likely, to come over the mind when the physique is at low tide; as in fasting, exhaustion, weakness from loss of blood or insomnia, or in the early stages of convalescence.

Second, if mystic experience has its rhythm, it shows little sign of regularity — it is not periodic. The worshipper's will and conscience take part in the affair, and not the organic wave alone: voluntary decision is interpolated, as in the circuit of nutrition. It is not true that mystic experience mechanically follows worship; there is a certain looseness of connection between prayer and its answer, which the passivity of the mystic implies. But the preparation of mind and the act of consent must enter into the history of the event at some previous time.

Third, there is no depression which corresponds in constancy and prominence to the mystic's elevation. The elevation of the mystic is not in such wise above normal that it must be compensated by a corresponding below-normal. On the contrary, it seems to be, in some sense, another normal. Something of its content and quality tends to become a permanent possession of consciousness; which would not be the case if it were simply

[1] See especially Godfernaux, "Cette oscillation constante du ton vital est bien, semble 't il, l'aspect physiologique propre du sentiment religieux . . . Quiconque éprouve le sentiment religieux est un extatique à quelque degré." Revue philosophique, vol. 53 (1902), pp. 164, 162.

an extreme, or "hyper-tension." There comes a time in the life of some of the mystics when the vision of God is, as they assert, a continuous experience, and the semblance of rhythm disappears.[1]

These considerations lead me to judge that the mystic's ascent and return are not to be understood as simply an unusually pronounced oscillation of vital tone. But perhaps they also imply that the rhythm itself is unnecessary. May not the very circumstance that the meaning of the mystic experience is to be built into the continuous level of consciousness, show that the two levels of experience belong together; that the alternation is accidental, and to some extent pathological? Delacroix, whose masterly studies of the mystics put us all in his debt, inclines to regard whatever rhythm there is as something to be overcome; and as something that is overcome in the long experience of the greater mystics.[2] After much painful experiment and mistake, such persons as Teresa, Madame Guyon, and Suso, emerge into a period of serene and powerful activity, from which the fitfulness, the heights and depths, the interruptions and disturbances, of the earlier enthusiastic devotions have disappeared.

But I must doubt whether this alternation is essentially pathological or whether it is ever overcome: I must doubt

[1] "My soul is, as it were, in a fortress with authority, and accordingly does not lose its peace . . . The imaginary visions have ceased, but the intellectual vision of the Three Persons and of the Sacred Humanity seems ever present." Teresa to the Bishop of Osma, May 1581. "Cette vie divine devient toute naturelle à l'âme . . . Ici l'oraison est l'action; et l'action est l'oraison: tout est égal, tout est indifférent à cette âme . . . Ici l'extase se fait pour toujours et non pour des heures." Madame Guyon, Torrents 232, 248. Quoted by Delacroix. Études, 143, 148.

[2] Etudes d'histoire et de psychologie du mysticisme, esp. ch. ii, vi, xi.

it if only from the fact that worship and mystic experience involve an exclusive occupation of attention which in the nature of the case is incompatible with simultaneous attention to other affairs, and vice versa. "When attention is turned in one of these directions, it is in some degree withdrawn from the other. I cannot at the same moment be conceiving of God as the only being of worth, and yet of my life — this fragmentary life — as itself a matter of worth. I alternate. . . . (One) requires a certain narrowing of his vision, a certain exclusion of the infinite aspects of his task, in order to perform that task well." Thus Professor Palmer states the situation.[1] If worship has any vital function to perform, it must alternate with other things, the necessity of rhythm lies somehow in the nature of my practical attention.[2]

[1] G. H. Palmer, The Field of Ethics, pp. 181, 173.

[2] The mystics found various ways for expressing a belief that some such alternation is not a matter of choice, but a result of the structure of human nature; as in such words as these:

"Now the created soul of man hath also two eyes. The one is the power of seeing into eternity, the other of seeing into time and the creatures, of perceiving how they differ from each other as aforesaid, of giving life and needful things to the body, and ordering and governing it for the best. But these two eyes of the soul of man cannot both perform their work at once; but if the soul shall see with the right eye into eternity, then the left eye must close itself and refrain from working, and be as though it were dead. For if the left eye be fulfilling its office toward outward things; that is, holding converse with time and the creatures; then must the right eye be hindered in its working; that is, in its contemplation. Therefore, whosoever will have the one must let the other go." Theologia Germanica, Winkworth, ch. vii.

To Plotinus and Pseudo-Dionysius, the two alternate directions of the mind had a metaphysical meaning: they symbolized the emanation and reflux which were supposed to make up the cosmic history; and more than this, they were parts of that cosmic rhythm itself.

Fénelon has his usual judicious comments to make on the notion of per-

I am driven therefore to look for further analogies among those normal alternations such as sleeping and waking, work and recreation, conflict and co-operation, society and solitude, hungers and satisfactions of various types. The fact that much of the early elevation is built into the later level of continuous living may be interpreted, in no very far-fetched manner perhaps, as akin to the assimilation of a meal. The experience seems in fact to have supplied the subject with a certain moral fuel as well as with cognitive material. His inability to bring its content to immediate expression is to be understood by the fact that this supply is still relatively external to him and requires a normal interval to be made his own; as in time it is made his own. Rhythm of this type would then last at any rate as long as the subject continues to grow. Approximate continuity is a sign of old age in mysticism; just as the gradual obliteration of the sharp rhythm of sleep and waking is a sign of physiological old age. Alternation lies deep in the nature of things psychical as well as physiological: it is the fundamental method of growth. I am inclined, therefore, to regard the mystic experience as a normal incident in the attainment of a new psychical level; and no exceptional incident, but one which in various

petual orison, or "spiritual marriage." "There is such a thing in this life as a state habitual, though not entirely invariable, in which the most perfect spirits perform all their deliberate action in the presence of God, and for love of him . . . This referring of all voluntary action to our unique end is the perpetual orison enjoined by Christ, and by Saint Paul when he said, Pray without ceasing. But this orison should never be confounded with contemplation pure and direct (which) has not the same species of perpetuity: because it is often interrupted by acts of the various virtues necessary to all Christians." Explication des maximes des saints, Art. XXV.

forms and degrees is a recurrent event in every person's life.

This may stand as a rude hypothesis which will place mystic experience in an organic relation to the rest of life. We may sharpen this conception by considering now the relative discontinuity which seems to exist between mystic experience and the ordinary level.

2. *Disconnection.* — The traditional religious mystic reaches a point of ecstasy in which he is as thoroughly detached from his waking world as is the sleeper. And as in the case of sleep, this disconnection follows upon a voluntary effort to be effortless, when his preparation has put him into the hands of some agency beyond himself. The absorbed thinker is also detached from the world, and the absent-minded man, and the person who falls into a "brown study": in some respects, the mystic's abstraction more resembles these than the laxity of sleep. But again, as in the case of sleep the sacrifice of time and of complete active consciousness is regarded as a natural means of conserving both life and time, so the mystic may be justified in regarding, as he does, his self-abandonment as a paradoxical necessity, not more remarkable than sleep, for maintaining his spiritual integrity.

Disconnection is the aspect of mysticism which the observer is most inclined to resent and condemn as abnormal. The mystic, on the other hand, has prized it most highly : for to be "carried away" is the chief sign that supernature has taken the place of nature. But both the critical observer and the mystic might profit by considering that the element of "mystery" or "ineffableness" in mystic experience is largely if not completely due to the fact of disconnection alone, not to any inherent mysteriousness or unnaturalness in the content of the experience. Psychologically, mystery is felt whenever there are two bodies of experience not in perfect communication, quite apart from the question whether the one or the other is inherently wonderful or weird. Mystery does not lie in either of the two bodies by itself; it expresses the effort of each to make terms with the other, and the beginning of success. It is the state of mind of one who begins to see. Mystery is thus the characteristic quality of every incipient idea, not yet wholly seized by the mind. And the mystic may be regarded, I think, as one who is confronted quite empirically with a body of new experience and idea in such wise that he is a possessor of two bodies of experience, neither of which he can doubt: both must be true, and he does not understand *how* both are true.

This is no uncommon state of mind. Such an expression as the following seems to me quite typically mystical: "How came this creation so magically woven that nothing can do me mischief but myself? . . . If I will stand upright, the creation cannot bend me." Here stands Emerson with the weight of appearances against him, sure of "the creation," yet equally sure of his own immunity; confessing that he cannot understand how both assurances can be woven into one fabric,— using therefore the word "magical." The mystic might be broadly described as the man who is willing to drop one world of assurance while he seizes another, confident that reality will harmonize them both, though he cannot yet grasp the idea which does harmonize them. Inability to bring the two experiences together tends, it is true, to cast doubt for a time upon the reality of the one not present: and the religious mystic is one for whom another world than this, or another stratum of experience, has gained such substantial certainty that the reality of everyday experience must suffer this kind of passing doubt. But the true mystic is he who holds to the reality of both worlds, and leaves to time and effort the understanding of their union. This kind of discontinuity in experience (such in part as Emerson pleads for in his arraignment of anxious consistency) seems to me a condition of mental soundness and health, as well as of mental growth.

There is some deep-going practical principle here concerned, whose existence we can note without at present trying to determine its law. It is a principle which suspends the operation of the ideals of reason, from time to time, without in the least questioning or supplanting those ideals. We must have consistency in the end; we must have connectedness; we must have unity: but for the sake of having this ultimate unity and order, anarchy and discontinuity must have their moment. That sort of self-possession which is made of continuous rationality must be held subject to self-abandonment, when the hour of empirical truth arrives. And the hour of truth is always present. Idolaters of self-possession, as we are: do we not see that every pulse of consciousness is full of the tumult and wonder of these plunges into the ununified and returns therefrom? that sensing, listening, accepting the hint of any honest emotion, every merest decision such as the instants of living are made up of — all of these involve some commitment to the unknown, some such willing embrace of a momentarily broken rationality? The emotion itself is but the call of the new idea which has its overt connections yet to make with this system of mine; passion is but a more impetuous commitment to an insight of larger scope and of larger destructive (and reconstructive) implications. All enthusiasms, whether of devotion or anger or love or courage, are alike in this: all alike spurn continuity and seize the insight which the moment offers as a new world of truth, whose unity with the old may be cared for in due time. And has not passion also such a tide as the mystic knows, which after the critical moment of consent substitutes its own motion for the will, now apparently passive, of the worshipper? Some *cult* of discontinuity, strongly resembling the mystic's breach with the world, we may thus see everywhere in the intimate working of our mental life. The disconnection which the mystic practises is so far countenanced, and vaguely explained.

The mystic, we may say, simply brings his discontinuity into the open and makes an avowed principle of it. We see why it is that no person whose god is convention and self-rule can be a mystic. In the typical mystic temperament we expect to find a certain openness of spirit, such as readily accepts a present inspiration as its law. The encasements of mental attitude in such persons are never fast-set: the limberness of their inner substance promises well for continuance of growth. At his worst, the mystic is impulsive and childish; at his best he retains something of childhood, its tenderness, its freshness of impression, its unsatiated wonder, its generosity: he has that simplicity and teachableness which are found in the very young and the very great. He may, for this reason, be a demonstrative person (the "gift of tears" was once regarded as a saintly attribute); or he may, for the same reason, seem to live in perpetual calm: in any case, he is one whose attachment in the Absolute is so secure that he has no fear in embracing any insight which can gain the consent of that side of his consciousness, though for the present it can claim no other. (Here perhaps we begin to break through into the theory of the mystic disconnectedness, and the continuity behind it; but we shut that prospect for the present, and return to our psychology.)

Some degree of openness to discontinuity in experience is evidently a part of deeper practical wisdom. But does this general principle, whatever it may be, valid for these partial ventures in experience, — does this principle explain or justify such radical and total disconnection as the mystic practises? For the mystic, strictly speaking, is the man whose disconnection is made between the whole system of things and ideas temporal on the one side, and the heart of the eternal on the other: whereas the subdued "mysticism" of our ordinary life merely flits from one body of ideas to another within that world-system. Radical mysticism, religious mysticism, with its sweeping negation and equally sweeping affirmation, seems to sever a man from his fellows as well as from nature: it tends to make him solitary, anti-social, and useless; to give him over to subjectivity. We are not inclined in our time to rate highly any solitary aspect of religious thought or practice. And yet I incline to think that just this radical social disconnection is also an essential part of mysticism.

3. *Solitude.* — All thoroughgoing mysticism is solitary, so far as human companionship is concerned: we must first be clear about that. There are phenomena of religious history that look much like mass-mysticism, and have been interpreted as such: religious dances, dramas, festivals, revivals, in which the white-heat of social consciousness becomes the generator of mystical enthusiasms. But even in these somewhat tumultuous and disorderly variations of our theme, the mass-consciousness forms the level from which the individual *departs:* he is not a mystic until his own spirit has made its solitary leap to God, like a tongue of flame out of the midst of the fire.

Much of what we call "social life" moves on a similar principle — that of passing from hand to hand a function which in any one hand is a solitary function: each one in turn becomes "it," takes upon himself alone the difficulty in question, learning by his own experience what otherwise he sees only from the outside. Whoever helps to sustain any social structure is alone just in so far as he is responsible: and he comes, for the most part, to his solitary social position through having wrestled with some angel in more literal isolation from other human ken. The initiate must go down alone into the grave; though initiation is on the whole a social ceremony. And so, whether we have in mind an orgy of Dionysus or a meeting of the society of Friends, it is individual seizure by the spirit which marks the moment of religious success.[1] We do not understand solitude until we see that it can ride on the back of any whirl of sociality however furious; its pang may be the more poignant because the utmost limit of common possession has been tested in an immediately preceding moment. He who merely imitates is but a false mystic —for the thing to be imitated is a burst of original impulse: he who is entranced by social suggestion is but a false mystic—for the inner core of what his social environment requires of him is the violent subdual of the social bond by the superior energy of the divine *rapport*. He alone is utterly unsocial who refuses when his own watch comes to go out and meet the absolute in the darkness. Solitude, I say, is the essence of mysticism: and, I add, the basis of its supreme social importance.

For it is the most dangerous things that are the most important. We of this age have come to fear solitude and with it all mysticism because solitude is the home of stagnant growths and morbid consciousness, because it is the crowning curse of all vices and itself a vice even in religion. We see in it only the danger of losing objectivity, which is indeed its essential peril. But consider the mystic's intention, which after all is the thing to be judged: his intention is that his absolute

[1] Though the early ascetics of Egypt lived in communities, their dwellings appear to have been individual, and each had its place for entire solitude. W. M. F. Petrie, Personal Religion in Egypt, p. 68. The same is true of the early monks of Ireland, so I am told by Mr. C. A. Bennett, who supplies me with the following note: "With many of their establishments were connected 'diserts,' lonely spots in woods or mountains, to which from time to time the individual monk might retire for solitary meditation, fasting, and prayer. The cenobitic never wholly replaced the eremitic ideal in Ireland." Cf. Gougaud, Les Chrétientés Celtiques, pp. 103-104.

Object shall gain in strength pari passu with his entrance into himself. Mysticism in its true character is precisely *the redemption of solitude:* it is the process which enters one step farther than we have yet explored into the heart of our own infinite subjectivity, and reclaims that new increment for the general use, in the form first of a deepened morality and art. If our own age with its growing sociality and immersion in the manifold is little mystical, it is also true of it that the power of evaluating solitude and therewith the depth of self-consciousness is little developed: in so far as this age of ours has flattened and shallowed out, it is because it has so far lost its mystical instincts.

I cannot doubt that the value which attaches to the partial discontinuities of living in our spiritual economy attaches also to the complete disconnection which the typical religious mystic practises: the latter is governed by the same law as the former. We cannot live well, I judge, unless there is something in our lives which offers us from time to time the possibility of absolute detachment and solitude: that which is necessary and useful in part is necessary and useful also in whole. The mystic is simply the person who does consciously and with the whole man that which we are all doing spontaneously and in fragmentary fashion in every moment of our effective living. Doubtless, then, the rhythm of mystic experience has its law, such as will place it with the other normal rhythms of experience. But as the mystic rhythm is the most comprehensive of all, I shall refer to this law simply as the principle of alternation; and shall now try to state its meaning.

CHAPTER XXVIII

THE PSYCHOLOGY OF MYSTICISM (*continued*) — THE PRINCIPLE OF ALTERNATION

THE principle of alternation, so far as the program of daily living is concerned, is neither abstruse nor unknown. Of the various goods which go to make up a balanced existence, we naturally treat each in turn as if it were a sole and sufficient object; we do not undertake to pursue them all, or many, at once. All good things do doubtless belong together; but each good thing, we recognize, is to be pursued separately. The difficulty lies in inferring from the parts to the whole: that is to say, in seeing that the alternation which is obviously necessary as between one partial object and another is also necessary as between all partial objects and *the whole*. But just this, I think, is what worship means: that the whole must become a separate object of pursuit, taking its turn as if it also were a part, as if it were *another* among the many goods of practical occupation. Let me illustrate this principle as we commonly recognize it among these many partial interests, and then carry it on to the total alternation of religion.

I

We may best appreciate the principle of alternation by what it is contrasted with, the principle, namely, that all things belong together and should be pursued together. To this contrasting principle we pay much respect: old dualisms as between soul and body, form and matter, God and world, have become tabooed in practice as they have become obsolete in theory. We believe in the *concrete*, in the soul that is one with body, the God that is immanent in the world: and we are inclined to make practical programs according to this belief. If soul and body belong together, we must cultivate both together. If man and woman belong together, we must educate both together. If all beauty is one beauty, then the highest art will be composite—we must have perfumed music, dramatic music, Wagnerian opera, or in German fashion, music with beer, Gemütlichkeit, and a fine outlook. But for the most part some sense of fitness saves us from turning our concrete doctrine too thoroughly into a program. Our inferences become fantastic; and without abandoning our belief in the concrete, we recognize a fundamental dualism or pluralism in the necessities of conduct. Reflection and action belong together, but we cannot carry on both at once, with success: each best finds its due influence on the other if each has its time of whole-hearted attention. We cannot endure form without substance, whether in men or books or things, nor substance without form; these also belong together and perfection in either will bring perfection in both: but not waiting for perfection in either, each must be acquired in its own way and time, by some degree of separate attention. In larger concerns, liberty and authority belong together: but in the course of history an expansion of one alternates with an expansion of the other, each developing characteristic abuses, preparing the way for an outburst of the other with more or less disturbance and passion.

The whole man, in short, is not to be found in any one moment — nor in any one man. The dreamer and the man of affairs are forever finding their way together; the spirit of peace is forever breeding with the spirit of war, in more successful syntheses of character:[1] yet specialization has its infinite work to do, — the concrete is its deposit, not its occupation.

So it is with all the antithetical goods of the world; and so presumably is it also with that most comprehensive antithesis between God and the whole world of visible work. I believe in the "concrete universal" as a metaphysical doctrine; God and the world belong together — neither is anything without the other: but from this true generality it no more follows than in the above practical matters that God and the world can yet be best known or won together. The concrete universal cannot either in this case or in any other be forthwith made into a maxim for historical conduct. God and the world, I maintain, must be worked in with one another forever: forever they must be pursued in alternation. We have now to follow out this theory.

II

In every art we recognize a distinction between technique and spirit. We care little for one without the other; yet we know that technique has its own right,

[1] In classic times, the pursuits of commerce and city life actually unfitted men for fighting; the antique contempt for the merchant was based in part upon a psychological fact. To-day, commerce has its good quota of combativeness; and an industrial country is never without an efficient army.

and must be cultivated, as if for technique's sake alone: the spirit has its own moment, in the intervals of technical study,—and the spirit represents *the whole*. Here the whole alternates with the parts.

The art of winning knowledge is not different from other arts in this respect. We know what the tools for intellectual discovery are—facts in infinite variety and extent, measurements, classifications, knowledge of all existing theories: he who would win truth must fill himself as full as possible of science, of history, of social motives, of the immense richness of the cosmos. But we know too that there comes a moment when these very things, his necessary means, become his poisons: this is the moment at which they become *himself*. The man becomes identical with his learning, is nothing but his learning: he cannot use it because he has lost sight of the thing it is *not*, he has forgotten what it is *for*. His technique cannot serve him unless he can see beyond it. That self must be withdrawn and re-oriented: it must turn its back upon itself, and revert to *the whole*.

This practical necessity is embedded in the very categories with which science carries on its work. It is in the psychology of our knowing processes that we find the barest and simplest view of this alternation in which the whole is one member. For as a process in time, knowing has to ply not only from fact to fact, from part to part of experience, but also between all such parts and some conception of the whole. Beside all the work of observation there is the work of hypothesis, the alternation between induction and deduction, laying hold on a whole and returning from the whole to the several parts.[1] The scientist is occupied with phenomena; but beside the phenomena, the concept of *substance* in some form or other (whether of matter, or energy, or law, or soul) must take a place as *one other object* of necessary attention. Any concrete knowledge of a society, a race, an age, etc., must be reached by a similar interplay of categories: beside the *extending* of knowledge, there must be a *deepening* of knowledge, an attempt to grasp the 'spirit' of things, their principle, formula, essence,—in brief, their *one*, their whole. It is not otherwise with our knowledge of individual men. If I wish to know a person, I must pursue acquaintance in two antithetical directions: I must learn to know him in what he does, at his periphery, in the various expressions of his action in the world of our common objects; and I must also learn to know him by the pursuit of his central 'substance,' by the intuitive seizure in intimacy of the unity from which all these plural deeds are derived.

And knowledge of the greater whole evidently follows the same principle as the knowledge of these lesser

[1] There is a tendency among logicians at present to make a concrete of induction and deduction as of everything else; and to assert that neither process exists apart from the other. Ostwald asserts that there is no deductive science, but there is *wohl* a deductive procedure, which must be understood in connection with induction. Well, let it be so: there is an inductive procedure and a deductive procedure, and these are two different procedures, and do in the history of research alternate with each other. That is all; whether we draw the lines of any science cleanly about one or the other procedure is of no consequence. The alternation itself will never be wiped out. Analogically speaking, the quest of induction is scientific *prayer;* and the discovery of a whole, in answer to such prayer, a scientific mystical experience. Inductions are not to be taken by violence, they are received in passivity. The question of induction is treated further in chapter xxxi below.

wholes. My world at its periphery is 'experience,' 'life'; at its center it is 'substance,' 'reality,' 'God.' We must know both aspects in turn, and conceive them as we can together. My total picture of this world is drawn like an artist's sketch—not by a line continuous and adequate in the field of vision, but by a series of lines which err, and which are broken in their course by recurrence to the (undrawn) idea. God is in the world, no doubt: the plural and visible aspect of things is divine also—that is, *if we are able to see it so*. But if we are to prosper in such an interpretation of the world (which certainly sets upon that world a high value) we need from time to time to have caught the original meaning of 'divinity' in some immediate experience.[1] We must recur to the whole.

Herewith we come upon the principle of alternation in its full meaning, which is best seen in the *history of the will*. In all our practical living we human beings are pursuing some total good under shapes and by means which are inadequate to it, and so partly false to it. We are obliged from time to time to reject what

[1] It is not accurate to say that we are unable to hold in a single view the many and the one, the appearances and the reality, the periphery and the center, the world and God. To some extent we must do this: in attending to the many, we may not lose sight of the one, at the risk of losing the many also; and in attending to the one we may not lose sight of the many, at the risk of the vanishing of the one. The one must always be known as the one *of these many*. The situation is rather this: that in the process of attending to and dealing with the many, the vision of the One *tends to vanish* and must be renewed by empirical presence of its object. Likewise, in lifting the mind to the One, the sense of the many, with which the One must be thought, tends to fade, and God loses all meaning to the mind that regards him. The exclusive direction of the mind whether to the many or to the One is a self-destroying process: whereas the alternating of attention may be a self-developing process.

we have done, to withdraw our forward-moving efforts, and revert to the whole: not because of the *fact* of error (for there are errors which may be remedied on the spot without change of direction), but because of the *type* of error, — it is an error which involves not only our tools, but our *selves*, the operators. We begin to get into our own way and so to defeat our own work. We can find no radical remedy except in getting rid of that self; and no radical way of abandoning that self except by reverting to the whole.[1]

This is, in outline, the meaning of the principle of alternation. There is something about our practical attention to any part or parts which turns self-defeating, and requires such complete abandonment of the parts, and reversion to the whole as religion has demanded, that whole which is different from all parts. And there is also something about practical attention to the whole

[1] The principle of alternation is the supplement of the *principle of relativity* both of knowing and of willing Both principles, of alternation and of relativity, are historical principles: they apply, that is, to *knowing*, not to *knowledge*. It is not knowledge that is relative; it is the temporal act of knowing. It is my momentary position as a being in time and space which determines that at any moment I may see but one side of a shield — and this limitation I cannot overcome. But such knowledge of the whole as I have leads me by alternating my position to repair the defect of my historical knowing. Now knowledge of the whole, such as guides this alternation between relative parts, is also a matter of degree. And in so far as I fail to overcome my relativity at any point, or find myself sinking deeper into it, I am forced to turn away from all parts, and directly seek a whole that will place them. Thus I alternate between whole and parts, and thereby transcend relativities as they make themselves felt. Every detail of psychical life shows this method of action. Attention in its minuter physiology is a rapidly alternating process, perpetually withdrawn from its object and instantaneously replaced; in the instant of its withdrawal having recovered a better poise and a steadier termination, having wiped away the film of relativity with which self and object had begun to obscure each other.

which turns self-defeating, and can only be recovered by occupation with the parts. Hence the movement of our temporal life must swing between them. But in order to see more clearly what is meant by this "reverting to the whole," we must look deeper into that self-defeating tendency which makes this alternation necessary.

III

It is a matter of common observation that every human effort produces something it does not want; and this by-product sooner or later checks the effort. We may even say that every effort produces something of the opposite of what it aims at: the strain to see brings blindness; the strain to think brings absence of mind; strained self-consciousness brings loss of self-possession; careful calculation invites failure; scrupulous morality develops the immoral; high aims bring specialization and deformity. These are facts, but what is the reason for them?

The reason, as I see it, lies as far back in the nature of things as the fact that the soul of man has a body, appears in space, and works out its destiny in time. Whatever is the cause and meaning of our physical existence, that same cause makes our temporal efforts self-checking and that same cause requires us to recover our spiritual integrity by bringing the whole down among the parts, and treating it as a thing of time and space like ourselves.

That which makes existence in time important to spirits such as we are is the power of *voluntary attention:* it is the specific mark of our individual selfhood, and it is also the place of our freedom. All the work of life, with its manifold interests, can be described as the sphere of our voluntary attention and action. This characteristic marks off all our occupation with the parts from our occupation with the whole in worship, which in the mystic experience itself becomes passive, that is to say, effortless. The contrast between mystic experience and 'life' is at the same time a *contrast between effortless attention and effortful attention.* But in this effortful attention we find the chief mark of our personal liberty; and it is just this liberty which is bought with the great price of *artificiality,* and separation from nature.

For in this voluntary business of life, we are not merely pursuing a good which is already made; we are constructing our good, we are *making* good. That same absolute good which the mystic simply finds, appears to our common action as something which we can win only by making it our own, reproducing it, or realizing it by our own labors. All practical life may thus further be described as a transition from a self that is given to us (by birth or otherwise) to a made-self. And it is here that we inevitably separate ourselves from nature. For all such practical constructive effort must have its plan, its aims, its standards; and whatever aims and standards we self-consciously adopt and define to ourselves as 'our good' are so many theories, types, generalities, — never quite the whole truth. Since we must model our conduct on some definite plan, *the practical will is necessarily theoretical,* and so far, abstract, incomplete.[1] We gain

[1] The will works in the concrete — that is true. But what it consciously sets up in the concrete world are its own ideas, mouldings and

firmness in the saddle of practical self-possession only by condemning to death a certain margin of our consciousness.[1]

This inherent defect in the operation of voluntary attention becomes more pronounced and radical as effort continues; simply because every voluntary effort, assuming as it must that its standards are adequate, that it knows what it wants, strengthens the assumption by acting upon it, and so deepens the breach between the artificial self and the natural self. We are never occupied with any object without becoming to some degree fascinated by that object and assimilated to it; as the object is partial, so we who deal with it become partial.[2] As a conscious, self-making agent, "the individual is always wrong"; yet, just as such a free, effortful, self-making agent, the individual must always assume that he is right.

We are thus, by "our finite situation," bound in a predicament from which our active selves cannot shake free, though the ultimate knower in us is not involved in it. Ambition and duty, all use of conscious freedom, all *work*, in short, develops of itself an inner opposition, or spiritual checkage. For this loss of margin, as the artificial self becomes identified with its own assumptions and objects, is a progressive impoverishment of

improvements upon a given reality, pseudo-individual objects, imitations of the concrete. Never yet has the conscious will of man constructed by its own effort alone a living being. Our explicit practicality, I repeat, is theoretical and abstract.

[1] Here commences the building of "subconsciousness." See the note on this subject at the end of the book.

[2] This is the "relativity" to which the human will is subject; we cannot act in the world of matter without becoming material; we cannot use our freedom without becoming to some degree a *thing*.

that *whole-idea*, whose use, as we thought,[1] gives all objects what value they have. In order that my various practical enterprises should go on well, it is necessary that my various ends should maintain their worth; and in order that they may hold their worth and interest, my whole-idea must be active in all my occupations — I must be thinking *with* my whole-idea, and efficiently. But the incident of voluntary activity is to undermine the effectiveness of this whole-idea.[2] And the result is a spiritual fatigue, analogous to, but neither identical nor contemporaneous with, physical fatigue.[3]

The symptoms of this spiritual checkage are not hard to recognize. They are simply the inevitable assumptions of action become hardened into fixed illusions. We find ourselves in the first place regarding the several objects of our pursuit as though they were *absolute*, real in themselves and good in themselves; and we cannot see them otherwise than with this exaggerated importance. We cannot bear to lose any of them; for every loss is a dead loss. And if we win, we are still dissatisfied, for every gain, too, is a dead gain, reaching no further in its value than the object then and there

[1] See above, chapter xi.

[2] Deliberate narrowing of the range of idea, in one's occupation with the part, is the essence of *sin*. Freedom may thus add to the breach between natural self and artificial self a positive barrier. For the present we may ignore this further element in the "separation between man and God."

[3] No doubt this fatigue of the idea is also physical in the same way that all spiritual limitation is physical: that is to say, there is a physiological expression for it. It is none the less a concern primarily of ideas; it has a necessity of the same order as that which makes us temporal beings at all. In the end it is a matter of religion, and can only be successfully approached from the religious quarter.

gained, leaving infinite further gains to be made. No gain is so great as to seem to me a gain of the whole. My world of will-objects has become *pluralistic;* and my practical problem has become essentially hopeless. Another symptom is *criticism.* For all work and construction must be critical, that is, selective. All voluntary activity takes up the critical attitude toward what is, and resolves to bring about something better, by first conceiving something better. The practical temper has to separate the good from the bad: and since its world has taken on this pluralistic and absolute appearance, the good qualities and the bad qualities of things and of men seem independent of each other. We think that we can have the one without the other and we insist on it. We have no interest in a possible union of the good and the bad; we draw a clean line between them; we are condemnatory and exacting, for the sake of our own standards. We grow mighty in discrimination, and terrible: we grow puny in synthesis and creative power. A further consequence and symptom is that our responsible temper finds nothing in the present that satisfies it. It is alienated from its present moment: it is *romantic,* in the sense that it seeks its good elsewhere, far away, in a place very different from anything it finds in experience. As the over-prepared, over-equipped, over-trained person, with his eye habitually fixed on some future moment as the moment of his action, is indeed prepared for everything except for the judgment "Now is the time"; so the soul over-steeped in actual work loses capacity to believe in the *presence* of the good worked for. Its sympathy flows forth with difficulty; and that attitude of "fusion" which we were recently describing as mystical in character, finds little scope for exercise. The one and good is not here — that is all.

All of these common symptoms of spiritual fatigue, I repeat, are nothing more than the habitual assumptions of action taken as whole truth. They picture nothing but the abstracted soul of the active man; the common materialism of strenuosity, deepened into a belief in the "abstract universal." All these symptoms sum themselves up in this: that I find *nothing individual in my world.* I find no present particular of which I can say — Here is the standard embodied: I find no object in which my whole-idea, with its high power of synthesis of good and bad, can find endless occupation. My universals have parted company with particulars. I find illustrations of value; things good in this respect and bad in that; specimens of general concepts; but no individual.

And losing contact with the really individual aspect of the world beyond me, I also lose contact with the individual in myself. My artificial self becomes the only self I am acquainted with. This self is built up according to self-conscious standards of criticism, universal in character, derived largely from my social consciousness, and passing current in the world just because I have thus dutifully universalized myself. It is a well-known selfhood — known, in fact, through and through, empty of mystery — well-behaved also, conventionally confirmed in its own successful technique of self-handling, the man of the city and of the world; betraying at every point the failure of privacy, of recourse to the individual I am, the sealing of spontaneity, the formal hardening of the heart, the unhumanizing of men by over-contact with humanity, the strain of general attitudes not wholly naturalized in oneself.

To live thus with the universal, the abstract universal of action, and with one's own artificial and dutiful embodiments thereof, is the beginning of death.

IV

The effort of work, then, provides for its own arrest. Work, simply as a voluntary application of ideas, does gradually disintegrate those values for which alone work exists. In all literalness life ceases to be worth living, and death in some shape will be *sought*. Into the midst of all effort, dutiful or otherwise, there must fall soon or late a sense of the aimlessness of work, a questioning and denial of worth-whileness, a consciousness of moral wear and tear in the determined pursuit of objects whose value is not wholly convincing, a need for recovering sincerity and spiritual poise.

And this new-born need, still of the same moral stuff that first launched the work, now reverses the direction of action, and turns naturally toward some object whose value is convincing without any effort, toward *enjoyment* in some form or other. Pleasure, recreation, friendship, the companionship of men and women, beauty — all these recall the outgoings of ambition and moral effort, and reunite a man with his natural appreciation. Something in common these all have with the quest of the mystic, and with the mystic experience itself. And *worship is the whole which includes them all.*

It is not primarily external failure which brings man to worship. It is simply the internal decay of the incentive of work, the drooping of the sails of ambition, the falling out of humor with one's own humor, the mysterious vanishing of the raison d'être of life as a sphere for the theoretical will.[1] And whatever recovers the worth of living by *recovering the natural vigor of the whole-idea* is worship, or a part of worship.

It may not be at once obvious how worship is related to all these other means for recovering our values? — there is much here that has no resemblance to worship, nor any visible need of it. For spiritual as well as for bodily fatigue, physical nature has its simple advice to give, and ancient human experience its rule of thumb. As the Egyptian proverb has it, "The archer hitteth the target, partly by pulling, partly by letting go; the boatsman reacheth the landing, partly by pulling, partly by letting go."[2] No man can earn the good by consciously mastering all its conditions; so the race long ago found out. Critical responsibility must be limited; physiology and the self-righting mechanisms of the world must do what self-consciousness fails and will always fail to accomplish. All such counsels of passivity, *laissez faire*, partial death, are parts of practical wisdom and have no apparent necessary connection with religion.

But these things all need religion to finish them just because they are relatively un-self-conscious. Our free and self-conscious personality ought not to be satisfied, and cannot be satisfied, with a restoration purely by

[1] All these, taken together with the sense of one's own responsibility for the result, i. e., that it is due to self-assertion. The sense of sin re-reads and complicates, but does not essentially alter, the problem.

[2] Instructions of Ptah Hotep to his son.

mechanism or by *laissez faire.* In fact there can be no such thing as a recovery of value which is essentially physiological or subconscious; the idea must be recovered *as an idea*, that is to say, consciously and intentionally.[1] Worship, we may say, is *the self-conscious part of the natural recovery of value;* it is that part, therefore, which assigns all other parts their place and meaning.

Sleep wins our consent without offering any account of its method or meaning — or perhaps a minimum account. In the pursuit of pleasure there is something more of the positive and intentional. To pleasure, friendly association, and art we turn still blindly and instinctively; but with some dawning grasp of the *idea* in what we do. There is a free and deliberate element in the reversal of action. In all of these we perceive the play of the universal in the particular, a natural union of the two given without effort, and rejoining us with the individual element in our experience.[2] But in

[1] This implies that in the complete alternation there is something of the voluntary self which is not abandoned: if this self is to know the meaning of its own recovery, it cannot be wholly in abeyance while the process of recovery takes place. There is something in all our artificial efforts which is absolutely right, and cannot be withdrawn: namely, the task itself of being self-governing, world-building, self-making beings. It is our nature to be artificial, and our right to be self-knowing: whatever postulates and selfhoods have to be negated and revised, they are not *these.* Freedom has the peculiarity that it can recognize its own relative failure, and define more or less clearly what it lacks; and in so far as it can define its need, it can consciously pursue it. Thus the preparation of the mystic never surrenders its intentionality, even when it is most passive.

[2] To Kant's mind, it is the communicability of the æsthetic judgment, the universal validity to which it aspires, that stamps it at once as an affair in which thought is engaged. But he cannot identify it with objective reason, nor with explicit reason; hence he explains it as a sub-

worship the idea has broken through and become explicitly an object of search; the soul deliberately seeks the One, the individuality of the world, as a present object of experience.

Everything that may still be to us an object of immediate and effortless appreciation will take part in this search. Hence worship naturally allies itself outwardly, as well as inwardly, with recreation, social enjoyment, and beauty. Worship uses these, and goes beyond them: it recognizes in them the absolute which is its own and discards the rest; puts behind its back all but the One which is in all, and is the condition of them all. This final, sacrificial aspect of worship — the negation, or rather subordination, of all partial loves — is the act which alone can make these loves immortal: it is the conscious possessing of their necessary condition.

Thus worship adds the touch of unity and self-con-

jective play of the faculties of knowledge in an "Erkenntnis überhaupt." "Also muss der Gemützustand der eines Gefühls des freien Spiels der Vorstellungskräfte zu einem Erkenntnisse überhaupt sein." And of what Vorstellungskräfte? "Einbildungskraft, für die Zusammensetzung des Mannichfaltigen der Anschauung, und Verstand für die Einheit des Begriffs, der die Vorstellungen vereinigt." Kritik der Urteilskraft, p. 62. We know, in general, well enough, what this means: the sense of the inner enlivenment, and lightening at the same time, of the action of our "powers" in the presence of beauty, as if a smooth place had been found and these powers were not more in harmony with each other than with the reality which they appreciate. It is essentially free play, and reflective, but not subjective.

Kant notes the relatively effortless, self-continuing character of the experience of beauty thus: "Sie hat (eine) Causalität, den Zustand der Vorstellungen selbst und die Beschäftigung der Erkenntnisskräfte ohne weitere Absicht zu erhalten. Wir weilen bei die Betrachtung des Schönen, weil diese Betrachtung sich selbst stärkt und reproducirt." Ibid., p. 68.

sciousness to the whole body of our natural spiritual recovery. It is, I repeat, nothing more than doing with the whole self, and consciously, that which in blinder and more fragmentary fashion we are doing at every moment of our waking lives, and especially in the moments of partial return, such as we have mentioned. The mystic is he who knows that his insight must be an event in time, and that it is his right as a self-conscious being in time to seek for it. The man who prefers to leave his religion in the obscure, in its diffused and partial forms, is the man who puts the prize of life upon vagueness and the unexplicit. The mystic, on the other hand, who adds worship to all the rest, the mystic is the man who prizes the overt, the definite, and the literal in religion.

V

The motive of the mystic, then, is something quite different from moral ambition. In the active part of the mystic's preparation for worship, the moral motive may still be visible: it may still be touched by a sense of the importance of work, of various humane interests, as if it were for the sake of these ends that one now turns his back upon them. The zeal of the mystic for self-purification, his moral scrupulousness, may be in part derived from his view of his own practical duty or his desire for success. But this is all something distinct from the love of God in its psychological meaning; and this meaning does not appear until the active stage of worship, which is "prayer," gives way to passivity in the discovery of an object of *effortless appreciation.* Unless the characteristic of pleasure, that is, of wholly spontaneous and original conviction of worth, enters into worship, the prayer has no answer and worship is to that extent a failure.

But in the mystic experience that is what happens. The object upon which the worshipper has bent his thought becomes actually significant of *the whole.* The mystic has found a present object which is able to gather into its own vortex all the meanings of his worldly work, and therewith to abolish the independent worth of that work. His idea of the world in its unity has, simply, become adequate to its synthetic task ; and the disunited segments find their way together: this is the whole secret of value. It would be just to say that the worshipper is at first moved rather by the desire to love God, than by that love as a ruling motive: and that the actual love of God is itself the success of prayer, simultaneous with the insight which the mystic obtains, identical with it.[1] The character of this experience is well pictured in a simple note in the diary of Tolstoy, whose mystical traits (though he would hardly be called a mystic) are closely allied with his powers of penetrating self-description:

"Yesterday," he writes, "I hardly slept all night. Having posted up my diary, I prayed to God. It is impossible to convey the sweetness of the feeling I experienced during my prayer. I said the prayers I usually repeat by heart, 'Our Father,' 'To the Virgin,' etc., and still remained in prayer. If one defines prayer as a petition or as a thanksgiving, then I did not pray. I desired something supremely good ; but

[1] "L'oraison s'appelle méditation jusqu'a ce qu'elle ait produit le miel de la dévotion: apres cela elle se convertit en contemplation. Le désir d'obtenir l'amour divin nous fait méditer; mais l'amour obtenu nous fait contempler." St. François de Sales, Traité de l'amour de Dieu, VI, iii, quoted by De Montmorand, Revue philosophique, vol. 57, p. 252.

what, I cannot express, though I was clearly conscious of what I wanted. I wished to merge into the Universal Being. I asked him to pardon my crimes; yet, no, I did not ask for that, for I felt that if he had given me this blissful moment, he had pardoned me. I asked, and at the same time felt that I had nothing to ask; and that I cannot and do not know how to ask: I thanked him, but not with words or thought. I combined in one feeling both petition and gratitude. Fear quite vanished. I could not have separated any one emotion,— faith, hope, or love,—from the general feeling. No, this was what I experienced yesterday: it was love of God, lofty love, uniting in itself all that is good, excluding all that is bad."[1]

The moving principle of Tolstoy's life at this time was doubtless a large human ambition, taking impulsive shape as a desire to perfect himself, and to "test himself"; and swinging perhaps only in this solitary instance within the circle of mystic worship. But this human ambition and this divine love are closely related to each other. We may say that beyond the limits of the mystic experience itself, the love of God takes on the form of human ambition; that these motives are, so to speak, allotropic forms of the same. They alternate with each other, as the hour glass is turned,—each one in turn becoming the life of the other. With the idea of God, one loves the world; and then with the idea of the world, one loves God again,—and the two loves, or ambitions, are of one substance, though they involve alternations in the history of the empirical will.

VI

For worship cannot last; it also has its type of self-defeat and death. The worshipper who persists in his

[1] Life of Tolstoy, Aylmer Maude, vol. I, pp. 63–64.

contemplation of the whole, thinking to establish himself permanently in the immediate presence of God, becomes an automaton, precisely as the determined worker becomes a machine.

'Automatism' of a very literal character is not only admitted but even boasted of by certain mystics who have professed to enjoy the constant vision of God. Madame Guyon reaches a stage of perfection whose chief marks are the absence of personal volition, the replacement of effortful voluntary action by spontaneous obedience to the suggestions of her religious sense, or fancy. She accepts the logic of the complete withdrawal of individual will and choice, namely, that all acts become indifferent: there is a will in the world and she has become the instrument of it, but with perfect passivity, without sharing in it, "laissant à Dieu le soin de faire naître les occasions et de les exécuter." "But why do you do this rather than that? I do not know. I give myself over to that which carries me on."[1] From this condition of mind there comes the "apostolic life," marked by an extraordinary facility in preaching and writing, capacity to do a prodigious amount of work, and to undergo great distress without protest from her own intelligence and will. Her life during this time has traits of largeness; but it is a largeness which is evidently consuming itself and lessens to a small end: it exhibits much free motion, but little effect; it produces much writing, elaborate commentaries on scripture, "Torrents" of various sorts; but how much of permanent worth?[2] To abandon conscious control of the

[1] Cf. Delacroix, Études, etc., p. 155 ff.

[2] Mme. Guyon's Œuvres complètes fill forty volumes. In it all, there

trend of work, to resign remembrance of what has been done and written, to live continually in the present moment only (in so far as these things actually occur) — here inspiration, real enough in itself, begins to decline into irresponsibility. The sad weakness of will and of voluntary thought which comes of it is sufficient comment on its general failure as a plan of life. "I find in myself no power either to decide or to execute; I appear to myself like a phantom." [1] We have no need to dwell on the failure of unremitting worship. We in our day have well perceived and overcome that danger. We need only note the fact.

Thus each aspect of life apart from its alternate becomes a mechanism. And the whole of human existence falls into two phases, work and worship; the domain of duty and the domain of love, respectively.

We have now outlined the relation which worship, as I believe, does normally bear to life at large: it is a necessary alternative to all our effortful willing and knowing, so far as these are living processes of empirical history. The principle of alternation tends to justify

is some genuine inspiration. Cowper (in a letter to Unwin, Aug. 3, 1782) says, "Mr. Bull . . has put into my hands three volumes of French poetry, composed by Madame Guion — a quietist, say you, and a fanatic, I will have nothing to do with her — 'T is very well, . . but in the mean time her verse is the only French verse I ever read that I found agreeable; there is a neatness in it equal to that which we applaud, with so much reason, in the compositions of Prior. I have translated several of them, and shall proceed in my translations," etc. The preface to "Poésies et cantiques spirituels" describes (doubtless with exaggeration) this verse as having been written "sans aucune réflexion. . . Ce lui était un gêne insupportable de faire la moindre réflexion." See Delacroix, p. 158.

[1] "Je ne trouve en moi nulle puissance de vouloir ni d'exécuter, et je me trouve comme un fantôme." Lettres V, p. 458; Delacroix, Études, p. 214.

the 'negative path' of the mystic by placing it in its organic context. Neither phase of the rhythm is justified by itself. Duty has no right over men apart from their religious experience. On the other hand, religion has no right apart from its descent into the world of effort. In reality, in the logical and eternal order of things, these two phases of experience belong together, and in time also are always finding their way together: but in psychological order, in the natural history of the mind, they fall apart, and must be pursued separately. Religion belongs with morals — yet the deeds of religion must alternate with the moral life and for a time displace it. Religion belongs with all the works of art and science and human betterment — yet it has its own moment which takes away from theirs.

Any given moment of life must choose between two goods, psychologically incompatible. On the one hand, the peace of the hermit, the silence of the forest, the exaltation of sacrifice, the mightiness of simplification and unity, the joy of self-abandonment, the calm of absolute contemplation, the vision of God. On the other hand, the variety and stress of life, the zest of common ends, the mastery of means, the glory of infinite enterprise, the pride of creativity and self-possession. The modern world as a whole has made its choice. But there is a better choice: namely, the choice of both. For the life of each is that it may lose itself, from time to time, in the life of the other. And this, which is obvious in things partial, is true — and even chiefly true — in things total.

CHAPTER XXIX

PRAYER AND ITS ANSWER

IN what has gone before, we have been so much engaged with the psychological bearings and analogies of worship, that the central purpose of the mystic's prayer and its answer have been obscured. It may be well, therefore, to state now in simpler fashion our view of prayer, and of the attainment which prayer reaches; not attempting to carry theory farther, but simply to relieve and clarify this central point.

Let us first consider what is meant by the answer to prayer, that is, the mystic experience itself, and then the nature of the prayer which finds such answer.

Mystic insight has been compared by William James with our occasional experiences of *realizing*, more or less suddenly, the meaning of words, sayings, points of view, which may have been familiar and empty possessions for a long time. Such realizing as this, we may observe, is never simply the discovery of the meaning of a general proposition. It is a flowing together, after some artificial separation, of universal and particular. I wake up to the meaning of an old adage, or of an opinion to which I have been hostile on prejudice, when I bring such a generality into connection with a concrete occasion. And the commoner mystical experiences begin, I believe, with the concrete occasion, only suggesting or foreshadowing the universal meanings which they have.

Experiences of this sort are not uncommon. They are but moments of greater mental integrity than usual, in which consciousness is more concrete, the associations and resources of the mind more instantly collected and fused into a total grasp of the meaning of its present object. Such a moment is apt to be disconnected from other moments just on account of its unusual synthesis: it is disconnected from our usual condition of disconnectedness. What surprises us in such a moment is that we are commonly so blind. Hence these moments are remembered, and become authoritative over other moments, as occasions when we have seen clearly, whether or not we can any longer recover that same clearness of view.[1]

Such an experience for instance, sporadic yet fairly common, is a sudden realization of the flux of time, the mystery of the past that is gone as if it had never been, and of the future moment that is sure to be, yet is wholly non-existent. So seductive is the occupation of the mind with generalities, and so practically useful the assumption that everything recurs, that the individual quality of time-units rarely penetrates to us — we act as if one moment could always be substituted for another. The

[1] Such experiences reach all degrees of clearness. The dominant idea which defines a passing 'mood' — and most certainly every mood has its idea, or vision — may be very obscure. Our various feelings, our marked experiences of pleasure and pain — though they never fail to become authoritative in our total consciousness of what the world means — are, singly taken, hard to read: we seldom think of them as moments of insight. We hardly recognize an experience as typically mystical until *the idea has broken through*, and our sense of its significance outweighs our interest in its present quality.

uniqueness of the present moment has to be discovered and rediscovered; it cannot be fairly seen without something like a religious reverberation; the poetry of many an Omar is in that simple fact. It is perhaps some such sense of infinite significance in mere present existence which leads Meister Eckhart to say that "He who stands continually in a present Now, in him God the Father begets his Son without ceasing."[1]

Still more frequent and still more typically mystical is the discovery of *oneself* as an individual; as when some summons drives home the question, Who are you? What are you? The assumption of an artificial selfhood, if we are right, is not an accident nor a pure vice — it is a necessary incident of duty. The idealist as well as the hypocrite may be suddenly confronted with a new vision of himself upon a rude demand to be "natural," or serious, or sincere. Such demands very frequently find only another self — not the real one; may substitute for the social self a more primitive and uncouth being, equally untrue, the self of my bad conscience or of my self-distrust — still, then, a theoretical self, though less theoretical than the made-self. The individual self is indeed hard to find, the self which *is*, deeper than all epithets. To come upon this individual is an event straightway known to be significant.[2] Inge quotes the following from Tennyson's memoirs:

[1] "Meister eghart spricht: wer alle cit allein ist, der ist gottes wirdige; vnt wer alliu cit do heimenen ist, dem ist got gegenwürtig; vnt wer alliu cit stat in einem gegenwürtigen nu, in dem gebirt got der uatter sinen sune an vnderlas." Wackernagel, Altdeutsches Lesebuch, col. 679.

[2] *What* this revelation of self may signify is a further question and doubtless differs at different times. It is likely to be an *egoistic revelation;* a vision of the infinite risk of being alive, and of the infinite right of the

"A kind of waking trance I have often had, quite from boyhood, when I have been all alone. This has generally come upon me through repeating my own name two or three times to myself silently, till all at once, out of the intensity of the consciousness of individuality, the individual itself seemed to dissolve and fade away into boundless being: and this is not a confused state, but the clearest of the clearest" etc.

But the best known of all experiences of the mystic type is that of discovering the individuality of another person.

We deal with men for the most part through their qualities and properties, that is to say, through their universal, describable, recommendable or condemnable sides; each man stands to us, or tends to stand, for a certain formula, quality, function, in semi-official manner. We have our theory of him; he plays his part in our artificial world, as one of many. We note in him many qualities, good and bad, interesting and perhaps contradictory; we wonder how all these characters are united in one being who feels no such variety in himself. The one quality that combines these many in a consistent identity we can neither describe nor convey; nor can we surely hold the memory of it except by return from time to time to his presence. But for

solitary self to be satisfied. It always includes in itself that more abstract vision above described, the uniqueness of the time-movement. Subjective idealism, and such practical philosophy as that of Nietzsche or Max Stirner, are unravelings of the purport of just such mystical experiences: and they are not false visions, for the stake of existence to the subject cannot be overstated, though it may well be disproportionately stated. The will to power and the will to save one's soul have much in common: and one as the other has immeasurable religious importance. In all such experiences, and the self-recovery that goes with them, it is the vision of the individual which marks the moment of mystic illumination.

the most part we are not concerned with this; the man is a function, and would be improved by the excision of his bad qualities; we could easily re-make him to his advantage, after the pattern of our own universal standards. Our critical judgment of him is, we have said, pluralistic and general: there is a miracle in him — that is, his individuality — but we remain outside the mystery, and willingly. For it is the business of men to fit well together in the work of the world, to be officers there, reliable working-universals.

But at times we are granted something like a mystic vision: it seems to us that we have come into the presence of the individual and have seen the miracle as such. We have found the other soul in its seclusion and simplicity — so we think; and we begin to appreciate the place even of its apparent defects in that synthesis which is itself. The critical attitude is no longer able to hold its negation against this interest in the person as substance — as something that is, and is one. The vision in fact begins to work upon us; we cannot forget it: we no longer attend to it with voluntary effort, but it forms a part of our consciousness and begins to make us over after its own pattern, as if it were active and we were plastic before it. This perception of the other as an individual being is love, in its special meaning. Love does not displace criticism: it contains it.[1] Love accepts the individual with his defects, because the One

[1] I perceive faults in my social acquaintances, but I do not make a practice of telling them their faults, because my relations with them are still subject to the abstract assumptions of our artificial selfhoods. But whatever fault I discover in one whom I love I make known to him: for thereby I address the self which I have discovered, simpler and greater than the self of that fault, and which can join me in being hostile to it.

which it has seen contains the inward remedy for those defects. Nor does love feel the need of concealing its own faults, for love of another involves also a discovery of the individual in oneself:[1] it is a presence of the individual to the individual, a "flight of the alone to the alone."

Love is a revelation like that of the mystic, full of significance. For in finding the individual, one has indeed found the individual's *idea*. That which explains and unites and largely justifies all these various and seeming-inconsistent qualities is some view of the world which he has, some hold on the absolute, some whole-idea. He is an individual vision of reality; and in knowing him, I do at the same time know his vision and make his vision my own. This is the central fact of all mysticism: namely, that the discovery of the individual is always a discovery of truth, of a powerfully synthetic idea, and yet not by the way of effortful thinking. That interest in another soul which we call love is not an interest in his idea as a matter of theory: it is an interest in *him* as an individual substance, a being which knows and is more than its knowledge.

All these common experiences, we say, are analogous to the mystic insight. And there can now be little doubt about the nature of that insight itself and its place among the rest. For what is the mystic experience but finding the idea of the whole, as love finds the idea of a person? Worship seeks the self of the world as an individual being; but in finding this self, it

[1] Love thus includes in itself all of those lesser or relatively abstract experiences which we have been describing.

gains, or regains, a tolerating conception of this world, a view which can make life as a whole once more acceptable, inviting, great. In this idea it is able not to sink but to suspend its criticisms of existence: it is not reconciled to defects, but it sees something more than dead fact, even some meaning, in their presence. The total sound of life sends up to it some echo of beauty; and it is able, without blindness, to become as it were a lover of the whole. For the idea which thus of itself absorbs our hostilities, binding our many and divergent judgments in powerful synthesis, is won not by the effort of the theoretic will, but by coming effortlessly upon the spirit of the world, as an individual being, simple, wonderful, and in close union with the individual in oneself.

These other experiences are not only analogous to the mystic insight: they are, as we have said, parts of it. All loss of value in the world is at the same time a loss of religious insight. All the artificialities of effortful attention strike first at the virility of the whole-idea, and dim the consciousness of God. All absolute criticism condemns the whole; all pluralism mutilates first the unity of existence; all romanticism adds to the burden of heaven. And wherever in all life the individual vanishes from my grasp, there has vanished first the individual God. Where men and self become abstractions, there God also becomes an abstract universal, occupying an official position in my artificial world, reduced to be dealt with in polite and deadly distance. On the other hand, wherever the individual is recovered, there is in some degree also a vision of God. God is the One of all these plural loves and pleasures; and it is the love of God which naturally includes and places all the rest.

But of all these objects, God is the only one always accessible to direct pursuit; the only one admitting such a conscious, voluntary cult as worship is. Our pleasures are so many discoveries; friendships, appreciations, loves generally, happen to men as by good chance: once they have dawned upon us, we may pursue them as vigorously as we will, but the appreciations themselves cannot be directly sought. It is only such vision of God as one at any time has that enables him to recognize the pleasant, the beautiful, in things and persons: the only net that can be spread for the loving of men and things is the consciousness of the absolute.[1] So far as these other objects retain their value, that is to say, their idea, we may turn to them; but their salt has a tendency to lose its savor, and cannot be salted again by its own kind. This is the root of our trouble. We know always that life is worth living; we know, too, that we have in us somewhere the power of appreciating it; we know that nothing is common or unclean, and nothing hopeless: only — we cannot see it so. We have lost our primitive joy in primitive things; we have lost our freshness of impression. It is no longer true that "the scent of a flower, the flight of sea-gulls round a cliff, the cornfield in the sun, stir us to strange and cosmic delights." And it is worse than useless, so we find, to try with might and main to *feel* in these

[1] As a command, the injunction to love one's neighbor would be meaningless unless the command to love God went before it. In the case of all other affections, I love what I must; in the case of this one I love as I will, hence it is subject to command.

things what we have once felt. Nothing is more common than this trying, and nothing more fatal. Yet the thing is there. There are great funds of enthusiasm and literal love of men and things in us, if we could but reach them. There is a love of life in us which we never let go. But that love of life, if we can discern its true nature, is at bottom a love of God: it is that mystic thread which "in the ground of the soul" is never broken. If we can regain that, all the rest will follow. And only by regaining that can we surely recover the rest. It is for this reason that we must add to all the other means for keeping or recovering our spiritual integrity, prayer. And what, in this present day of grace, does prayer mean?

It means, in the first place, that we maintain our discontent, returning again and again to the demand that our existence shall find itself justified in our own eyes. The first practical principle of religion is to hold without weakening the right of every individual life to know its own worth. We must not let reality go, this reality which has produced us, until it satisfies us: it must yield us the idea which unites what we most deeply desire with *what is*. This is the prayer of Jacob; and in a fundamental sense it is the first prayer of every human being. We are right in wishing to see first and be loyal afterward.

It means, in the second place, that we understand clearly to what self this right belongs, and cultivate that self. This right to see does not belong to our complex and strident personality which goes about, thinking by omnipotent effort to earn its happiness and its certainty. It belongs only to that in us which is simple and sincere. The sincere is that which is moved by necessity not by effort (no feeling is sincere which is made by will): the genuine will is the will which goes forth from effortless attention, that is to say, from love — and that is to say, from sight. We have the right to see first and be loyal afterward only because *unless we see we cannot be loyal*, nor in any sense sincere or moral. No determination to be a lover of life, no resolve to fight down desire or grief or regret or aversion, no attempt to transform one's own nature, can succeed by dint of the effortful will alone. But sight does its own transforming: sight turns the energy of our own desires into the work of their own re-making. It is thus an effortless self, and therewith a necessary will, that we have to seek. And for the same reason, it is a simple self, not involved in our artificial distinctions.[1]

To be able to command this simple and sincere self is the critical condition of religious insight. Hence (thirdly) we in this day must still follow, in some fashion significant for ourselves, the negative path of all the mystics. We require the sight which cannot come through trying to see; we must try, then, to put ourselves consciously where sight must follow. We must

[1] This world is so made, not only that a simple view of the whole is possible, but that our mastery of the world may proceed, and must proceed, from this simple view outward. The idealist philosopher has been inclined to conceive the subject as ruler of the object: in this case, to 'return into oneself' is to return to the seat of ultimate power, and to find the law-giving principle of things, that which is *a priori* in both thought and practice. But it is rather the simple than the subjective that we must learn to appeal to, the simple which is both subjective and objective, and whose *a priori*, or 'anticipated attainment' is concrete.

deliberately review and reject, from time to time, whatever is falsely artificial and self-assertive in our outgoing purposes; we must track, as far as we can, the points of our own partiality. We must, even in this modern world of ours, know how to shake off the prepossessions of our theoretic wills; to regard all ambitions and duties for the time as non-existent; to reduce all reality to the primitive terms of self, universe, and the present moment (wherein everything begins from the beginning). In this stark, original selfhood, detached from action and from the warping of the interests of action, we view all that active career as in a drama, as the life of another, in the light of what we can then and there muster of the whole. Its loves and hates rise up before us in a more universal frame. We must recall especially whatever is still to us of effortless value, whatever we do still sincerely enjoy and love, and we must pray for the vision of the whole of which these various goods are fragments, and upon which they depend as their absolute. I use the word 'pray,' because, in the end, there is no other word which conveys that attitude of will in which effort is so combined with non-effort, and self-assertion with consciousness of absolute dependence. Nor do I know why this word should be translated into anything more scholastic. The insight we require is both a right and a gift, the justest gift in all experience; we dare not be too proud to comply with its evident conditions. We must know that in doing these things, we are already using a degree of mystic insight: we are relying upon an attachment to the whole which is too deep in us to be lost or overcome; we are striving to 'enter into ourselves,' to recognize this attachment for what it is, the love of the God of that alienated world. This is prayer.

And the answer to prayer is whatever of simplicity, of naturalness, of original appreciation, is brought into our view of things by this act of obedience of the mind to its absolute object. In proportion as our prayer is honest, we shall find ourselves less thinking, and more seeing; and we can turn again to meet experience with so much better poise and understanding. How full, how instantaneous, how overwhelming may be the vision of the deity of the world and the worth of one's own part in it, no one can say: certainly it is beyond the province of philosophy to prescribe. Neither can it be told when or through what apparent accidents the deeper insights of our experience may occur. Philosophy can only point out the fundamental law of religious life, the right to see first and be loyal afterward; and interpret in its own abstract language the conditions of that vision.

But the meaning of the mystic experience is prophetic. It anticipates an attainment still to be won; it can be held only by proceeding to that winning. Worship is false unless it is sanctioned in turn by the life that follows it. This sanction is twofold. First that it does not undermine, but rather supports, the world of other aims. The mystic must return not less a lover of men, but rather a lover in more intense and human fashion, because it is only the true worshipper who can find the world genuinely lovable. The vision of God must give the reason for all the irrational attachments of life, all the sacrifices of self to brother, state, or cause. It furnishes the answer to the last Why of duty. To be 'loyal afterward' is the first sanction of true worship: and also the condition of further insight. It is by the alternation of loyalty and worship that each life must hold and increase its individual level of value.

The second sanction of worship is, that the worshipper does not merely sustain, but creates. All beauty, as Plato thought, incites to reproduction. It incites perhaps to something more than reproduction — to origination. Some superabundance there is in the vision of God which sends the seer back not to the old but to the new; not with a release from old grievances, but with something like a hunger for pain and difficulty. The edge of the tool of will is restored, and it is eager for world-making. The man is able to fight, to oppose and suffer; he is endowed with grit, with faith. This is the moral result of true worship.

And this, I believe, is the whole inward response to prayer. The mystic has reverted to the One, and now returns to the many, more real than before, more potent. That which can happen only with the consciousness of God is an act of God: and I cannot doubt that it has been with the mystic even as he says — namely, that God has given to him something of Himself. By just so much as the ultimate meaning of things becomes present to him, by just so much is he capable of bringing new values back to earth; not in explicit form at first, but as an enhanced quantity of being in himself, as a renewed grasp of the quality of the goal. In this way is the mystic freighted with the future; and the fruit he may gather in his own person, or may spread abroad in the world merely in the form of his own quickened hold on life and love of it, in the form of the "Holy Spirit," to be applied and gathered by others.

But the whole meaning of the answer to prayer, and so of prayer itself, cannot appear until we have reviewed those fruits of which the mystic experience contains the prophecy.

PART VI

THE FRUITS OF RELIGION

PART VI

PRELIMINARY

IN times gone by, the more remarkable experiences of the mystics were unhesitatingly read as direct communications of God to the human mind. The content of some of these experiences has been deposited (together with much else) in the various sacred writings of the world, as revelation. Other such experiences seemed to signify commands, and found expression chiefly in action: their record is to be found in history, as the inspired works and prophetic deeds of men. In religion as we know it to-day, we hear little of either revelation or prophecy: answer to prayer, such as it is, seems to have taken on a more private interest. Yet I have no doubt that in some form or other these are still the fruits of religion: so far as religious experience has become intelligible to us, it has been as a development both in idea and in will. And further, I have no doubt that these results are acts of God: for that is an act of God which cannot happen without turning the mind to God. I shall therefore discuss the fruits of religion under these heads: revelation, inspiration (religious creativity), and the prophetic consciousness.

These are the results of religion as they appear first in the life of the individual, and through the individual contribute to the wealth of mankind. It is through the individual that religion achieves those results in history which first drew our attention (chapter ii), and whose theory we are now ready to develop. But there are further fruits of religion, more distinctively historical in character; results which appear in the structure of the social environment wherein the religious consciousness must live and breathe. It remains for the concluding chapter to outline these over-individual fruits of religion, and their effects in the general movement of history. Thus we touch upon the edge of another aspect of the work of God in the world, suggested in part by the term providence, and in part by the term salvation in so far as this saving must come to the individual from the outside, through the medium of his spiritual environment. Here we shall find a necessary supplement to the inner answer to prayer; and also a view of the function of those historic mediators which the universal spirit of religion forever inclines to transcend, and forever returns to by an inward necessity hard to understand.

CHAPTER XXX

PECULIAR KNOWLEDGE AND CERTAINTY: REVELATION AND DOGMA

IN speaking of revelation we have in mind that *knowledge* which is the especial product or by-product of religion; we have to ask what it is that the mystic knows, which cannot otherwise be known. We have in mind also those sacred books. They form a peculiar body of literature: unorganized, obscure, repetitious, unscientific, powerful, immortal. In this present chapter we shall have in view both this ancient literature and contemporary religious experience; and shall undertake to interpret the one by the other.

The mystic both in his preparation and in the experience that supplements that preparation, is a world-destroyer as we have seen: and his return must be a re-creation of a world. The mystic is always *original* in the sense that he feels obliged to make his world consciously his own, to build up everything for himself from the beginning. But this may not mean that he has any novelty to offer others; on the contrary, being much occupied with first principles of world-building he may never come so far as the world otherwise has come. Tolstoy well shows this quality of the mystic as knower: the imperious necessity of rejecting all previous accomplishment of men; of reducing the world to anarchy, and building all up again from chaos. His life is spent among the rudiments, not without great result, but without ever perceiving the worth of his own temporal present: a huge, fertile, world-moving anachronism. Such in general is the case of genius, controlling the future not by any complete grasp of its own age, but by a recovered hold upon the ancient and eternal. And such, in general, is also the case of the mystic; whose chief concern is not to find things new to men at large, but only to find the Ancient of Days as a God revealed personally to *him*. The mystic is, in the first place, an original knower of old truth.

What the mystic knows is, first of all, that which he intends to know, namely God: and in so far as he is a mystic pure and simple he knows nothing else than God. There is nothing new about this knowledge except its relation to him: what he knows he knows certainly, in his own person, and for himself.

Nevertheless, he seems to regard his old truth as of general interest: he treats it as if it were a veritable mystery, and as something which could not otherwise be known to men than through his announcing it. He is not in any way abashed by the multitude of his predecessors who have been publishing the same thing. The typical mystic seems to be innocent of all historical comparison in this respect: history always begins with him, and flows outward in all directions. He speaks his mind as if he were the first to speak, and as if all depended upon his speaking.[1] It is because of this

[1] There is, of course, a psychological necessity here at work. No man can keep a truth as *his own* without trying to impose it upon others. If it is a truth, this revelation, it is a knowledge of mankind's god, not of

circumstance that the systematic truth-seeker, who measures revelation by stages, finds the literature of mysticism and of all religion curiously repetitious and

any private god of the worshipper ; and it must show itself true in their confirmation of it. A certainty which cannot be recovered in the certainty of other moments and of other men is a defeated and dying certainty. For his own sake, if for no other, the mystic has been driven to become a propagandist of his old discoveries.

This necessity of corroboration casts doubt upon the absolute certainty of the revelation itself. The mystic experience seems to carry with it a great surge of certainty : the mystic knows that "This is God"; there is a sense of arrival, of having touched goal, that seems to banish all possibility of doubt. This moment becomes the standard of all certainty ; it is an "illumination." Yet, the mystic himself frequently falls into doubt, in later moments, about the authenticity of his experience ; it may have been due to the devil, or to imagination. If he thus belies his own original assertion of immediate certainty, what credit can it have on strictly non-partisan grounds ?

The mystic needs to judge the truth of his experience by its bearing on other experience. If it accords with life generally, he will in the long run regard it true ; if it cannot be made to harmonize with experience otherwise and with thought, he must abandon it. Hence there can be no immediate certainty, we are sometimes told ; assurance is conferred on the mystical experience by its external relations, by the entire system of living truth into which it falls. The truth of the world is necessary to give certainty to the truth of God. "It is the possibility of comprehending these experiences," says Delacroix, "of living them, of utilizing them in action, which here serves as a touchstone of their truth. Intuition is of no value save in an ensemble with which it accords." Études de psychologie, etc., p. 380.

I agree with Delacroix that without a system of experience there would be no certainty of anything ; and that harmony with world-knowledge is needed to establish the certainty of God. But since we have judged that the certainty of this world is derived from the certainty of God in the first place, the world can hardly withhold its consent. The world is not otherwise known than as the world of this God ; God is not otherwise known than as the God of this world : the two knowledges are of one piece — the mystic cannot be mistaken. The intention of worship, which gives the whole experience its identity, has its continuous object, the known God present in all experience : this is the absolute constant in the process, and hence not subject to doubt. Thus it is possible to be empty, defying serial arrangement, recurring again and again to the same point. But there are reasons for this peculiarity and we shall do well to look into them: emptiness and antiquity have their own way of becoming fertile.

In the first place his repetitions are justified by the character of the truth which he has to announce. For his truth is a truth which has to be verified individually by every new human being. The ancient truth of the mystic is nothing else than *the truth about originality*, about what it is to own one's own soul. The knowledge of God as the worshipper has it is the opposite of everything that can ever become merely traditional in religion. No matter how true an idea of God religion may hand on, the true *idea* may constitute a wall which keeps God out, if it is adopted as an idea simply, —that is to say, as a repetition of other men's insights,

certain *at the moment*, without waiting for later corroboration or later doubt. I know of no certainty which is not certainty at some moment or series of moments; certainty also must have its temporal existence. We must remember that in these experiences, to which we give the name of mystic simply because in them the individual finds himself consciously at one with the whole of things, the world is not absent: it is with one's world-knowledge that one now knows his world-unity, or God. The system of ideas is in no sense abandoned, but rather in the liveliest use, though not thought *of*. Hence it is that the mystic may be certain in his moment, immediately.

But to keep this certainty in all later moments is a problem for those later moments. Systematic agreement and alternation are necessary to hold what has in a moment been gained. The meaning of that experience is the meaning which it can keep throughout all such oscillations of thought; it is the invariant which survives and becomes defined through the long course of trial and error which all this system-making and comparison involves. Both statements are true—one may be wholly certain of the presence of God; and yet one must keep this certainty, novel or not, by communicating it.

as a universal idea. God, who is truly said to explain man to himself, must explain *me* to *myself*. What I require to find in a god is that "This is what I have wanted; this is what I have been meaning all the time; the world as I now see it is a world in which I as a primitive, various, infinitely discontented will can completely live and breathe." This is what the mystic is trying to make plain — that the idea, as a universal, is not sufficient for any man to live by.

Hence the chief burden of his revelation (as if of the idea's own never-resting conscience) is that religion must exist as experience and not as idea only. There is nothing in sensation which physical science cannot exhaust, except the experience of having sensations: in the same way, there is nothing in the mystic experience not expressible in idea, except the experiencing itself. This is the chief part of the mystic knowledge which cannot be otherwise known, namely that *the mystic experience is possible.* Monotonously and age after age, men rediscover and reannounce this invariant truth, as if they were calling on men to exist, to live, to save their souls. And what is it to save one's soul, if not to be original in this sense (and in what follows from it)? From this point of view the reiteration of the mystic is justified.

But there is a further reason for the mystic's persistent celebration of time-worn axioms. Repetition, which is abomination to science, is not necessarily an abomination to the sense of beauty, nor to the sense of gratitude, certainly not to the lover, and for similar reason not to the worshipper. Individual interest can never recur often enough to its old theme; and 'revelation,' though it is a contribution to truth, is not, in its first intention, a contribution to science.

There is no topic so much discussed among friends, and none so inexhaustible, as that invariant relation of which they have the fact before their eyes, — friendship. Friendship doubtless stimulates the mind, but chiefly to feed upon itself. As for lovers, the world knows what secret topic occupies their conversation, and upon what theme they bring forth endless poetry. Song and poetry are forms which infinitely repeatable truth must take: they thus become the mystic's specialty, and revelation must consist largely of the song of God. "He hath put a new song in my mouth," says the Hebrew mystic — a song whose novelty does not appear in its name — "even praise unto my God."

Not infrequently it appears to the mystic that this poetical repetition has become the whole purpose of his existence. "Thou hast put off my sackcloth and girded me with gladness to the end that my glory may sing praise to Thee and not be silent." A more literal confession is found in those newly unearthed "Odes of Solomon." "As the work of the husbandman is the ploughshare; and the work of the steersman is the guidance of the ship; so also is my work the psalm of the Lord: my craft and my occupation are his praises, because his love hath nourished my heart." [1] And the English translator of these Odes refers in his preface to the similar expression of Epictetus: "Well, then, since most of you have become blind, ought there not to be

[1] Ode 16, quoting with some freedom the rendering of Mr. Harris, Cambridge, 1909.

some man to fill this office, and on behalf of all to sing the hymn to God? . . . If then I were a nightingale, I would do the part of a nightingale; if I were a swan, I would do like a swan. But now I am a rational creature, and I ought to praise God: this is my work; I do it, nor will I desert this post so long as I am allowed to keep it; and I exhort you to join in this same song."[1]

The mystic consciousness is *self-preoccupied;* and the knowledge that comes from it is very largely knowledge of itself.

This self-absorbed character of mystic knowledge may explain why the mystics have so much to say about "the truth" in the abstract, without suggesting what the truth is. The mystic knows the Truth, so he assures us: but he seems to spin hopelessly about this point, and to come forward very slowly with any statement of its contents.[2]

May it be that the mystic is more sure *that* he is sure than of *what* he is sure, — except that he is sure

[1] Discourses, Book I, ch. xvi. Tr. Geo. Long.

[2] The Odes of Solomon may again illustrate the point:

"He hath filled me with words of truth, that I may speak the same. Like the flow of waters flows truth from my mouth, and my lips show forth his fruit. And he has caused his knowledge to abound in me; for the mouth of the Lord is the true Word, and the door of his light." (Ode 12.)

"He glorified me by his kindness, and raised my thought to the height of his truth. Herein he gave me the way of his precepts; and I opened the doors that were closed; and the bars of iron which I was about to break in pieces melted and dissolved before me — nothing appeared closed to me, because I was the door of everything." (Ode 17.)

With how much show of substance, and yet how empty of definable content is all this celebration of "the Truth."

of God and of his own relation to God? In these matters, the *that* actually precedes the *what*, both in time and in importance.

In politics, as Walter Bagehot has well shown, there is a moment of development at which it is more important that there should be *law*, than that there should be *good* law: any law at all, at this moment, is good law, because law is better than disorder. There is a moment in religion, also, at which any God is a good God; any absolute is a good absolute; any certainty at all is a matter of supreme importance. This moment cannot last, either in experience or in reason; but it is enough to give color to the primary religious attitude. Any certainty is better than no certainty; it is good both for the mystic and for his hearers to have touched absolute assurance, on no matter what subject. To be certain has a pragmatic meaning in any case; the man is disposed to resolute action in general, and his resoluteness is able to communicate itself. The presence of the *form* of assurance in the world, is the presence of some emptiness that will gather to itself its own filling in time; as many an unequipped good-will by practising *assurance* has in time acquired some substance of efficiency, in medicine and elsewhere. And who knows but that the various pretences through which boys grow into youth and manhood show also some natural precedence of the form over the matter: any form at all is some matter — such seems to be the rule, a germ which in honest soil will grow. I dare say that this preliminary *law* of Bagehot's is a child of this same religious *assuredness* which alone in this world is capable of absolute command.

Let the mystic, then, be certain of his "the truth," his "God's truth," and do not enviously require him at every turn to say what the truth contains. No one insists more than I that it must contain something, and can be no pure ineffable zero, but in human language we must be willing to wait for its deposit, and even to put up with much error. The church, let me say, is always right in claiming to be infallible. Any church which modestly declines such pretension, any mystic who in his main point admits that he may be mistaken, does thereby stamp itself or himself as fraudulent. For if one knows God, he will also know that he knows (so truly testifies Spinoza); hence, although not every one that claims certainty is true, every one that disclaims it is false. It is among the certain ones that all true prophets will be found. It is among the infallible churches that all true churches will be found. What the church chiefly has to learn is not to be infallible in regard to *too much.*

The infallibility of the religious institution proceeds from the certainty of its mystics; it is better that they also should not be certain of too much, should be willing to abide in the region of being sure chiefly that they are sure of "the truth," of the absolute. But the mystic feels the clamor of the crowd for bread; he has, besides, his own internal emptiness which must be filled; he trembles on the verge between being rightly sure of his residual object, and being wrongly sure of some more visible content. As a matter of natural history, the mystic, in practical affairs, is apt to carry his assurance too far. The defect of his virtue may be, that he becomes absolute on too slight provocation. He is the sturdy will, which in decline may become the temperamental dogmatist. It is never easy to deal with a will of this sort, which supposes itself to be founded on an original source of truth at once immovable and inaccessible. One can only watch its career (once its certainty invades this world of sense) as of a thing of Nature, closed in general to common instruction; and be grateful for any tendency which it may show to coincide with reason. But the indomitable and unreasonable person is neither a result of mysticism nor a cause; he is a well-known natural product, widely distributed: and while his natural firmness may be magnified by the sanction of religion, it must at the same time be rendered safer and truer by the essential tendency of worship to universalize the mind and bend it to reason. Indeed, is not mysticism the natural antidote for over-mightiness of personal will; and perhaps the only protection of society, in the end, against its most vehement members? For if the Strong Man in his solitude is not in company with the Absolute Other, his solitude is indeed absolute, and wholly menacing. The worshipper by the nature of his profession, must first humble himself before his object, and with all his strength suppress his strength, until it begins its assertions at the zero of all historical content. None but God can reach the all-mighty will in its solitary origins. It is the destiny of religion to find that difficult and all-important center of a just infallibility, which curbs and defines all absolute assurance, without disastrously abolishing it.

It is well for the mystic to dwell chiefly upon his

absolute certainty of the absolute, and of his wholly original relation to ancient reality. But his revelation cannot stop here, because his experience has legitimate bearings on other experience, and he is obliged to trace them out. The mystic will become a knower of things new as well as old.

Of this new knowledge, we have here to say that it comes to the mystic in the course of his return to the world, unsought by him. He has known God from the standpoint of the world; now he begins to know his world from the standpoint of his new experience of God. As after every new experience the familiar experiences to which one returns are lit up with unfamiliar light, shining out strange and reborn: so as the mystic resumes his occupation with the many things, he finds that "all things have become new," and this novelty he will learn how to distil into the stock of human wisdom at large.[1]

It is natural that these new impressions should be read first in their religious bearings, and so contribute first to the dogmatic enrichment of religion itself. From such impressions arise those dogmas which have to do with the world and man. If all things do contain 'memorials' or reminders of God, the mystic will see in that fact a divine origin of the world; and in time these same reminders will take shape as a doctrine of the divine Word or Logos. And as he finds reminders, he finds also *obstructions to the reminding:* here

[1] Says the Ode-writer: "My heart was cloven, and its flower appeared; and grace sprang up in it; and it brought forth fruit to the Lord. . . . And everything became like a relic of thyself and a memorial forever of thy faithful works. For there is abundant room in thy Paradise, and nothing is useless therein."

begin his condemnations, his contributions to law and prophecy.[1]

This way of making judgments is a very common one; it is what we might call, judgment by compatibility or incompatibility of mood. All of our earlier moral judgments are of this sort. A dominant personal relationship (say of child to parent) governs one's attitude to all sorts of things, not so much through verbal command, as through a perception of what would harmonize or jar with the conscious quality of that relationship. The recurrence of the presence of the person gradually defines the judgment. In the case of the mystic, the various approaches which he makes to his God after meeting his world and judging it, become so many questions to which he finds a *yes* or *no*, according as his consciousness of God is accessible to him or not. God shows thereby what he loves and what he hates; and though there is much weary guessing as to the reasons for the presence or the absence of divine favor, yet in the course of time inductions emerge, "experimental wisdom" of fairly stable sort. These resulting judgments are thus due to what F. B. Jevons has happily called "supernatural selection," in contrast to the natural selection of survival by actual utility.[2] And all such judgments, social, cosmological, and moral, are at the same time judgments about the nature of God; are so many developments of the knowledge of God, made possible by this continuous alternation in experi-

[1] This process also we see in the Odes of Solomon: "And I forsook vanity, and turned to the Most High my God, and I was enriched by his bounty; and I forsook the folly which was diffused over the earth — yea, I stripped it off, and cast it from me."

[2] Introduction to the history of religion, ch. viii.

ence. The mystic's preparation is an epitome of such empirical judgments about God, that is to say, of the kind of disposition which God will favor. Thus the mystic contributes little by little to the dogmatic content of religion; and these dogmas have their own methods of trial and selection.

In this origination of new judgments, the mystics have done their harm in the world,—being sure of things that are only partially true. We thought that the mystic would do well to be slow in concrete creativeness. But taking the whole bulk of dogmatic utterance together, we must still judge that the harm done is infinitely less serious than would have been the harm of losing that same material and the assurance with it. The mystic's blunders have their indispensable truth; and partial truth may be pragmatically truer than the completely guarded statement. Most mystic utterances are untrue; as, for example, most of Emerson's statements are untrue. His continual volley of the small cartridges of dogma is a symptom of mystical habit; they are a minor rill of mystical enlightenments. And doubtless to his own knowledge and intention many of his statements are partial. He writes *esoterically*, that is, for the reader who has the sense and good-will to supply the cautions and conditions for his statements. That word of his already quoted, "No one can harm me but myself" is esoterically true, empirically untrue; but how far superior to all such guarded and accurate statements as we might make of it. The valid doctrines of the church are in the same case; their truth is literal, but esoteric. It is capable of complete translation into philosophic propositions about the world and man and the Absolute,—in the course of infinite time. But meanwhile it conveys truth to the man of good-will and insight; indispensable truth; would we could also say, "and nothing but the truth."

The mystic gives us the *thing* which is to be modified. There are many who can supply the modification; but who else could have pulled down from heaven that substance? In the positive dogmas of the mystic we find absolute truth getting its *first relations to facts:* its second and third and subsequent relations will be found in time; but meanwhile we have the thing, and men can live by it. It is the mystic's function to set *theses* into the world, crude positive theses; *antitheses* will come of their own accord: but the thing that wins immortality, after all the corrections of thought and experience, will have personal identity with that original thesis.

Of the mystic's knowledge, then, in summary survey, we have to say this. That the contents of 'revelation' are twofold. There is first the certainty and praise of God, and of the mystic's relation to God; this knowledge moves within its own circle, and has no apparent fruit nor progress, being to an external view self-absorbed and empty, not much else than certainty of certainty. But secondly, there is the positive contribution of the mystic and prophet to the concrete spiritual wealth of mankind, a creativity to which we can discern no limit.

Thus it is that the knowledge of God which is in intention the end of the mystic's knowledge is also its beginning. The knowledge of the oldest becomes the parent of the newest knowledge. And not alone in the domain of religious truth. For in the light of this experience all other experience, we say, has become changed and of new meaning. Many of the judgments which the mystic now coins, judgments contributory to science and the arts, will appear to him *unparented.* They simply arise in his mind. The same, I think, may be said of all our unparented knowledge, that knowledge which we attribute vaguely to 'inspiration,' and of which we speak dogmatically, saying, "It must be so": all such knowledge has as one parent this same original knowledge of the eternal. This will be the thesis of our next chapter.

CHAPTER XXXI

THE CREATIVITY OF RELIGION: THEORY OF INSPIRATION

FROM time to time the methods of religion have impressed us as being methods fit for the origination of new thought and of new value, if any such thing is possible on this planet. And I believe that we must recognize in worship the very process through which religion becomes historically fertile in the sense of our first speculation regarding the rôle of religion in history.[1] It is our purpose now to enter as we can into the logic and meaning of the creative event, and to sketch its re-echoings in life generally.

For creativity has its method and logic; not such as binds it or predetermines it, but such as gives it root, lodgment, and effect. Any valuable creativity is far removed from pure chance or irresponsibility in things. It has its place and its conditions, just as in the world of organic life, creation and birth have their own assigned organic method and quota of energy in the economy of the life-cycle: whether or not it is an easy matter to define the parentage of novelty, some parentage it must have. The world that shall be emerges from the world that is by the appearance of the purely new; yet that emergence is subject to some control and consent of the world that is: unless the present in

[1] Chapter ii.

some fashion loves and desires the future, the future will bear no progeny. In so far, a theory of origination is possible; and what is more to be wished for than insight into creativity?

It is an old observation that moral and cognitive ideas tend to form self-perpetuating systems; they grope toward equilibrium, working-harmony with each other and with experience, until they strike an arrangement which goes on reproducing itself, not leading beyond itself by any further stroke of experience. This is the settled *character*, of men, races, states, times.

The structure of such a moral system was hinted at in several places by Aristotle. Thus in the Nicomachean Ethics (II, 2), "Strength is produced by eating much food and by undergoing much severe labor; and no one can do this so well as he who is strong . . . (similarly) by abstaining from pleasures we become temperate, and when temperate are best able to abstain. . . . (In general) that same class of actions which develops a given virtue is itself furthered and energized by that virtue." Aristotle is observing that virtue somehow is presupposed in acquiring virtue; that it must aid in its own acquisition;[1] conversely, that if it is absent we are shut out from it, as he who has no strength is shut out from that working and eating which produces strength. These systems, circles, groups,[2] have thus an apparently fatalistic character. Only he

[1] An observation that might have reconciled him with Plato if he had pursued it farther.

[2] Groups in the mathematical sense, defined chiefly by the rule that

who is already temperate can become temperate; only he who is already wise can gain wisdom. Aristotle himself will admit to the study of ethics only those who are already mature and well-trained, prepared to admit the necessary first-premises for his reasonings. The good he defines with a deliberate circle as that which the good man judges to be good; the good man being defined, in turn, as he who values what is really good. Thus the good and the good man adjust themselves to each other, and recognize themselves each by the other. There is no appeal from their position; nor, on these principles alone, is there any way of knowing whether what the "good men" of any time, or of all times, regard as good is really good. For our blind-spots perpetuate themselves as well as our true visions: every type of character has a conception of the good which it sustains and is in turn sustained by. Hence every type, good or bad, tends to lose the power of self-criticism: the 'best' has no way of discovering its own defects. There is no way here for growth, novelty, creativity.[1]

The ultimate resistance to any innovation is this approximate self-sufficiency of the set of ideas, moral and other, which we already have, the tendency of

a combination of any two elements of the group according to the characteristic operation of the group produces always another member of the same group, never an object falling outside that group.

[1] Whatever is, in the world, whether defective or not, tends to assume the form of organic completeness, mutual self-support of parts, self-propagation, and thus to justify its existence by immanental structure: whatever is *pretends to be right.* On the other hand, whatever pretends to be self-sufficient, and to justify itself only by its group form and self-propagating powers, is to be suspected of defect: whatever *merely is*, is wrong.

that set of ideas to reproduce within its own kind, exclusively. In so far as we are stupid, we can only stupidly try to overcome stupidity; in so far as we are selfish, we make selfish efforts to escape the rewards of selfishness — as by giving to charity for the sake of treasure in heaven; in remorse for falsity, we try to right ourselves, yet anxiously preserving our face: and we observe, in others if not in ourselves, that defects are not overcome by this kind of trying. In just such futile endeavors is not our total humanity bound, in so far as it hopes for any genuine originality in whatever direction?

But group-enclosedness can in some cases be destroyed, as vortex-rings are destroyed, by a touch from outside the group — a touch positive enough to be disorganizing. And in so far as we can trace the inner process of creative thought, such as history has so far known, we find just such group-burstings taking place; and we can discern, I believe, something of the conditions under which such burstings and originations occur.

It is indeed only in recent times that invention has been conjoined with the power of self-description; and with the willingness to be autobiographical: but we need few instances to put us in possession of the principles at work. For invention is, in essence, no rare event; every soul of man that lives and works in the world is creating at every moment of his life some infinitesimal rill of novelty. We need then only such examples of creativity as may bring us to consciousness of what goes on in ourselves. We shall find that the moments of creation are moments in which the old is not less, but more, intensely present to consciousness; it is grasped as a whole, and *realized*, as for the first time; and in that realization we shall see emerging a dogma of rejection, "This (old position) cannot be the truth," "This cannot be so." Which negative dogma will make way for a positive dogma — equally unparented so far as that moment discerns — "This contrasting thing must be so," and herewith the new idea has its footing in the world, born as something *necessary* — having therefore a parentage though as yet unnameable, a parentage which we may be able to make evident.

We may take a few instances from Tolstoy, — a mind richly creative, dogmatic, artistic and withal trenchantly autobiographical in all his works, making it possible to follow with advantage the beginnings of new ideas. Here is an extract from his diary, written after seeing an execution in Paris, long before his political opinions had begun to take shape, — an early and negative item in the creation of those opinions:

"When I saw the head separate from the body, and how they both thumped into the box at the same moment, I understood, not with my mind, but with my whole being, that no theory of the reasonableness of any present progress can justify this deed; and that though everybody from the creation of the world on whatever theory had held it to be necessary, I knew it to be unnecessary and bad."[1]

Another instance from his educational journal, on punishing a boy in his experimental peasant-school for stealing, by hanging a placard on his back:

[1] This and the following extracts from Tolstoy are taken from Aylmer Maude's Life of Tolstoy.

"I glanced at the face of the punished boy which had become yet paler, more suffering, and harder than before, and I thought of convicts; and suddenly I felt so ashamed and disgusted that I tore the stupid card off him, told him to go where he liked, and became convinced — and convinced not by reason, but by my whole nature — that I had no right to torment that unfortunate boy; and that it was not in my power to make of him what I and the inn-keeper's son wanted to make of him. I became convinced that there are secrets of the soul hidden from us on which life may act, but which precepts and punishments do not reach."

In Tolstoy's religious development, his new ideas emerge with the same unparented certainty, as he has recorded his experience in "My Confession." Let me quote instances along the way of that remarkable progress.

"One can only go on living when one is intoxicated with life; as soon as one is sober, it is *impossible not to see that it is all a mere fraud*. . . . Sooner or later my deeds will be forgotten, and I shall not exist. Then why go on making any effort. . . . How can men fail to see this?

"I now see that if I did not kill myself, it was due to some dim consciousness of the invalidity of my thoughts. I, my reason, has acknowledged life to be unreasonable. But how can reason, which (for me) is the creator of life, and (in reality) the child of life, deny life? *There is something wrong here*.

"Then I turned my gaze upon myself, on what went on within me, and I remembered that I only lived at those times when I believed in God. As it was before, so it was now: I need only be aware of God to live; I need only forget him or disbelieve in him, and I die. . . . 'What more do you seek?' exclaimed a voice within me. '*This is he*. He is that without which one cannot live. To know God and to live is one and the same thing!' . . . and the light did not again abandon me."

And now, having won for himself this ancient truth, he finds insights arising in him of a more novel character, but with the same dogmatic abruptness. *It cannot be*, he thinks, that believers of other confessions than that of the Greek Church are without true religion ; whence it follows that the church must be wrong in condemning them. And with regard to war, and executions,

"It was *impossible not to see* that killing is an evil, repugnant to the first principles of any faith. Yet they prayed in the churches for the success of our arms ; and the teachers of the faith acknowledged killing to be an act resulting from the faith."

The whole spiritual history of this man is a series of like unparented inspirations. And it is not otherwise with minds of greater psychological sophistication creative in other fields. Psychologists are seldom autobiographical, by some strange contrariety ; but Fechner, who is of their greatest, does often write in confessional vein, and here is a passage much to our present purpose.[1] Sitting on a bench in the *Rosenthal* at Leipzig on a warm sunny morning with plenty to occupy his senses, he falls to musing as follows :

"A strange illusion is this. At bottom, all before me and about me is night and silence : the sun which so dazzles me is in truth but a dark ball, seeking its way in darkness. . . . In this universal darkness and desolation and silence which embraces heaven and earth there hover certain beings who but singly and inwardly possess brightness and color and sound, — mere points probably, which emerge out of the night and sink back into it, without leaving behind them any vestige of their light and sound ; who see one another, though nothing

[1] From the opening of his book, Die Tagesansicht gegenüber der Nachtansicht.

between them is lighted; speak with one another, though nothing between them resounds. So it is to-day, so it was from the beginning, so will it be to all eternity."

Now comes to Fechner the view of the natural man in all its vehement contrast to this world-picture, which to Fechner is but the Weltanschauung of his age by general consent. This natural man

"believes that he sees objects about him because it is actually light about him; he does not believe that the sun begins to brighten the world first *behind his eyes*. . . . His illusion, furthermore, will certainly never yield, no matter how firmly established (by consensus of science and philosophy) may be the knowledge that it is illusion. May it not be that this knowledge is itself an illusion? Is it not the truth that endures longest, — and is not that which longest endures *the truth?*

"Must not that Night-view shrink in fright from itself if with a faithful mirror before it, it could know that it is itself which it sees therein? Nay, had the world at first seen the entire hopelessness and footlessness and vanity of that view with the clarity which came to me in that hour, it had never been able to win its place as a World-view. And though clarity is the last thing in these matters, the last thing will be clarity. As surely as day follows night, so surely upon that Night-view of the world a Day-view must follow, which will give foundation to the view of the natural man — not contradict it. And the world will appear in a new connection, in a new light, and under new and positive points of view."

Here is the beginning of Fechner's new idea, which with true prophecy he indicates as the idea of the generation succeeding him, the view which in our own way we have tried to take possession of. This idea also comes to its originator as a dogma, an "It must be so," namely, that the view of the natural man, this persistent view, is the true one.

We need look no further for instances of the creative event: these may be typical of all, whether in art or morals or science or religion.

In all these experiences of dawning novelty, we may observe the same sharpened consciousness of the old or usual idea, the idea with reference to which the new is defined as new and different. This old idea is, as we say, freshly *realized;* which means, freshly connected with reality, especially with the reality which the thinker is conscious of in *himself*—that which is realized is "brought home," made a conscious part of his own vivid and literal present world. And this old idea, in being realized, is at the same time repudiated; repudiated, not with any pure and blank negation, but in favor of some positive thing which in time will make itself known. In this realizing and repudiating, the new thing is already asserting itself, and doing conscious work. These are the psychological phenomena which in various proportions always surround the birth of novelty.

And the event of this birth itself is to be traced, as I think, to this touching to the quick of *self-consciousness:* the old idea has penetrated to the self; the self has been stung by it; and in the *reflexion* thereby occasioned, the new thing is engendered. It is when Tolstoy finds himself "ashamed and disgusted"—judging himself; it is when Fechner lets the "natural man" in him spill his scorn on the futile theorist of his habitual selfhood; it is when some deep-set love of life and reality reaches a point of wrath and habit-breaking, or in other moods, of wholly joyful inertia-killing; it is in such moments that creation takes place. I wish, then, in the first place, to connect the event of creation with the event of *reflexion*,—that is, with the emergence of a *self*-consciousness out of a consciousness that is pursuing in all smoothness the lines of the empirical object-world.

In reflexion, the focus of consciousness shifts in such a way that without losing wholly from sight the object with which one has been engaged, the interest now attaches, not primarily to that object, but to the self in its relations with that object. These reflexive movements of consciousness are, in general, occasioned by some *defeat* in the ordinary inertias of the mind. As when, in speaking, one becomes aware of throat, or difficulty of words, or clothing. As when the hunter returns empty from the day's chase, reflecting that, after all, what he wanted was not so much the game as the pursuit. Or, as when in success one comes to the end of an absorbing task, and finds himself at a loss what next to do: he is for the moment "thrown back upon himself" as upon a being who during the absorption has been forgotten—his reflexion is occasioned by the defeat of his usual habits of occupation and attention.

And in all such occasions the organic function of reflexion seems to be precisely the demand of the situation for something new. The continuous thread of my empirical self-consciousness is no doubt due to some permanent friction in applying my existing stock of ideas to experience, and the persistent demand for creativeness thereby occasioned. We should expect reflexion to have something to do with creation. And for the further reason, that the Self stands permanently *outside* all those closed or closing groups of mental and moral habit; the more perfectly self-sufficient and self-propagating these groups become, the more they fuse with the object-world —becoming object of self hence different from self— though in their perfect working not reminding the self of itself. He who can revert to himself is free from all groups, and has in himself that which can disorganize them and see beyond them. The only question is, how one is able to revert to himself, that is, how reflexion is possible. For if defeat is the only occasion for reflexion, and a self-sufficient mental group does not meet with any defeat, we are still unable to free ourselves from its bondage, through our inability to reflect. *How is reflexion possible?* Is not this the question to which every critique of creativity must come?

Now my proposition is that *the power to reflect depends upon the power to find your Absolute,* in the last resort upon practical religion. It is through alliance with the Absolute that man is able to reflect: it is through his reflexion that he becomes creative of novelty, system-destroying novelty.

Of reflexion generally, we know that it is not under direct and complete control of the will. Self-consciousness is subtle and elusive; self-knowledge, or significant self-consciousness, is the most difficult of knowledges. Success in seizing that in self upon which one would turn, in self-analysis, self-expression, discerning of one's actual motive or actual state of feeling, depends upon a certain gift, a genius of self-capture, a skill in fixing the retreating shadow; and for this there seem to be no rules of technical procedure. We only know that the Other Mind is the chief aid to self-knowledge, the only environment in which it can attain high development. Socially-fostered reflexions may bring the individual to the general level of social-self-knowledge: they cannot, however, lift him above that level, and it is precisely this social closed-group which it is most important to break through. Here we revert to a principle already appealed to in another context: that there is no criticism of any self or system except in present view of a positive content beyond them. And that which is outside every finite system, "the Not of all that man can think or say," is precisely the absolute with which religion seeks and gains vital alliance. If God has once been known, the world and the self must thereafter be seen under the survey of this experience. I am able to reflect upon any world-self system because and only because I have already experienced something beyond it. It is Tolstoy's certainty of God that gives him power to criticize the Church. It is Fechner's sense of the validity of some more primitive world-view that separates him from the accepted "Night-view." In brief, all of my partial reflexions are *parented by some previous total reflexion.* But total reflexion, that is, reflexion upon the whole of things temporal, is precisely a definition of the cognitive side of mystic experience.

And conversely, reflexion might be defined as a partial mystic experience. For reflexion, like worship, abandons the forward and outward direction of attention, and reverts inward, seeking by denial to separate itself from immersion in the object which occasions that reflexion, and succeeding only in so far as its denial is supplemented by a positive vision of the reality which that object does not contain. Reflexion also illustrates the principle of alternation ; self-knowledge and object-knowledge growing by intervals of self-abandonment each in the other. And the motive of worship, so far as it is a rejection of the world, we thought to find, even as the occasion for reflexion is found, in some friction in the usual objective processes of the mind. *Reflexion is the generalized form which worship takes in our experience:* it is, so to speak, the agent for the dissemination of religious attainment throughout the body of experience. It has no necessary religious character; for this belongs only to the total reflexion. But all such partial mystical movements are dependent for their vigor and sense upon the total alternation of consciousness, and what it can grasp of the Absolute and its quality. Our "scent for reality," our "grip" upon fact and value, are our experience of God as being thought with. At any given time this sense of reality is as a possession of the individual, inalienable from his personality, his own definition and character, the most intimate fact about him, wholly independent of his piety or intentional relation to God. But the conditions for the maintenance of this "instinct," for its perpetual regeneration, and withal for its growth, require as in the case of every instinct that we take self-conscious possession of that which is by nature present; that this which is thought with shall be renewed also by being from time to time thought of and made an immediate experience.[1]

[1] In simpler, but more barren fashion, the logic of novelty may be exhibited thus :

Assume a point, A, which shall be outside every particular system of thought or character, outside every group ; and adopt the general prin-

The scope of our principle will be extended when we observe that *induction* is a mental process akin to reflexion. It has been regarded as typical of all invention, — this process of induction, whereby the mind arrives at a new law, a new synthesis, a new *aperçu* of essential likeness, a new simile or metaphor, a new hypothesis, a new speculative order among the facts of experience. Induction is sometimes described as a movement from parts to whole or to universal: worship and reflexion may be described in the same terms. Induction is not compellable by rule; this also it has in common with mystic experience and reflexion. No fixed method can be laid down in logic whereby the law of a given set of phenomena can be determined. There are good ways of preparing yourself to discover such laws and likenesses: but when you have followed all the 'inductive methods,' you must wait for your gift. The problem 'To find the common element in a given group of objects' has no solution; there is no general formula for discovering integrals. Even simple observation is a gift, simple observation being the elementary operation in induction; and simple observation may serve to show the kinship we are asserting:

ciple that any such system, B, when seen from the standpoint of A, changes its character, becoming for experience, say B′. With these two assumptions we have defined at once the conditions for an infinite progress in B. For as B by reflexion from A becomes B′, so B′ by reflexion from the same A becomes B″, and so on. Thus endless novelty springs from recurrent contact with that which is eternally the same. The second of these assumptions is equivalent to the principle formally touched upon, in chapter xiv (The Need of an Absolute) : namely that Sein with Bewusstsein gives Werden. This logical scheme is accurate so far as it goes, but has nothing to say of the quantitative or qualitative values of the changes in question, nor of the psychological conditions under which B is viewed from the standpoint of A, nor of the growth of A within its own identity.

I observe nothing unless I question; and I question nothing unless I conceive a thing as being other than it turns out to be. What I see at the theater and what you see there are different things; because you are conscious of more ways in which the play might have been better or other than it is. You note a trick of carriage or voice which you trace to a certain training or racial origin; I observe nothing but a carriage and a voice — it does not occur to me that they have any peculiarity, that they could have been different. I have no questions ready, — I do not see outside of them. Simple observation is a gift: and is great hypothesis-making a gift of any radically different sort than this of conceiving the thing otherwise, — that the apple should not fall, or the earth not be a plane, or the center of things elsewhere than where we are? In one case as in the other, one is helped by all manner of acquaintance with facts, experience, imagination, training, "spreading the divine net"; but making thereby no fore-fated capture of the divine idea. We will ascribe the successful result neither to chance nor to industry; shall we say to *genius*, thereby asserting that our induction has some parentage, we know not what? Precisely so; and what is genius again, but that same "scent for reality" wherein reflexion has its source also?

As reflexion is a judgment upon my self as a whole, so induction is a judgment upon some external self or class as a whole. Induction is external reflexion; and reflexion is internal induction. And for the most part these operations are simultaneous, parts of the same mental movement. It is one and the same thing to become aware that "All the objects about me are inanimate" as to become aware that "I am alone"; the former is an induction, the latter a reflexion. To observe that "All these books have fine print," and to locate in my eyes a subtle discomfort, are probably not two mental operations, but one. It does not flash upon my mind in any case that "All A's are B" without a simultaneous exposition of self-consciousness, like the recovery of a lost name. Ability to invent, to induct, to discern likenesses, depends on a degree of consciousness which is at the same time power to reflect, to detect what it is in me that is restless and groping for further predicate-giving. The inventive artist, poet, musician, has his moments of prelude to idea-making in which *musing* he can hardly tell whether he is scrutinizing his objects or the stirrings in himself. Reflexion and induction are of the same fabric, and have the same conditions for success. Every induction is *induced* by a prior induction, ultimately by a *total induction*, or judgment about the whole of things,—none other than my whole-idea, derived from whatever knowledge of the whole and of God my experience has built up for me. Every induction is at the same time a deduction, then, —an "It must be so," parented, though from the background of consciousness, by an insight which in its origins is religious.

Worship then in its most generalized meaning is the genus of which reflexion and induction, including simple observation, are species; and mystical movements of the mind, reversions to that which is relatively total, in infinite replication and variety, make up one half of the whole of mental life. Herewith I think we have taken into view in principle all phases of creativity and invention. Invention can never be the result of a direct effort to invent, if only because the thing to be invented is not yet seen. No one by taking thought can increase his stature; he must apply himself to that through which the increase of stature may come: and he who would invent would best put himself about invention by strengthening his hold on reality. He who would be creative in any direction would do best to pursue that from which alone creativity can result, a personal knowledge of the Absolute. This is that "guidance of God" for which men may legitimately pray, and expect answer. When the holy spirit is come, he shall lead you into all truth; and not otherwise is new truth, or new value accessible to mankind. Thus religion is fruitful through worship: and may we not also say, it is the one fruitful thing in the world?

Whatever religion adds to human wealth is not poured in, as an extraneous gift: it comes in continuity with what that individual has known before. No man by means of his religious insights can be transformed from ignorance to learnedness. The fruits of inspiration are not such as labor could secure: hence they neither displace labor, nor produce "unearned increments" in the field of human exertion.

It is true that certain of the mystics have claimed much *imparted* knowledge, even of the informatory order. Teresa claims to have received, through her devotions, the powers of description and literary expression, and of penetrating the meaning of the Mass, though

Latin was to her an unknown tongue. The friends of Boehme, it is said, would bring to him words from foreign tongues whose meaning he would divine from their sounds. But granting to the full the historic accuracy of stories like these, we have not made these individuals learned. A type of education they do accomplish, quite germane to the type of their mighty efforts in self-discipline, — an education, namely, in self-knowledge and in human nature generally, such as any person with similar original effort might hardly fail to win. But whatever self-development the mystic receives, he receives not without his own activity; and hence there will be no complete breach of continuity in his knowledge.

So evident has it become to us that the inspirations of religion bear the marks of all existing limitations, — of character, of times, of opinions, — that products of such alleged inspiration have been interpreted as the deification of one's own thoughts otherwise established. The mystic, it is said, is governed by his expectations. The God he sees is the God he has been led to define to himself, by tradition and reflection. The ideal he reaches is his own ideal, that is, the ideal of his time, modified by his own individual quality, and elaborated by his own thinking. The practice of prayer is a means, we might think, of selecting from one's stock of ideas certain ideas to which we wish to give a special potency and control; and through some process of auto-suggestion, fixing these ideas in the seat of power. We cannot doubt, as we review the history of sainthood, that each saint in turn has reinforced in himself by his devotion his own clarified personal equation, and the sentiment of tradition. In mediæval saintdom what do we find in saintly character but the reproduced pictures of still older saints, the types of perfection embodied in older eulogies?—a certain *corporate flavor* which gives us, indeed, the mid-age fragrance and romance; but also the mid-age mustiness, softness, impure purity, and flabbiness of soul,—all that type of mind which in these latter days Nietzsche has so effectively condemned, to the great surgical benefit of Christendom. Where else in history can we find so distinctive a spiritual mannerism fastened upon a thousand turbulent years with successful solidarity? Religion, on this showing, might well qualify as an apt instrument of spiritual conservatism, perhaps even of tyranny, little fitted to encourage originality of mind. In no case does the good of which the mystic catches sight seem to depart by any great gulf from the best good of his time.

Herewith the mystic finds himself accused, and not for the first time, of opposite faults: of turning in a fast circle, and of detached individual caprice. The truth of which seems to me to be this: that before he can be original he must first be as unoriginal as possible, must first make fast whatever he can fix upon as tenable in his spiritual environment. All of his negations are in the interest solely of the best he yet knows; and so far as his preparation remains primarily his own activity, he gets no step beyond the best he knows. Of himself he can accomplish nothing but continuity, even of the most binding type: no one can be more conscious than he of his inability to "pass beyond himself." His best efforts do but tighten about him the net of his own limitations. Hence the mystic's vision of the good will change slowly, for the most part: but the important matter for us, at present, is that it *changes at all.*

In antagonism to rash claims to supernatural enlightenment, free from human limitations, it is well enough to point out the abundant presence of these ties. When X boasts of complete novelty, it is proper for Y to exult over every sign of antiquity he can discover in it: but, on the whole, this is not the most genial and profitable of occupations. "Give me a *difference*, a new departure," says the dialectician, "and I will show you a likeness in the midst of that difference." Good: that is clever, and sometimes important—but does it banish the miracle of difference? Since for some reason (not wholly good) continuity seems the self-explanatory and obvious aspect of our living, and the miracle of the world to lie in its production of novelty, it is an obligation to make our scientific most of any spark of novelty that may be emitted by any process whatever. In worship and its results we see everywhere limitation, limitation even exaggerated; but limitation *in the process of overcoming itself.* The right and wrong of the traditional moral quality will infect the act of worship; but ask how this traditional error is to be put off, how historically it has at last been put off—and we shall find that it is this very act of worship which (in some form or other) is the appointed way of escape from it. Worship is undoubtedly a bad thing, when bad men worship —and all men are bad: but he who would therefore abolish it abolishes his only hope of better men.

The worshipper's God will contain a magnified image of himself—that is inevitable. But the act of bringing one's view of self into conjunction with an actual consciousness of the Absolute is an act which must do something to disrupt the limitations of that idea. The worship of God in human form is never identical with the worship of man. The known God-function tends to disjoint the humanity of the thing worshipped. What the worshipper has before him is not man, but man denied; man at war with all that is false in his own humanity; man overcoming himself; man *in Untergang*, as Nietzsche would have it, giving way to Superman. This process depicted in the heavens takes place in the minds of the worshippers; and their own humanity exposed to the blast of their own experienced absolute becomes newborn, a thing different by some slight increment from what it was before. Every man knows the true God, that is our first premise; let his God-pictures be what they may, they are all doomed and dying pictures, pictures of the man that is being put behind, on the way to the man that is to be.

Would I persuade my neighbor to put off his defects, his faults of vision, his hereditary quirks and hatefulnesses, I can accomplish nothing effective and central but this — to show him himself in the light of his own absolute. For to find this absolute, as the mystic finds it, he has been obliged to reject what he can of his empirical trappings, and most of what I despise in him has been detected by himself, if not in his own preparatory introspection and katharsis of the passions, yet in his return from the contemplation of Deity. How shall he detect *the rest?* How shall he overcome what is so abominably rooted in him that he carries it to heaven with him and spoils my prospects of enjoying life there? He may never see it; in which case I must either wish him dead, and well out of this fair universe with all his foulness, or else I must wish him once well in the fresh air and sun, with a more complete negation of himself, through a better hold upon his own absolute—I must wish him a better mystic. The only ultimate appeal of man to man is built on man's grasp of God. And what I can see to be true of my neighbor is not less true of myself.

In whatever field the originator may act, or the reformer, or the creator, his procedure will be the same. It is as he *re-takes* his world, having for the love of God turned his back upon it, that his world appears to him new with a novelty which he is himself giving to it or eliciting from it. He is the bearer of a treasure of "recollection" not essentially different from that of which Plato speaks; and under these rays whatever object he turns upon becomes cognitively and morally fruitful, full also of value and life. This is not the work of the impersonal idea; it is the work of a personal experience; and in so far as this vision of the absolute is his own vision, colored by his own individual quality and resonance, his new endowment is but a deeper spring of that factor which we sometimes call 'temperament,' sometimes 'instinct,' sometimes 'genius.' His creation is still his own, and bears the stamp of his individuality. His relation to his absolute has not obliterated him, nor overmastered him: enabling him to reflect, it has given to him himself; enabling him to create, it has given to him a freedom which might well be called freedom in the concrete.

Nor does the creator create without the aid of that

world to which he is contributing. Creating means nothing but bringing to birth in particular historic fact and context. Though the creator begins by destroying, that which he can never destroy nor wish to destroy is the definite sensible existence upon which he must knit his novelty. The true element in everything false is the fact that it has existed, and has occupied a place in the world of particular things; it seems just to say that it is the false thing (as thing, not as false) that is the *other parent* of the new, in parentage giving up its life to that which replaces it. Of all fields of human creation that of the *historic deed* exhibits at its best this continuous descent of the idea into the particular; and creative historic action is the supreme moral achievement. The mystic in historic action is termed the prophet: in a study of the prophet we may span the final term of religion's work in the world.

CHAPTER XXXII

THE PROPHETIC CONSCIOUSNESS

WE have seen through what channels religion contributes to the wealth of human life, not creating anything for men, but creating men, conferring on them power and freedom to create. We have now to take the one important step which remains to complete our view of the effective insertion of religion in the world: namely, to enquire how human happiness and misery are affected by religion and worship. It is the ultimate problem of practical religion, and indeed of all practical thought, to make reckoning, not with the *general principles* on which this world is framed and furthered, but with the actual *data of fortune*, the particular shapes and configurations of happening, as fate or providence pile them up about us and with apparently random distribution. It is a matter of the last importance for any view of life whether it leads men to find their welfare within the stream of historic circumstance, risk, accident, or outside of it — even though just outside. Our philosophy and our religion take one hue or another according as we regard our particular fortunes as matters of chance, whose evils we must know how to transmute and be superior to; or as themselves necessary elements and ingredients of our welfare.

I

Mankind very early overcomes the illusion that his happiness is dependent upon the possession of particular objective things wherein values lie.[1] The first use life makes of reason is to distinguish between the thing and the value: we are not bound to honey in order to get sweetness; nor are we bound to sweetness to get savor for our food; nor to savor for satisfaction. By a long course of experience in which our desires are greatly generalized and provided with an immense gamut of substitution, the world of values begins to float apart, like a world of ghosts, between self and the world of things, gaining embodiment in this object or in that only by a stroke of will. No man's happiness is bound to the possession of any particular thing unless he himself freely binds it thereto.

And if personal choice rather than necessity must determine the objects of my pursuit, it is personal choice that must hold me to any adopted pursuit; my whole relation to particular things, persons, objects beyond myself, becomes arbitrary, tentative, liable to repudiation. It is only my will, not my view of objective necessity, that holds me to any given historic course. No particular thing or definable object is necessary to my happiness. And, alas, no particular thing or definable object is sufficient for it. There is a thorough absence of correspondence between values and historic objects. A certain alienation from history results in this way simply from universal experience.

And, in the main, this freedom from things has been an advantage. So great is the contingency in the matter of historic success in controlling any particular

[1] The outline of the following argument was first stated in an address before the Phi Beta Kappa Society of Leland Stanford University, entitled "The Necessary and Sufficient Conditions for Human Happiness." Parts of that address I have used in this chapter.

object, so difficult the acquisition of assured power, so elusive these visible vessels of our values, especially those more precious living objects of love and social pride, that no degree of independence has been thought too great. Religion for the most part has found it well not to diminish but to emphasize and enlarge this natural separation of ours from the material and particular prisons of our happiness.

Philosophy, too, has worked in the same direction; reminding men to what extent each one is the maker of his own happiness, to what extent all the necessary conditions for happiness lie within the self, and not at all out there in history and circumstance. To be "philosophical" is nothing other than to practise this belief. Every age has its seer who renews this ancient doctrine. We listen to him and believe him: it seems that all assurance of happiness depends on finding it a wholly inward affair, and even that all justice requires it. For in so far as welfare depends on external things, some of its conditions will be beyond control: those who succeed will succeed in part by leave of circumstance; and there will be those that fail without fault of their own, and without recovery. Hence men have always demanded of the sage, "Teach us to be happy," as if this were indeed an art open to every one who can possess himself, let fortune be what it may, an art of the inner man, not of external mastery.

Hear the words of Maeterlinck, who with inimitable union of power and art has made this doctrine a living force in our own time: "It is true," he writes, "that on certain external events our influence is of the feeblest; but we have all-powerful action on that which these events shall become in ourselves. Nothing befalls us that is not of the nature of ourselves. The event in itself is pure water that flows from the pitcher of fate, and seldom has it either savour, or perfume, or colour. But even as the soul may be wherein it seeks shelter, so will the event become, joyous or sad, tender or hateful, deadly or quick with life. I do not pretend that destiny is just. (But) there is nothing in the world more just than happiness, nothing that will more faithfully adopt the form of our soul, or so carefully fill the space that our wisdom flings open."[1] The controlling conditions of welfare lie within, and not in that current of outer event, the current of history, or as Maeterlinck calls it, of *destiny*.

And have we not in our own analysis of value concluded that worth is conferred on things, not by their intrinsic qualities, but by that with which we think them? It is the *idea* that creates what beauty, what desirability of any kind, things seem to possess; it is not in their power to rob us of this,—it is not in their power to make or mar our happiness. Happiness, may we say, is the idea of the Whole in unhindered operation upon experience. He who knows God knows how to be happy in this world, having in himself both the source of positive value and that by which all pain can be transmuted.

We tend, I say, to believe such doctrines as these; it seems that we must believe them, or condemn the world. On the other hand, we feel uneasy under them. They seem to leave us without a full and sufficient

[1] Wisdom and Destiny, tr. A. Sutro, pp. 28, 29, etc.

warrant for historic action and effort. These are, after all, stoical doctrines at heart; the stoic would have us sufficient in ourselves: and yet, if we examine the sources of his strength we shall find that the stoic sage is depending upon a sense of intimate kinship with that very destiny to which he professes himself superior. "Nothing for me is too early or too late, O Universe, which is in time for Thee." That which makes it possible for such a thinker to open himself to affection and to experience is a magnificent faith in something outside himself. Such a shut-in-ness as can encounter no solidity of value in the world beyond, and is without assurance of any other victory than that of its own poise or of its own value-creations is necessarily without power of self-abandonment. The pride of creatorship in this realm of values, which is indeed the highest prerogative of our individual selfhood, may turn to the veriest curse at the moment when the goods in our hands appear to us as *nothing but our own creations*. Creation is a solitary business; we are therefore not surprised to find here and there a soul, lofty in this citadel of inner values, smitten with the horror of imprisonment in its own freedom, ready to accept any touch of fate, ready to cry out, "Strike, sacred Reality," if it may but regain the sense of validity outside.

Self-sufficient we cannot be. And this truth our theory of value has taken into account. For that whole-idea cannot be had by any but the completest exposure to the world of objects; nor can the vigor and integrity of that idea be maintained by any self-enclosed determination of the will, but only by resorting to its source in experience. Nevertheless, the conditions for happiness do still lie outside history, do they not? The current of particular event has no decisive importance for our welfare. We love life; but we love it as second-best, as a region wherein the idea meets resistance. The mystic has found his absolute object by help of negation after negation; he is free not indeed from reality, but from all particulars; he waits as one whose chief good is delayed — as one reconciled with God, and also as a fruitful and useful citizen, but as one who has no absolute treasures laid up here where moth and rust corrupt, and where the thieves of circumstance break through and steal. What has our mystic, then, to do with fortune?

II

In order to answer this question, we shall have to develop a stage further our account of the inner nature of happiness. Happiness we know has its quantitative variation: it increases with the body of idea we can bring to bear on any subject; it is in large part a matter of horizon. The happy man in any situation is the man to whom that situation is no cave, who in the midst of it can hold his broader bearings, bringing to it the quiet sense of affairs and, in the end, of eternity. The institution in which I am a conscious factor; the state, which flings over a petty personal existence a large dome, a dome of concrete inclusiveness and eternity, any totality of which I form an actual part, the crowd in which I am able to lose myself, even the sense of my own insignificance as a forgotten cog in the wheels of universal event — all of these add to the quantity of my happiness. But while happiness may be much or little, there is here no account of *unhappiness*, which is a matter of quality not of quantity of experience. It is the question of unhappiness that we have now to face.

On its inner side, I think we must say of unhappiness that it is in all cases a matter of conscious conflict, that is, of *divided attention* or distraction. I am unhappy whenever my idea is torn between two or more objects that claim it. For instance, he who is unable to bury himself in anything because of the simultaneous demands of everything else, is clearly in so far simply unhappy. If guilt causes unhappiness, it is through the disruption of selfhood caused by the unbanishable call of ignored obligations. If sorrow is unhappy sorrow, it is because of some persistent conflict, as between a beloved past and the insistent present objects of attention, the unwelcome necessity perhaps of living on and away from that past. And even of physical pain; if it is able to suspend happiness for a moment, it is because it half succeeds in pinning consciousness within the focus of its own event. More than half the pain of pain is the imprisonment of personality, and the unequal struggle of the spirit to get free and be itself. Unhappiness is dividedness of mind.

And this notion of unhappiness is corroborated by the fact that whatever wipes out our fragmentation and induces in us a wholeness of attack gives back the happiness which is continually slipping from our grasp. Such, in general, is the function of recreation and art, of worship and all its partial analogues, so far as they bear directly on happiness, not merely to enhance our idea, but to reunite its fragments. Art instils into us its own unity; and especially music, which combines the movement of a restless will with the peace of a completed totality. It matters not how we regain our singleness of thrust — whether by the ascent of a hill, or in prayer, or through a book or a human being: the ground of the blessedness of such a moment, and of the moments of action that issue from its canopy, lies in its power to recall the divergent channels of our attention into unity, to "make us whole" from center to limit of our mental range, for the purposes of the next undertaking. Psychologically speaking, happiness may now be described as the continuous *undivided* consent of my whole-idea to the experience or activity at hand; and the empirical mark of happiness is concentration, or enthusiasm of action. To the happy man, things and deeds appear worth while; his actions meet the mark, and rebound to enhance his energy for the next stroke; whereas those of the unhappy man strike, if at all, like spent bullets, or shatter, and contribute nothing to his self-continuance. Whatever restores wholeness in action restores happiness.

Happiness, on this showing, does certainly not depend immediately on external things at all, but upon our own inward mode of dealing with them. If it were within our power to throw the whole force of our idea, at will, upon any object: there could be no content of experience however hideous, or painful, or spiritually grievous, which could make us unhappy. But is it possible, or even conceivable, that attention could be so brought *within* the will? There is something paradoxical even in such a supposition. For if it were true, then no event of failure could dethrone any one's happiness; we should be unable to attach unlimited importance to the outcome of any finite enterprise; that is, we should be unable to give whole-hearted attention to the enterprise; and hence, by hypothesis, we should be unhappy. For we can give ourselves with but half a will to undertakings whose failure can alter no real value. It seems a condition of happiness that happiness should be destroyable by failure; otherwise we could hardly treat any present task as worth the effort of our whole will. The type of attention requisite for happiness seems to depend on a belief during the course of any effort that the object thereof is *worth* my whole devotion : and I cannot at the end of such effort, if I fail, thereupon repent my belief or change it. There is some sophistry well known to proverb and fable in allowing defeat to contradict the theory of the endeavor — namely, that the grapes were really worth having. Defeat, then, must necessarily split attention, leave me divided between this fact to which I must attend because it is the present reality, and that not-present object to which my whole effort and belief had prepared me to attend. Defeat must necessarily split attention and create unhappiness, unless in some way it is possible, in the pursuit of definite ends, to combine an unlimited attachment with an unlimited detachment.

III

That such paradoxical attitude is possible is indeed suggested to us by certain familiar facts of experience. Something like a union of perfect attachment with perfect detachment does exist in the consciousness of the good sportsman, or of the good experimentalist. To the good sportsman, defeat in any contest must not leave bitterness behind, nor either diminish the entire enthusiasm for the next attempt. As for the good experimentalist, his failures become sources of satisfaction to him just in proportion as he has spent every effort to make them succeed: for the withholding of any effort leaves it uncertain whether or not the failure is a genuine failure, and need not be tried again; here, perfection of attachment is evidently a condition for completeness of detachment. And we can see, also, that these attitudes are largely applicable to fortune generally. To some measure, the happiness of life depends upon a perfection of the game spirit: to "get into the game" accepting its rules and its risks, has been given as the best available rule for human happiness. Something hypothetical or even histrionic seems to enter into our conduct with this temper; we assure ourselves that we are staking our whole souls on this issue or that, but we know in our hearts that we are not; we know that defeat, if it comes as it always may, will not destroy our integrity of spirit, and therewith our happiness.

So much the wisdom of life suggests; and it leaves us indeed external to history, superior to it, even in a relation of *moral irony* toward it. We play as if our treasure were there, knowing that it is not; and we must so play, or lose even that happiness which, in striving, we have. Is this a satisfactory attitude toward history? Is drama, play, a certain inward duplicity in our enthusiasms, tolerable *on the whole*, as perhaps it may be tolerable in tentative fragments of living? Is "the game" our last adjustment to destiny? Is it not rather itself a division of mind, and a fundamental unhappiness; an alienation, even though a subtle one, from the world in which we must perforce act, from the particular to which we must perforce attend?

The modern forms of stoical doctrine exhaust all ingenuity to overcome this breach and to reunite with active history the soul which they have fundamentally detached therefrom. They assure us that welfare lies in the pursuit, not in the winning; from which it follows that we must mightily pursue and act even though nothing is to be captured. Or we are shown that the world of particulars and accidents is here to produce in us the moral temper, to develop the soul: it is, as Fichte would have it, the externalized material of our duty—whence we must strenuously open ourselves to experience for the love of our character, regardless of empirical outcome. Or, after all, the great interest is just knowledge and consciousness itself, which can never be subserved by any withdrawal from facts nor injured in their untowardness. This is Maeterlinck's point of view, and it seems to me the best possible statement of the case: "To the sage, truth can never be bitter. He finds more pleasure in the attempt to understand that which is, than in the attempt to believe that which he desires. There is no gain in shutting out the world, though it be with walls of righteousness." Consciousness, self-knowledge, knowledge of man and of reality, —this is the great result of our insertion in history—nothing else matters. "Destiny has only the weapons we give her. She is neither just nor unjust, nor does it lie in her province to deliver sentence on man. She whom we take to be goddess is a disguised messenger only, come very simply to warn us, on certain days of our life that the hour has sounded at last when we needs must judge ourselves." In all the literature of Stoicism there is no finer conception than this of the way in which the disenfranchised soul is yet held in whole-hearted attachment to the detail of fortune.

But the ruses are not successful; the will cannot thus be decoyed into unreserved espousal of the pursuits of life. The world of common action having no part in the absolute end, being there as a means only, becomes touched with a sense of incomplete reality or illusoriness, such as we discern in the atmosphere of Maeterlinck's earlier writings. It fails to hold that concentrated allegiance of the idea which is necessary to happiness. The inadequacy of the stoical principle even in its best forms has impressed itself on our racial instinct, and the world generally has taken refuge in another principle, that of *altruism*, or *vicarious happiness*. Success there must be, but it need not be *my* success: mastery of fortune there must be, but it need not be *my* mastery. Let me but know or believe in some power that is controlling or shall control physical event and history; then the event begins to have a meaning: and I can find my happiness in the assured victory of that power, though free as any stoic from the need of victory in my own person. History has entered into the absolute goal of things as a member; and all history thereby becomes contributory and important.

IV

The language of the altruistic principle is familiar to us. It is the language at once of resignation and hope. It is the language of the patriot: "I may fail, but the idea of liberty must conquer"; "This measure of mine may be defeated, but the policy or cause must triumph." It is often the language of the scientist; or again of the parent who regains in his sons the hope for all that he has not himself accomplished. Such vicarious happiness must be, in fact, the greater part of the actual joy of any living man; for no one can reach maturity without identifying his happiness to some extent with the welfare of his friend, the success of his party, or the establishment of his opinion, quite apart from any prosperity of his own. The scope of this principle is universal; and taken together with the prevalent belief that all cosmic affairs are so connected that they form a single history in which all can participate, it offers a plausible solution of our dilemma — to many minds, the only possible solution. For in such an interconnected world as this, every being must lie open to every other: vicarious joy can be no more actual than vicarious suffering, so long as we take into our survey anything less than the whole movement of life. The same knowledge or sympathy that brings in upon me the joy of remote triumph brings in also the more pungent distress of the many near defeats. In the race there can be no perfection till all are perfect, no complete happiness till all are happy. What sure triumph, therefore, can there be for any except in the common end, indefinitely distant, the end wherein all triumph; and what present happiness can there be save in that consummate vicariousness of interest which makes the goal of all history the justification for all that now is?

This principle has its religious heightening; it is even the sum total of what many understand by religion. Thy will be done: is not this the act wherein the individual definitely identifies his own success with the success of the Highest, rising thereby superior to his own fortunes without being dissevered from whole-hearted historic action?

And it has also its philosophical expression. It seems to me that Royce has brought this principle of altruism to its philosophic fulfilment. It is indeed impossible to seize fragments from a thought so vast and organic as his without danger of misrepresenting it; but I must venture to quote from a chapter wherein, dealing with our interminable struggle against the evils of our finite existence, Royce summarizes the conditions which may secure to us such happiness as we can certainly command.

"In all this my own struggle with evil, wherein lies my comfort? I answer, my true comfort can never lie in my temporal attainment of my goal. For it is my first business, as a moral agent, and as a servant of God, to set before myself a goal that, in time, simply cannot be attained. . . . Wherein, then, can comfort truly be found? I reply, In the consciousness, first, that the ideal sorrows of our finitude are identically God's own sorrows . . . and in the assurance, secondly, that God's fulfilment in the eternal order is to be won through the very bitterness of tribulation . . . through this, my tribulation." And as for the less noble ills that "seem not to have, for our present consciousness, any ideal meaning . . . Our comfort here lies in knowing that in all this life ideals are sought, with incompleteness and with sorrow, but with the assurance of the divine triumph in Eternity lighting up the whole."[1]

Thus to conceive my finite experience *sub specie æternitatis* is not merely an emancipation from evil, it is our essential and positive achievement of happiness. It is the experience in which "our temporal life is even now the expression of the eternal triumph"; and through this act of knowing I become an actual partaker in that triumph. It is this conception of the eternal which makes a vicarious happiness possible: and it is vicarious, in so far as my present relation to that will is one of loyalty primarily, not of comprehension; my present attitude to fortune, one of resignation, not of control. What this eternal triumph is, I do not know; I only know that it is real: and this, for Royce, is enough. "Strengthened by that knowledge, we can win the most enduring of temporal joys, the consciousness that makes us delight to share the world's grave glories and to take part in its divine sorrows."

V

These truths do deeply touch the original springs of human happiness. Such knowledge of the eternal Purpose and loyalty to it must be a great part of any real welfare. Vicariousness of mind is wholly necessary to happiness; ensuring the widest scope of that idea-world whereby all things must be appreciated that are appreciated. Have we not already found in altruism the

[1] The World and the Individual, vol. ii, pp. 407 ff.

largest possible contribution to personal welfare;[1] and in companionship the experience which can transmute all pain?[2] Vicariousness is wholly necessary; and were it not for that fatal separation from one's own immediate concerns, might be regarded as sufficient. But the vicarious principle cannot heal this division; hence it is not final.

For vicarious happiness is, by its nature, independent (or relatively independent) of my personal success in any present undertaking. So far from supplying an adequate motive for treating this present business as of infinite importance, it is essentially a refuge from the contingencies of that business. It does not remove nor evade misfortune; but when misfortune comes, it relieves it by distributing the shock through the whole range of my vicarious interests. He who loves the whole has resources beyond himself in his own evil hour. But the question of that particular evil is not met; one is simply lifted above it or borne through it by his attachment in the absolute. One is consoled, but not restored to confidence in the worth of his own action. Our principle has no launching powers; its attitude toward evil and misfortune is essentially passive: it is always one of comfort after the fact, never of adoption before the fact.

But surely we have not attained human manhood with reference to the ills of our destiny until we can go to meet them, instead of waiting in philosophic discomfort for them to surprise us. He whose deed is dragged from him is not owner of that deed; and he who must pass out of his own conscious will for comfort, cannot wholly return to this same conscious will for the coun-

[1] Chapter xi, p. 136. [2] Chapter xv, p. 222 ff.

sels of positive action. No man, I venture to say, can be wholly happy in defeat unless he foreknows and goes to it, not as Napoleon to his island, but as Socrates to his death. Not resignation, but *renunciation*, is the greatest and last of the virtues in presence of the ultimate enemies of our fortunes. And not blank renunciation, but renunciation made significant by some consciously known purpose which in the midst of defeat is not defeated. Only thus can the will return wholeheartedly to the charge. No vicarious or indirect mediation can supply me with the necessary integrity of interest in this present undertaking. In short, no man can be happy, nor ought to be, without a conscious control of his own fortune; without a fundamental and necessary success of his own in dealing with the world of objects beyond him.

This is a hard saying: for it demands what both altruism and stoicism have assumed to be impossible, a power over facts even in the midst of our finite circumstances. Nevertheless, I believe that we must either make this requirement, or abandon the attempt to find happiness in the world. This latter course is always open to us, and is virtually adopted by most; but at a greater cost than they think, that of relinquishing the hold of religion upon human history.

Altruism, not less than stoicism, leaves me unsure of the worth of my present act and purpose: that present act is liable to be defeated by an event, which even though it reveal to me the will of God or my own deeper will, must hold over my undertaking a shadow of invalidity. I can never taste the quality of genuine happiness, namely, perfect belief in and devotion to my own undertaking. I am a necessarily diminished and divided being: I am to act, but another than I is to succeed. And not less than in the case of stoicism does such an attitude impose upon myself and upon my world, in time, an air of unreality. For while God and Nature first become real to me because they determine me; they can only remain real, in so far as I also can successfully determine them, and as I intend. Men's mental horizons always tend to shrink beneath what their passive experience shows them as real; they tend to coincidence with the sphere of their conscious efficiency. Religions of nature and of humanity appeal to men chiefly because here are purposes whose meaning we think we can share, and effectively promote, even as we intend. The earth is real to me in part because it resists me; in part because it yields to me and I can recognize my own works in solid rock. Were there no sure succeeding there, earth and I would speedily become unreal to each other. Reality must be defined as the region wherein I can identify my happiness with my own success; not alone with the success of another.

Indeed, I can only know and understand an Other in so far as our object-worlds, and our objective goods likewise, are the same: hence, in whatever sense God is to triumph in history, in that same sense must I triumph also. In some degree, as we have seen, every soul of us knows the whole, and feels in his own limbs the thud and the impulse of the engines of reality: it must be possible, then, for our wills, to the same degree, to contain the will of the universe. We must be able to reach a kind of maturity in respect to God himself, in which we are ready to assume the burden not only of omniscience — as we continually do — but also of omnipotence, with regard to some fragment, however minute, of the historical work of the universe. In such a moment the act which we should utter would be known as a completely real act; and since we cannot separate our own reality from the reality either of our objects, or of our deeds — we too become for the first time completely real.

To require this of the world is to require what we may call *the prophetic consciousness.* By the prophetic consciousness I do not mean a knowledge that something is to happen in the future, accomplished by forces beyond myself: I mean a knowledge that this act of mine which I now utter is to succeed and hold its place in history. It is an assurance of the future and of all time as determined by my own individual will, embodied in my present action. It is a power which knows itself to be such, and justly measures its own scope. I do not say as yet that an assurance like this is possible; still less that it has ever been attained: I say only that it is necessary for happiness — that without it this region of historical fact must stand condemned as outside the sphere of either justice or reality. Apart from the possibility of prophetic consciousness, this region must be to our wills a "realm of chance" — just such a realm as Hegel and Royce and Howison agree with James in accepting — impenetrable to the Spirit, and ultimately repellent to the Spirit; wherein, therefore, the Spirit can never be wholly naturalized and at one with its own existence.

VI

If this demand for prophetic consciousness seems preposterous, it is chiefly, I must think, because our various philosophies of life have persuaded us of its impossibility; and we will be reconciled, even though half-heartedly, with what is attainable — a bowing-down which is the modern form of devil worship. Further, the love of *power*, of which this prophetic consciousness is but a sublimation, is associated in theory with the ruthless, the violent, the competitive, the relentlessly self-assertive, as in the philosophies of Hobbes and Nietzsche. Only a few can command success of this sort; and that at such moral cost that we repudiate the ideal, and seek our happiness in some other faculty. But may it not be that this instinctive love of power which is in every human creature needs only to be raised to the dignity of prophecy to lose both its cruelty and its incredibility? May it not be that these philosophers of the *Wille zur Macht* have but labored to preserve to us our confidence in the chief moral element of our nature?

For when we consider the facts of life, such an experience as this, a knowledge of necessary historic command of fortune, is neither hypothetical nor unknown, nor yet confined to the careers of violence. Moments of world-shaping prophecy are indeed rare enough in the records, even if the records are to be believed. And yet it is not meaningless that men whom we otherwise respect have, in certain critical passes of their experience, claimed this for themselves; they have left it at least ideally open to our attainment. Do we not recall utterances of Ptah Hotep, of Socrates, of Alexander, of Dante, Spinoza, Montesquieu, Hugo, Froebel, Pitt, Browning, Disraeli, sent out in the teeth of hostile circumstances, asserting a sense of invincibleness in their historic position? There are false prophets also; but we ask only whether there be any true ones. And we have not to depend on the reports, perhaps the boasts, of others' experiences. We may assume that whenever a supreme type of experience is possible to human nature, it will have numerous analogues and anticipations scattered throughout our common experiences. If the prophetic consciousness is possible, it will not be left without a witness here.

I am inclined to think, as I examine our ordinary commerce with physical facts and with social particulars such as history is made of, that our consciousness of command is the rule, while tentativeness and defeat are the exceptions. *Skill* is possible in a thousand ways; and skill is an experimental dealing with facts which has reached the point of assurance. Active life, like the life of thought, is built on the basis of concrete certainty. Our conscious enterprise is three-fourths experiment; but it steps out from a vast substratum of the indubitable. If our bodily existence is itself a kind of instantaneous and perfect command over a limited range of physical nature, our active existence has a like range of primitive certainty which defines the level of the species. A man is he who can infallibly exercise or acquire a certain minimum of assured power over facts, in work and speech and habit; man is defined by a certain high level of assumable power. The child must be taught to doubt, not to be confident of success; the proud prophetic attitude is the native air of our existence, and can no more be wholly cancelled by our numerous defeats than can our consciousness of deity.

But our more significant prophetic experiences lie on the other side of experiment; they come to us as skill assimilates itself to nature, and imitates the fundamental certainty with which it fuses. A well-defined and limited consciousness of power seems to me to be the essential fruit of mature self-knowledge. May not an orator command his audience, and know that he must do so, as simply as a child commands the ear of a parent? In such powers we all share. For all language, and all expression of every kind, is just such a process of making historic and actual certain experiences which at first are but private meanings of my own: and in so far as I can be sure that these private meanings are indeed universally valid, I may undertake with certainty to utter them. If I know, as I do, that my own experience of physical nature is an experience universal and sharable, it may be that beliefs, emotions, reasonings, principles, should appear to me with a like universality. And it is not uncommon to see men so convinced of this necessary acceptance of their idea that they are willing to persist in uttering it in face of universal repudiation, sure at the same time that they know their fellows better than they know themselves. Often we find our poets dealing in just such generous prophetic insistence with our common lives, knowing that what they express is no private sentiment, but the typical and universal sense of man. We remember, among others, the "Non omnis moriar" of Horace; and of Shakespeare,

"Yet do thy worst, old Time." And this of Francis Thompson,

> "I hang 'mid men my needless head,
> And my fruit is dreams, as theirs is bread:
> The goodly men and the sun-hazed sleeper
> Time shall reap; but after the reaper
> The world shall glean of me, me the sleeper!"

The more visible modes of prophecy, however, appear in those regions of experience where human happiness reaches its common height, namely in the more intimate personal relationships. No one is lover who does not prophesy: and this prophecy reaches its summit in the most presumptuous of all commands, "Follow me." In all friendship we say we have the debt of loyalty, and find our happiness in loyalty: yet loyalty is that one element of mutual living which nothing but a prophetic consciousness can explain. Nothing but a prophetic consciousness, a foreknowledge of the power of success in this difficult relationship, can justify the vows of marriage as they have been made: and any less binding vow is so much less than moral. Love itself seems to have such prophetic bearings, whether truly or falsely; it summarizes and discounts all obstacles in advance, and instates itself in unquestioning command of life and body. Love at least must postulate prophecy.

Our prophetic experiences begin in our immediate personal context. Our first acquired and conscious historical powers are powers over the free agents of history — our fellow persons. From this focus our prophetic range spreads itself outward, largely through the conductive medium of men and institutions, until it reaches and claims the services of all matter. Prophecy accepts and stands upon all these acquired and distributed powers, such as they are, and fuses them into single deeds, addressed to particular situations, deeds which know their place and their meaning, and which shake themselves free from the contingencies of the progressive experiments of mankind, for the purposes of their own moment.

Moreover, the consciousness of historic validity is not limited to such single deeds as these. The form of command, as power perfects itself, tends to become non-assertive, silent, and immediate, conveyed with the temper of attitude and action: and as personality acquires this more perfect poise, the exercise of prophetic power may become continuous, not simply concentrated in climactic performances. The effect of such silent and continuous command may be nothing more than this, that *things grow* in its presence. But this, if we have not been mistaken, is what chiefly happens in the presence of God. This also is historical action.

VII

These are the common foundations of our action. And if there be any such thing as a more total and significant prophecy than these, it will have the same structure as they: it will be the whole of which our various experiments are parts. Happiness may be identified with success in the utterance, not of fragmentary meanings here and there, but of some total meaning; the indelible historic expression of a self. It cannot fail to be at some high cost that a man may come to recognize his own total and universal meaning, and impose that upon the course of things. Some complete commitment to that aim might well be necessary. And such commitment will not leave him to suffer that pain alone which may reach him by diffusion; it will put upon him the necessity of courting pain, even of creating pain for others where none now exists, rousing them from their ease and exciting their wrath. It is well for us that every man has his quantum of the belligerent spirit; for it is as necessary to our happiness to have found and defined our proper antagonism as to have found and defined our proper love. Enthusiasm can exist on no other terms; for enthusiasm is not energy merely, but energy conscious of a potential difference. When we have caught the spirit of this kind of detachment we discover that the outer dimension of ourself varies with the greatness of the thing we are over against quite as truly as with the greatness of the thing allied to us. We take a fierce joy in the power to perfect that detachment by simplification, by renunciation, demonstrating to ourselves that we have the power to renounce, to deny, to oppose — to send our plowshare deep, so that when it moves, as it must, a huge segment of sluggish, inert earth will be disgruntled and displaced. We find re-entering into our souls those lost virtues of war and asceticism — virtues which can never be artificially fostered or reclaimed.

In such a temper as this are strangely combined the self-sufficiency of the stoic, the universality of the altruist, and that righteous love of power which our own age at once celebrates, fears, and decries. The prophet is the realization of all these human motives; and it is he whom all these have in mind as the superman, who is also the sage, and the man wholly happy in his historic context. Is it not he whom Maeterlinck has in mind, even while he praises the stoic virtues? "To those round about us there happen incessant and countless adventures, whereof every one, it would seem, contains a germ of heroism; but the adventure passes away, and heroic deed is there none. But when Jesus Christ met the Samaritan, met a few children, an adulterous woman, then did humanity rise three times in succession to the level of God." This is that "consciousness of self" which "with the greatest of men implies consciousness up to a point of their star or their destiny"; and not alone because "they know in advance how events will be received in their soul," but because in addition to this they also know *what they will do with these events*, and what stamp history will carry as it falls back from that encounter.

Shall we not acknowledge, then, that the prophetic consciousness is a wholly credible experience, abundantly indicated in the ideals as well as in the instincts of men as the concrete conception of happiness? And if we regard it as necessary for happiness, we do not thereby wholly condemn our experience even as we find it. It is certainly not necessary for happiness that every undertaking should succeed, that there should be no failures: it is only necessary that as our buffeted lives labor for the most part between our two great refuges — stoicism and vicarious satisfaction — it should still remain open to us to believe that these lives may have some total historic meaning, and that this meaning can, through whatever discipline or observance, be brought to consciousness and valid expression. If we can believe this, history can never become wholly alien to us.

But how and when does the hour of such total prophecy arrive? Is there to be a moment when not alone the hero, the patriot, the sage, but the simple man of quiet life and plain speech, may lay aside the attitude of humility, cease to admit his possible failure, and take control of the history which at that moment is enacting itself in his presence? Must there come to every one an hour when the connection between the success of his cause in the world and the success of his own deed lies clear before him, turning vicariousness into cowardice; when he knows beyond doubt that the arc of the destiny of that idea must now coincide with the swing of his own arm? In what form does prophecy arrive? And how is the prophetic consciousness possible?

VIII

My answer is that the prophetic consciousness is possible in the same way that reflexion is possible, in the same way that a total present judgment upon the world is possible. The prophet must know himself; and he must know his world, not in detail but in so far as it is relevant to his purpose: such knowledge as this must come to him through his relation to the absolute. The prophet is but the mystic in control of the forces of history, declaring their necessary outcome: the mystic in action is the prophet. In the prophet, the cognitive certainty of the mystic becomes historic and particular; and this is the necessary destiny of that certainty: mystic experience must complete itself in the prophetic consciousness. The lightning of Zeus is not released until already it is forefated to strike the earth; in this transaction heaven and earth must break away together. So whatever certainty the mystic acquires means and foretells a positive overcoming of the world: he can only keep his certainty by making it visible to himself in historic accomplishment. Prophetic power is the final evidence to each individual that he is right and real; it is his assurance of salvation; it is his share of divinity; it is his anticipation of all attainment. Hence it is that the greater mystics have been great founders, great agitators, and have if not a heavenly immortality yet unquestionably a mundane immortality. There are no deeds more permanent than those of Buddha, of Mohammed, of Jesus. And innumerable lesser deeds of equal validity have completed the substance of these mighty frames. The deeds of the mystics constitute the hard parts of history; the rest has its day and passes.

The love of history has not usually been reckoned among the virtues of the mystic. The mystic is precisely the timeless and unhistorical being, even in the midst of his creations. It is no concern of the artist that he produces to-day or to-morrow, for this company or for that. I admit the paradox. The carelessness of time is the chief evidence of the artist's historic security. If he is a true creator he addresses *history itself*, with all its accidents. Socrates does not write, nor does Spinoza publish his chief work; but each in his own way cares sacredly for the viability of the link between himself and the concrete future.

Retreat from history is the mystic's temptation. And he who dwells in the universal alone becomes false; the unhistorical mystic is a liar: he has hidden himself from the truth which is only in the fact. But the falsity of mysticism is the beginning of its end.

The next swing of the alternation of mind brings the scientist, who is the mystic confronting the fact with his absolute. Objectivity of mind is the most germane fruit of religion; and science becomes possible only through long discipline of worship. Man cannot at first bear a perfect contact with nature, nor conceive a wholly physical causality; none of his early hardships give him the sense of *fact;* his fancies stand between him and the possibility of a fully physical experience. It is only the developed spirit that can bear the fact in its nakedness. It is only the modern mind that can define causality. Truthfulness is a wholly modern virtue, born with the Renaissance and its respect for the objective event. And the Renaissance is the mediæval mind turned upon nature; it is worship turning to discover the sacredness of history. The historical virtues, truthfulness and economic integrity, are the latest moral products of spiritual advance, the especial deposits of the Christian temper in religion.

And indeed it is only the mystic who *ought* to be historically moral; for to him alone can the world as it is, in its very particulars, be sacred. The unfriendly shapes of fortune are the chief occasions for faith; only faith is right in exposing itself to them without reserve: and faith is but the love of God, the prophetic consciousness, confronted by the particulars of history. It is only the mystic, I say, who is wholly bound to history, and therewith to truth and honor.

There is such a thing as losing one's soul: and that is, rejecting one's call to prophesy. For if there be any immortality beyond this present scheme of things, it is not in abstraction therefrom: the destiny of our own deeds, great and small, is an integral part of whatever future there may be for us. To deserve to endure is the only guarantee of enduring. I have no faith in an intrinsic indestructibility of the substance of consciousness. One life is given us; another may be acquired.[1] Immortality, I venture to think, may be the chief and total object of the prophetic consciousness. But if so, it must be a consciousness of such command of nature as he only has who can wholly accept nature as it is; of such superiority to the catastrophes of history as he only has who can unreservedly live out into this present history, knowing it, even to its last hard fact, as *his* sphere of divine control.

Professor C. A. Bennett calls my attention to a remark by Edmund Gosse in an essay on Malherbe to the effect that in the sixteenth and seventeenth centuries it was the fashion for all poets to claim immortality. When prophecy becomes a convention, the virtue has leaked out of it; but it was presumably some original virtue that inspired the imitators.

[1] See on this point Frederic Palmer, The Winning of Immortality.

CHAPTER XXXIII

THE UNIFYING OF HISTORY

OUR historic existence with its immense contingencies we take for the most part with a certain poetic remoteness: we only half believe in it; we hope well of it — that is to say, we hope well of the luck that seems to prevail there. We live still in a semi-savage dreaminess, incredulous of the distant contingency, incredulous therefore of the present moment, veiled from the actual conditions of action, circling at planetary distances about our own practical center. The fanciful is too real to us, the real too fanciful. The evil that is in this world, and especially in this spirit of meaningless accident — the luck which we hope will be *for us* good luck — this evil does not rouse us: it benumbs us, rather, and confirms our somnambulism. This is our ingrained irresponsibility, our original sin.

It is the last fruit of religion to produce, or approximate, a prophetic consciousness, that is to say, a natural historic consciousness, wholly wakened, literal, and real, capable of seeing the divinity of its own present fact and acting upon it. It is the work of faith to face the bulk and detailed circumstance of nature, banish its luck, remove its mountains. Religion must labor long, but aims at last to bring about such a faith, literal, prophetic, responsible.

But we are right in our incredulity, so long as

religion comes to us only as a psychological necessity. The conditions for prophetic control of fortune lie without as well as within, far out on the borders of the universe. Science and the State, under the encouragement of faith, may banish luck gradually to these borders: but from them, luck streams back upon human life — distributed, perhaps, in its incidence, yet none the less menacing and vast. Unless the original sources of history, the ultimate arrangements of natural facts, the configurations of physical things which set the last limits to the hopes of all living beings, are already subject to some other control than our own, there is no such thing as absolute certainty of historic action. I cannot hasten the missile that has once left my hand; every workman must leave his work at last to a world that he can no longer govern; the whole race of prophets and world-builders stands helpless in the presence of a wider agency whose name is either Fate or Providence. Without the coöperation of an environment not less than infinite, the best prophet comes at last to zero — the worse because of his concrete hopes. The mystic must give reason for his dogma that there is no "realm of chance"; that beside the work of God which we have been tracing in the individual mind, there is a supplementary work of God in the world beyond the human will, — there at the origins of the plot which all events work out. Thus the theory of religion rests back upon cosmology and the philosophy of a wider history for its final justification.

I cannot here follow out into this wider world the question of the right of the religious consciousness in its immediate practical assurance. But at least one principle prevailing in that world is already in our hand, and I will touch upon it in closing. So far as our own human history is concerned — a small part, no doubt, of our total environment — we can see that the religious will tends to create the conditions for its own success. Note what these conditions are.

It is in our human environment, as we said, that our natural will-to-command finds its first successes: our power extends from this center outward. Yet taking the human world as a whole, it presents a problem to prophetic ambition not less baffling than that of the control of nature: in fact, these two problems are precise counterparts of one another. Dealing with the social environment has always the guidance and encouragement of response, pro and con, which nature lacks. On the other hand, dealing with nature has always this element of satisfaction, that nature is a single order, persistent, invariably faithful to its own principles whether against us or for us. The obstacles to prophetic confidence in dealing with the human world consist in the absence of just these qualities. He who intends to accomplish something permanent must appeal to an environment that treasures and faithfully conserves values. The fluid mass of free wills conserves nothing, holds itself bound to nothing. A world which can promise to conserve must itself be unitary and eternal: it must have a principle of persistent identity and reliability like that of nature. To introduce into this mass of free individuals an order, unity, and inflexibility of purpose like that of nature would indeed be something of a miracle. Yet without this, the prophetic attitude is not justified: this, as I see it, is precisely what the prophet must require. He must *find in the current of history a unity corresponding to the unity of the physical universe, or else he must create it.* And what I want to point out is that it is just such a conscious unification of history that the religious will spontaneously tends to bring about.

We can see that the type of power which we have called prophetic, unlike that power which Nietzsche celebrates, tends not to compete with and destroy the like power in its neighbors, but rather to develop and to propagate it. As laughter begets laughter, and courage courage, passing from mind to mind and crystallizing a social group or a social world upon its own principle, so does the world-conquering temper of religion beget its like. No human attitude is more socially contagious than that of worship, except the practical attitude toward facts which comes out of worship: namely, enthusiasm for suffering, conscious superiority to hostile facts of whatever sort or magnitude, knowledge of their absolute illusoriness, so far as they pretend finality, — in a word the practical certitude of the prophet. When religion has thus acquired a clear-sighted and thorough *contemptus mundi*, religion begins to be potent within this same world of facts: it was within the scope of the stoic to become impregnable, but the religious spirit finds itself more than impregnable, — irresistible. The prophetic attitude begins at once to change facts, to make differences, to do work; and its first work is, as I say, its social contagion: it *begins* to crystallize its environment, that is, *to organize the social world upon its own principle.*

And if this temper is actually spread through the

social world (not rising and dying out like the wave of laughter, but reaching the threshold of self-perpetuation), something more has happened than the dissemination of a *type of will* by 'social imitation'—namely, that *environment* is created which this same type of will requires. The human world has taken on a certain unity of mind and purpose; for whatever may be the special field of action of any religious will, every such will must desire that unification of the conscious world as a necessary part of its own purpose. So far, all have common cause. Every prophetic will is something of an environment for every other; as the group widens, and pervades human life with its principle, it becomes, as an environment, more adequate to its task, and may reach complete adequacy.

We may conceive some such group as becoming fully conscious of the nature and extent of this task; and adopting as its own special responsibility the extension of its own unity, for the sake of making this same will accessible to all men. It would thus make it, so to speak, its own prophecy that prophetic will shall be possible; that no human being shall be obliged to let his prophetic impulses die for lack of that unity in the human world which must justify them. This, I believe, is the essential purpose of the *religious institution*. It is this purpose, as I conceive it, which brings religion to earth in the form not simply of a system of truth, not simply as a type of personal experience, but in the form which religion everywhere takes, that of the positive historic body with work to perform.

Positive religion in its primitive phases *makes history possible*, cultivating what we might call the tribal and national memory. In its more developed phases, it tries to achieve a more general, non-political, but none the less historic solidarity among men. It undertakes, we may say, to do for the sporadic prophetic impulses of men what the State does for their sporadic impulses of justice and public power. Let me develop this idea a little.

As I look over the circumstances of religious development, I observe that there are four striking changes in the religious consciousness which usually occur together: as religion becomes 'redemptive' (that is, world-overcoming in one way or another), it detaches itself from the national life, it begins a universal propaganda, and it refers itself and its adherents to some distinctive historic object or person as the beginning of its temporal undertaking (and so, as a special point of irruption of the divine into history). Thus Islam points to its shrine and its sacred book; the Buddhist convert must take refuge in the Buddha, as well as in the doctrine and the order; Christianity asks men to regard its founder as the unique way to God. How are we to understand this remarkable concurrence of characteristics at this stage of development?

It is the analogy of the State which best helps me to understand what these things mean. The political organization affords to the individuals under it what Bagehot well describes as a "calculable future." In the State I have some prospect of a tangible immortality. I acquire property that may affect in one way or another my children's children. I promote laws, perhaps, that influence more or less all lives to come within the scope of that government. I can do my small part anywhere in art or industry or science with a sense of worth; because the State is there to give permanence to the growing treasures of one generation after another. The State *lends to my deeds its own permanence,* so far as these deeds are legitimate and within its own province.

In the same way the religious institution (I am speaking now of the ideal, as reflection shows it to me, certainly not of the entire body of instituted religion as it now is) — the religious institution seems to exist to lend its own permanence and immortality to the deeper and wider prophetic purposes of men. In severing its fortunes from those of the State, it assures to the individual his right to live and take part in an infinite history, though outside all States, and in spite of the defects of all earthly States. It stands between the creative individual will and that unordered, or unstably ordered, human social mass, before whose free mobility and passion that will is indeed in a hopeless plight.

Religion defies the clash and decay of the political attempts of men, whose mission in their own sphere is similar; but it is historic religion which chiefly renders those political attempts hopeful. Religion from primitive times the protector of the stranger, the market-place, the truce, is the forerunner of international law; because it alone can create the international spirit, the international obligation; it alone can permanently sustain and ensure that spirit.[1]

[1] By such super-nationalism in religion, national individuality is not obscured, but rather promoted. We require a world-religion just because we do not require, nor wish, a world state.

It is this function, as I think, which the greater religions have more or less clearly perceived. They propose to bring into human affairs that most general unity, not interfering with nor displacing any more special undertaking, without which no such special undertaking — whether of art, or of science, or of law — is worth while, being without promise of permanence.

We customarily think of the religious institution as a way of arranging for *the social side of worship.* Worship is imperfect unless when I worship, I am joining the race in worship.[1] Instituted religion has accordingly made worship public; at its best, it does much to join the minds of all sorts and conditions of men in worship, of all present human worshippers, and with those of the past and of the future. Further, we think of the institution as *an educating body*, or as propagating the religious type of mind by that social imitation we were speaking of. But we usually fail, as I think, to see what the institution does to justify that type of mind; namely, that it brings to the individual soul not only its moral ideal, its psychological norm, but also the *kind of world* wherein such a mind can alone rightly assert itself. It is a unified and responsible world, one which cares for the individual in his concrete character, and will bear out his rightful will to endure, — a human world which religion itself has made.

It is a sign of the good faith of the institution that

[1] We have regarded worship in its mystical aspect, as a solitary adventure of the soul: but we have also noted from time to time that before the mystic may make his lonely flight to God, he must assert as fully as possible his unity with his human spiritual context. Unity with the Absolute becomes significant in proportion as the worshipper is first one with the spirit of God as already established in the world.

it brings to the individual, who seeks assurance of his own absolute worth, its assertion of its own power and permanence. It encourages him to prophesy, only in so far as it itself is based on prophecy. It asserts its own universal scope and indestructibility — the gates of hell shall not prevail against it. If this is a true assertion, the individual may always knit his prophetic action to that. The attitude which as a solitary being he could not rightfully assume is made possible to him by this external agency which is throwing over all history its most general unity, bringing men everywhere to a singleness of mind and a singleness of purpose. Through that agency, and not otherwise, he may win, in the language of religion, his (historic) salvation, the forgiveness of his ingrained sin.

In our current consciousness, we feel little need of these external assurances, nor of the institution which offers them. The sense of sin grows foreign to us: the suggestion that we any longer require what our fathers called salvation strikes with a note of unreality. We feel ourselves morally secure; and historically, — as secure as need be. But when beneath this over-socialized surface of consciousness we penetrate to the actual basis of such certainties as we have, our self-respect, our belief in human worth, our faith in the soul's stability through all catastrophes of physical nature, and in the integrity of history — this history of ours — forever, we must recognize there a mass of actual deed, once for all accomplished under the assurances of historic religion. A *system* of deed, I might rather say, organized about a prophetic purpose once planted in history and now perpetually reproducing itself all around us.

The work of positive religion is largely silent; like the work of positive law, it is as great in what it prevents as in what it noisily accomplishes — perhaps greater. But the work is there, and if we are just we shall acknowledge it. Our confidences with regard to history must be built in history as well as in universal thought, — in both of these, welded together. Unless we can discern at its silent work in human affairs this power, self-consciously eternal, actively communicating its own scope to the feeble deeds, the painful acquirements, the values, the loves and hopes of men, we have no right to such faith as we habitually assume. And without such faith there is for us no valid religion.

EXPLANATORY NOTES AND ESSAYS

I

NOTE ON THE SUBCONSCIOUS

IT is well to emphasize the fact that subconsciousness is not an endowment but an incidental acquisition, due to strain of voluntary attention. It is a by-product of determinedly self-conscious life. No infant has a subconsciousness: no adult is without one.

Our subconsciousness at any time may be roughly described as that remainder of consciousness which persists outside the sphere to which in our various practical efforts we deliberately narrow our interest. And this remainder has two divisions which must be sharply distinguished in thought, though in fact they blend into one another.

We may define these two divisions by their relation to the voluntarily conscious self: the first is *allied* with it, the second is more or less hostile to it, or *critical* of it. The former part, the allied subconscious, is called subconscious chiefly because it is not being thought *of*, though it is being thought *with*. It contains the instincts that we inherit and the habits we form; also the memories we store, and all the system of ideas with which we do our apperceiving. It contains the habits of appreciation we build up, and the habits of decision — in short our 'character.' It is an active organ in all experience, and can at any time become an object of reflective scrutiny. Though many an element of memory, of attitude, of my controlling ideas and deeper instincts, may evade the grasp of my pointed attention at any moment, there is nothing here that is essentially inaccessible, nothing that may not become part of the focus of consciousness. It is not 'split-off' from the central stream of attention: its objects are the same objects, its world is the same world, with that of the artificial or central self.[1]

The other aspect of subconsciousness, the critical, is the part to which the name is more properly applied. It is a consciousness of objects which *we*, the artificial person, have chosen not to be conscious of. It is the unchosen or repressed, marginal life of the mind, maintaining an existence of protest, like a sort of bad conscience. What our artificial efforts exclude from notice is not utterly excluded; we are not so free as we seem in the self we make. It is impossible to condemn to oblivion any small voice in us without in some measure being conscious of that voice; and especially if we condemn on less than full conviction we cannot help being aware that our condemnation is hasty, and this element of our consciousness remains in communication with the excluded strand, and keeps it alive, as it were surreptitiously.

Thus it is that old habits of observation continue to do their work without separate urging. Things which I have once noticed, or collected, or otherwise valued, I continue subconsciously to take notice of, though I may have outgrown the interest, or may have become ashamed of it. There is an extraordinary cunning and minuteness about this aspect of subconsciousness. It is the watch-dog of the mind. It may take note of time, observe faces, remember the numbers on houses or bank-bills, the names of streets, the turns of stairs, passing shadows, flitting expressions of the eye and voice: it is faithful, as the photographic plate is faithful, to slighter impressions than the artificial self can discriminate. For doubtless the limits of voluntary interest have reduced the fulness of the reports which our senses may make to the artificial self. Our eyes and ears are capable of far more than we can now get from them; the remainder, up to the limit of their sensitivity, may still be kept in a subconscious record. But again

[1] Since subconsciousness, as I believe, is a division *within* consciousness, the proper contrast is between the subconscious and the artificial self, not between the subconscious and the conscious.

we must say that this faithful and relatively mechanical observer in us takes note of nothing that has not at some previous time been important to the self-conscious mind, whether of the individual or his ancestors. Its world, though supplementary, is still the same world as that of the artificial self.[1]

[1] There is in reality, as I have said, no sharp line between the 'allied subconsciousness' and the 'critical subconsciousness': whether any given experience, noted by these persistent habits of observation, becomes critical, or merges itself with the allied 'apperceiving mass,' is a question chiefly of the kind of exclusion which relegates that experience to subconsciousness. It may be an exclusion of antipathy; it may be an exclusion of simple limitation of interest (in which case, the subconscious criticism amounts only to this, that 'These things also ought to be taken into account'): or again, it may be an almost wholly passive exclusion. Professor Angier, in commenting upon this note, makes this distinction very clear and graphic. He writes: —

"As I take it, many of the occurrences of life which apparently do not impress explicit consciousness at all, toward which at any given time we react in no accepting or repressing way whatever, slide into the subconscious where they find congenial connections and become part of the reservoir of what you call the 'allied subconsciousness.' In traveling, for instance, I imagine that many of the scenes through which we go, which never enter the focal point of consciousness, nevertheless contribute richly to the final attitude with which our travels leave us; and later, in recalling these travels, they furnish a background for our memory image or for our conversation.

"Is there not a difference between those things which we have "chosen not to be conscious of," i.e., repressed, and those things which have simply not entered the field of explicit choice at all? This seems to be a real distinction. Those things which do not enter the field of choice, but nevertheless casually make their impression on the subconscious, do not necessarily, perhaps not at all, constitute part of the critical subconsciousness. To my mind it is only those things to which we are either instinctively or through deliberation averse that become our subconscious monitor and critic.

"It seems to me that we meet two types of personality based on this distinction: one, the genial, tolerant man who impresses us as reeking with a rich and friendly co-consciousness which gives subtle color and tone to all his sayings and doings; and the other one, whose helping co-consciousness is meager, but whose critical or antagonistic co-consciousness is rich."

This protesting part of subconsciousness has great variations in its volume and strength as compared with the self-conscious stream running along beside it. It has its periods of fulness and of emptiness; it has its own methods of relief, finding its way back to the central self. We may describe briefly the circumstances that fill it up; and then these methods of relief.

1. *Strenuousness.* Clearly, whatever tightens the strain of conscious attention will increase the burden of the subconscious. The natural materialism of determined action; the stern selection for world-building purposes of *fact* having a specified degree of solidity and resistance; these make quick work of all trailing "clouds of glory," and relegate them to the subconscious where they maintain a ghostly existence. What men call sentiment has to spend much of its life in this Coventry: it has little chance while "business is business" —and probably ought to have little chance.

Insistent 'reasonableness,' i.e., strident logical pose where ideas are far in advance of possible idea-connections, richly contributes to the subconscious, and correspondingly impoverishes the artificial self. Note too that it is the nature of reasonableness of this sort to seem to itself right and self-sufficient: the circle of ideas that pass censorship becomes fixed; they make themselves a closed group. The voice of the excluded margin is timid, unarmed, merely advisory, at a political disadvantage. It is easy for the focus to become tyrannical, to refuse due representation to the counsels of the subconscious; so that a parallel stream of judgment which might silently mingle with and modify the course of decision is cleanly excluded and put into hostility. Thus the focal center of life hardens, polishes its surface, and tends to perpetuate its own quality.

Severe mental concentration produces apparent oblivion to external happenings; but in reality a division of mind which adds to the subconscious. If long continued, certain segments of memory and of the technique of common living may be split off, temporarily or permanently.

Moral and religious strenuosity has the same result, and particularly when one wages war against an entire aspect or conception of oneself. Dr. Prince's Miss Beauchamp shows very well a type of zeal which must result in highly charged subconsciousness. As a child "her mother exhibited a great dislike to her. . . . On the other hand she herself idealized her mother, bestowing upon her almost morbid affection: and believing that her mother's lack of affection was due to her own imperfections, she gave herself up to introspection, and concluded that if she could only purify herself and make herself worthy, her mother's affection would be given her." [1] As she comes under Dr. Prince's observation "she is possessed of a conscientiousness which at times has proved embarrassing to her friends. It is carried sometimes to a degree that may be characterized as morbid. For instance, while in college she was the recipient of a scholarship; consequently she considered it her duty, in return for this benefit, so diligently to apply herself to her studies that it was impossible for teacher or physician to enforce sufficient recreation, or even the rest and hygienic measures which were absolutely necessary to keep what little health she had." Further fragments from Dr. Prince's notes: "morbid pride . . . refinement of thought and feeling beyond the ordinary . . . she took everything intensely . . . mentally and morally stubborn." The depth and coherence of Miss Beauchamp's subconscious life must be attributed very largely to this extraordinary will together with the equally extraordinary definition of its own problem.

This is not to condemn the strenuous life; on the contrary, only through strenuous attention can the standard of definition and factualness be set to which it is the aim of all idea to conform; I only point out the inevitable incident of that strain. Any action at all, any dealing with things, is a strain

[1] Morton Prince. The Dissociation of a Personality, ch. ii.

outward, involves some artificial limitation of judgment, some over-influence of physical standards, and will require compensation. The subconscious is simply the internal register of the compensation required, and will obviously increase in fulness with the degree of free-will put behind the action.

2. *Suppression of critical comment.* There are various ways and various motives by which our spontaneous criticism of people and things gets huddled out of sight, and may be so effectively suppressed as to become subconscious. Thus we incline to suppress *self*-criticism; the self of us which "knows better" when we want to depart from common sense or common duty, the self to which our moral gadflies appeal when they assume that every man knows what is right, and come toward us rather with indignation than with persuasion; the self which we call conscience or mother wit; this self is capable of being suppressed — that is to say, so systematically hushed that it learns its place and ceases to interfere. In such cases, our bad conscience does literally take up its abode in subconsciousness. We suppress also criticisms of others, of institutions, opinions, etc.; we choke down dislikes, wrongs, fears, doubts, scruples, on the theory of our artificial self when it holds that these negative feelings ought not to exist. Theoretical policy, especially social policy, must in the main be affirmative; succeeding policy must be blind to minor hindrances; health must ignore disease: and these fair resolves run much danger of building up a critical subconsciousness, producing a bland and false personality. One is parted from the truth of his own aversions. One begins a régime of duplicity, and may end by losing all personal grit and valency. An especial case of this suppression is that of the knowledge of guilt of a past act which I regard as unconfessable: it may be a trivial matter; or it may be a criminal record, a character overcome and hidden from sight; or it may be no moral thing at all, but a physical or mental peculiarity, or a defect in one's pedigree or origin which, as one thinks, simply must not be known. Suppressions of this sort contribute

richly to subconsciousness, and incidentally to the clinic of the psychiatrist.

3. *Organic growth.* The assumption that the artificial self is sufficient unto itself makes difficult the entrance of new ideas into consciousness, especially of new attitudes toward life as a whole such as growth brings. Whatever is new in the field of idea is still weaker, as against the central self, than the usual marginal idea; for the most part these incipient developments can gain recognition only through the channels of dream, imagination; they so far gain the conscious ear as to call the mind away from actualities, from time to time, to a world of vague but alluring phantasms which turn into nothing real. Hence it is that adolescence, which is peculiarly a time of theory-grasping as well as of growth, is subject to subconscious accumulations and to dreams, and so to more or less disturbing processes of relief. On the other hand, these new ideas have this advantage over other types of subconscious burden that they are waxing in force rather than waning, and are destined at some time or other to find their way to the center.

The rejoining of the artificial self with the subconscious self is an event for which nature has not failed to provide certain instinctive methods. For each of these ways of accumulating there is a way of discharging: I think it is true that all of the major rhythms of conscious life involve some rise and fall in the subconscious pressure. I wish to point out that all of these methods of relief involve *finding an object which is common* to the conscious and the sub-conscious self.

1. For strenuousness the natural remedy is a general lowering of activity, repose. Wherever the strains of artificiality and attention can be released, as in privacy and the ease of friendly intercourse, the subconscious begins to find its way back to the focus. This type of relief reaches its natural end in sleep. In sleep, voluntary attention is abolished; the mind

is acting on no theory of the good, and no theory of itself. But in sleep it cannot be said that consciousness is abolished; it is rather the case that consciousness has attached itself to an object which is common to all interests, conscious and subconscious, namely, the individual self. And by relating themselves to that object, without interference from the theoretical will, the various strands of mental life tend to resume their natural relations to each other.

2. For suppression of comment the natural remedy is a generally heightened activity, excitement, orgy, passion.[1] Passion might almost be defined as a rapid release of subconscious strain under heightened attention. It occurs when some object in the conscious field arouses an idea belonging to that strand of the *allied* subconsciousness which is keeping this part of the *critical* subconsciousness alive. We commonly observe that in anger, long suppressed comment finds its way to the surface: criticisms which one had resolved never to utter come to the fore and join in the summary destructive flux. More accurately speaking, anger is the flood itself, the rapid synthesis of the disowned ideas with the idea which has here found its object. But any agitation tends to enlist wider and wider areas of mental resource, and so to bring subconsciousness into working relations again with the artificial self, just as by aid of heat or solution chemical unions may take place, and equilibria be established, which otherwise would remain indefinitely *in posse*. In excitement, one passion makes opportunity for another; and orgy may end, not only in general exhaustion, but also in the general harmony and unity of the entire creature. Thus, amusement and recreation do their part in relieving subconscious pressure.

3. What organic growth contributes to subconsciousness is a kind of suppressed comment; and its natural relief is also a kind of passion. This passion occurs when the dreams, in

[1] There is, of course, no strict one-to-one correspondence between these types of relief and the types of accumulation of strain. Thus suppressed comment may also be relieved by repose, or by change.

which the growing motive had been finding vague expression, 'come real'; i. e., when in the waking world an object appears which at the same time recalls and satisfies those groping ideas. This, of course, is what happens in 'falling in love.'

4. But beside these instinctive methods of relief there is another, namely that of *deliberate reflection.* Experience in this matter, as in all matters, brings about the possibility of conscious control of the process of reuniting the disjoined fragments of selfhood. One learns to recognize in himself the malaise of subconscious pressure, and to turn upon himself with the demand, "Well, what is the matter with me." Such a person is delivered from the more drastic and physiological upheavals, just so far as his power of self-analysis reaches. If he can find the *idea* which commands both the conscious and the subconscious, he can do intentionally what nature does instinctively. Thus, confession and self-confession relieve the strain of suppressed comment, and in such wise that one knows what has happened to him — in so far, with better result than by the way of passion. The deliberate practice of sincerity and prizing of the 'natural' self are habits which to some extent may prevent the accumulation of rebellious residues. Resolute facing of the fear or the doubt which dogs one's peace; consciously planned occasions for meeting and removing grounds of injury or dislike: in all these ways, and in many others, consciousness holds in its own power the methods of reunion with the critical subconsciousness.

But there is no such thing as a complete displacement of nature by art in this matter: the squarely reflective restoration of selfhood reaches but little way. It is but a process of seeking, or as we might say, of prayer; it cannot surely command the reconciling idea; and even so, it does not so much displace the natural methods of repose, excitement, and love as it does meet these half way, and recognize their place in the conscious system of life.

It must have become evident that the subconscious or "subliminal self" is only another name for that natural self of which we have been speaking; the self which in effort we lose, and tend to harden a superficial crust against. Whatever releases subconscious ideas into central consciousness does so far relieve spiritual fatigue; and vice versa, whatever relieves this fatigue does at the same time rejoin these two partially divided aspects of conscious life. It will therefore be possible — though of no great advantage — to express the meaning of worship in term of this relation between subconsciousness and the rest of consciousness.

Characteristic of worship is the necessary place in it of the method of *deliberate reflection;* this constitutes the active part of worship, or prayer. And in the passive side of worship, the mystic experience itself, we find qualities which resemble those of all the 'natural' modes of recovery, — rest, excitement and love: worship is a natural synthesis of all of these; the elevation of the mystic is a state at once of passion and of peace. This might be inferred apriori from the fact that the idea of God is one to which no item of consciousness, whether split off or not, can get out of relation; it is an idea which belongs permanently to that self which stands prior to the divergence between the artificial and the subconscious.

The religious ecstasy or orgy is a product of religious specialization. That is to say, worship ideally speaking is capable of fulfilling all the functions of the other means of re-integrating selfhood, whether of love, or of amusement, or of sleep itself (as witness the exploits in comparative sleeplessness of Madame Guyon, of Philip of Alcantara, and of many another): and if one must, or will, confine himself to this one method of spiritual recovery, mystic ecstasy is quite normal. We avoid it, and on the whole prefer to avoid it, by a differentiation of worship in which our mystic experience is diffused among the several more instinctive rhythms. I do not doubt that the distrust shown by certain of the stricter sects toward amusements, especially toward dance and the theater, is due not so much to the alleged inherent sinfulness, of these amusements, as to the circumstance that they actually substitute for, and so diminish the intensity of, the specifically religious mysticism. It is a clear modern instance of the 'jealous God'; and this jealousy is justified in so far as pleasure is disposed to ignore its dependence upon the whole-idea for existence.

The language of subconsciousness need not misrepresent the facts of religious experience. With the descriptive skill of James or of Pratt it conveys much truth which could hardly otherwise be so effectively expressed. But it almost inevitably misleads. For it hardly fails to suggest, first, a division that does not exist; and second, a superhuman resource which is different from the resource of our simple waking selves.

As to the first point, we must insist on the fact that there is no subconsciousness which is *out of consciousness*. The 'allied subconsciousness' is an organ of consciousness; and the 'critical subconsciousness' is present to the 'allied subconsciousness' in the same way that the artificial self is present. The 'allied subconsciousness' is simply the comprehensive self whose object is 'the whole.' After many years of observation, Janet finds himself doubting whether even in hysterical patients there may not be a self which envisages both the normal and the dissociated segments of consciousness. He thus states his own present questionings: "Does not the hysteric herself possess a sort of insane belief which makes her relinquish certain phenomena? Up to what point is she sincere in her declarations of ignorance? Does she not to a certain extent deceive herself?" etc.[1] And what may hold good in such abnormal deepening of the cleft between the artificial self and subconsciousness, I cannot doubt to be true of our normal relation to subconsciousness — namely, that we are conscious of our 'subconsciousness' all the time. The subconscious is not something which we should think of as a distinct gland of psychical life, accumulating its own stores and occasionally

[1] Subconscious Phenomena, p. 66.

overflowing into the central self. The subconscious is the deposit of our own logical sense, our own value-consciousness and moral judgment, our own metaphysical instinct, in short, of our own whole-idea, in its unceasing criticism upon the judgments of our partial, strenuous, and artificial self. It contains the opposite, or antithesis, which our artificial self at any moment needs to justify it and make it completely true; it contains, therefore, the next turn in the dialectic of experience: — all of Hegel's categories may be conceived to spring up in order out of subconsciousness.

And this may serve to correct also the second misconception which the language of subconsciousness arouses, namely, that we have here a mysterious and superhuman faculty of knowledge. Not that it leads us to think too highly of our capacities. That reflection of von Hartmann's is hardly too sanguine, however absurdly it is expressed: "Let us not despair at having a mind so practical and so lowly, so unpoetical and so little spiritual; there is within the innermost sanctuary of each of us a marvelous something of which we are unconscious, which dreams and prays while we labor to earn our daily bread."[1] Well, so there is; only, we are not unconscious of it. Subconsciousness has indeed infinite resources, but they are *our* resources — they are the resources of the infinite idea such as we in our normal waking capacity do rightfully possess, and such as we shall in time learn to command.

[1] Quoted by Hart, Subconscious Phenomena, p. 106.

II

THE RELATIONS BETWEEN IDEA AND VALUE UNDERSTOOD THROUGH BIOLOGY.[1]

IT is a besetting fault of our constructive thinking to overestimate the load which a distinction will carry. We prove that conscience is uniquely different from the calculus of values and think we have saved ethics. We discover that theoretical judgments and judgments of appreciation are fairly independent, and hasten to found philosophies of religion upon the breach. With these and other dichotomies we renew the experience that unless we have something more than a difference, what we accomplish is simply to insulate our ethics and our religion. What tempts us repeatedly into this dead corner is, I believe, the conviction that mind must be studied on its own ground: whereas the truth is that regarded thus intimately and ideally the objects of our inner experience tend to fall into just these fruitless disparities.[2] In my own

[1] From an article published in Psychological Bulletin, Vol. v, No. 5 (May 15, 1908).

[2] The more contemporary psychology exerts itself to be purely experiential, the more it finds itself busied in listing the 'irreducible' elements of the mind. This is true particularly of German psychology where good judgment is less likely to interfere with consistency of method. It might save some trouble to observe that all aspects of the mind as pure experience are irreducible. Pleasure is pleasure ; Begriff is Begriff ; reason is reason ; nothing is identical with anything else — not even with the aggregate of its elements ; everything is simple and unique. It is well to note this truth, — to insist on it is to spin on our boot-heels. An irreducible is an object of which we can only say that it is what it is ; of this material no science can be made. The tendency which isolates these objects has something idealistic about it, perhaps ; but since it has nothing but the 'given' to offer, it is necessarily dogmatic and exclamatory. Only a genuine idealism can afford to be thoroughly materialistic in its first explanations.

attempts to gain relief from such situations I have found myself moving, more or less clearly, in the direction of physical theory.

I have come to believe that there is a certain inevitable logic in this. Our inner experiences, our oughts, our happinesses, our values, even our pleasures among themselves, must as objects of thought remain miscellaneous furniture, each turning its back to the other in default of common understanding, unless we can bring some finely indifferent unit of order and comparison into them. The first business of all explanation is to express a thing *in terms of what it is not* — an event in terms of its cause, truth in terms of process, sensation in terms of motion. Other things equal, the more alien in nature the terms in which a thing is expressed the more successful the explanation: the thing has its roots in the utmost corners of reality — the demonstration is complete.[1] Now nothing is so admirable in its categorical indifference to the concerns of the spirit as is physical nature. It has no member either in the psychical movement or influenced by it. It is a seamless garment of interweaving threads; it is what the mathematician calls, in a word, a closed group, and the physicist, a conservative system. This complete conceptual independence it is which chiefly qualifies it for serving as a terminus of explanations for the peculiarities of spirit. Its alien quality (once it is admitted to be a part of the same world with spirit) insures that no aspect of consciousness will be unrepresented in the physical system; there will be nothing even in the relation of

[1] The difficulty always is to see that such explanations explain. To explain a thing by what it is not — that is to explain one mystery by another. But is there nothing illuminating about that? The company which miseries are said to love lightens them; mysteries love company also, and for a similar reason. If we are satisfied to look no longer for the supports of the earth because a group of unsupported planets can be self-supporting we must be prepared to recognize similar relations among facts. Every datum, taken alone, is dark, just because it is ultimate. This stranding upon 'data' is empiricism's weak spot, and its opportunity. The thing that relieves data of darkness is, not more data exactly, but the group-form into which data assemble themselves.

consciousness to its world of objects and to other subjects which is not shown in its field *by some exact metaphor*. That is to say, — the elements of consciousness which on their own separate ground are mutually repellent, find themselves mirrored in a homogeneous world no part of which can get out of relation to any other, and from which, therefore, if we have the key to the metaphor, those relations can be read and understood.

But this logical hint is enforced by a more substantial consideration. It is reasonable to suppose that the answer to any question will be found in the context of the phenomenon that calls forth the question. There are good grounds for thinking that whatever plurality the mind shows, whatever temporal movement and flux, is due to its entanglement in nature; or, to read the same relation from the other end, nature may be the temporal and plural life of the mind. So of each several aspect of the mind. Conscience, for instance, has no variety, no application, no career, except for its commerce with our 'empirical' instincts and desires; and desire, in turn, has no variety nor development, except in the toils of a differentiating organism. Very probably, also, conscience splits off from desire or desire from conscience on some rock of nature. Hence without any assumption as to which of the two, nature or mind, is the prime mover in this differentiating process, we should naturally look for our principles of synthesis *in that same region of things which reveals the cleavages.* Genetic surveys have always the advantage of showing the emergence of the thing in its 'natural' relations — in the case of conscience, for instance, it will be found in the company of those desires and impulses with which it is destined to concern itself as regulator. Nature can give no sign of conscience except in the midst of its business. We have not first to deduce the thing and then its application; but if we find it at all, we shall find the application first and the thing in the heart of the application.

Now to decipher the physical substratum of mind, what we most need is a distinction of categories. Not every aspect of consciousness is presented in the physical context by a separate organ or process; we must be ready to appeal to the higher physical categories, the configurations of organs and processes, accelerations of processes, and other differentials and modifications of energy. What nature shows us is not simply a metaphor of consciousness (and hardly that — for its language is all but literal), but it shows us *a finished analysis* of consciousness. We know that whereas in itself pleasure is simple, conscience is simple, and nature is simple, the attempt to express one in terms of another brings out the subtleties of each; and we shall not expect to find every unitary mental state marked out in the body by tangibly colligated physiological phenomena. We should be guided much more truly by the principle that *psychical categories are complementary to physical categories.* The first aspect of a psychical *one* will be a physical *many;* this physical many will have its physical unity also, but that unity will not be in the same class of objects with the many — will be found in physical functions which are the more derivative in proportion as the psychical category is more substantial. The unity of the 'self' may thus be the last thing for which the simple physical expression is found (no pineal body among other bodies), though that simple expression necessarily exists. The processes which belong to a self are naturally more widely dispersed and more various than those which belong to such imperfect and fragmentary unities within a self as 'an experience,' 'an idea,' 'a pleasure,' etc. In the interpretation of the *freedom* of consciousness we have a clear case of the complementary nature of physical and psychical categories. The freedom and initiative of consciousness is represented in nature by the obedient regularity, sometimes called the *necessity*, of physical sequence. This is the only basis upon which the relation of the free spirit to nature can be made intelligible. In a machine whose parts have any slack or lost motion the eye will discover the origin of pushes and pulls by the direction of the slack. But in a machine all of whose connections are perfect, so that there is not even infinitesimal slack in any part, it is impossible for observation to discover whether the wheel is pulling the piston or the piston pushing the wheel. Nature as a mechanism certainly offers no visible suggestion as to the seat of its original impulses; it simply goes its perfect way; and this alone it is which enables me to accept unreservedly the testimony of consciousness that itself is the active and original thing in the world, all else being ultimately passive. With this understanding the chief difficulty in all biological accounts of conscience is relieved — how, namely, out of natural law, that is, out of absolute obedience, can come the dictator. It is just *because nature is the region of perfect obedience* that the dictator has to 'come out.' In all strictness, dictatorship is simply the permanent outside of nature; and nature gives birth to conscience as it were, by way of confession. What we see in nature is the gradual perfection of the receiving organ, so that freedom acquires growing significance as life moves on; but some receiving organ is always there, the regular is the continuous signature of the free. We have therefore *no separate place* to make in our account of value or conscience for freedom, since it is completely expressed in the character which makes nature nature.

The term 'idea' will play the fundamental rôle in the theory I have to propose, and it will be desirable to sketch its physical interpretation before attempting the further question of the nature of value-experience. I shall attempt in the end to show, through these physical expressions, that values and conscience are *functions in the life of 'ideas,'* and to point out definitely, in the same language, what these functions are. Our disjointed world of facts, appreciations, and duties, may then be seen in some intelligible shape and connection on a basis other than metaphysical, though at every point the shapes of nature are but the intaglio of the spirit.

I. The Biological Equivalent of 'Idea'

If our interpretation of freedom is valid, the fact that any given physiological apparatus works 'mechanically' creates no presumption that it is unaccompanied by consciousness. Consciousness is not introduced into the biological series at the point where mechanism fails to meet the needs of adjustment, because there is no such point. Hence 'instincts, however truly explained as congeries of simple automatisms of tropic character, may at the same time represent some element of consciousness. Such an element would necessarily be a 'universal' or *general idea;* for the instinct is related not to individual objects, but to a type or class of objects, in such wise that *whatever* object affords the proper stimulus releases the appropriate action. To consciousness the stimulus would appear not as 'this individual object' but rather as 'a specimen of this *kind* of thing' toward which such and such a line of action is desirable.

The repetition of the stimulus would present to consciousness 'another specimen of the same type,' and the similarity of response might connect itself for that consciousness with some quality common to the two particular objects; but we who look on can see that the *identity of the idea* lies not primarily in any objective characters of the two experiences, but rather in something which the organism carries around with it, and which *exists when there are no 'experiences'* to set off its train of behavior. I wish to show not only that there is a biological equivalent for the permanent identity (sometimes called the 'timelessness') of the idea, and for the native difference between an idea and 'an experience,' but also to show that the idea has a more continuous presence in consciousness than the experiences in which it is subsumed from time to time. An idea is in fact never absent from consciousness; the prevalent belief that it vanishes and reappears is a confusion between the idea and the experience. Recognitions of objects are intermittent; but our ideas, it should be evident, are not what we think *of*, they are what we think *with*. Now whatever else the unity of a consciousness may mean, it also means that there is no isolated action of ideas, but that I think with all of them at once in each moment, though the 'bearing' of any given idea upon any given experience may be very remote.

But beside the ideas that correspond to instincts, that is, to the various modes of regular, quasi-official dealing with objects, there is a set of ideas of a different sort, which I may call the *field-ideas*, such as the idea of extension, or of the physical continuum, or of a particular friendship, or that important symbolic idea 'the whole of things.' These do not correspond to any outlinable instincts; their biological expression must be sought elsewhere. But inasmuch as the field-ideas develop in close concomitance with the development of the instincts, the nature of the biological expression may appear by considering the *interaction* of instinct-ideas in the course of evolution.

The evolution of ideas in its most general biological character may be summarized as a matter of the *balancing of instincts* — that is, of the emergence of 'secondary' or counter-instincts, which act together with the 'primary' instincts as more general instincts than either alone. Such a pair will be represented in consciousness by *a more general idea*. Now we have to note that every time one instinct has been balanced by another, consciousness has acquired not only a new type or class of objects, but also an idea of much greater scope than that corresponding to either of the two instincts separately. Just as my present impulse cannot be checked by the suggestion of something future without making me aware not merely of the two points in time, but more or less dimly of the stretch of time between; so the generalized habit of modifying the present impulse by the consideration of future contingencies cannot be established without making the idea of the *time-field* a correspondingly firm element of my conscious vista. So in proportion as I learn to modify my reflex upon what is here by the suggestion of what is not here, the idea of *space* becomes a mastered range of mental vision. The logic of the process is this; that whenever an x meets its *non-x*, x having been my largest class, the two can coexist in the same mind only as parts of some 'universe of discourse' whose scope will in general be very much greater than x. The development of an inhibitory instinct, therefore, can never mean the setting of one suggestion against another simply, but it means opening *a whole field of possible variations* where before there was but one fixed line. This whole process of balancing instincts, impulses, suggestions and associations means that the mental range is becoming more complete. Man's peculiarity in biological terms is his extraordinary balance — throughout his being he stands on two feet. It is this same peculiarity which in psychical terms is expressed in his extraordinary capacity for gripping large totals, and at last for coming to use the category 'the whole.' The use of this category is reason.[1]

Now any one of these vista- or field-ideas, as we may call them, varies greatly in vividness. This vividness will be a function of the intensity of the x-impulse and also of the intensity of the *non-x* suggestion. The consciousness of time, for instance, is *made vivid by the conflict* between the claims of a pungent present and a pungent future. Let me suggest that a vivid representation of a future moment and therewith of the time-field, whether voluntary or resultant, stands for an expenditure of actual physical energy; and that the continuous and easy presence of future and past to our vision represents a high level of *potential energy* in the nervous elements concerned. In general, I would propose that the extent of the ideal-whole in whose presence a conscious being lives and to which he adjusts his action is biologically represented by the potential energy of the nervous centers.

II. The Theory of Value-Experience

The earliest and simplest instincts seem to be of such sort that the 'perception' of the stimulus and the 'gratification' of

[1] The effect of the counter-instinct in developing a field-idea shows itself in the phenomenon of *hesitation*. Now the resultant of two instincts is just as determinate as the action of one. Hesitation means not that two possibilities interact, but that a range of possibilities has to be run over as a relatively independent object. Man's fitness for reason is concomitant with his pre-eminent fitness for hesitation.

the instinct are one and the same process. Dealing with its object either by contact or by immediate reaction the subsumption of the general idea *is* the satisfaction. Despite the immense veiling of the phenomena of pleasure and pain by the complexities of development, the profuse demarcation of states of consciousness as 'ideas' which are neither instinct-ideas nor field-ideas but perhaps fragments thereof, I believe it can be shown that *all pleasure is still of the nature either of subsumption* (wherein an idea, or a conceptual whole, is applied to one of its instances) *or of induction* (wherein some instance or group of instances are provided with a conceptual whole which covers them). The joy of making a successful induction and the satisfaction which a child takes in applying a new word, are typical of all our positive values.

I cannot here make attempt to cover the field of value-experience, nor to account for all the well-known anomalies of our feelings of pleasure and pain. I shall review simply in very rough outline a series of phenomena which seem to me fundamental in the sense that any theory which will explain them will explain the rest in the long run.

1. Pleasures connected immediately with the senses and with the several physiological functions have their marked rhythmic intervals; and the longer the period of intermittency, the greater, in general, the volume of the pleasure (Spencer). This dimension of pleasure seems to be a function of the nutrition of the organs concerned.

2. Pleasure is itself a destructive and exhausting process. This is a natural inference from (1). Pleasure heightens life — that is, it quickens expense; it draws living to a focus as a flame creates its own draught. The intensity of a pleasure varies directly with the rate of destructive metabolism.

Pleasure may 'accompany states in which the organism is being built up' (Royce, and many others); but the process of building up is incidental to the pleasure itself, a biologically fortunate incident indeed, but having no representation in consciousness. The actual succoring of the organism occurs later in time than the pleasure and affects first of all parts quite different from those concerned in the pleasure. In the long run pleasure is normally profitable to the organism ; it usually accompanies only such expense as the body is happy to restore; the drain affects primarily funds which have been appropriated for that particular purpose ; and these circumstances have something to do with differentiating pleasurable expense from painful expense. But *per se*, pleasure is a drain.

This is a clear instance of the complementary relation between physical and psychical categories above noticed. As an experience, pleasure is indeed a filling up of the cup, the supplying of a need. And the deeper the draft upon vital resources, the greater the fulfilment of desire. This holds true to the limit. Only that delight can ultimately satisfy and fill the soul which drains the body to the point of death. Indeed, all joy is akin to death; the fortunate drone unites with the queen, and dies — a rapport symbolic of all pleasure.

It is, in part, confusion between these inverse psychical and physical categories which has misled so many of the best observers into the belief that pleasure is a psychical accompaniment of physiological construction. It is extremely doubtful whether such construction enters into consciousness at all.

3. It follows from (2) that the expense in pleasure is not confined to the organ immediately concerned with the object which is the occasion of the pleasure. To a certain degree, change of object will renew pleasure, and variety of object preserve it; but there is evidently a common store which every pleasure draws upon, independent of the particular organ or object. A person thoroughly exhausted in one joy is ready to enjoy nothing else but Nirvana.

4. The quality, 'pleasure,' is a function neither of the special nor of the general exhausting process alone, but of some relation between them. Pleasure is at the same time a *central* and a peripheral experience.

In psychical language, pleasure requires attention. The

physiological design of consciousness must be one of concentration. However wide the range of a person's affairs his whole interest must be recalled to the simplest experience he would enjoy. The process of 'becoming absorbed,' let us say in music, is at first a conflict with the inertia of other trends of interest: they must all fall into line at last. The intensity of the pleasure depends upon the perfection of the focus, that is, upon the absence of competition among objects of attention. The person is *all in the pleasure*, no matter if it be a 'mere' sensation.

5. But if it is important for the perfection of the experience that other interests cease to compete, it is equally important that they *continue to exist.* The quantity of the pleasure depends on the completeness of the recall, but it also depends on the presence of interests to be recalled. Pleasure is a function not simply of the fact of focus, but also of the amount of stuff concerned in the focusing. In this respect, different pleasures, so far from being competitive, depend each one on the existence of the others to give them magnitude: every pleasure has one dimension which varies directly with the number of instincts, or desires of possible kinds of pleasure — and not simply with the degree of differentiation, but with the ground covered by the differentiated interests, that is, with the range of the objects. In other words, pleasure is *a function, among other things, of the idea-horizon;* any given pleasure echoes into the whole cavern of a self, and varies in quantity with the volume and resonance of that cavern. Even within the career of a single pleasure it is noticeable that as absorption becomes complete and the circumference of the circle of consciousness begins to contract, the pleasure has passed its culmination, and will tend to zero until the interruption of another object of attention dissipates it.

All this points to the hypothesis that in all pleasure our 'field-ideas' are at work (not as thought of, but as thinking). The 'circumference of consciousness' is a variable which corresponds exactly to those changes in the vividness of the field-ideas which we supposed to represent a certain tension or potential in the centers. And this tension, we said, was in turn a function of the competition of impulses. For example, the extension of time-vista both foward and backward which marked the earliest economic advances of mankind, is concomitant with the growing possibility of inhibiting a present impulse by the idea of a future value. The continuous subjection of impulse to the consent of all the possibilities in a time-field means indeed an interference with pleasure in the sense that each claimant for attention has to *struggle for possession ;* but it means that every object which gains this attention is the source of a pleasure whose value is greater than that of an undisputed enjoyment of the same object in proportion to the enhancement of the time-idea. In physical language, every increase of the potential energy of the centers increases *all conscious values* in the same proportion.

What the physiological processes are which play themselves off in the actual business of enjoyment, I can here do no more than hint. All pleasure is rhythmic and tends to self-maintenance. A *mood*, for example, which is a value-experience on a somewhat roomy and deliberate scale, becomes pleasurable in proportion as it learns the arts of life, as melancholy feeds and reproduces itself from node to node of its rhythm. The quality we call 'pleasure' is deeply connected with this formal character of the processes involved (a character which makes of them precisely what the mathematicians mean by a 'group'). On the conscious side, it will be evident by a little observation, that the change which occurs when a trying experience after repetition becomes pleasurable, may be described as the acquisition of an *idea* under which each element of the experience is subsumable as it rises. When for instance anxiety in a given situation gives way to confidence, we have acquired on the intellectual side, *vista*, and on the practical side a readiness to meet with appropriate action whatever type of event may arise in the course of the experience. So with a mood: it is implicitly a *Weltanschauung*, and it lives by the process of corroborating its theory of things in the events that pass its focus; in this *commerce of its idea with the instances* of life lies its satisfaction, be it a gloom or a glory. I propose that the same is true of *organic pleasures*. In them, nature has embodied in structure the *idea* concerned; she has solved the problem of that particular evil for us (for doubtless all the destruction which is at the heart of consciousness is an organic problem); and the idea she uses will be most difficult to drag into the foreground of vision. But that the idea is present in physiological concentration, and can in time be read, no one who follows the spiritual progeny of any instinct can question.

My thesis then is simply this: that all pleasure is essentially a process of intercourse between an idea and its instance. The field-ideas of any consciousness will be concerned in all of its pleasures; and each of these pleasures will have as one of its dimensions a quantity which varies with the effective range of its total field, or, biologically speaking, with the potential energy of the centers.

III. The Theory of Conscience

Since Spencer, much has been done by way of distinguishing conscience from those types of inhibition which more or less closely resemble it and ally themselves with it. The work of describing psychologically the unique characters of conscience is in the nature of the case always unfinished; but it will be sufficient for our purposes if, by way of a phenomenology of conscience, we may make clear the separation between conscience itself and the *load* which conscience carries or adopts.

The load is the relatively changeable aspect of conscience. Every individual in the course of his career makes numerous changes in the points of scruple which constitute the burden or application of his conscience; the race has done the same thing on far greater scale. Perhaps the first burden and certainly the most permanent protégées of conscience are the 'secondary instincts' — but they are not conscience. This load makes use of all accessible means of support: pains, punishments, associations of approval and disapproval, and all the well-known instruments of social propagation, so that in the contents of conscience as we find it in ourselves there are motives traceable not only to our own education and experience but to every stage of our historic and phylogenetic journey, motives in which the aspirations of the Orient, or even the sorrows of those remote pre-moral ancestors whom Spencer invokes, are among the comparatively recent relics. But all this is something other than conscience. No theory indeed is complete which does not explain the circumstance, remarkable enough in itself, that conscience has the capacity of allying itself with all this material — that it is able so early in human history to lend effective support to a struggling secondary instinct, and to turn the natural disadvantage of the remote consideration into some sort of equivalent chance for survival. But the first point is to distinguish the thing itself from all its adoptions; and I shall resume very summarily what seem to me the most significant points in that separation.

1. Conscience has nothing to do primarily with the way we feel about any specifiable *kinds of action*. For it is a more central affair than can be described in terms of a connection between types of action and such elements of experience as might adhere, by association, etc., directly to these types.

Nothing is more astonishing in the earliest history of the moral motive than the speed with which it shakes free from peripheral lines of association and becomes an organic attitude to action in general, which it requires some use of subsuming intelligence to apply to particular kinds of action. The function of those *third parties* to the moral situation which appear so early in moral development — the alleged first ancestor, the totem, the lawgiver, etc. — is primarily that of supporting conscience in this central position, the position, that is, of relative independence of the 'types of action' and thereby of more or less freely variable application to them. Psychologically expressed, the thought of an action has to pass through the thought of this third party, with the régime he represents, before that action or kind of action is considered right or wrong.

2. The painful quality which we attribute to the motive side of conscience is also a part of its load; that is, it is adventitious. Conscience is necessarily painful only in so far as all hesitation, or the halting of immediate satisfaction, is painful. Whatever traces and suggestions of past pains and punishments conscience bears with it must be referred to its accretions, not to its nature. The sort of check which conscience imposes upon action is more nearly like that which some inarticulate presentiment of a greater good might impose upon a definable good. But strictly speaking, conscience has nothing to do with represented pleasures any more than with represented pains, nor with any represented utilities of an inheritable sort, as will appear from the following.

3. Conscience resembles the æsthetic consciousness in being a continuous source of new requirements, not traceable to any 'lessons' of previous experience. If it were the record in us of experiences of any sort already finished and organically digested it would tend to fading rather than to finesse. But nothing more than conscience is subject to explorative origination, and to the sport of virtuosoship.

The theory of the biological aspect of conscience which I have now to propose is simple. It depends upon the theory of ideas and values already developed, and needs but one further preliminary, — the proposition, namely, that any *flux* in consciousness is, or may become, itself an object of or factor in consciousness.

Just as we have impressions not only of distinct static objects, as stones and trees, but also of *processes*, as dawning or waning of light; so we have awareness not alone of high spirits and low spirits, but also of the rise and fall of spirits, if these changes are sufficiently rapid; so also, of the flux of vigor, of the loosening of attention, etc., — sometimes even of waking or falling asleep. I presume that every flux in consciousness is in some measure an object of consciousness, for consciousness is by definition, 'that region in which appearance and reality coincide'; though it may well be that few fluxes are separately registered and noted.

Now if our theory of values is sound, the most significant of all fluxes in any consciousness for the integrity of its values would be a flux in the effective range of its field-ideas; for we proposed that the field-ideas were factors in every particular experience of value. Physically, every pleasure has for one of its factors a coefficient of potential tension in the centers; and the potential capacity of these centers has been very gradually extended as instincts have balanced each other, the most sensitive index of this growth being the range of effective bearing of our field-ideas upon the immediate business of living. Any act which rejects the bearing, let us say of the future upon the present, wilfully obscuring the time-vista and tending to diminish its efficiency in consciousness, will strike a blow at the degree of all values in that consciousness. It will do so, moreover, in a way of which the agent can at the time have no inkling.

Conscience, I believe, is the perception of this differential; that is, on the physical side, it is a recognition of the flux, real or virtual, of potential capacity in the nervous centers; on the side of consciousness, it is a sense of flux in the valid bearing, or efficiency, of my field-ideas. Or, since all field-ideas in the same consciousness must come, as we have said, to an understanding with each other, so that they act as parts of a single field which we may symbolize abstractly as 'the whole,' conscience may be described simply as the perception of flux in the awareness of the whole.

In this description the word perception is open to valid objection, inasmuch as the consciousness which is experiencing the flux in question does not interpret its experience in terms of any such flux. The change which affects 'ideas,' consciousness always tries to interpret as a change in 'experiences,' referring its uneasiness to the agency of mysterious *objects*,—the 'third parties' above mentioned. It would perhaps be better to say not that the flux is 'perceived,' but that this actual flux has become a separately effective agent in consciousness, leaving undetermined how consciousness, in its more or less bedevilled efforts to construe to itself what is happening, shall report these effects. On the biological side the language seems to me sufficiently precise. I make no attempt to portray to my mind the ultimate physical occurrences — an attempt which would be presumptuous with far more knowledge of these processes than I can boast: I am content to state what I believe to be the true *genus* of the event itself. To say that we are aware of a thing, is to say, biologically, that the representative of the thing is doing some work within. The work which conscience does, we thought to be inhibitive in character. Now wherever there are field-ideas at all, there are fluxes of field-ideas as a matter of course: but *conscience begins when this flux begins to be itself effective*, through whatever apparatus. Biologically, therefore, we may say that the 'recognition' of the flux above described consists in a *resistance* to a negative flux wherein the capacity of the centers is diminished. The biological equivalent of conscience is: *A resistance to any tendency to diminish the potential capacity of the nervous centers.* If this supposition is valid, it should at least accord with the phenomena of conscience which we have brought forward.

It is evident that conscience would from the start be independent of external experiences associated with any special 'types of action.' Conscience would work just as decisively in inhibiting an action which threatened our field-integrity in an entirely new and unheard-of way, as it would in the case of a thoroughly conventional mode of offence — perhaps better. But any external sign of disapproval upon an action undesirable in this intimate way would add its definite 'no' to the less definite 'no' of conscience; and any considerable group of such tangible corroborations of conscience would form a body of fusions which even to skilled psychological observation, if it were of the prevalent point-blank variety, would defy analysis. Conscience pure and simple is distinguishable only in its work of initiative and variation.

And we can see further how conscience would have an æsthetic and super-useful character. As a sense for a differential, it would vary with powers of discrimination; it would be a function of 'fineness of fiber.' It is entirely conceivable that a prodigy of conscience should appear in the midst of a relatively rough-shod community, which could not be the case if conscience were the vanishing echo of an already fixed racial inheritance. But while conscience outstrips utility, it is not hard to see that it would tend to be useful. For the field-ideas are but signs of the adequacy with which consciousness presents to itself its world. Conscience at any time stands for a superabundance of adaptation. But, as in many other cases, nature has had to adapt herself *generously* because there was no way whereby she could adapt just enough and no more.

Finally, we can see that as it would be impossible for early man to discover the nature of the evil that threatened him in his troubles of conscience, so it would be impossible for him to express it accurately in terms of any known good. Its voice in him, until he seized upon the sticks and straws of 'empirical' corroborations, would be chiefly that of inarticulate resistance, a check which gave no clear reason for its presence, a categorical imperative or forbiddal. But in so far as he tried to make plain to himself the uneasiness at his center he would have to connect it with the widest objects of his Weltanschauung — his future, his ancestors, and his spirits. For these remotest objects are only the outpost stakes which we have set as marks of the widest total mental ranges we have thus far conquered. The sense of duty as a strain indicates that the range of 'the whole' is being enlarged. The sense of pleasure which at length displaces duty in that same type of action may mean that this degree of totality is now secure. But unless we suppose that a man's mind can reach a complete adequacy of view, the sense of duty can never, as Spencer suggests, be expected to disappear.

The final test of any such theory as this will be found in its ability to explain the history of the evolution of conscience. This immense task must be reserved. What I have here aimed to do has been accomplished — to show the natural relations of ideas, values, and duties, through the medium of their common biological context.

III

THE KNOWLEDGE OF INDEPENDENT REALITY[1]

IF it has been the fault of realism to give the object of knowledge an independence which makes it meaningless, it can be no sufficient ground for idealism as a positive doctrine to refute a meaningless independence. It is not enough to bring forward the ever-ready "Ich denke, welches alle meine Vorstellungen begleiten kann," or Royce's "Ich will, welches alle meine Vorstellungen einnehmen kann." For while the idealist may say, after the mathematician's fashion: 'Give me any object, however independent, and I will show you an ich-denke, or an ich-will, which can take it in,' the realist may always rightly reply: 'Give me any ich-denke, or ich-will, however capacious, and I will show you an object whose being is independent of that very thought.'

For it is an act of reflection which discovers the ich-denke as including the object; and by reflection upon your reflection you rediscover the primitive relation of externality between your mind and its objects: you are unable to make an idea of your idea except by recognizing something which is not that idea.

Now philosophy can have no permanent interest in a game of who shall speak last. While if we decide the matter by enquiring who has spoken first, the realist carries the day: the 'first intention' of the mind is that it deals with objects independent of its own thought for their being. And no matter how successful you may be in showing what interest the subject may have in the objects which it finds, this interest is so

[1] Reprinted in part from an article published in The Philosophical Review, Vol. XIX, No. 3, May, 1910, under the title, "How Ideas reach Reality."

far *secondary*, in respect to the existence of the independent objects, that it would be precisely the same interest were the objects as different as can be imagined. Your 'ich-will' has no power to determine what the objects shall be; it assumes that they are there to be accepted.

That the original and naïve attitude of the mind to its objects requires to be interpreted, we must assert with idealism. But it seems clear to me from considerations like the foregoing, that the interpretation cannot be so readily found as by taking the object up bodily into the subject through the reflective turn so typical of idealistic reasoning. The idealist reflection shows successfully that nothing can be real for us in which it is not possible to trace the mark of ourselves and of our interests. But this always leaves it possible that the same objects may bear other marks at the same time; and that these other marks are the defining characters of their objectivity.

The whole life of knowledge can best be understood, I believe, as an intercourse between the self and an independent reality. An analysis of cognitive experience should show what this means, and how idealism in extending the I-am to the entire scope of the I-think is rendering meaningless the conception of selfhood. Knowledge implies a complete breach, at some point or region, in the wall of the self. Let us consider whether any such region can be defined.

There are reasons for looking for such a region first within physical experience. Some of these reasons have recently been put forward by M. Bergson. Largely the same reasons were touched upon by Kant, whose uneasiness about empirical idealism came in part from the same quarter; and it may not be amiss to recall briefly these familiar considerations. The entire weight of our judgment of Wirklichkeit, Kant asserts, hangs upon Wahrnehmung.[1] We may make to ourselves conceptions as we please of things according to the categories (for

[1] Postulate des empirischen Denkens überhaupt.

instance, of things so related that the condition of one thing carries with it a definite condition of the other things); but from these conceptions we can never know what actual things stand in that relation, nor can we understand how they can be so related, until we refer to physical experience.[1] Of our knowledge of change, a strong point with M. Bergson, Kant says, that in order to represent to ourselves Veränderung, we are obliged to make use of Bewegung, or change in space, for an illustration: without this we cannot make even the general meaning of change clear to ourselves, for it is something whose possibility is quite beyond the grasp of the 'pure understanding.'[2] In sum: however much *a priori* knowledge may be possible, we have actually no working ideas at all without "Wahrnehmung, mithin Empfindung"; and this click of sensation is required to give the note of reality to any part of the system of experience, categories and all.

But as with idealists generally, so with Kant: while we hear him speaking boldly about 'external reality' in quite realistic vein, we have always to expect from him the annulling stroke, "Yes — but what do you mean by external reality?" Kant has not failed to express himself on this point, most radically of course in the "Widerlegung des Idealismus." The reality which we know in physical experience, he says in effect, is outer, not only in the two senses commonly accepted by idealism,

[1] The following sentences from the Allgemeine Anmerkungen zum System der Grundsätze are noteworthy, partly because of the use of the expression, 'objective Realität' instead of 'Wirklichkeit,' and partly because Kant is speaking of the reality not simply of individual things but of the categories themselves — that is, of things *as conceived:* "Es ist etwas sehr Bemerkungswürdiges, dass wir die Möglichkeit keines Dinges nach der blossen Categorie einsehen können, sondern immer eine Anschauung bei der Hand haben müssen, um an derselben die objective Realität des reinen Verstandesbegriffs darzulegen. . . . Noch merkwürdiger aber ist, dass wir, um die Möglichkeit der Dinge zu Folge der Categorien zu verstehen, und also die objective Realität der letzteren darzutun, nicht bloss Anschauungen, sondern sogar immer aeussere Anschauungen bedürfen" (2d ed., pp. 288, 291).

[2] Allgemeine Anmerkungen, etc., 2d ed., p. 291.

namely, (1) that objects in space are outer to each other, and (2) that the system of nature confers upon some objects not now present to my perception the same reality which is attributable to these present: but also in a further sense which not even the personal ich-denke can engulf, namely, (3) that here we find this very personal self, in so far as it is a peculiar individual, in the *process of being made.* As a knower — so we might interpret the argument — I am as a whole a being with numerous peculiarities: I have not only a time-span, and a time-rate, but a very definite and particular time-span and time-rate. And so of many another element in my make-up — the special tension of my desires, the numerical coefficient of tenacity in my attention, and the like. Now if these peculiarities require explanation, they cannot be explained by anything within the self, because they affect and define the self as a whole; but the truth is that we know these peculiarities in experience, and we know them only by knowing something else at the same time, namely, an outer reality which is measuring itself against myself, and whose point of contact is found in sensation. I have no peculiarities which are not first peculiarities of something not-myself. Whatever may be the nature of this reality, here, in sensation, I see as it were my own measurements, my own peculiarities being borne in to me. The material of sense is, in its first moment, not-self-stuff, and only in its second moment, as elaborated in my forms of experiencing, does it become part of my own being. The physical judgment, then, juts out into the idealistic night — it works in a realm where selfhood is metabolic, non-monadic.

The essential point in this position of Kant's might be formulated in this way. You, the idealist, may legitimately attribute to, or include within, any self, so much as that self can understand and reproduce, and no more. The self, at your own rating, is to be defined by mastery, by self-consciousness, by self-sufficiency. And since this power of conscious control fades out as it approaches the particular, and never penetrates the particular, you must admit a final limit to the individual self at the point where experience becomes particular, that is, at physical experience. But reality has always, as one of its factors, particularity: whatever we think of as real we endow with the qualities of the reality which plays upon us in sensation, in so far as sensation is one of the maxima of experience, setting the standard of pungency, definiteness, completeness of detail, determinateness to the last point of enquiry, all-thereness; whatever we believe real we regard as continuous in these respects with the reality thus presently touched, and in such wise continuous that this present moment is regarded as real by infection from or derivation from the rest of reality. Thus the successive points of our contact with reality arrange themselves in what we call a 'history,' a succession of moments marked at every point by these characters of particularity and surprise. Moreover, whatever reality the self has is measured by the prior and independent reality of the objects with which it deals; nor do we finite selves ever acquire a reality which can subsist apart from our sensible objects. Dreams, imaginations, volitions, may be regarded as our several degrees of experimentation in being thus self-sufficiently real. But with the highest success of these experiments, namely, in successful action known to be such, our reality remains in large part centripetal; we continue to live only by keeping open the avenues through which that independent being is communicated to us. Hence, in sum: the self does not *include* reality. Reality is beyond the self; not a distinction within the self. What we can claim of reality is a point of contact, a surface of osmosis, in sensation: this is the border between the reality original, and the derivative reality of myself; it is 'the immediate' and also 'the ultimate,' the last point within and the first point without. Our experience is metaphysical (or perhaps better, metapsychical), not phenomenalistic; but of the independent reality we possess only the 'that' which we immediately experience as we experience our own limit; we possess no 'what' whatever. Such is the Kantian answer to empirical idealism of physical experience.

In recognizing sensation as a point of vital contact with an independent reality the above argument seems to me final. But it is not clear to me that this reality is found only in sensation; the irrationalistic conclusion is too hasty. It may or may not be true that 'There is nothing in idea which was not previously in sense'; but it is also true that 'There is nothing in sense which cannot be taken up into idea.' From which it would follow that we may have not only sensations, but also *ideas* of independent reality. Whatever objection there might be to this doctrine would seem to come from taking the distinction between idea and sensation, or immediate experience, in too ideal and artificial a manner. The fixed gulf between idea and sensation is perhaps as great as any chasm in nature can be; but still it is a natural chasm, and the functional relation between the two is likewise natural. What this relation is may be illustrated by a political analogy.[1]

The state is an effort of society to become fully self-conscious and self-controlling; its ideal is so far identical with that of the individual mind. The state deals with its natural data — namely, its physical and economic status, its customs and traditions — just as the self does with its natural data, its sensations and instincts: — it turns them into ideas. The state calls its own ideas, however, by the name of 'laws' (or institutions, which are congeries of laws). Now a law is always either an experiment, or a statement of the conditions under which experiments must be carried on. The rigidity and fixity of a law is only such as is necessary for a satisfactory

[1] It is remarkable that the state furnishes present philosophy with so few analogies. For the state is still, as in the days of Plato, the most perfect visible example of the mind in its dealings with reality; while the things which have happened in politics, and in our understanding of politics, since the time of Plato, ought to render the analogy even more fruitful for us than it was for him. The philosophic value of analogy as a prelude to exact argument, keeping the argument proportionate and mutual, has increased rather than diminished with the multiplication of philosophic differences.

experiment. In order to know how life works we must proceed by assuming that we already know, and holding to the assumption until it is proven wrong. So the ideas which we individuals make are either experiments or conditions of experiment: they are so many ways of assuming that we already know reality. Now there are three points in this analogy which are important for our present enquiry:

I. The law is not something else than the custom which it transforms into an institution: it is the custom itself acquiring the power of speech and so of political entity.

When once there exists such a thing as a political world, a world wherein modes of action survive at last only by convincing some established organ that they ought to survive, then every custom is bound in time either to become an institution or to disappear. To be translated into law is only the process of entering the new status, of acquiring the new powers of self-defence and self-maintenance. So the idea is not something other than the instinct or the sensation. It is the identical thing, with newly acquired powers of speech and of influence upon action. To become idea is the fate which is imposed alike upon all sensations and all instincts because of the fact that there is such a forum in nature as a 'mind.'

Hence, while we may have, for example, ideas of things static, and sensations or intuitions of things changing; we have just as truly sensations of things static and ideas of things changing (it being understood that the sensation knows not what it is sensation of). There is no element of experience present to sensation which is not also present to idea. The idea is the experience made politically potent with reference to other experiences; it is the experience freed from the barriers of its historical context, able to combine with other experiences as determinants of action, without regard to original position in space or time. The idea endows the experience with a real faculty of transposition, akin to the assumed revolvableness and superposableness of the geometrical magnitudes; and nothing else than this new capacity of relation is meant by the fact that the experience appears to a mind. Hence, if there be any such thing as an immediate experience of time, there will necessarily be such a thing as conceptual time also; and this conceptual time will not be a different time, but identically the same time, with the new capacity of being regarded in segments, transposable, comparable, measurable.[1]

In general, the idea is the experience itself, made an active part of the conscious unity we call a self, understood by other experiences, and understanding them in turn.

II. All laws are subject to error and revision except the laws which contain the conditions of experiment.

A law contains besides the representation of a custom also a judgment, or enactment, which sets that custom in a positive position in the public life. The implied judgment may be thus interpreted: "In this enactment the custom, or impulse, or interest, in question is given its rightful meaning, force, and bearing in the public life in general." This judgment, which is the experimental side of the law, may be in error; and its error can be corrected only by the same reality which the law undertakes to entertain, namely, by custom, economic fact and human nature as found in the tendencies, customs, and feelings of the populace.

The constant flux and revision of positive law is (supposedly) the renewed attempt to determine the true political interpretation of this same reality. Whatever scope there is for originality in public life, it cannot lie in the invention of new material for that life, but only in the mode of voicing this permanent material. Hence while the power of originality

[1] It seems a wholly deplorable misuse of language to say that because conceptual time or metrical time is artificial, it is therefore not the 'real' time. As well say, because the family as now instituted is an artificial family, it is not the real family. It may not be the ideal family, nor the original family; but I know not where to look for the 'real' family except in the idea of families — as they are.

lies with the successful utterer, the source of originality itself is in the people, in their dumb feeling of wrong, and in their dumb anticipation of the direction of right. They are the social sensation and primitive fact. They are the primary and permanent reality which in correcting the errors of law, constitutes the goal and object of all original law-making.

Correspondingly, in the individual mind, sensations and feelings are the Demos. All ideas are subject to error, with the exception noted: and the reality which corrects them is met in sensation. Further, as Bergson rightly says, there can be no personal originality apart from this Demos of experience. The best originality of the mind is but the truth of nature; it is the master stroke of release, the release of nature into the condition of idea. But what is thus released is still the same reality which was present to sensation; were it any other the intention of the idea itself would be defeated.

III. Laws which contain the general conditions of experiment, that is, the laws regarding laws, law-making, law-correcting, and law-enforcing, which together are the constitution of a state, are not subject to error in the same sense in which the positive law is thus subject, and so not subject to correction in the same sense.

This part of the law differs also in this further respect from the positive law: That it does not seem to appear as part of the reality met with in external sensation, in the original facts of society: it is in a peculiar way the state itself, it is the new thing which has happened to make all the work of social self-thinking in law necessary. We might say, after the old epistemological formula: the customs and predicaments of natural society contain all the subject-matter of law — except the political constitution itself.

Nevertheless, constitutions also are subject to secular evolution. There are such things as unnatural constitutions; hence there is such a thing as a natural constitution. Is it possible that in the datum of state life there is anything which might serve as an original and slow corrective to the constitution? May it be that the principles of administration that become customary in the family, and in the collective meeting of economic emergencies, constitute the reality, as it were in the form of sensation, which the state announces as idea? It cannot have been otherwise[1] and it is not otherwise: the sense for authority and the logic of authority in elemental human nature is authority for the state in its interpretation of authority. The constitution of the state is the state itself, and yet it conforms to an external reality which is part of the datum of its existence. The customs to which it gives political birth are already in their crude form, *administered* customs. Not only the positive part of the law, therefore, but the law of the constitution itself, the relatively a priori part of law, has its external object in experience to which it must conform, and from which it receives continuous instruction.

So also with the mind. It has its principles of experiment which are not subject to correction and error as are its common predicates. These principles of experiment, the ideas of cause, substance, and the like, are *the mind itself* in its dealings with its sensations. Nevertheless, these also are not wholly nor primarily internal. They are first part of the reality of direct experience. For this experience is never experience of physical nature alone: it is experience of *administered nature*. The mind has *mind* as part of its real object; and its ideas of ideas are not originally got from views of *itself*, but from views of its very external reality.

This is a hard saying; but it is the truth. The reality which we touch in sensation is nature *known*; and hence nature already endowed with the characters of the idea. The objectivity of the world extends to its space, its causality, its matter, its energy; and we have no other system of nature than that which we find already established in experience. This reality which we experience and which we know to be independent, is not an unknown being, giving rise to sensation,

[1] See especially on this point, G. Tarde, Les transformations du pouvoir.

and so to physical experience, and so to reflexive experience; but it is a full-fledged world of nature and thought. Our original experience is just as truly an experience of other-mind as it is of other-things; and the independence of the other-mind, and of the other-things, are one independence.

If we are right, then, the idea reaches independent reality in the same way that sensation reaches it. Experience is experience of independent being, known both in sensation and in idea at once.

So far, I have tried to state and illustrate a doctrine, not to prove it. But it is capable of proof; and the proof takes the form of the historic ontological argument. The ontological argument is a way of inferring from an idea to a reality. "Because I have a certain idea," so it runs, "there must be a reality which corresponds to it." As it stands it certainly cannot apply to all ideas. To apply it, it is necessary to distinguish first between the ideas which are hypothetical in character and expect correction, and those which are not thus tentative; this distinction we have already sketched. But to put it strictly; For every idea which expects correction there is another idea determining how that correction must come, and hence not subject to correction at the same time and in the same sense. And since there are some ideas subject to correction, there must also be some ideas or idea not subject to correction at all. In the rough, these stable ideas are the ideas which guide my constant experimenting. I do not try here to deduce them, nor to decide whether they are one or many. We know well enough in what direction to look for them: they include some constant elements in the spatial, substantial, causal, and social aspects of my world. But the point which I wish to make, and which constitutes the necessary amendment of the historic ontological argument is this: These ideas guide me only in so far as they are at the *same time idea and experience*, the idea in question being no other than the experience recognized.

For whatever may be the variable and whatever may be the

constant elements in my present idea, that portion of it which is still subject to error, and so subject to correction, is experienced in no wise differently from that portion of it which is not subject to correction. For example, in so far as I experience *cause* at all, I experience it all as one real fact, and *there is no type of error to which this idea is subject which can refer me outside the precinct of this same objective reality for its truth.* Hence we may say: Whatever idea I have of causality, in that sense there is a real causal relation between things. Or, because I have an idea of space, space is real. Or, again, in whatever sense I can think, or imagine, or deny the existence of a fellow-mind, in that sense the fellow-mind is real, and an object of my experience.

If this thesis seems incredible, let one imagine what it would be to experience, in the most satisfactory manner conceivable, another mind — let us say 'to be within another mind'; let him then compare the imagined experience with his present experience — and let him state, if he can, in what essential respect these two experiences differ. Until such statement can be made, I need not hesitate to assert as I have done, that our original experience of independent reality is an experience of nature known by an independent knower. And now let me summarize what this independence amounts to, and in what way idealism is modified by admitting it.

The most general statement that can be made is this: That real objects are independent in whatever sense we can imagine, or think, or enquire about, or deny, their independence. The existence of 'the independent object' is in fact the most general subject-matter capable of ontological proof. The independence of any object is the independence which I do in truth experience in it; and if I wish to know more nearly what that experience amounts to, I can look nowhere but to those ideas which refer to that experience. Let me return for a moment to our illustration.

The independence of the real object, in the case of the state, means in part this: That nature pursues her way in spite of the laws if the laws are wrong; but that if the laws are right, she pursues her way more easily. If this be true her independence is limited. The laws, in fact, are organs of nature at the same time that they are organs of the state. And because this is so, they learn to express the very independence which their object maintains. Nothing is more conspicuous in the history of law than its progress in the definition of the status and technique of an independent citizenry; it comes to confer upon them a kind of individual separateness of being which they originally neither had nor desired. In the ideas of property, in the specialization of labor, and especially in the use of money (by which we are given a kind of solitude in the use of goods inconceivable to early man), the state seems to be introducing human nature to its own independent character, and so giving rise to more of that independent ferment to which it must submit its own demands.

And now, in the case of the idea, we have to say likewise, that the idea is at the same time an instrument of the self and an instrument of that very reality which it is regarding as its object; and that the idea has its own way of presenting to the self the independence of that object. How boldly language has come to attribute independence to the various objects of experience; how thoroughly 'substantive' our nouns have become in their grammatical relations; how unhesitatingly we confer a kind of absoluteness upon each thing named, as if it might exist in its own right. And this assumption, as it is meant, receives the pragmatic sanction: it works; it continues to work better as the world grows old; and it alone works. It works because it is the truth of reality; because it successfully expresses not alone the ultimate condition of all experiment, trial, and error, but at the same time the most primitive fact of experience itself — the experience of that not-myself which is permanently making me. And in this sense, rather than in the reflective sense, the truth of nature, even in her independence, is to be found in the idea, and in the idea alone. The real independence of the object is the independence which I learn to attribute to it; it being well understood that it is not a matter of my choice whether or not I do thus attribute independence to my objects. The independence is a matter of experience first, and of idea afterward. But now, more specifically, what does this independence mean?

It means, in the first place, *priority of being*. Not necessarily temporal priority (though this is part of it), but originality; the kind of priority which I instantly experience as I find myself being made. The real is the source of myself, both as particular being through my historical context, and as a being with ideas. In this experience, I see beyond the self that is being made: my knowledge runs out in advance of my existence, and lays hold on what I am not. It is at this point that idealism, if we have been right in this argument, will have to suffer restatement. *We cannot identify I-am with I-think.* It is possible to experience and to think being which is prior to me, which is in reality not-me. The I-think has a scope which exceeds the I-am by one remove.

True, there is nothing in what I-think which can be excluded from me; what I know is in the process of becoming me, in so far as I am able to appropriate it. The I-think represents the explorative, reaching-over function of my being; it is my spiritual metabolism — by it I take root in the soil and breathe in the air of the conscious world beyond, and assimilate it to myself. Thus though all reality be in truth spiritual, the finite knower knows realistically; the being of the object is prior to his own.

In the second place, independence means *necessity and authority*. The reality is that which, in knowing, I cannot change, that which corrects my errors, and that which determines how error shall be corrected. My objects as they come to me in history are my fate. My general 'will to be rational' or to 'accept the will of the world' has no force to determine what they shall be. My attitude to reality as it particularly is (except for my will that there be a particular reality) is not one of constructive willing, but one of refusing to reject; and I continue to refuse to reject, that is, to 'hope' or to 'believe,' in part because I know the ontological relation between my will and the will of the whole. This knowledge does not abolish the authority of facts; it makes me willing to accept that authority and to win what power is possible to me through obedience thereto.

There is a third aspect of the independence of objects which is a mutual (commutative) independence, and which is best illustrated by looking at our state from the other end. Given a sovereign, the several inhabitants of a territory are more independent of each other than before, or else less so. That is, — some distant ones are brought into a significance which they had otherwise absolutely lacked; while the adjacent ones are able to ignore the proximity of one another, as otherwise would be impossible. Perfect sovereignty makes neighborhood an indifferent relation. The independence of each other which citizens thus acquire is the counterpart of the nearest approach to a realistic independence which the world of knowledge can show. The kind of independence, namely, which is visible in particular facts, items of information in general, contents of purely arbitrary memory. These fragments bear upon me only by way of the general fact of sovereignty, the reality to which we belong in common; they come but vaguely, distantly, and by virtue of the habitualness of my mind, under the scope of my will. Thus arises the third meaning which independence may have: To say that an object is independent of me may be as in (1) and (2) the other way of saying that I am dependent upon it; or it may mean (3) that the object has no bearing upon my other present objects except through the distant medium of 'the reality.' In this tertiary and derived sense, independence of *me* means independence of myself as an object to myself, and is mutual. The chair which I do not want I can put out of the room without making any significant difference either to the chair or to the other chairs in the room, or to my own empirical self. This is the freedom of parts with reference to each other, which is due to their common dependence upon some absolute third.

To sum up: The independence of the object is such as is correlative to my various types of dependence, and to my peculiar type of independence. The idealist is always right in turning upon the realist with the demand: 'But what do you mean by independence?" The realist is right in insisting that an allegation of meaning in answer to the question does not swallow the object up into the subject, the distinction between what I am and what I think being a persistent one for finite subjects. The force of the idealistic criticism of realistic epistemology is confined, so far, to showing up inconsistency or impossibility of thought. And we return thus to Spinoza's definition of substance as 'That which is by itself and is conceived by itself'; not because logic controls Nature, but because logic *is* Nature, in the only form in which Nature can now be approached by human consciousness.

IV

NOTE ON LEUBA'S THEORY OF THE NATURE OF THE MYSTIC'S LOVE OF GOD

IT is from the point of view of the principle of alternation that I would judge the theory of Leuba, who in several well-known articles [1] has done much to supply the lack of a psychology of the mystic's motive. He has rightly distinguished the two sides of this motive. The ambitious element appears to him as a fixed necessity for moral perfection, a "tendency to the universalization of action," amounting in some persons almost to hyperæsthesia of the moral sensibility. The element of love on the other hand appears to him under a very earthly guise, as a need for satisfying the instinctive affections, a need for "organic enjoyment," in which a thwarted human desire finds an ideal route to its satisfaction. The divine love, on this basis, is a form of the pursuit of subjective pleasure; no wonder that it seems to Leuba to be inconsistent with that other fundamental motive, the moral ambition so often expressed in the severe asceticism of the mystic's self-discipline; no wonder that the mystic's development is read by him as an elimination of Eros, a conquering of love, "a reconstitution of the individual under the influence of the disposition toward universalized action, wherein he may reach entire deliverance from the desires of the natural man."

I cannot but believe that this apparent conflict and incompatibility of motive has been created by Leuba himself, through the view he takes of the nature of the divine love. At the same time Leuba is fundamentally right in recording the con-

[1] Revue philosophique, vol. 54 (1902, II), pp. 1 ff. and 441 ff.; vol. 57 (1904, I), pp. 70 ff. Mind, N. S., vol. 14 (1905), pp. 15–27, etc.

trast between these two motives: incompatible they are not, but antithetical they surely are. And it is easy for the antithesis to become an antagonism: on the organic level, love and ambition do look in opposite directions. The practically obvious thing about love is that one turns away from work; and the motive which is at bottom a wholly moral demand for the renewal of the worth of work may easily be mistaken for a denial of that worth: love, ignoring its own nature as transmuted ambition, enters into a false competition with duty. And duty may respond by forgetting that it is nothing but transmuted love. Thus the antithesis becomes a practical hostility or opposition, creating falsely partisan moral philosophies, rigoristic on one hand, epicurean on the other.

This apparent conflict which is evident in things partial is also possible in things total: it entangles the mystic not less and not more than other men. The love of God then becomes a path of dissipation, antagonizing moral ambition: but it is not true that this is its natural character. We are bound to define the motive of mysticism by its normal condition, if it has one — even though this normal condition has never yet been realized. And we are still more bound to give the mystics credit for their best achievements, and for their deepest discriminations. No one who reads the mystics can suppose that they have been unaware of precisely this danger; nor that they have been undiligent in guarding against it. They have seen, and precisely stated, the truth that the highest possibilities of experience are also the most perilous. Let me quote a passage from Tauler on this point:

There are those who have lost their way in the spiritual life, because they have undertaken to live this life after their own conceit, without the direction of God. They have a desire to taste inward spiritual comfort; but this desire (not wholly freed from subjectivity) becomes in them a veritable spiritual unchastity: for it is nothing other than a natural inclination or love which is bent and crooked inward into itself, seeking in reality *its own comfortableness.* Outwardly, these two types of love, the natural and the divine, are as like as two hairs of the head; but in their inward meaning they are wholly alien. For the true lover of God offers himself up wholly, together with everything he has and is capable of; and cannot tolerate the thought of any other appeasement of his longing than the ineffable Good, which is God himself. The others fix their minds upon the blessings and sweets which they demand from God, and if they fail to get them they are beside themselves with impatience and violent clamor. What they desire is a type of rest and comfort naturally pleasing to all creatures: and such an experience is possible to any person who knows the art of emptying himself of imaginations and impulses. Let a man but separate himself from all contingencies and from all works, and there will come over him in this state of emptiness a peace which is very great, lovely, and agreeable, and which is in itself no sin since it is part of our human nature. But when it is taken for a veritable possessing of God, or unity with God, then it is a sin; for it is in reality nothing else than a state of thorough passivity and apathy untouched by the power from on high, which any man can attain without special grace of God. It is a purely negative state from which (if one in arrogance calls it divine) nothing follows but blindness, failure of understanding, and a disinclination to be governed by the rules of ordinary righteousness.[1]

It has never been easy for human nature to sustain its love at the level of true worship; it has never been easy to keep integrity in presence of that seductive movement of reflection which seizes upon an experience and forgets its first intention; there is a statistical certainty of some lapse, and this, if Delacroix is right is precisely the thing which necessitates the long agonies of the second stadium of the mystic's life cycle. The important point, however, for a fair scientific theory is this: that mysticism has its own corrective within itself. It recurs to the essential identity of its love and its ambition.

To know that the love of God is of the same substance with moral ambition decides some questions about the psychological nature of that love. But it does not decide the worth of Leuba's thesis that it has close psychological kinship with the love of man and woman. It would be necessary in a

[1] Freely taken from Predigten, II, pp. 335–339 (ed. 1841).

complete theory to show the wide differences of these two as well as their striking likenesses; but there is no more important scientific task than to define with accuracy the extent of this likeness so universally recognized in literature and history, in the imagery of the mystics themselves. To my mind it is the principle of alternation which defines this likeness. Beyond doubt, the mystic's exaltation sweeps up into its own current whatever in the thousand-fold alternate swingings of human nature moves in its own direction, — not as their product but as their master. It would indeed be surprising if the sexual nature of man, with its movement away from the sphere of deeds to the sphere of substance, with its strong tide away from the particular to the over-individual and racial, with its suggestion of total, infinite, and yet immediate worth, did *not* more quickly and completely than any other human impulse discover in worship its ultimate meaning and law. This must be the case: not because the love of God is at bottom sexual love, but because sexual love is potentially love of the divine. As to the details of Leuba's theory, I leave them to be dealt with by his competent critic, De Montmorand.[1] But the main criticism to be passed upon that theory is only that it is not the whole truth; and in this case anything short of the whole truth is untrue.

The whole truth lies surely in this direction — that *all* of our human impulses and loves are akin. And the psychology of mysticism waits less for an analysis of the love of God than for an analysis of all other human desires. It is not this love but those that need explanation. The love of God is the one natural instinct of man: worship is the one deed which answers as an echo all other deeds in history. Upon one point the psychologies of Plato, Augustine, and Spinoza are agreed: that all special desires are refracted desires for the Absolute Good. We moderns with superior analysis have not yet regained in our own tongue these results. We need to know

[1] Revue philosophique, vol. 56 (1903), pp. 382 ff.; vol. 57 (1904), pp. 242 ff.; vol. 58 (1904), pp. 602 ff.; vol. 60 (1905), pp. 1 ff.

the "laws of the transformation and equivalence" of desires and values: then we shall see how they may be one and all, not suppressed by, but paid over into the all-consuming passion of religion. Both Leuba and his critic fall into the error of supposing that in the perfecting of mysticism some side of human nature is put under, some dissociation or amnesia has been accomplished, so that the "lower centers" never again assert themselves. All this seems foreign to the facts. For all reasons I should prefer to think that in mysticism the needs of sex, together with all other needs, are understood and satisfied; that all the hundred voices of human desire are here brought to unison. With this understanding and not otherwise can I see how religion is to fulfil its assumed functions: to keep from mutual estrangement the primitive in us and the far-civilized; to offer individual souls — malformed in the specializations of our social order, or mutilated in its accidents — the possibility of complete personality; to unify in wish and will, as reason does in principle, the whole moral existence of man.

INDEX

INDEX

Italics indicate words or phrases used in this book with special meanings.